An ARCHBISHOP
for the PEOPLE

An ARCHBISHOP for the PEOPLE

The Life of Edward J. Hanna

Richard Gribble, CSC

Paulist Press
New York/Mahwah, N.J.

Photographs and cover photo courtesy of the Archives of the Archdiocese of San Francisco, California. Used by permission.

"Countering Federalization of Education in the United States," *Records of the American Catholic Historical Society of Philadelphia* 108, nos. 3–4 (Fall and Winter 1997–1998): 23–52, reprinted by permission of American Catholic Studies, Journal of the American Catholic Historical Society. www.americancatholicstudies@villanova.edu.

"Social Catholicism Engages the American State: The Contribution of Edward J. Hanna" originally appeared in *Journal of Church and State* 42 (Autumn 2000): 737–58. Used by permission.

"Urban Apostle: Edward Hanna and the City of San Francisco, 1912–1925," *Southern California Quarterly* 86 (Winter 2004): 369–90; and "A Rough Road to San Francisco: The Case of Edward Hanna, 1907–1915," *Southern California Quarterly* 78 (Fall 1996): 225–42. Used by permission.

"Church, State, and the Immigrant: The Multiple Contributions of Archbishop Edward Hanna," *U.S. Catholic Historian* 16, no. 4 (Fall 1998): 1–18. Used by permission.

Cover design by Joy Taylor
Book design by Lynn Else

Library of Congress Cataloging-in-Publication Data

Gribble, Richard.
    An archbishop for the people : the life of Edward J. Hanna / Richard Gribble.
        p. cm.
    Includes bibliographical references and index.
    ISBN 0-8091-4405-0 (alk. paper)
    1. Hanna, Edward J. (Edward Joseph), 1860-1944. 2. Catholic Church—Bishops—Biography. 3. Bishops—United States—Biography. 4. National Catholic Welfare Conference—History. I. Title.
BX4705.H247G75 2006
282.092—dc22
[B]
                                                            2006023749

Published by Paulist Press
997 Macarthur Boulevard
Mahwah, New Jersey 07430

www.paulistpress.com

Printed and bound in the
United States of America

This book would never have been completed without the support and significant assistance of two men, Dr. Jeffrey Burns, archivist of the Archdiocese of San Francisco, and Father Robert McNamara, archivist and historian of the Diocese of Rochester. It is to these two fine men and scholars that this book is dedicated.

CONTENTS

Photographs follow chapter 8, on pages 203 to 207.

Preface and Acknowledgments

I first learned of Edward Hanna in the fall of 1987 when I began to conduct research on Father Peter Yorke and the San Francisco labor movement in the early twentieth century. Over many years my interest in Hanna grew stronger as I studied in depth the American Catholic Church and the significant contribution he made to its progress in the realms of church and state. His rare ability to successfully minister to vastly different groups and to be appealing to all was an attraction to me. While I read varied accounts in brief of some of the aspects of Hanna's life, it was amazing to me that to date no scholar had made an attempt to produce a full biography of this highly significant churchman and civic leader. During the past seventeen years I have had the opportunity to delve more completely into all aspects of Hanna's life, producing essays that have attempted to go beyond the efforts of other scholars. This biography is the final step in a long journey to bring to light for scholarship the life and contribution of a man who was so beloved by all constituencies that he can truly be called an archbishop for the people.

The pursuit of information in the completion of this effort has sent me to numerous archives and historical repositories where many dedicated people have been instrumental in aiding my quest. Dr. Jeffrey Burns, archivist for the Archdiocese of San Francisco, was the one who first introduced me to Hanna and his contribution to labor history in San Francisco. Over the years my numerous trips to the archdiocesan archives have been aided by his dedicated service and total support for the project. Without Jeff's assistance this project would have been impossible. When I started doctoral studies in American Catholic history at the Catholic University of America I learned of Father Robert McNamara in Rochester and his lifelong interest in Archbishop Hanna. Through his encouragement and personal assistance, including the use of his personal research on Hanna, setting up interviews, careful reading of essays, and gracious welcome on research trips, I was able to compile Hanna's life history in Rochester. The archivists at the Catholic University of America, especially Mr. John Shepherd, were also of great assistance in numerous trips to Washington, DC. John was able to direct me in many ways to find additional information, especially associated with Hanna's work as administrative chairman of the National Catholic Welfare Conference. In Los Angeles, Monsignor Francis Weber was gracious and very helpful, especially in trying to determine the full story of events at the end of Hanna's career in San Francisco. Librarians in the California History Room of the San Francisco Public Library and the Bancroft Library at the University of California at Berkeley were also of great assistance with gathering information for local newspapers and various manuscripts and documents.

The completion of a project of this nature is not possible without the support of family, friends, and certain organizations. Professor R. Scott Appleby, while serving as director of the Cushwa Center for the Study of American Catholicism, was gracious in providing significant funding for research trips. His own interest in the subject led him to encourage me to complete my research and to write a definitive work on Hanna. Stonehill College in North Easton, Massachusetts, where I live and teach, provided several summer grants that allowed more research trips to be completed. My religious community, the Congregation of Holy Cross, provided a nurturing and supportive environment as well as time to work toward my goal. Most especially, in this vein, the Brothers of Holy Cross at St. Francis High School in Mountain View, California, provided me with hospitality and much support for three summers while I did research on this book. Lastly, my blood family, my parents, Richard and Dorothy Gribble, and sisters, Barbara and Judy, as well as good friends, most especially Sister Tania Santander Atauchi, CDP, have been a constant source of encouragement in all my academic endeavors. I thank them for their time, love, and support.

Richard Gribble, CSC

INTRODUCTION

Historians of American Catholicism have always assumed and described in varied ways the uniqueness of the Church's roots in this country. Concepts of religious pluralism, democracy, and republicanism have been major factors in how Catholicism was planted and grew in an environment totally different from its European parent. Implicit in America's foundational documents is the belief in the separation of church and state, canonized in the First Amendment to the Constitution, which states in part: "Congress shall make no law respecting an establishment of religion, or prohibiting the free exercise thereof." In theory the establishment clause was instituted to assure religious freedom and to prevent the formation of a state religion, as had been the norm in Europe. In practice, however, the First Amendment has become a constitutional guarantee that the two great institutions of church and state will remain separate. Nonetheless, American history is replete with questions and issues that could not be resolved by only one entity; the intersection between church and state was inevitable.

The American Catholic hierarchy has from the time of John Carroll been involved with state affairs and issues, most especially when members of the faith are involved or secular issues or laws impact on Catholic teaching. For example, the historian Vincent Lannie has described the efforts of Bishop John Hughes to win state funds for Catholic schools in New York.[1] Hughes and Bishop Patrick Lynch in Charleston lobbied the Vatican for the North and South respectively during the Civil War. Cardinal James Gibbons not only personally petitioned the Vatican on behalf of the Knights of Labor, but was also a personal friend of President Theodore Roosevelt, who once commented about the archbishop, "Taking your life as a whole, I think you now occupy the position

1

of being the most respected, and venerated, and useful citizen of our country."[2]

In the twentieth century leading Catholics continued to be involved with many state issues. John Ryan, Peter Dietz, Francis Haas, and George Higgins were four of the most prominent "labor priests" who supported the rights of organized labor, articulated by Pope Leo XIII in his famous 1891 encyclical, *Rerum novarum*. As described by his biographer, James Gaffey, Bishop Francis Clement Kelley of Oklahoma spoke and wrote about oppression of the Church in Mexico. Francis Cardinal Spellman in New York energetically campaigned against Communism, supporting the efforts of Senator Joseph McCarthy among others. In a more collective sense the National Catholic Welfare Conference (NCWC), from its inception in 1919, frequently ventured into the secular realm on issues of education, immigration, recognition of the Soviet Union, and Church oppression in Haiti and Mexico. More recently the National Conference of Catholic Bishops (NCCB) has weighed in with pastoral letters on the issues of war and peace (1983) and the economy (1986).

Edward Hanna, a priest from Rochester, New York, and archbishop of San Francisco from 1915 to 1935, presents an exceptional example of one Catholic prelate who operated with great success in both realms of church and state. One contemporary described Hanna in 1926: "From his first coming, the great Metropolitan has identified himself with the interests of the State, civic and religious, never glancing back from his ploughshare, but ever forging ahead."[3] His ability to uniquely combine great intellectual acumen, wise judgment, a sense of fairness, pastoral sensitivity, ecumenical understanding, and commanding a respect among his peers and priests that was rarely seen allowed him to achieve significant results for both church and state. It is totally appropriate, therefore, that a complete chronicle and analysis of his accomplishments for American society as servant to church and state be presented.[4]

Edward Hanna (1860–1944) lived during a period that was rich in historical significance for the nation and the Church. As a youth in Rochester, New York, there is no indication that he was touched in any significant way by the Civil War, Reconstruction, or the onset of the Gilded Age. As a servant of both church and state in the early twentieth century, Hanna was influenced, however, by the Progressive movement, which "sought to improve the conditions of life and labor and to create as much social stability as possible."[5] The concurrent rise of the Social Gospel and its emphasis on the need for society to right the wrongs wrought by industrialism was another significant influence on Hanna, both personally and indirectly through his boyhood friendship with Baptist minister Walter Rauschenbusch, considered by many to be the leading proponent of the movement. Additionally, the excesses of the 1920s followed by the Great Depression would directly impact Hanna's life work as archbishop of San Francisco.

Church events also had significant influence on Hanna and the progress of his life and thought. He came to educational and intellectual maturity during the Americanist crisis (1885–99) and was suspected of theological Modernism, which came to the forefront when Pope Pius X, through *Lamentabili sane exitu* and *Pascendi Dominici Gregis* (1907), condemned this more intellectual approach to Catholicism as the "synthesis of all heresies." He served as archbishop during a period described by William Halsey and other historians as a time of disillusionment for much of the nation when Catholics sought to defend the values and principles of American idealism against the onslaught of various forms of irrationalism.[6] Attacks on the family through the promotion of birth control and challenging the rights of workers were only two of many areas that Hanna addressed in the civic and sacred realms. Social Catholicism through the promotion of Catholic Action was another significant issue that impinged upon the ministry of Archbishop Hanna.

Considering the significant positions he held in both church and state, it is a historical lacuna that Edward Hanna to date has not received a full biography. The first historian to investigate Hanna's contribution to American Catholicism was a fellow Rochester priest, Robert McNamara. McNamara's publication record on Hanna is limited to a broad summary of his life in a 1963 essay in *Rochester History* and a short reference in his history of the Diocese of Rochester,[7] but his interest in Hanna was keen and research on his life, especially extensive interviews of several people who knew him in Rochester, is voluminous. I have also completed several essays on various aspects of Hanna's life.[8]

Despite the lack of a full treatment of his life, several important aspects of Hanna's contribution to society have been described in various amounts of detail in essays and monographs. Hanna's brush with Modernism, which forced his name to be dropped from contention for the coadjutor position in San Francisco in 1906, has been described in some detail by several historians. R. Scott Appleby describes the Hanna case as an example of Modernism in America. Michael DeVito and Thomas Shelley look at this incident from the perspectives of the *New York Review* and St. Joseph's Seminary at Dunwoodie respectively. Gerald Fogarty, SJ, reviews the accusation of Hanna as a modernist from the perspective of Catholic biblical scholarship in the United States. James Gaffey describes the events looking at Patrick Riordan's attempt to obtain Hanna as his coadjutor.[9] Hanna's role as chairman of the Administrative Committee of the NCWC has also been described by many historians. Hanna's efforts to protect Catholic education against the onslaught of anti-Catholicism in Oregon and federalization have been chronicled by Douglas Slawson and Thomas Shelley. Slawson and Paulist John Sheerin have presented the fight by Hanna and the NCWC to aid the persecuted Church in Mexico in the 1920s and 1930s.[10] The archbishop's significant efforts in San Francisco's labor front have been described by me, by Michael Kazin, and by William Issel and Robert Cherny.[11] Hanna's leadership with the California Commission of Immigration and Housing has been addressed in doctoral dissertations by Christina Ziegler McPherson and Anne Marie Woo-Sam.[12] Hanna's efforts at the behest of President Franklin Roosevelt to arbitrate a paralyzing West Coast dock strike in 1934 are outlined by the historian David Selvin.[13]

This book adds depth and context to the work of other historians and fills in the many missing pieces of Hanna's life to provide a full portrait of a great American Catholic. Hanna's life and service are historically relevant for several reasons. The sheer number of commissions and boards he served on, his active membership in civic and service groups, and many other activities demonstrate his tireless energy and the wide scope of his service in sacred and secular realms. Hanna was petitioned by every facet of society because he was perceived to be fair and just. He shunned the ivory tower of ecclesiastical rank to be constantly present to the average person on the street. Yet, his experience and acumen also made him the choice of high-ranking religious and government officials to lead the NCWC and to lead numerous commissions seeking answers to problems with immigration, worker wages and strikes, and unemployment. His open attitude to all also made him acceptable to people of all faiths and levels in society. Hanna can truly be called an archbishop for the people through his wide appeal to all constituencies and his pastoral, nonprejudicial, and professional approach to the resolution of conflict. Archbishop John Mitty, Hanna's coadjutor, on the occasion of Hanna's retirement summarized his appeal and contribution:

> Through the gift of these personal qualities he has done much in this community to bring the members of it, separated by so many interests and traditions, into a better mutual understanding and a closer social union. His name has been synonymous with kindness, gentleness and courtesy and will be held in loving benediction by thousands of friends and admirers who will follow him with every wish for joy and happiness.[14]

This monograph is a chronological and systematic presentation of Hanna's life and contribution to American society. Chapters 1 and 2 describe Hanna's youth in Rochester, his formation for priesthood, his ministry as priest and professor, his civic activity in Rochester, and his eventual elevation to the episcopacy, although delayed due to his association with Modernism. Chapters 3 through 5 describe Hanna's work in the city of San Francisco, including his advocacy for Catholic education, his active involvement with numerous civic and church organizations that served the poor and youth, his leadership in a series of wage arbitration boards in the 1920s, and his significant ecumenical efforts. Hanna was clearly loved by his priests and by the people of San Francisco, Catholic and non-Catholic alike. Chapters 6 and 11 present Hanna's efforts in the civic realm for California and the nation. The archbishop served as a charter member and president (1923–35) of the California Commission of Immigration and Housing, headed the State Unemployment Commission, and chaired the State Emergency

Relief Commission during the Depression, and led a three-man panel that settled a violent agricultural workers' strike in California's San Joaquin Valley in 1933. Hanna's appointment as chairman of the National Longshoremen's Board and his resolution of the great West Coast dock strike of 1934 is also chronicled. Chapters 7 through 10 analyze Hanna's many accomplishments as chairman of the Administrative Committee of the NCWC. Serving from the conference's inception in 1919 to his retirement in 1935, Hanna guided the nascent body to offer the Catholic response on the significant domestic issues of immigration, federalization of education, and the distribution of birth control literature and paraphernalia. On the international scene Hanna led the NCWC's efforts that rejected America's recognition of the Soviet Union in 1933 and championed the restoration of Church rights in Mexico in the 1920s and 1930s. Chapter 12 describes Hanna's retirement to Rome and his death, the one area of his life that, due to lack of extant data, remains somewhat of a mystery.

Edward Hanna was an archbishop for all people, serving civic and religious sectors of society with equal vigor and expertise. While many Church officials have been active in the civic realm of society, few have made the impact that Hanna did. Fewer still have been equally adept in the religious realm. Hanna, therefore, presents a rare blend of service that was accomplished through his wide appeal. Whether the need was from church or state, the call often went to Edward Hanna, who responded generously to the betterment of society. Hailed by many contemporaries and historians as the most beloved prelate in the history of San Francisco, he was truly an archbishop for the people.

Chapter 1

THE ROCHESTER PRIEST

Irish textures have been deeply woven into the life and culture of America's people. The spirit of celebration, evident from the almost universal appeal of identifying oneself as Irish by heritage or association on St. Patrick's Day, reveals the widespread influence of Irish culture in the United States. The Irish immigrants who flocked to America's shores in the early to mid-nineteenth century brought their Catholic faith with them. Irish Catholicism was steeped in moral rigor and dogmatism, and it emphasized the letter of the religious law over its spirit. By force of numbers and by the assumption of positions of authority in Church and society, Irish Catholics, as Lawrence McCaffrey has stated, "have played…an important role in directing the American Church, urban politics, and the labor movement."[1]

Irish influence in the American Church was present from the outset and grew over time. During the era of immigration, English-speaking Irish men and women were better able to assimilate into American life than Germans, Italians, and eastern Europeans were. More important, the American hierarchy was dominated by Irish or Irish-American prelates, many of whom fostered American values of liberal democracy, popular sovereignty, and the separation of church and state. It is this ethnic understanding of Catholicism that formed and influenced Edward Joseph Hanna, Irish-American, priest, archbishop, and church and state leader. Hanna used his intellectual acumen, sense of fair play and justice for all peoples, and charismatic personality to make significant contributions to church and state, on both local and national levels. Edward Hanna was an archbishop for the people who gained acceptance and recognition in all circles of society.

The Nineteenth-Century American Catholic Experience

American Catholicism of the nineteenth century was characterized by an apologetic defense against nativists, by massive migration, and by a quest for self-understanding in a new land of opportunity. The era's waves of nativism and anti-Catholicism varied in form, but the persistent message was that Catholics could not make good Americans. At times the animus was manifest in violence, such as the burning of the Ursuline Convent in Charlestown, Massachusetts, in 1834, the Philadelphia riots of 1844, and the repugnant behavior that met the visit of the papal representative Archbishop Gaetano Bedini in 1853. Copious anti-Catholic literature included the lurid tales of women religious published as *Six Months in a Convent* (1835) by Rebecca Reed, and the infamous *Awful Disclosures of the Hotel Dieu Nunnery in Montreal* (1836) ostensibly by "Maria Monk" but actually written by a group of Protestant ministers. Numerous other books, periodicals, newspapers, and pamphlets described Rome as the whore of Babylon.[2] In the political sphere, the Know-Nothing Party, a derivative of the Order of the Star-Spangled Banner, founded by Charles B. Allen in 1849, was active in an anti-Catholic campaign from 1852 to 1856. The party swept to many local, state, and congressional victories while asserting that no Catholic should hold public office.[3]

Massive waves of immigration to America's shores in the nineteenth century added to the anti-Catholic animus of the nation. The first significant period of immigration, from 1830 to 1860, was dominated by an influx of Irish and Germans, many of whom were Catholic. The Irish in general were poorly educated, with no marketable skills. Native-born Americans, including some Catholics, argued against their presence because they competed for unskilled labor jobs. Additionally, many Irish immigrants landed on the rolls of government assistance, placing a drain on limited community resources. Many Germans, because of the language barrier, were more resistant to assimilation, within both the Catholic community[4] and the nation as a whole. The second wave of immigration, from 1880 to 1920, brought many eastern and southern European

Catholics to America, and the resulting problems of assimilation, job competition, and religion triggered the formation of the anti-Catholic American Protective Association.[5]

While American Catholics searched for acceptance in their newly adopted land, they also were absorbed in a quest for self-understanding. The same factors that pushed Catholicism to create a defensive apologetic in spirit and action accelerated its need to establish an identity within American society. If the myriad peoples, heritages, and nationalities with the common bond of the Catholic faith were to persevere and succeed, they would need the comfort of an identity. Nativists habitually stated that Catholics could not be good Americans because their fealty to Rome as a foreign power conflicted with loyalty to the United States. Immigrant Catholics were stereotyped as old-world priest-ridden monarchists or, paradoxically, as anarchists fomenting revolution. To counter such arguments, many other Catholics stressed the close compatibility of American principles with those of Catholicism. Catholic converts Orestes Brownson and Isaac Hecker, the latter the founder of the Congregation of Missionary Priests of St. Paul the Apostle (the Paulists, 1858), argued not only that Catholics could be good Americans but also that Catholicism was the religion most compatible with American democratic principles.

Central to the self-understanding of Hecker and his fellow Americanists was an incarnational concept of church, with its concentration on divine immanence in the history of American Catholicism.[6] Amid a growing middle class with a vast array of charitable and educational institutions and parish and diocesan societies, these assimilated Catholics stressed the positive character of American society, claiming that American Catholics would make significant and formative contributions as the nation began to gain international status and prestige.

Edward Hanna: Family and Youth

The Hanna family of Rochester, New York, was of Scottish descent, but for many generations before immigrating to the United States they had lived in Ireland. Edward Hanna Sr. was born on

9

November 8, 1819, between New Castle and Belfast, County Down, the son of Nicholas Hanna and Margaret Lennon. Hanna was a descendant of the Reverend Hugh "Roaring" Hanna, one of the great Ulster Orangemen, who is memorialized by a statue outside St. Enoch's Presbyterian Church in Belfast, where he served as a minister.[7] Edward Sr. received an excellent education, especially for his day. As a youth he moved to England seeking greater economic stability but, in 1838, after the death of his parents, immigrated to the United States. He traveled by canal to western New York, settling in Rochester, where he obtained work as a cooper (shoemaker). There he met Anne Clark, the daughter of Bernard Clark and Mary McCabe. Anne was born on March 31, 1835, in County Cavan, Ireland, and immigrated to the United States during the great potato famine of 1845. She was also fortunate to receive a finishing school education with natural science, music, and needlework as the curriculum. Described by her children as "a saint," Anne was well respected for her work with the poor, assisting the Sisters of St. Vincent de Paul and St. Mary's Hospital. Edward Sr. and Anne were married at Immaculate Conception Church in Rochester on September 18, 1859.[8]

The newlyweds wasted no time in starting a family: a son, Edward Joseph Hanna, the first of five children, was born on July 21, 1860, and was baptized three days later at Immaculate Conception Church. Since Hanna's extant personal correspondence is limited to a few letters over many years, it is not clear what relationship the future archbishop had with his brothers, Frank and James, and with his sisters Margaret, who later married William Basset, and Anna, who became a religious of the Sacred Heart. However, we do know that during his tenure in San Francisco, Hanna financially assisted Frank's lumber business and presided at the funerals of his sister Margaret in 1930 and her husband, who died quite prematurely in 1917. It is also clear that Hanna corresponded with Anna, who resided in convents in Seattle, Washington, Providence, Rhode Island, and St. Joseph, Missouri.[9]

Hanna was a happy youth who realized his privileged status. The family lived in a comfortable three-bedroom home on Brown Street in central Rochester. Hanna was grateful for his family, especially his mother and father, whom he described as "excellent parents who knew the proper medium between all play and no work, and all work and no play."[10] From his earliest days the seeds of justice and the concept of fair play were planted in Hanna. Additionally, the close bonds of family were manifest in important ways. These values became the seedbed from which his later career as servant to church and state gained sustenance and strength.

Like their parents, Hanna and his siblings received quality schooling. Hanna began his education in 1867 in the common or public school system, attending School #2 in Rochester. From the outset he demonstrated the intellectual acumen for which he would later be well known, advancing four grades in the course of one academic year. A local paper commented, "From the time he [Hanna] first attended what was then by courtesy called a public school, he showed remarkable intellectual attainments and devotion to study."[11] After one year, however, his parents, heeding the edict of the local ordinary, Bishop Bernard McQuaid, to attend Catholic schools,[12] enrolled Edward in the Cathedral School, operated by the Irish Christian Brothers, where he studied between 1868 and 1875. There he came under the direction of Daniel B. Murphy, who took special interest in young Hanna and prepared him for high school.[13]

Hanna attended Rochester Free Academy (RFA) for his preparatory education. Initially the faculty, feeling Hanna was too young for the academic program, encouraged him to take a business course of study, which he completed with distinction in 1876. He was then enrolled in the classics course, which he completed three years later, graduating as valedictorian of a class of twenty-two students and speaking at his commencement ceremony on June 27, 1879. His speech on Irish nationalist and abolitionist Daniel O'Connell was well received. As the local media reported: "Mr. Hanna is a natural orator. He declaimed his oration in a manner that would have done credit to a more experienced speaker and was a most creditable effort. We can compliment Mr. Hanna on the tenor and delivery of his production."[14]

Walter Rauschenbusch, the salutatorian and commencement co-orator, was a boyhood friend of Hanna and later became a leading proponent of the Social Gospel during America's Progressive Era. A Baptist from birth and by conviction, Rauschenbusch experienced the plight of the poor in America firsthand through his work as a pastor in the Hell's Kitchen district of Manhattan. Returning to Rochester in 1907 as a professor of church history at Rochester Theological Seminary, Rauschenbusch became an overnight expert in the Social Gospel and a national celebrity through the publication of his first book, *Christianity and the Social Crisis*. He capped his brief career in the Social Gospel spotlight with *A Theology of the Social Gospel*, published shortly before his death in 1918. Rauschenbusch's contribution to the Social Gospel was synthesized by Reinhold Niebuhr, who called him "the most brilliant and generally satisfying exponent" of the movement.[15] Hanna and Rauschenbusch lived close to each other and were good friends during their days at Rochester Free Academy, being two of the original nineteen founders of the Alpha Chapter of the Pi Phi Fraternity. After graduation, however, they went their separate ways and their close friendship dwindled to occasional contact through a few extant letters. While both men distinguished themselves as champions of the downtrodden, the letters reveal that Rauschenbusch felt Hanna was too sheltered in his education. He wrote, "I wish I could take the Jesuit spectacles off his nose and take him around the world and make him see life as it is, instead of the caricatured image his teachers show him—I always feel as if we do not half understand each other."[16]

Hanna's obvious intellectual acumen was matched by an equally strong faith, as exemplified by his active participation at St. Patrick, the cathedral parish of Rochester. Hanna came to the attention of Bishop Bernard McQuaid, who used the youth as an altar boy at special liturgical functions, including the dedication of churches and the laying of cornerstones. Hanna's attraction to the Church was also noticed by a boyhood friend, Katherine Conway, but she did not see anything striking about his participation:

> It was generally assumed that his thoughts were on the priesthood, yet he was the gayest of the gay, and not even the most familiar friend would have ventured to force the sealed door of the sanctuary of the boy's heart. It was noticed that he was a frequent communicant; otherwise there was nothing unless, perhaps, his close application to his books, to distinguish him from his other mates.[17]

Conway went on to say that Hanna was "one of the ablest at [the] Cathedral School with a fine dramatic and humorous gift."[18]

Like others, McQuaid was equally impressed with Hanna's intellectual acumen, especially as he looked toward his future need for professors at his dream diocesan seminary in Rochester. Thus, when Hanna was eighteen, McQuaid accepted him as a diocesan presbyterial candidate and sent him to Rome to be trained for pastoral ministry and to obtain a doctorate, qualifying him as a future professor.[19] Hanna left for Rome in October 1879. A local paper reported: "Mr. Hanna leaves Rochester with the well wishes of a host of friends for health and happiness in the old world. His recognized ability leaves no doubt of his eminent success in his chosen profession."[20] He resided at the North American College but took classes at the Urban College. Instead of beginning to study philosophy immediately, Hanna decided to spend his first year studying rhetoric and languages. He reported his status to McQuaid:

> My progress during the year just passed was not, perhaps, as great as it might have been, still for the most part, I tried to employ my my *[sic]* time as well as possible; and though I did nothing at all brilliant at the examinations, nevertheless I obtained pretty good places.

He also thanked McQuaid, speaking of his hope for better progress in the future:

> I assume your Lordship that I will, with the assistance of Heaven, put forth my best efforts to make use of the opportunities you have so kindly afforded me, so that should it one day be my lot to go forth hence and as a priest to battle with the busy world, I may not be found wanting.[21]

Hanna's decision proved to be very wise, for it made him fluent in Latin and Italian and paved the way for his brilliant academic career.[22]

Hanna next entered into philosophy, with the scholastic system of Thomas Aquinas the norm following Leo XIII's 1879 encyclical *Aeterni patris*. He capped his two-year program with a masterful thesis on Aquinas. Hanna's acumen was noted by professors at the Urban College, who invited him to participate in a public philosophical disputation, as an "objector," before the Holy Father and twenty-two members of the curia. Hanna reported that "although it caused a little anxiety, still [it] required no great labor."[23]

In November 1882, Hanna transitioned to his study of theology without skipping a beat. His academic program lasted three years and consisted of the standard repertoire of classes in ecclesiastical history, scripture, moral and dogmatic theology, and canon law. We can gain some insight into Hanna's life as a seminarian from a letter his boyhood friend Walter Rauschenbusch wrote after visiting the former in Rome: "Ed Hanna is doing finely, standing first in his class." Two years later Rauschenbusch again reported,

> From Ed Hanna I had a letter dated August 17, but it was so full of a compendium of Roman Catholic systematic theology that it fairly squelched me for a time and I have not the cheek to answer him with my low gossip. He has received all the orders, had the "character *indelebilis* as priest," is bound to eternal virginity, etc.[24]

Once again Hanna's academic acumen was recognized by his instructors. Father Edward V. Boussard, SJ, commented, "Mr. Hanna is the first scholar there [Urban College] and one of the brightest men ever educated within its walls[.] His Latin debates are the wonder of the Americans in Rome....He [will] undoubtedly leave Rome with the highest honors ever given a student of this College."[25]

As Rauschenbusch had indicated, Hanna received his minor orders as his time in Rome continued. On reception of the subdiaconate, the first major step toward priestly ordination, Hanna commented to McQuaid,

> Although most unworthy of so exalted a dignity and fearful of the weighty responsibilities thereto annexed, still our Lord seemed to give me courage to take the step and now that it is over I can only hope and pray that I may not prove recreant to

the grace I have received nor unfaithful to you and our diocese to which I have bound myself.[26]

Hanna was ordained to the priesthood on Trinity Sunday, May 30, 1885, at the Cathedral of St. John Lateran by Archbishop Giulio Lenti. Hanna gave thanks to McQuaid for the privilege received: "If today I am numbered among the elect of God, it is due to you who so kindly received me among your privileged sons."[27]

Following his ordination Hanna continued his doctoral studies in sacred theology (STD) to attain the credentials to teach on the college level and thus be qualified for McQuaid's future seminary. Hanna's major professor at Urban was Archbishop Francesco Satolli, who in 1893 would make history as the first apostolic delegate to the United States. In July 1886 Satolli arranged the first public theological disputation at *Propaganda Fide* in fifty years. (*Propaganda Fide* was the former name of the "department" for evangelization of the Roman curia.) Hanna and fellow American Edward Pace, who would distinguish himself as a professor at the Catholic University of America[28] and had been Hanna's co-defender in 1882 on a philosophical disputation on Aquinas, answered questions posed by the assembled professors and curia, with Pope Leo XIII in attendance. The questions dealt with the knowledge, will, and power of God. The pope was so impressed with both student priests that he conferred the doctorate *honoris causa* without the need for exams or dissertation. One Rochester paper summarized Hanna's accomplishment: "During his career as a student in Rome, Doctor Hanna made the most brilliant record ever won by an American student."[29]

Hanna stayed on in Rome one additional year, working for Satolli as an examination reader at *Propaganda*. The young priest was willing to assist his mentor only if McQuaid agreed and only provided it would not hinder his activity and duties at the North American College. He explained to McQuaid that if he had thought only of his own needs and feelings he would have declined the offer, "but as it was asked by Prof[essor] Satolli as a personal favor, it would seem ungrateful to refuse considering his past kindness to the College and to me in particular." In July 1887 Hanna left Rome and returned to Rochester to begin work in his home diocese.[30]

The Rochester Priest

The Diocese of Rochester, New York, was established on March 3, 1868, by order of Pope Pius IX. The diocese, initially consisting of eight counties but growing to twelve in 1896, was carved from the See of Buffalo. Bernard McQuaid, a Newark, New Jersey, priest, was consecrated bishop on July 12, 1868, and installed as Rochester's first local ordinary on July 16.

Upon his return to Rochester, Hanna took up residence at the Cathedral Parish of St. Patrick while teaching at St. Andrew's Preparatory School, which McQuaid opened in 1870 as the feeder for his still-hypothetical seminary. Apparently Hanna's reputation for academic achievement preceded him, for almost immediately after his arrival in Rochester he was offered a position at the fledgling Catholic University of America, opening that fall. The church historian John Tracy Ellis claims that Bishop John Keane, the newly appointed rector of the university, badly wanted Hanna, offering him the chair of dogmatic theology. The offer seems to have been extended while Hanna was still in Rome, since Satolli suggested that he accept it; however, Hanna's loyalty to the diocese and McQuaid, as well as the ordinary's disapproval of the offer, led Hanna to decline the invitation.[31]

While Hanna's daily activity at St. Andrew's kept him busy between 1887 and 1893, it was his pastoral ministry at St. Patrick's and his work in the local community that advanced his reputation in the diocese and the city of Rochester. He became a popular and well-known preacher, as noted by a local paper: "His [Hanna's] panegyric of the titular St. Patrick, preached in the Cathedral, is regarded as one of the finest examples of sacred oratory."[32]

His sermons give some insight into Hanna's ecclesiology and his understanding of the person of Christ. Hanna was able to look at history and realize that the Church, while at times battered and bruised, was able to withstand the storms of life:

> Thus through tempest and sunshine has the ship bearing Jesus sailed on with its precious burden of souls on to the port of eternity. Thus it has been lashed by wind and wave, thus it has

kept on its enduring course. Thus in every trial has it come forth victorious, because of Jesus' presence there.

In this same sermon, after reviewing the Church's history in combating heresy, he was confident for its future: "Let the experience of the past be our answer. Let her undiminished vigor fill us with confidence. Rage the storm will, but in our own time, Jesus will calm the tempest."[33] Foreshadowing his theological understanding that would raise questions in 1906 about his possibly modernist beliefs, Hanna offered some ideas on the knowledge of Jesus, both human and divine, in a sermon, "The Doctrine of Christ." He asked the question, "Is the doctrine of Christ simply the doctrine of men, or does it bear upon itself the impress of divinity?" He acknowledged that Christ's knowledge was "more sublime than the doctrines of man" and "it has not the blemishes and imperfections found in the writings of the philosophers" and "is a more complete system than ever came from the hand of man." Yet he concluded that "Christ could not have acquired such learning in a more natural way" than through the human condition.[34]

Hanna's intelligence made him an effective preacher, both pastorally and as teacher, but it was his understanding of the human condition and his long hours in the confessional that gained him the hearts of the local Catholic immigrant community; Italians in particular appreciated the fluency he had acquired from his many years in Rome.[35] Consistent with Catholic theology of the day, Hanna professed a somewhat negative human anthropology and worried that youth might not be ready for the challenge of the world. He exhorted them:

> Young men and young women, hope of our coming generation, be not seduced by our world and its allurement. Put on the armour of Christ that you may resist when temptation presses. Be men and women of faith. Be loyal to your Master, Christ.[36]

He realized that the human race was in a contest against evil, that "sin will not turn to the virtue of purity without a hard fought battle." He warned his listeners, "But not to hear God's call is not only folly but dangerous [and] suicidal to our souls. The classes of men who neglect the divine warnings are many."[37]

Human frailty and consequent sin had a solution, however. Hanna professed the efficacy of reconciliation and promoted the sacrament of penance. He proclaimed, "We must…diligently examine our conscience, confess what we have recalled, be sorry for the past and, at least with the sorrow of attrition and purpose, [try] not to offend God whose mercies to us know not numbers."[38] Hanna translated his theology into a pastoral sensitivity that made him extremely popular with the faithful in Rochester. One contemporary account is illustrative:

> Go to the Rochester Cathedral on any Saturday night for the last twenty years and the confessional of Dr. Hanna was surrounded by the poor and sorrowful after all others had left for the night—a motley crowd waiting for the word of comfort and consolation which ever came, and never tired, but patient always with the patience of Christ.[39]

Hanna's effectiveness in the confessional was indicative of his kindness, a trait that was observed by all who encountered him. On the occasion of his consecration as bishop and his move from Rochester, one report stated, "Always he has been kind. If all the loving kindnesses that he has wrought could be transformed into flowers and laid at his feet, they would form a pathway for him across the continent to the Golden Gate."[40]

Hanna's pastoral presence at St. Patrick's was not his only ministerial function beyond his work as educator. Throughout his tenure in Rochester, Hanna served as a judge of matrimonial cases and as one of the chief examiners of junior clergy.[41] Clearly, Bishop McQuaid wanted to fully utilize his star Roman-educated priest, even though the seminary he dreamed of was not yet a reality.

In 1875 McQuaid had begun to plan for a national seminary in Rochester. The bishop envisioned a college seminary along the lines of Seton Hall in New Jersey, which he started in 1856 while serving as pastor of the cathedral parish in Newark and as assistant to Bishop James Roosevelt Bayley. Due it seems to financial constraints, it was only in 1879, however, after returning from his *ad limina* visit to Pope Leo XIII the previous year, that McQuaid seriously took up the idea of an independent seminary. Remembering the modest seminary at Fordham, which he attended in the 1840s, McQuaid intended to break the "old-time consecrated miseries and needless suffering on the part of seminarians" with a modern building. He spoke of his dream in an 1881 pastoral letter: "The seminary will become the central pivot of ecclesiastical work, the nursery of priests, the home of learned professors devoted to theological studies, a sacred place that in time will grow in the affection of priests and people."[42] By 1886 McQuaid had raised $18,000 for the project, allowing him to purchase a twenty-acre lot on Lake Ontario for $10,000. To supplement his building fund McQuaid obtained pledges of an additional $60,000 from clergy and laity. He engaged Andrew J. Warner, one of Rochester's leading architects, to design an imposing Victorian Gothic building. Construction began on St. Bernard's Seminary in 1891; the chapel was dedicated on August 19, 1893, and classes began on September 4, 1893.[43]

Hanna, who held the chair of dogmatic theology, was one of eight members of the original faculty at St. Bernard's. The others were Andrew J. Breen (scripture and Hebrew), Andrew B. Meehan (canon law and liturgy), Owen McGuire (mental and moral philosophy), Prosper Libert (natural science and librarian), Ludlow Lapham (English and German), Eugene Bonn (music), and James J. Hartley (pro-rector). All were priests save Lapham and Bonn, who were laymen.[44] Hanna was generally well respected by seminarians and staff as an excellent teacher. The historian Frederick Zwierlein, who was a seminarian at St. Bernard's during Hanna's tenure, wrote, "Dr. Hanna was a brilliant Professor of dogmatic theology, a good pedagogue and spoke Ciceronian Latin better than I heard anywhere in Europe." Another former student, J. F. Goggin, commented that at times Hanna did not sufficiently prepare his lectures, but he was a good teacher, "when he worked at it."[45]

All agree that Hanna made every effort to befriend seminarians, serving not only as professor but as mentor. As professor of dogmatics Hanna taught such courses as God the Trinity, God the Creator, the Incarnate Word, the One God, and numerous courses on the sacraments.[46] Breaking with tradition, he addressed the students by their first names and was ever willing to engage in sports, especially baseball, with them. One former student commented on Hanna's personality: "Affable with all, students included, and [he] cultivated this affability and charm." Students referred to him as *"refugium peccatorum,"* a reference to the fact that students who were in trouble would always receive a hearing from Hanna. Like the faithful at St. Patrick's Parish, the seminarians found Hanna to be an excellent and very pastoral confessor.[47]

While most agree that Hanna was a fine teacher, there are mixed reactions to his scholarship. His intellectual brilliance was never an issue and his native ability from his Roman record was clear, yet several former students have questioned his work ethic. One student stated,

> He had a natural brilliance, but like many another so gifted he coasted along on that, and never was a student; [he was] always a better teacher than a scholar. What he knew he could put across well. At the same time, he was not averse to posing as a most learned scholar. Had he applied himself to continual study it would have been easy to be so in fact.[48]

Some claimed that Hanna was "not especially deep," deriving many of his ideas from Michael Ryan, a colleague at St. Bernard's, and others.[49] A former student, Edward Byrne, commented, "Ryan stimulated Hanna to do the continual study which he was failing to do, and he introduced him to zestful knowledge of new philosophical notions."[50] Additionally, it was claimed that the information for Hanna's essays in the *Catholic Encyclopedia* project came from others, especially a book, *The History of the Incarnation*, which Hanna used in class.[51] Frederick Zwierlein has summarized Hanna's presence at St. Bernard's: "Hanna was an excellent seminary man: no scholar, but a fine pedagogue....He was also kindly to the seminarians, acknowledged them in passing, and was favored as confessor by many."[52]

While a professor at St. Bernard's, Hanna took two sabbatical leaves for educational purposes, as well as summer study. In 1901 he traveled to Europe, spending some time in Rome and then studying Anglicanism at Cambridge in England; in 1906 he studied at the University of Munich. Additionally, he spent three summers in Europe studying German and theology.[53]

In addition to his growing renown as professor and priest, Hanna enjoyed a generally harmonious relationship with Bishop McQuaid, who had groomed him for St. Bernard's. As we have already seen, Hanna demonstrated his gratitude by turning down the chair of dogmatics at Catholic University. In 1901 when William Henry O'Connell left his position as rector of the North American College to become bishop of Portland, Maine, Hanna was offered the vacant position, but again he declined out of loyalty to McQuaid, who was rumored to want Hanna as his successor in Rochester.[54] That same year Hanna's mentor from the Urban College, Francesco Satolli, was proposing him for several vacant sees in the Philippines, but Hanna discouraged the effort, preferring to work with McQuaid to stabilize St. Bernard's academic status: in 1890, he traveled with the bishop to Rome to petition *Propaganda Fide* to grant the seminary the authority to issue degrees. Eleven years later, while on sabbatical, Hanna was told by McQuaid to check on the status of the request. Finally on March 22, 1901, Hanna informed McQuaid that St. Bernard's had been granted permission to issue degrees, in recognition of McQuaid's personal worth, his loyalty to the Holy See, and his interest in seminarians and in the education of priests.[55] Clearly, McQuaid trusted Hanna in securing this critical permission needed for the development of St. Bernard's.

The sole but significant disagreement between the two men came in 1905 when McQuaid began to look for a coadjutor. The bishop feared that Hanna's broad-based popularity would subject him to divided loyalties as local ordinary when the inevitable battles between people arose. The crucial reason for McQuaid's rejection of Hanna as coadjutor—and the source of the rift between them—was the priest's attitude toward the bishop's edict forbidding the sacraments to families who didn't send their children to Catholic colleges or universities. Hanna was friends with P. B. Murphy, a teacher at the Cathedral High School who decided to send his daughter to Cornell, a move that drew the bishop's ire but Hanna's approval. McQuaid was concerned that Hanna would be unlikely to carry out McQuaid's policies as coadjutor, since he had not supported the bishop's policy on higher education. Hanna expressed his feelings to his former rector at the North American College, Bishop Denis O'Connell, now rector of the Catholic University of America: "He [McQuaid] knows that I would not deny absolution (just think of it) to the Father or Mother that sends his daughter to Wellesly [sic] or Smith or any other secular college."[56] While McQuaid told the consultors creating the *terna* that he could not choose anyone linked to the Knights of Columbus (thus eliminating Hanna, who had strong ties since the organization's formation in Rochester in 1896), Hanna knew the true reason for his exclusion. The incident was a significant cross to Hanna:

> I was hurt, not because they did not want me, but because the Bishop who has never in his life kept from me a single thing would allow my name to be bandied about from Maine to California, would allow me to be put in seeming opposition to him and not vouchsafe one word....How strange it is that the Bishop should close his career endeavoring with all his might to antagonize me? If he only knew how little I prize the prize he thinks he possesses, he might relent.[57]

Thomas F. Hickey was named McQuaid's coadjutor on February 18, 1905.

Hanna's exceptional work as educator and parochial minister gained him popularity, but it was his active involvement in the public sector, beginning almost immediately after his return from Rome, that distinguished him from other church ministers and set a lifelong pattern. Hanna's civic work is seen mostly in his advocacy for immigrants, especially Italians, for whom he possessed a great fondness. Hanna was a member of the Board of Directors of the New York branch of the North American Civic League for Immigrants, a group that helped Americanize and assimilate various immigrant peoples into local communities.[58] Hanna worked closely with the Italian community, numbering between fifteen hundred and two thousand, serving as their social justice champion and general spiritual leader. While teaching at St. Andrew's, he successfully campaigned for the Italian population's educational advancement, but it was his ability to secure jobs and serve as advocate that truly endeared him to the Italian community. The *Rochester Evening Times* reported, "Did a poor Italian need a job? Dr. Hanna knew every employer in the city. Was some other poor son of Italy entangled in the meshes of the law? Dr. Hanna was his defender and court interpreter."[59]

Hanna also exercised a significant pastoral presence within the Italian community. He nurtured the development of Italian national churches in the diocese and was active in the cathedral parish, preaching regularly in Italian and hearing confessions.[60] One commentator summarized well Hanna's contribution to the Italian community: "There was not a parish in the diocese in which he had not, during his vacation, collected the poor Italians from the highways and the byways, made them acquainted with the local pastor, prepared them for the sacraments, and persuaded them to send their children to Catholic schools."[61]

In Rochester, Hanna began another lifelong passion: his efforts on behalf of workers and organized labor. He summarized his early views on the labor-capital struggle in a January 1898 sermon:

> With the problem of poverty is closely allied the problem of labor. Christ taught by his example the dignity of lowly labor. "The Carpenter's Son" [taught] and by precept and practice did the apostle enforce the same. And if we are to put down the restlessness so evident about us, the strife between capital on the one hand and labor on the other, it can only be by putting into practice the teaching of Jesus Christ which tell alike to master and men what is just and true and right and avoidable to success in this life and the life to come.[62]

Hanna's most significant foray into this perennial battle was his efforts to settle a strike of construction workers, most of whom were Italians, in 1910. Working with labor leaders Anthony Micheli and J. Russell Bursilleri and with Mayor Hiram Edgerton, Hanna was able to quench violence by physically challenging a group of strikers, saying they could advance their rightful cause only by nonviolent means. Not one violent action was reported. Although a deal had been brokered between workers and owners for a one cent per hour wage hike, the strike was settled only when Hanna convinced contractors to make the raise effective immediately and not at the end of the work season, as owners had originally proposed.[63]

Hanna's reputation as a man of compassion, justice, and fairness, plus his experience with labor and immigrant groups, made him the natural selection to head a committee investigating sweatshop conditions and other alleged irregularities in Rochester's clothing industry, which were reported in a June 14, 1912, *New York World* story. The Chamber of Commerce promptly formed a special six-man commission, chaired by Hanna, to investigate and to report actual conditions. Hanna was a member of the Board of Trade, but it was his "integrity and broad sympathies" as well as his experience that made him a natural selection.[64] Acting in teams of two, the committee spent the next four months inspecting 139 local clothes manufacturing sites, checking such things as ventilation, heating, lighting, cleanliness, and bathroom facilities and taking note of minors who were working and the wages being paid to all employees. The committee's thirty-eight-page report, which detailed its findings, was generally favorable, demonstrating that the *New York World* story was at best an exaggeration and at worst a fabrication. The most notable and consistent problems were insufficient ventilation, lack of pneumatic cleaning systems, inadequate heat for winter and cooling for summer, and lack of cleanliness. The report recommended the removal of all outside privies and stoves as heating apparatus, and mandated several hygiene improvements. However, overall the committee found that conditions for 86 percent of the workers were good or excellent.[65]

Hanna's work on the committee was recognized by Henry Morgan, chairman of the Rochester Chamber of Commerce, who spoke of the priest's "splendid work as chairman." He continued, "It is such work as you and your colleagues on the committee accomplished that has made the reputation for efficiency during my administration as President of the Chamber."[66]

Hanna's participation in the labor-capital battle was only one part of his widespread efficacy in the civic realm. His success was due to his wide appeal to all constituencies of the local community, his strong sense of justice, and his affable and kind disposition. In

1910, when he celebrated his twenty-fifth anniversary as a priest, a local paper referred to him as "one of the best known Catholic clergymen in this [eastern] section of the country."[67] He was perceived to be a friend of the poor, an upright man with a gentle and humble manner who never placed himself above the people. The impression Hanna made on others was beautifully summarized on the occasion of his consecration as bishop:

> They [the people] thought of him not as the greatly gifted, but as the greatly gentle. Great is the power of learning, but greater still the power of loving. Here was and is a gentleman in the truest and tenderest sense of the word, a man not only that will inflict no pain, but a man also that will spend himself to spread happiness.[68]

Another Rochester observer commented on Hanna's universal appeal,

> During the twelve years of my sojourn in Rochester, years in which I had ample opportunity to see and know what manner of man the Auxiliary Bishop of San Francisco is, I know no one so intimately linked with all kinds and conditions of humanity and always for the advancement of some good cause, as he.[69]

The number and variety of civic groups and organizations to which Hanna gave his expertise and time was significant and became a trademark of his priestly style that would continue throughout his life. Between 1901 and 1912, he was highly active in the Society for the Prevention of Cruelty to Children, serving as vice president of the Rochester chapter beginning in 1904. He was a founder of the Rochester Public Health Association and served as its permanent vice president and chairman of the dispensing committee, hosting an annual dinner for the physicians and staff of the association to encourage their work.[70] Again presaging future endeavors in San Francisco, Hanna demonstrated special interest in children's needs, especially antituberculosis campaigns. He also assisted other groups, including the Chamber of Commerce, the Select Literary Club of Rochester, and the Rochester branch of the

Archeological Institute of America. In 1908 he was named to a task force to amalgamate the disparate charitable agencies in the city; the United Charities of Rochester, the result of the task force's efforts, was chartered on May 17, 1910.[71] Hanna was also a charter member and unofficial chaplain of the Rochester Council (#178) of the Knights of Columbus from its beginning in 1896 until his departure from the city in December 1912.[72]

Hanna's intellectual acumen gave him access to a select group of the city's leading citizens through his participation in the Fortnightly Club, an organization founded on January 26, 1882, at the home of Dr. Charles E. Fitch. Originally six members, the group had expanded to twelve by the time of its first official meeting on February 23. The club was "a meeting of gentlemen interested...in social and literary purposes" who met approximately every two weeks during the fall and winter months and discussed academic ideas through the research and delivery of papers at their gatherings.[73] Hanna was invited to join this elite group in 1898, the first Catholic priest to be so honored; he remained a participating member until he left Rochester in 1912. Extant records show that during this period Hanna gave eleven papers to the group over a wide range of topics, but his February 6, 1906, presentation, "The New Apologetic in the Roman Catholic Church," may be his most significant. Although the paper has not survived, the title reveals that Hanna, like most Catholic theologians of the day, was aware of modernism, the new theological trend that was causing a stir in Europe, which, as described fully in chapter 2, delayed Hanna's progress to the Church's episcopal rank.[74]

The Fortnightly Club provided Hanna with both an academic outlet outside of St. Bernard's and access to some of the most significant members of Rochester society. Hanna described the club's significance for him:

> It was good for me, wrapped as I was in my own dogmatic position, to be obliged to defend it against the objections of right-minded men, who were looking for the truth as anxiously as I was. It was a unique collection of men, and it will ever be good to remember that I was honored by a place among them.[75]

The repartee that Hanna enjoyed with the Fortnightly Club and Hanna's ability to gain varied perspectives on many issues are best illustrated by his relationship with Algernon Crapsey, rector of St. Andrew Episcopal Church, whose modernist views led to his removal from the church. One observer noted their clash, yet their common passion:

> It is difficult to conceive of two men with less in common than Dr. Crapsey and Dr. Hanna—the Episcopalian socialist and the devout Catholic scholar....In theology they stood at opposite poles. On the relations of Church and State, and of religion to public education, they were squarely divided. Yet, by means of common sympathy with the underdogs, similar beliefs in the rights of labor, instinctive preference for the poor over the rich, they were much alike. Both loved God and man, but had different ways of showing it. On the cause and cure of poverty, the one might quote Karl Marx or Henry George, the other the encyclicals of the Popes. Both men knew how to get close to workingmen and how toi [*sic*] make friends with children. Each recognized in the other a keen mind and a kind heart. That was enough.[76]

Hanna's association with the Fortnightly Club continued after his departure from Rochester. On December 10, 1912, the club met, but instead of the normal paper presentation, they paid tribute to Hanna by electing him an honorary member, the first of the club's history. Hanna missed the group's camaraderie, and whenever he was in Rochester in later years, he did his best to connect with the club, attending dinners in his honor in September 1914 and November 1915.[77] After assuming the reins as archbishop in San Francisco, he still expressed his affection and longing for the group:

> I am still with you in spirit and my memory goes back gratefully to the old days with the Fortnightly. It was a privilege to associate with you, one & all. Also for me it was a development and an education. You seemingly knew little of my training and attitude of mind, and I in the presence of perfectly honest,

outspoken men had a free opportunity to tell the...truth of the principles and of the line of action I had espoused. Then I would always remember with great joy the kindness with which, when I was a total stranger, the elders of the Club took me to their hearts.[78]

Hanna continued to attend Fortnightly meetings whenever his travel schedule and the club's meetings coincided.[79]

Conclusion

Edward Hanna's years in Rochester, from his youth to his first twenty-seven years as a priest, were joyful days filled with accomplishments that presaged his future career as archbishop of San Francisco. Always the gentleman who cared for those who had less, Hanna used his talents to serve God's people in many realms. His intellectual acumen, recognized by Pope Leo XIII, as well as many contemporaries, was exercised most significantly as an educator, first at St. Andrew's Preparatory School and then, beginning in the fall of 1893, at St. Bernard's Seminary. A professor of dogmatics for almost twenty years Hanna was well known and loved by students in the classroom, but he was also well respected as a confessor. In a foreshadowing of his future episcopal career he became highly involved in civic affairs, working especially with Italian immigrants, helping to mediate strikes and heading a commission to investigate alleged irregularities in Rochester's clothing industry. The city of Rochester, while a comfortable environment, could not hold this man of great potential forever. But Hanna's road to the episcopacy and San Francisco was not an easy one, casting a shadow upon him, his scholarship, and the Diocese of Rochester itself. It is to this story that we must now turn.

Chapter 2

THE ROUGH ROAD TO SAN FRANCISCO

Intellectually brilliant and popular among varied constituencies, Edward Hanna had made a deep impression within the highest circles of church and state, both in the city of Rochester and beyond. As an educator at St. Bernard's Seminary, one of the more significant national training grounds for Catholic clergy in the United States, Hanna had the respect of his local ordinary and hundreds of seminarians and clergy that he trained. As friend and advocate for the Italian community in the city, chairman of the commission investigating possible irregularities in the clothing industry, and the first Catholic priest to become a member of the prestigious Fortnightly Club, Hanna had also gained the respect of the civic realm of society. He seemed marked for future greatness, but the first stretch of his journey to the archbishopric of San Francisco would be quite rocky, with some unexpected twists and turns. Yet Hanna was not one to shy away from challenge, so he persisted on the path that would lead him to the West Coast and his reputation as San Francisco's most beloved archbishop.

Theological Modernism in Europe and the United States

American Catholicism received a severe warning on January 22, 1899, when Pope Leo XIII's Apostolic Letter *Testem benevolentiae* was sent to Cardinal James Gibbons. The letter was issued to correct "certain contentions which have arisen,…which disturb the minds, if not of all, at least of many."[1] Pope Leo labeled these contentions "Americanism," a progressive movement that promoted a distinctly American understanding of the Church. Americanism had split the hierarchy along partisan lines. The progressives were led by Cardinal James Gibbons of Baltimore, but the campaign was championed by Archbishop John Ireland of St. Paul, Minnesota, with support from Denis O'Connell and Bishop John Keane. The conservative force was led by Archbishop Michael Corrigan of New York and his suffragan, Bernard McQuaid. Initially the Americanists had triumphed in their progressive stance,[2] but Leo's edict challenged the spirituality and basic axioms of the movement.[3]

Although Americanism as understood in *Testem benevolentiae* had been condemned, the movement's ideas lived on. Michael Gannon states that although the condemnation may have dampened American Catholics politically, socially, and ecumenically, intellectual circles ranged farther and more freely than ever before, "seeking to know whatever was true in the relationships between religion and the new physical and historical sciences."[4] Articles in the *American Catholic Quarterly Review* and the *American Ecclesiastical Review* described the latest intellectual investigations, such as advances in scriptural exegesis, historical science, and evolution studies in Europe.

European Catholic scholars continued the progressive thought initiated in the Enlightenment and fostered by the rise of rationalism. In an attempt to break out from a scriptural historiography perceived as stagnant, the scholars generated a new apologetic that was eventually labeled "modernism." This progressive theological understanding was based on two pillars: (1) the use of the historical critical method in the study of scripture and (2) belief in the development of doctrine. This form of higher criticism was seen as challenging to the faith and was swiftly condemned by Pope Pius X in 1907 with the publication of *Lamentabili sane exitu* (July) and *Pascendi Dominici Gregis* (September). The British theologian Cuthbert Butler wrote after the condemnation, "Xtian origins, New Testament, History of Dogma, etc.—have been made impossible for a priest, except in the most narrow apologetic terms."[5]

While the writings and history of European modernists such as Baron Friedrich von Hügel, Alfred Loisy, and George Tyrrell,

SJ, have been well documented, American modernism has received less attention.[6] Recent efforts have centered on two avowed American modernists, John Slattery and William Laurence Sullivan.[7] Additionally, Thomas J. Mulvey, a Brooklyn priest, and Dr. Henry Poels, a professor of sacred scripture at the Catholic University of America, have been classified as modernists.[8] The most complete analysis of theological modernism in America, by the historian R. Scott Appleby, demonstrates that modernist ideas were circulating in specific intellectual centers and seminaries and were found in the writings of specific Catholic intellectuals, thus refuting the earlier claim of historian and archivist Thomas McAvoy, CSC, that modernism never formally existed in the United States.[9]

The European apologetic that forced Pius X to issue his aforementioned 1907 documents began to appear in America around the turn of the century. Prior to 1900 the most noted censure of modernist thought was directed against the work of John Zahm, CSC. In *Evolution and Dogma* (1896) Zahm admitted that the development of the universe and all it contains was under God's direction. In 1898 the Vatican censured Zahm. In order to ease tensions and to avoid having the book placed on the Index, the Congregation of Holy Cross, Zahm's religious order, removed the book from circulation.[10] Earlier Zahm had been affiliated with Denis O'Connell's "Liberty Hall" in Rome.[11] His thought thus represents the transition and continuity between Americanism and the new apologetic of modernism.[12]

The foremost center of this new intellectual activity in America was St. Joseph's Seminary at Dunwoodie in Yonkers, New York. Archbishop Michael Corrigan had invited the Sulpicians to head the faculty at St. Joseph's in 1896.[13] During their tenure the Sulpicians gathered a distinguished and progressive-thinking faculty including James Driscoll, president of the seminary from 1901 to 1909, noted scripture scholar Francis Gigot, and dogmatic theology specialist John Bruneau. Francis Duffy and John Brady, who were also theological progressives, served on the philosophy faculty.

St. Joseph's principal contribution to the advancement of modernism was its sponsorship of the *New York Review*. Started and promoted by Duffy and Brady, with the support of Driscoll and Archbishop John Farley of New York, the *Review* began publishing in 1905 and was the finest American Catholic theological journal of its day. As editor of the *Review*, Driscoll encouraged scholars to submit articles that stimulated intellectual inquiry, especially the higher criticism then popular in scholarly circles. The *Review* emphasized the reconstruction of theology rather than promoting the new apologetic alone. Michael DeVito in his critical history of the *Review* states:

> Those professors believed that the expressions of revelation are culturally conditioned and that the Church in their day was failing to communicate the Dogmas of the Faith to the modern world because it was using the expressions and philosophy of a past age....The Dunwoodie professors believed that only an *aggiornamento* in the Church would reconcile the ancient Faith with modern science.

Farley told the editors to go ahead "by all means," saying that it would "render an invaluable service to the Church as well as be a fine witness to the scholarship of his seminary faculty."[14]

American Catholic theologians accused of modernism demonstrated the clash of ecclesiologies between the institutional Church, represented by Pius X and *Pascendi*, and modernity, as expressed in the United States by Driscoll, St. Joseph's, and the *New York Review*. Traditional Catholicism had viewed the Church, as revealed by Jesus Christ to the Jerusalem community, as an immutable deposit of faith that tradition had made clear. The Neoscholastic synthesis, as stated in the aforementioned *Aeterni Patris* (1879), protected this belief. Disciples of nineteenth-century liberalism and romanticism, outgrowths of the Enlightenment and the French Revolution, viewed tradition differently. For these more rational thinkers, the deposit of faith given by Jesus was not static and tradition was not its guardian. Rather, tradition articulated the fuller development of this revelation, with scientific methodologies in scriptural exegesis and systematic investigation seen as shedding more light on this development. The perceived threat of modernism in undermining the deposit of faith placed the pope on the defensive and caused him to act.

The Need for a Coadjutor Bishop in San Francisco

In March 1901, Pope Leo XIII authorized the presentation of a *terna* for the position of coadjutor to Archbishop Patrick Riordan of San Francisco, who had asked for help when the pressures of governance caused health problems. One year later, in March 1902, after receiving advice from fellow prelates, Riordan completed the *terna* with George Montgomery, his former chancellor and secretary as *dignissimus*. On September 5, Montgomery was appointed as Riordan's coadjutor with the right of succession, but less than five years later, on January 10, 1907, Montgomery died unexpectedly from complications of diabetes and appendicitis.[15]

Riordan wasted no time in initiating the process to seek Montgomery's successor, obtaining permission from Rome to submit a *terna* at his earliest opportunity. The archbishop wrote to Bishop McQuaid in Rochester, seeking his opinion on Edward Hanna, whose success in the 1886 theological disputation before Leo XIII had become legendary. While seeking information on Hanna, Riordan listed certain qualities that he wanted:

> He should be physically strong, have a good business mind, and while an orator is not needed yet a man who could present the truths of our religion to our people and one who will take an interest in Seminary and school work. I shall be only too glad to give him a free hand in doing whatever he wishes to build up the Kingdom of our Master on this Coast.[16]

McQuaid recommended Hanna without qualification, expressing complete faith in his priest and congratulating Riordan on his choice. Riordan replied to McQuaid, "I am grateful to you for your letter about Dr. Hanna and it is just what I always heard from others. You know better than anybody else and your recommendation carries a great weight with me."[17]

Archbishop Riordan also enlisted the advice of Denis O'Connell, who knew Hanna well from his days as rector of the North American College. Riordan wanted to know if Hanna was "strong in health,...a fairly good business man,...a man who is active for souls, zealous in the ministry." O'Connell, now rector at the Catholic University of America, was happy to recommend one of his former star students for the coadjutor position.[18]

Riordan's investigation convinced him that Hanna was the right person for the coadjutorship. He wrote to McQuaid, "There is no doubt whatsoever about Dr. Hanna being first on both lists."[19] Hanna was listed as *dignissimus* on the *terna*, with Richard Neagle of Boston and John J. Lawler of St. Paul as the alternates.

Despite Hanna's earlier rejection by McQuaid for the coadjutor position in Rochester, support for the priest's candidacy met no initial opposition. The American hierarchy lined up to pledge their support not only for Hanna but for Riordan, who was highly desirous of the priest's selection. Cardinal James Gibbons and Archbishops Ireland, Patrick Ryan, and John Glennon all sent letters of recommendation to Cardinal Girolamo Gotti, prefect of *Propaganda Fide*. Riordan himself led the forces supporting Hanna. Ostensibly in the east to attend a Board of Trustees meeting at Catholic University, Riordan continued on to Rome for his third *ad limina* report to the pope, where he planned to lobby on Hanna's behalf while keeping a close watch on events.

Additional supporters materialized in Rome. The American apostolic delegate, Archbishop Diomede Falconio, felt that Hanna would be selected.[20] Thomas Kennedy, rector of the North American College and a classmate of Hanna, planned to lobby, especially with former apostolic delegates Archbishops Francesco Satolli and Sebastiano Martinelli.[21] Gotti himself told Riordan that "very strong letters in favor of H.[anna] had reached him."[22]

As the time approached for *Propaganda Fide* to meet, it seemed that Hanna would be approved. McQuaid was supremely confident in writing to Riordan, "In my mind there is absolute certainty of your obtaining a coadjutor of your choice."[23] Riordan became so confident that he invited McQuaid to preach at Hanna's forthcoming consecration.[24]

That confidence was shattered in the fall of 1907. As early as the spring of 1906, Alexis M. Lepicier, OSM, professor of dogmatic theology at the Urban College, had used his classroom to challenge Hanna's orthodoxy based on a series of articles entitled "The Human Knowledge of Christ," published in the *New York Review*.[25] In December 1907 Cardinal Gotti asked Lepicier to formally critique the essays,[26] and the *terna* was formally submitted on August 16, 1907. But even before that, Hanna realized his articles were causing problems.[27]

Francis Duffy had invited Hanna to write the articles for the *Review* and had published them in the first volume between October 1905 and March 1906.[28] Both Duffy and James Driscoll were interested in establishing an association between Hanna and the *Review*. Originally it was hoped that Hanna would serve as associate editor, but due to his commitments at St. Bernard's, Hanna was not interested in the editorial position.

Lepicier's accusations were highly ill timed for Hanna.[29] The publication on September 8 of *Pascendi Dominici Gregis* filled Rome with electricity in seeking out "both authors and propagandists, [who state] there is to be nothing stable, nothing immutable in the Church."[30] The modernist rebuttal to the pope's encyclical raised the specter of excommunication for all, "authors, printers and abettors" of the new apologetic.[31]

Riordan instantly mounted a campaign to save Hanna's candidacy, but the situation only grew worse. He asked McQuaid to write to Satolli supporting Hanna and suggested that Hanna himself write to Satolli and Gotti, expressing amazement at the challenge to his orthodoxy.[32] However, in December the Rochester press reported that sources in Rome were describing Hanna as "being infected with Modernism." Worse still, a second accusation was made against Hanna, this time for an essay entitled "Absolution," which he had written for the newly published *Catholic Encyclopedia*.[33] Andrew Meehan, St. Bernard's professor of moral theology and canon law, who was in Rome on sabbatical, reported, "Hanna's affair is 'una bruta cosa.'...They don't charge him with heresy, but with not speaking out....It amounts to this: that they are sorely disappointed in him."[34]

The source of the accusations against Hanna came to light in late 1907, when Meehan and Salvatore Brandi, editor of *Civiltà Cattolica*, reported that the complaints against Hanna had come from America.[35] McQuaid initially assumed the plot was against St. Bernard's and the success it had achieved: "His [Hanna's] enemies here in America are likely to be some who have been unfriendly to St. Bernard's from the beginning. Our success has made many enemies; other seminaries will have to change their methods and improve their standards."[36] As the new year dawned, it was learned that charges received at the office of the cardinal secretary of state, Rafael Merry del Val, had come from Rochester. One week before the scheduled *Propaganda Fide* meeting, which was to act on the Hanna recommendation, Meehan wrote in distress to McQuaid, "It has been said here in Rome that one of our own number at St. Bernard's was opposing Dr. Hanna." Meehan further reported that Riordan knew the source of the complaint.[37]

Stung by the possibility that Hanna's accuser had come from within the St. Bernard's faculty, McQuaid immediately ordered the faculty to sign a written proclamation stating that they were not involved in the delation. When the document was released, the only member of the faculty who had not signed was Andrew Breen, professor of sacred scripture.[38]

The revelation of Breen as Hanna's accuser was a shock to McQuaid, who promptly removed Breen from the faculty.

> The best interests of St. Bernard's Seminary require that you should withdraw from it. I would advise that this act of withdrawal should be your own. Should no bishop be willing to receive you into his diocese, I will then name you to a parish of Rochester, though I am strongly of the conviction that another field of labor would be preferable as a means to a rehabilitation and a new start in life.

McQuaid felt betrayed, telling Breen, "I have lost all confidence in you,...and can, therefore, never trust you again. Enter some other seminary and strive to repair the past. Let your chief aim be to save your own soul."[39] Breen resigned from the St. Bernard's faculty and was initially assigned to Sts. Peter and Paul Parish in Rochester. In

February 1909 he was made pastor of St. Patrick Parish in Mount Morris, New York.[40]

What motivated Breen to bring accusations against Hanna? Sources suggest three possible answers to this difficult question. The most common explanation for Breen's action was envy, caused partly by Hanna's popularity with students[41] but mostly by Breen's dismal academic record compared to Hanna's brilliance. McQuaid had asked Breen to obtain a doctorate in scripture, but after twice failing to produce satisfactory dissertations for the Biblical Commission in Rome he returned to Rochester with a *licentiate.* Bishop McQuaid deplored Breen's apparent "insane jealousy,"[42] which led to a personal attack on Hanna. In an unusually angry tone, McQuaid wrote to Archbishop Farley,

> I have shown unusual forbearance toward Breen, who is so self-conceited that he is unable to appreciate it. Breen is possessed with insane jealousy of Hanna. For four months he plotted against the latter in an underhanded way. It is only when he was unmasked that he repented. How could I trust such a man in the future?[43]

McQuaid said that Breen's "jealousy of Hanna, and of everybody more popular than himself was his only cause."[44]

Breen's claim that Hanna held "loose views on some essential tenets" was a second possible rationale. He informed a friend in Rome about Hanna's writings well aware that his was not the popular view but claimed: "The people care little for orthodoxy."[45] Breen explained in detail his motivation and rationale for action:

> What I did in my correspondence with Rome, I did not in any malice....There are times when loose theories of religion are the fashion. They do not benefit the world; on the contrary they tend to destroy all religion. Feeling persuaded that the revered candidate in question held certain views dangerous to the Church, I sent a specimen of these to a friend in Rome. I did not write to the Propaganda nor to any Cardinal. I wrote a letter to the Most Reverend Archbishop Riordan expressing my views. No word was said reflecting on the revered candidate's

character. I detest some of the theories of the revered candidate while esteeming the man. I expressed to the Most Reverend Archbishop my regret that I had mentioned this obstacle to the election of the candidate. Now, I may have been unduly alarmed, but certainly I had some cause, for Rome had declared that the articles produced [by Hanna] gave a "painful impression." In view of this I feel an injustice has been done me by declaring that I am "the guilty one." My conduct was not secret. I wrote in good faith and at the dictate of my conscience. My superior could have had a complete statement of my action at any time for the asking. I know that mine is not the popular side of the question. The people prefer affable kindly people to those of stricter orthodoxy. But [as with] all events, this which I have honestly written should be considered in judging me.[46]

Meehan reported to McQuaid, "I believe that Dr. B[reen] is honest in the matter from his viewpoint at least to a certain extent."[47] Breen wanted Rome to examine Hanna's writings. He stated, "If he [Hanna] is not sound in orthodoxy he ought not be made Archbishop. If he is sound, Rome will give him the post. No injustice will be done him."[48] Another interesting theory about Breen's motivation is that he was simply a pawn in a plot hatched on the West Coast to keep East Coast Church influence out of San Francisco. Although there is no extant evidence to verify the claim, some at the time of the delation suggested that Breen was contacted by West Coast bishops and asked to serve as their "agent." Additionally, several Church officials in San Francisco were touting the Irish-born labor priest Peter Yorke for the coadjutor position.[49]

Edward Hanna's Theology

Breen's accusations against Hanna require an analysis of the latter's scholarly writings. As stated earlier, the New York Review, which sought to be "a journal of ancient faith and modern thought,"[50] led the progressive assault on theological study in America. Michael DeVito, the Review's chronicler, describes the journal as a new venue for discussing the Christian faith according to the styles and experiences of contemporary life.[51] The *Review*'s promoters were aware that its method of theological reconstruction might be challenged.[52] The journal pushed forward, however, publishing articles in its first volume by George Tyrrell, SJ, and William Sullivan, CSP. Given these developments, Hanna's essays in the *Review* implicate him as a modernist by virtue of his association with the journal and its modernist contributors.

Hanna's first essay, "The Human Knowledge of Christ I," puts his entire effort in perspective. He begins by acknowledging the dangers inherent in such an investigation,[53] then summarizes the opinions of earlier theologians on the question of Christ's human knowledge: some admit to a limitation of knowledge; others claim there was none. Hanna closely examines the kenotic theory, which questions whether Christ possessed the beatific vision from the outset. He concludes:

> Some kind of kenosis must be admitted....One can see readily how the accepted Kenotic Theories affect the question of the human knowledge of Christ and how a "depotentiated logos" theory must give us in Christ only a human consciousness even though such consciousness is supernaturally illuminated to the highest degree.

This essay draws no conclusions on the questions raised, a pattern that would continue in all of Hanna's initial *Review* articles. In answer to the kenotic question, Hanna states that since the Church has made no definite decision, after an analysis of the literature, he too will draw no conclusion. He writes: "Seemingly the Church has given no definite decision. It is a question then that must be settled so far as may be for the present, through a careful study of the Scriptures, the Fathers and the theologians."[54] Although the article draws no conclusions, it does not challenge the three "chief difficulties" of the modernists, as expressed by *Pascendi*: scholastic philosophy, authority of the fathers and of tradition, and the magisterium.[55]

"The Human Knowledge of Christ II" analyzes the basic question under investigation through a review of scripture. Overwhelming evidence exists in the Bible favoring the superior knowledge of Christ. Hanna, however, discusses texts that shed doubt on Christ's perfect knowledge, including the idea of Jesus' growth in knowledge (Luke 2:40, 52) and his apparent ignorance of the date of the Parousia (Mark 13:32). As with his earlier effort, Hanna states that scripture gives no answer as to whether Jesus possessed the beatific vision from the outset. Hanna, therefore, draws no personal conclusion, stating that it is impossible to know the mind of Christ.[56]

In this essay Hanna makes an important distinction between the human lack of knowledge that may have existed in Jesus and ignorance on the part of Christ. He states that it is possible to conclude that Jesus the human person grew in knowledge without claiming that errors in teaching resulted from any possible limitation in knowledge. He writes,

> It is one thing to say that Christ grew in knowledge, that as a man he did not know all things; and quite another to say that he erred in giving expression to certain ideas—that he said certain things which he thought to be true, but which the further development of knowledge has found to be false. To state this means to say that he was deceived, and that, though unwittingly, he deceived others.[57]

Hanna's second essay subtly challenges the tradition of the Church, analyzing the scriptural record to imply that Jesus as God might not have known all things from all time. Although he uses the text critically, Hanna's analysis does not support the immutability of God in all things, a position that violates tradition. Additionally, Hanna's scriptural orthodoxy is suspect when he questions but does not challenge the Mosaic authorship of the Pentateuch.[58]

Like the first two installments of "The Human Knowledge of Christ," the third summarizes previous literature on the question at hand, namely, the opinions of the fathers and doctors of the Church on two specific passages, Luke 2:52 and Mark 13:32. Although he argues that others have at least implied some limitation to Christ's human knowledge, Hanna draws no conclusions.[59] Hanna's failure to draw personal conclusions in this and former essays was seen by the Vatican as symptomatic of the modernist approach.[60] The historian of American theological modernism R. Scott Appleby summarizes Hanna's theology in his series on "The Human Knowledge of Christ": "Applying a developmental model of human knowledge to the question of Jesus' own self awareness, Hanna concluded by 1906 that Jesus grew in knowledge of his divine mission and implied that he shared the cultural limitations of his contemporaries."[61]

Hanna's *Catholic Encyclopedia* articles also require a review. In his essay entitled "Absolution" he outlined both the history and the practice of sacramental absolution in the Church. Speaking of the development of doctrine, Hanna wrote, "But it is one thing to assert that the power of absolution was granted to the Church, and another to say that a full realization of the grant was in the consciousness of the Church from the beginning."[62] This written analysis of the concept of absolution was consistent with his classroom approach to the subject.[63] However, his essay on "Penance" makes specific reference to *Lamentabili sane exitu* and maintains no development:

> It is therefore Catholic doctrine that the Church from the earliest times believed in the power to forgive sins as granted by Christ to the Apostles. Such a belief in fact was clearly inculcated by the words with which Christ granted the power and it would have been inexplicable to the early Christians if anyone who professed faith in Christ had questioned the existence of that power in the Church.[64]

Lepicier, who had criticized the "Human Knowledge of Christ" essays, saw a conflict between *Lamentabili* proposition 46 and Hanna's statement on absolution. The decree had condemned the idea of a gradual development of Church authority concerning absolution,[65] yet Hanna allowed for such development by intimating that the full consciousness of absolution was not present in the church from the outset. In addition to the specific proposition of *Lamentabili* with reference to absolution, *Pascendi*, which Lepicier supported, condemned Hanna's advocacy of the development of doctrine several times.[66]

The Delation of 1908

The Congregation *Propaganda Fide* met on January 13, 1908, to decide the Hanna case. Different sources said different things about the attitude of the Congregation as its members assembled. The *San Francisco Examiner* and *Rochester Post Express* were confident that *Propaganda* would approve Hanna at the scheduled meeting,[67] but Andrew Meehan was not optimistic, telling McQuaid that the Italians were sure to turn Hanna down.[68] *Propaganda* met without raising the issue of the coadjutor position in San Francisco. It was obvious to all that the congregation had intentionally postponed the decision so that the allegations against Hanna could be investigated further. After a long effort to personally lobby the Roman officials, Riordan was "sorely disappointed" with the delay.[69]

Despite the delay, it was commonly believed that Hanna would eventually be named as Riordan's coadjutor. The press reported that Hanna was still the most acceptable candidate on the *terna* and should be named by March 13.[70] Riordan left Rome confident that once the furor had died down Hanna would be selected. McQuaid could find no problems with Hanna's writings, declaring that in all likelihood he would be consecrated soon after Easter.[71]

Why was McQuaid so ardent and forceful in his support of Hanna throughout this affair? One view says that McQuaid believed Hanna had been wronged in his delation. As an ardent conservative in the Americanist crisis ten years earlier, McQuaid was a defender of papal authority and orthodoxy. Since *Pascendi* had mandated bishops to report any people or writings that seemed modernist in perspective,[72] McQuaid's failure to report Hanna indicated that he found Hanna's writings unexceptional. In his opinion, Hanna was merely restating old arguments. The bishop wrote Merry del Val,

> I am not asking to shield Dr. Hanna from the consequences of heretical teachings if of such he has been guilty, but after extensive inquiry among the ablest theologians we are unable to see where the heresy exists. To overshadow for life such a man as Dr. Hanna, whose faith, charity to the poor, piety and every priestly virtue are known everywhere, would be a calamity.[73]

McQuaid's personal relationship with Hanna may also help explain his unwavering support. Many facts demonstrate the bishop's personal affection for Hanna. As a seminarian Hanna had been "picked out" by McQuaid for study in Rome, grooming him for a future in education. In 1909, when McQuaid was on his deathbed, he gave his episcopal ring to Hanna, saying he would need it.[74] On the other hand it was McQuaid who had rejected Hanna in 1905 as his own coadjutor due to a clash of ecclesiologies.

Most probably, however, McQuaid's primary reason for ardently defending Hanna was to preserve the reputation of St. Bernard's Seminary. When accusations challenging Hanna's orthodoxy became public, McQuaid worried about the consequences for the seminary. He wrote, "If this charge had any foundation it would implicate St. Bernard's Seminary and myself....St. Bernard's...cannot afford to incur the slightest suspicion of weakness in the Faith, or in any degree lose the confidence of the Holy See. St. Bernard's stands for what is sound and pure in morals."[75] He also argued that the theology taught at St. Bernard's was sound:

> I know my professors well, as I am constantly with them, and I am sure that there is no tinge of unsoundness in their speech and thoughts. Nearly all of them have been educated at the Propaganda and under Cardinal Satolli himself, and if per chance one of them took up a liberal tone of speech, others would make short work of his speculations.[76]

McQuaid's eagerness to preserve the seminary's reputation also motivated his dismissal of Breen following the revelation of his accusations. As rector of the seminary McQuaid needed to support the theology taught at his institution. Thus, it was imperative that Hanna's orthodoxy be supported and that Breen be dismissed. As McQuaid wrote, "In arriving at these conclusions [that Breen must be dismissed]...I am governed solely by a conviction of duty toward the future welfare of the Seminary."[77]

Breen was convinced that McQuaid's response to Hanna's case was driven by his desire for the glory that Hanna's appointment would shed on the seminary and that this desire blinded McQuaid to the errors in Hanna's essays.[78] McQuaid's defense of Hanna was supported by the faculty and students at St. Bernard's. Eleven members of the faculty, all save Breen, signed a letter that in part read: "We, the undersigned, declare each one for himself,…that this accusation, so detrimental to the good name of Dr. Hanna, [and] of the Seminary and the Rt. Rev. Bishop as well, merits our most earnest condemnation."[79] When the news of Hanna's delation reached the seminary, the surprised students met and wrote a letter of support for their beloved professor:

> Resolved—That we, the entire student body of St. Bernard's Seminary, having had every opportunity of observing both his theological teaching and his practice of Christian virtues, take this opportunity to express our commendation of him as a model instructor and true priest, deserving and inspiring our initiation.[80]

Many officials in Rome and members of the American church hierarchy joined in the defense of Hanna's orthodoxy. Riordan fought hard for Hanna, asking Gibbons, Farley, and O'Connell to promote Hanna's candidacy on their forthcoming summer visits to Rome and personally lobbying for several months with Vatican officials.[81] Satolli, although somewhat infirm, continued to support his former student,[82] as did Salvatore Brandi and Abbot Francis Gasquet.[83]

Given the turmoil caused by Hanna's articles, one has to wonder about his motivation. When asked by Duffy to submit "something theological" why did Hanna choose such a controversial and dangerous topic as the human knowledge of Christ? Hanna left no personal papers, but one letter does reveal his motivation in writing his essays for the *Review*. In correspondence with *Propaganda Fide*, Hanna stated,

> If I erred, I erred in method, not in doctrine. Apart from us the Protestants held a doctrine called "kenosis" which truly negates the divinity of Christ; apart from us the Protestants and Modernists hold that Our Lord had erred especially in reference to the day of judgement. I have written these articles to defend the divinity of Our Lord against the Protestants and

to affirm him free of every suspicion of error against some Modernists....I was only writing an academic dissertation.[84]

The failure of *Propaganda* to act in January prompted Satolli and Riordan to ask Hanna to write two additional articles to answer the objections raised against his essays "Absolution" and "The Human Knowledge of Christ."[85] St. Bernard's faculty also strongly suggested to McQuaid that Hanna write articles clarifying his position and answering the objections raised.[86]

Hanna did publish two articles in the *New York Review* responding to the accusations made against his orthodoxy. The fourth and final part of Hanna's series on "The Human Knowledge of Christ," written to settle the objection that Hanna had drawn no conclusions in his earlier series, summarizes what he said earlier. He asserts that Catholic theology and tradition admit the limitations of Christ's human nature as essential to a finite and created human but deny that these limitations led to error. He acknowledges, along with St. Thomas Aquinas, a real growth in the earthly knowledge of Christ. Hanna's technique in this essay is similar to his former efforts, tracing the teachings of theologians throughout the centuries on Christ's human knowledge. The tone of the article, however, is less bold. He writes, "The same Catholic tradition confirmed in our day by the Syllabus of Pius X [proposition 33] excludes any possibility of error in the human knowledge of Christ."[87]

Hanna explains that the fathers did not teach *ex professo* in their understanding of Christ's knowledge. He also upholds the tradition against the modernists: "Nor does the tradition adown the ages give the slightest help to the Modernist who would admit possible error in the words and in the thoughts of Christ."[88] The article concludes with fourteen summary propositions based on the fathers and theologians he had presented in the essay. Therefore, unlike his earlier essays, in this essay Hanna does draw conclusions, although they are based solely on the writings of others.

For the same issue of the *Review* Hanna also wrote "The Power of the Keys," clarifying and modifying ideas from his *Review* essays and from his article on absolution in the *Catholic Encyclopedia*. Hanna is clear that the tradition is to be upheld and doctrine is to remain immutable. He openly attacks the modernist tendency to

45

admit error in the knowledge of Christ. He does draw conclusions, although again they are based solely on the writings of others. Hanna is more cautious than in earlier works, distinguishing between the unfolding of the practice of absolution and its consciousness in the Church. He admits to a gradual development in the use of penance but states, "There existed in the Church *from the beginning* the power to forgive and to retain sins and that this power is clear from the words of Christ" (emphasis mine).[89] The historian of St. Joseph's Seminary, Thomas Shelley, says that although Hanna virtually repudiated his earlier views, "they were not sufficiently reassuring to remove all doubts about his orthodoxy."[90]

Did the *New York Review* publish Hanna's new articles to prove its own orthodoxy? This question must have occurred to Driscoll, Duffy, and others associated with the journal. Hanna's articles directed the Vatican's attention to the *Review*. The *New York Times* reported that the Vatican had ordered the journal suppressed, although Driscoll denied the claim. Certainly the Holy See would look more favorably on the *Review* if a contributor reversed his negative position regarding more traditional orthodoxy.

Reaction to Hanna's new essays was mixed. Satolli was satisfied, but others thought Hanna needed to clarify his stance even further.[91] Reaction to the new essays came to an abrupt halt, however, when another article, written by Hanna and published in 1906, came to light. The essay, "Some Recent Books on Catholic Theology," published in the *American Journal of Theology* placed Hanna at odds with Cardinals Merry del Val and Gotti.[92] Riordan was informed:

> A thunder[bolt] stroke *[sic]* our house! I am informed that another article of Dr. Hanna in an all Protestant Review was denounced to the Holy See. I do not know what kind of article it is, but the Card[inal] Secretary of State and the Prefect of *Propaganda* are now "absolutely" opposed to Dr. Hanna.[93]

The newly discovered essay effectively erased any good that may have resulted from the recently published *Review* articles.

Analysis of the essay, which reviews leading contemporary theologians and summarizes their ideas, resurrects the specter of modernism. At several points, Hanna admits to development in Roman Catholic tradition and doctrine. An illustrative passage states, "The Roman Catholic religion may be considered as a theology representing the adjustment of divine revelation to the growing intellectual needs of mankind."[94] Moreover, in what might be seen as a rebuff to Vatican officials, Hanna concludes his essay in a somewhat arrogant tone:

> These few extracts culled here and those from works that are current in Roman Catholic circles, will perhaps be indicative of the trend of the new apologetic. The novelty does not seem to frighten the intelligent among Catholics. They seemingly desire to embrace the truth in whatever form it comes.[95]

After a summer of waiting, the nomination of Edward Hanna as coadjutor bishop of San Francisco came to a merciful end. On September 7, 1908, the cardinals of *Propaganda Fide* voted to reject the entire *terna* submitted by Riordan. Theoretically the document was rejected on grounds that it had not been properly prepared; the true reason was more subtle. Riordan explained that the entire *terna* had been rejected to save embarrassment to all concerned, especially Hanna, who would have been seen as condemned if only the section involving his nomination had been rejected.[96]

Hanna's rejection prompted negative reactions in Rochester, including one from the Reverend S. Fraser Langford, at Parsells Avenue Baptist Church:

> One of the saddest things that has happened in recent years to the Catholic Church has been the willingness of the Pope to listen to the charges of modernism against one of the broadest minded and most powerful thinkers of our city. I feel that a great loss has followed the failure to appoint Doctor Hanna to the Bishopric of San Francisco. Such acts rob the Church of the respect of his thinking.[97]

Following Hanna's rejection the Holy See acted quickly to fill the vacant position in San Francisco. Riordan asked that Denis O'Connell, rector of the Catholic University of America, be appointed. Eventually a new *terna* was written and on December 16, 1908, O'Connell was assigned as the new auxiliary bishop in San Francisco, a position that did not give him the right of succession.[98]

Appointment as Auxiliary Bishop of San Francisco

On January 12, 1912, O'Connell was named bishop of Richmond, Virginia, an appointment that created another opening in San Francisco and spurred renewed efforts by Riordan to bring Hanna west. Riordan, who had known the previous summer that O'Connell would be leaving, wrote to Daniel Hudson, CSC, at Notre Dame asking his advice on the candidacy of Dennis J. Dougherty, who was local ordinary in Jaro, Philippines.[99] Riordan wanted a coadjutor, but when Cardinal Gaetano De Lai, prefect of the Consistorial Congregation, informed him that only an auxiliary would be sent, Dougherty's name was dropped, since the appointment would have deprived him of a see; that's when Hanna's name resurfaced. Because the storm of modernism had subsided since Breen's allegations prevented Hanna's appointment the first time around, Hanna's name now moved to the top of the *terna*.

In late October 1912 Riordan and Bishop Thomas Hickey of Rochester were informed that Hanna had been selected as his auxiliary in San Francisco. The news came as a surprise to the Rochester diocese, since "it was not generally known that Dr. Hanna's name had been under consideration for the appointment."[100] Riordan was elated, telling Hanna, "I cannot tell you how much joy all this has given me—nothing ever gave me greater happiness in my life."[101] Riordan gave full expression of his feelings to Daniel Hudson:

> It was a great triumph and my heart is full of joy, for my own sake and for his [Hanna] also, for until now he was under a cloud, and evil minded people were disposed to carp at him because he had been rejected a few years ago but I kept my counsel and remained loyal to him, and at last, for his sake, I brought him through triumphantly. He is a wonderfully good

48

man, learned, and full of apostolic zeal for the building up of the Church, and I am not one to curb activities in that direction. I shall give him a free hand when he comes out to me.[102]

Hanna was consecrated bishop at St. Patrick's Cathedral in Rochester on December 4, 1912. The apostolic delegate, John Bonzano, was consecrator, acting with twenty-one other bishops, including Denis O'Connell, James E. Quigley of Chicago, and Thomas Hickey, who preached the sermon. Numerous invited clerics attended, including Edward Pace, Hanna's classmate from the North American College, and Riordan's chancellor, John Cantwell, representing the Archdiocese of San Francisco.[103] At a banquet following the consecration Mass, Cantwell welcomed Hanna to San Francisco:

> Bishop Hanna, you are coming to no mean city; you enter upon a fair inheritance; your lines have fallen in goodly places....In the name of the clergy of San Francisco, we welcome you to a land rich in Catholic traditions and in the memories of Spanish chivalry. You come to us with [an] Apostolic Commission, and anyone so coming, the clergy of San Francisco will be there with warm hearts and extended arms. You will strengthen the arms of the archbishop and prolong the usefullness *[sic]* of a great life.[104]

Hanna thanked all present, but closed with a special note of gratitude to the clergy of Rochester, who had nurtured and enriched him: "To the priests of the diocese I would say that I came to you over twenty-five years ago inexperienced and poor....I go from you rich in experience gained from the education of your lives."[105]

Conclusion

Edward Hanna was forced to traverse a rough and rocky road to San Francisco. His prominence as a Church scholar and his reputation in the civic community brought him to the forefront when Archbishop Patrick Riordan petitioned the Vatican for a coadjutor following the death of Bishop George Montgomery. Hanna's port-folio made him a logical choice and he seemed a sure bet for the appointment until officials in *Propaganda Fide* were apprised of the content of recent academic writings of Hanna published in the modernist-leaning *New York Review* and the *Catholic Encyclopedia*. When it was discovered that Hanna had been delated by one of his fellow professors at St. Bernard's, the incident became a *cause célèbre* pitting Hanna's many American supporters against the prevailing antimodernist Vatican hierarchy. In order to protect Hanna and St. Bernard's Seminary, the priest's name was summarily removed from the *terna* when, after a full year of debate, it was clear that his appointment was doomed. Nevertheless, Hanna survived to fight another day, and, in 1912, when the auxiliary position was again vacant in San Francisco, Hanna was appointed with no problems and much fanfare.

Hanna's consecration as bishop and appointment to San Francisco initiated a long and distinguished career in the Church and city by the Bay, the state of California, and the United States. Utilizing his Rochester experience, Hanna moved west to serve God's people with compassion and justice in the realms of both church and state.

Chapter 3

The Archbishop of San Francisco

Although his arrival was delayed, Edward Hanna's journey to San Francisco changed him from a scholar priest to a prelate nationally known and respected in both church and state. Hanna hit the road running in San Francisco. Within weeks he was actively engaged as an auxiliary bishop and shortly thereafter began his long association as mediator and administrator with various city and state groups. Hanna's attractive personality drew people to him and made them notice his multiple gifts. He used these talents to serve the local and national Church, supporting Catholic education, parochial ministry, and the American ideals of freedom and democracy, which were severely tested during World War I. Highly respected for his energetic approach to his duties, he represented the church in San Francisco for more than twenty years, as the nation experienced the War to End All Wars, the Roaring Twenties, and the dark days of the Great Depression.

San Francisco Background

By the mid-nineteenth century the city of San Francisco had traveled a circuitous course from obscurity to fame, seemingly overnight. In June 1579 Sir Francis Drake landed north of the bay during his famous circumnavigation of the globe, but only in November 1769 did José Ortega enter the bay. Seven years later the first Spanish colonizing party founded the Presidio and Mission San Francisco de Asis. San Francisco remained a small pueblo during the mission period, but in January 1848 James Marshall discovered gold at Sutter's Mill, some 150 miles northeast of San Francisco, transforming the city's history overnight. By the end of 1849 the small town of one thousand had become a small city of twenty thousand. The historian Tom Cole has captured the flavor of the city: "San Francisco...was the prototypical boom town. Gold dust scented the air. New and old money, ambition, and a bone-deep sense of adventure fueled a nonstop machine of excitement and anticipation."[1] Ten years later, after a minor lull when gold reserves ran low, silver was discovered near Virginia City, Nevada, and once again San Francisco benefited, financially and through growth.

The city's boon-and-bust existence continued through the next fifty years. The Church, established through the Spanish missions, became more formalized with the arrival in December 1850 of Joseph Sadoc Alemany, OP, who served as bishop of Monterey (though he kept a protocathedral in San Francisco) until 1853 when he was appointed the first archbishop of San Francisco. He erected his cathedral parish, St. Mary's (today Old St. Mary's on the corner of Grant and California Streets) in 1854. Financial prosperity after the Civil War brought fame and fortune to many including railroad tycoons Leland Stanford, Mark Hopkins, Collis Huntington, and Charles Crocker. The opening in October 1875 of Billy Ralston's Palace Hotel, described as "probably the fanciest and most outlandish hostelry of its time," was the perfect example of opulence. Golden Gate Park—the dream and product of principal architect William Hammond Hall and his successor and longtime (fifty-three years) park superintendent, John McLaren—grew from a sand dune in 1870 to one of the largest and best-known municipal parks in the country. Prosperity, however, led to crime in the form of the Barbary Coast's gaming houses and bordellos. Citizens responded through vigilante justice during the Gilded Age. Officials in San Francisco's growing municipal government also could not avoid civic corruption. Tom Cole wrote, "San Francisco in the 1880s and 1890s was a city in which civic virtue was as rare as a snowstorm." Meanwhile, by 1890 the city's population had risen to 300,000, making it the eighth largest city in the country.[2]

San Francisco's history was transformed, however, on April 18, 1906, at 5:12 AM when a significant earthquake and resultant fire destroyed a large portion of the center of the city. The initial shock actually only generated 20 percent of the damage incurred; the resultant fires, which raged unchecked for three days, led to the destruction of 500 city blocks, including 28,000 structures and over 450 deaths. Financial loss estimates were between $300 and $500 million.[3] Despite the unparalleled destruction, Archbishop Patrick Riordan, representing the attitude of most San Franciscans, proclaimed on April 27 to the Citizen's Committee:

> I am a citizen of No Mean City, although it is in ashes. Almighty God has fixed this as the location of a great city. The past is gone, and there is no use of lamenting or moaning over it. Let us look to the future and, without regard to creed or birth, work together in harmony for the upbuilding of a greater San Francisco.[4]

At the time of Hanna's appointment as auxiliary bishop, San Francisco was rising like a phoenix from the 1906 disaster. Symbolically and physically the city was rebuilding. On December 28, 1912, Mayor James Rolph led fifty thousand San Franciscans to hail the advent of the city's first public transportation system, known as the Muni Railroad. In 1912 as well the city's voters approved an $8 million bond issue to finance a new civic center complex on the site of the old city hall destroyed by the fire. The city hall, designed by the firm of Arthur Brown and John Bakewell, was the centerpiece of a complex that included a main public library, exposition auditorium, state building, and opera house. The auditorium was opened in January 1915 and the city hall was dedicated later that year on December 29. Rolph also was responsible for municipal efforts to bring potable water to San Francisco from the Hetch Hetchy Valley, some 170 miles east of the city. While water did not flow into the city from this project until 1934, it was Rolph's efforts during the early years of his long nineteen-year tenure as mayor that allowed the project to go forward.[5]

The truly remarkable event, however, that captured world attention that San Francisco had indeed been resurrected was the Panama-Pacific International Exposition (PPIE) of 1915. In January 1911 Congress named San Francisco the official site to host the World's Fair to celebrate the opening of the Panama Canal. While the city of

San Francisco had little to do with the project's construction, Rolph made the exposition the centerpiece of his campaign for mayor. Six hundred acres of tidal land was purchased by the Exposition Company and made ready by landfill provided by the rubble of buildings destroyed in the earthquake. A distinguished group of architects was engaged to construct the exposition's many edifices, including the centerpiece, Palace of Fine Arts, designed by Bernard Maybeck, and the 432–foot Tower of Jewels, which featured fifty thousand tinted pieces of glass and was illuminated by thirty-six tinted spotlights. The fair, which opened on February 20 and closed on December 4, drew over 18.7 million people. The Jesuit historian Bernard McGloin has concluded:

> Even though it had been preceded by the impressive Midwinter Fair of 1894, and was to be followed by the Golden Gate International Exposition of 1939, there is solid room for the opinion that the "PPIE" of 1915 was, all things considered, just about the best of them all.[6]

Almost the entirety of Hanna's time in San Francisco was contiguous with Mayor James Rolph, who in many ways dominated the era. In fact, their association was so close that many Catholics believed Rolph to be one of their own, until he was seen attending a Masonic parade. McGloin has written, "It would not seem an exaggeration to say that, from 1912 to 1931, San Francisco was in a measure, 'Sunny Jim' Rolph while, in equal measure, 'Sunny Jim' represented the best in San Francisco."[7] Practicing the politics of personality par excellence, Rolph, who was convivial, impeccably dressed with a carnation boutonniere, and full of vigor and affability, ran for mayor in 1911 with three construction goals: a new city hall, a public water system, and improved street car transportation. By the end of his first term two of the three goals were attained and the third in process. Historians William Issel and Robert Cherny comment on Rolph's accomplishments during his first term: "Rolph used the new street car line, like the new city hall and the PPIE, to promote a sense of unity and accomplishment, and he welded these feelings of unity and accomplishment to his own personality." More generally they conclude: "Rolph...rejected the narrow definition of municipal government and refused to limit the city government's role merely to the provision of some essential services…and to the franchising of private companies to provide other necessary services."[8]

After Rolph's first term, however, while his effusive personality and love for the role as mayor never diminished, his zealous style of leadership shifted to a more presidential style, seeking a less active voice and being content to reign over an increasingly factious municipal political scene. Rolph redefined the office of mayor during the 1920s. Issel and Cherny write: "From the war [World War I] onward, Rolph exercised less and less executive leadership, increasingly left administrative duties to others,…and preferred leading parades and hosting starlets."[9]

The Auxiliary Bishop of San Francisco, 1912–1915

Shortly after his consecration in Rochester, Hanna boarded a train for the trip west, arriving in the port of Benecia on December 21, 1912. Archbishop Riordan and a retinue of distinguished guests greeted him at the station. Hanna expressed his appreciation, pledging to assist Riordan in any way possible:

> In a city of the size and importance of San Francisco, with its promise of the future arising out of the reality and vigor of its present, it is impossible for anyone to be idle. I am *[sic]* come as a help to the Archbishop. Archbishop Riordan has a great work here, and I am delighted to get into harness and pull with him for the glorification of God in a city that has been built in God's own country.[10]

San Franciscans' first impressions of Hanna were consistent with the affable, kind, and intellectually serious attributes for which he was known in Rochester; clearly, Rochester's loss was San Francisco's gain. One local commentator wrote, "The advent of Bishop Hanna will mean an accession in culture, in help to works of charity, in matters of education, in spirituality." Another wrote, "His Grace is distinguished by an intelligent cautiousness that is rather more rare in clergymen than it might be."[11] Besides his eminent qualifications for the hierarchy, his charisma appealed to his new ecclesial and civic community. One observer stated that Hanna had

> the kind of head one loves to see on the shoulders of a friend. His look is the look that puts heart into the poor fellow who is down; he is genial, affable, winning, without so much as a hint of condescension which sets the spirit of a sensitive person on edge.[12]

The *Monitor*, San Francisco's archdiocesan newspaper, summarized local opinion: "Bishop Hanna is a man in whose presence you cannot pass one hour without coming away improved in mind and refreshed in spirit. He is interested in everything, but most of all in humanity, and that in particular, on the side which brings us nearest to our Maker."[13] Hanna's affability quickly made new friends for him. When asked about his impressions of Hanna, Riordan admitted, "Well, he's made more friends here in a year than I have in 42."[14] Hanna's initial impressions, related to a Fortnightly member, emphasized the contrasts he observed in his new environment:

> There is a world all new to me on this western coast. The men here are more progressive, more radical, more individualistic than we are at home, but they have not our culture, they have not our poise, they have not our finish either in thought or action.[15]

Riordan wasted no time putting his new auxiliary to work in the archdiocese. On Christmas Day, 1912, Hanna presided for the first time in the cathedral. He went to various parishes and schools to celebrate confirmations, the first at Notre Dame School in San Francisco on March 30, 1913. He also presided at cornerstone layings, the first being Notre Dame des Victories on May 18, 1913, and church dedications, with St. Anne Church in Lodi being his first on July 27, 1913. The new bishop also substituted for Riordan at ordinations, conferring orders on three men from St. Patrick's Seminary, the archdiocesan seminary in Menlo Park thirty miles south of the city, on June 23, 1913.[16] In the summer of 1914 Hanna traveled to Rome as Riordan's representative for his periodic *ad limina* visit with the pope. Although Hanna found Pius X in good spirits and surprisingly well, he died a few days later. Hanna was the last visiting bishop to see the pope.[17]

It was no surprise to any who knew him that Hanna almost immediately became actively engaged in the public sector of San Francisco. In June 1913 Governor Hiram Johnson made him a charter member of the California Commission of Immigration and Housing, an organization for which he served as vice president from 1913 to 1923 and as president from 1923 to 1935.[18] Only one year after his arrival, Hanna was elected president of an executive committee formed by local leaders of church and state to investigate the significant problem of unemployment in the city. Hanna's reputation and personality made him the clear choice to lead the committee. The *Monitor* reported, "Under his [Hanna's] direction and leadership remedial measures were adopted that lessened the gravity of the situation."[19]

The Archbishop of San Francisco

On December 27, 1914, Patrick Riordan died of natural causes; his funeral was held on December 31. The next day, Thomas Conaty, bishop of Monterey-Los Angeles, called a meeting of the archepiscopal council to begin creating a *terna* for the now-vacant metropolitan see. Conaty sought advice from the suffragans of the archdiocese and then conferred with Hanna in San Francisco.[20] Many assumed Hanna would be named as Riordan's successor. Thomas Shahan, rector of the Catholic University of America, wrote Hanna: "I trust when next you have occasion to help this most holy enterprise it will be in your own jurisdiction as Archbishop of San Francisco. Here in the East we all look upon it as practically assured and we are only waiting for the public announcement."[21] The vicar general of the archdiocese, John Cantwell, also assumed Hanna would be selected. In February he wrote, "We are all anxious here, at the present time, waiting for the successor. Unless the unforeseen and unexpected happens, our good Bishop Hanna will be permitted, please God, to remain with us." Three months later he was even more confident: "I do not think there is any doubt but that the bishop will, in the course of a few days, receive his appointment."[22]

On May 20, 1915, word was received in the archdiocese that Hanna had been appointed the local ordinary by Pope Benedict XV. John Bonzano, the apostolic delegate who had consecrated Hanna as bishop in December 1912, informed him of his appointment through official correspondence on May 24.[23] Pope Benedict XV wrote to the bishops of the San Francisco metropolitan: "We commend you to render to the same Edward Bishop, Archbishop elect, due obedience and reverence according to the sacred canons, in order that mutual good will between you and him may produce abundant fruit for the good of souls."[24] Hanna's reaction revealed his humility and his desire to follow his predecessor's path. He addressed his fellow priests, "I shall carry on and perfect the good work begun by the late Archbishop Patrick Riordan. And when I say I'll do that, can there be any loftier pronouncement?" Speaking to the laity, Hanna voiced his constant pastoral aim: "If I can help you to be apostles of the things that are worthwhile, if I can help you to rise above the race for power and live for the things that never die, I shall be happy."[25] Hanna continued his episcopal duties, conferring minor orders (porter, lector, exorcist, acolyte, and subdeacon) at St. Patrick's, ordinations at St. Mary's Cathedral, and traveling to Chicago to preach the funeral Mass for Archbishop Quigley, to whom Hanna had felt indebted since he had attended Hanna's consecration in Rochester.[26]

Edward Hanna was installed as archbishop of San Francisco on July 28, 1915, with the apostolic delegate John Bonzano again presiding along with seven copresiding prelates. Bonzano, reading the Bull of Installation from Benedict XV, directed his words toward Hanna:

> We have a firm hope and confidence that [with] the right hand of the Lord assisting you propitiously, the distinguished Church of San Francisco in California may be governed advantageously by your pastoral industry and fruitful zeal, and that it may receive a prosperous increase in spiritual and temporal things.

Speaking on behalf of the clergy of San Francisco, the chancellor of the archdiocese, P. J. Cummings, stated:

> We know your Grace, we know the manner of man you have been amongst us. We know the tireless energy, the courage, the high ideals, the strong trust in God which you bring to your work. We, therefore, look forward to the future with unbounded confidence, persuaded that with the Divine blessings your administration of the See of San Francisco will be, in all things, unto the strengthening and building up of the kingdom of God in our midst.[27]

Hanna gratefully asked for assistance from all the Church constituencies as he assumed the reins of the archdiocese:

> If you will help me, all unworthy in my great office, I can see rising from this western see a San Francisco greater than the dreams of its greatest men.…Your presence here is a harbinger of success, a proffer of help without which my great mission must fail. If you help me and I am true, great good may come to San Francisco, good to the State, good to the nation and the world.[28]

Because of problems caused by World War I as it raged in Europe, the conferral of the pallium on Hanna was delayed until October. Bishop Joseph Glass of Salt Lake was the principal celebrant at the Mass, together with Bishops Peter Muldoon of Rockford, Illinois, and Thomas Grace of Sacramento, California.[29] After the ceremony, Mayor James Rolph, who would have a long and close relationship with Hanna in San Francisco and California, hosted a formal reception for the new archbishop. Rolph noted that Hanna, who was well known outside San Francisco, was "a man of learning as well as a man of wide experience in the school of human nature. He is ever ready to give unselfish service. It is the keynote of his character. He is an indefatigable worker, and yet always a man of buoyant spirits, good nature and democratic disposition."[30] Hanna received congratulatory messages from all fronts, including his Fortnightly Club associates in Rochester. One person, noting his "suffering of some years ago," looked forward to a possible red hat for the new archbishop.[31] O. K. Cushing, president of the Associated Charities of San Francisco, who would work closely with Hanna on the State Unemployment Commission between 1931 and 1932, wrote of "the great pleasure and gratification [of]...your appointment" and "the good fortune that has fallen to the State of California, particularly to the city of San Francisco, in your accession to that high office."[32]

The Personality and Ideas of the Archbishop

As Hanna assumed control of the archdiocese, the way that others perceived him began to follow a definite pattern. He was described as a man with a "singularly attractive personality...which showed itself in the constant stream of his courtesies to every one, from a casual acquaintance to the friend for years." He possessed piercing dark eyes with a certain twinkle. He was also gifted with a winning smile and a soft sympathetic voice; he was kind, affable, friendly, and courteous to all he encountered.[33] He had an extraordinary memory, which one person described as "an archive of condensed biographies, each precisely labeled and docketed, like so many questions in a scholastic 'summa.'"[34] Hanna was known to be generous, "a leader in philanthropy [whose] charity knew no restrictions; it does not distinguish between race, color or religion, but seeks the welfare of all, irrespective of accidental differences."[35] His sense of justice forced him to look at issues from varied perspectives, giving him a more liberal trend than most churchmen. An editorial written three months after his appointment as archbishop summarized how he was perceived by most people:

> Archbishop Hanna has given to every office assigned him the best he had and he has thought no duty too humble....Perhaps his duty is rendered sweeter by the affection he has for all persons, especially the poor and fallen ones. And yet with the Archbishop's tenderness there is a mingled dignity and firmness of character which those acquainted with him have not failed to notice.[36]

Hanna's sense of duty and commitment to others was characterized by a laudable work ethic and the virtue of self-sacrifice. Many noted that he was an "indefatigable worker,...never idle, and apparently never tired," who at times had to be told to slow down. His sincere unselfish nature, simplicity, and strong character were appreciated by all stripes in society.[37] After his death a tribute by his successor, John J. Mitty, summarized the open and ecumenical way that Hanna approached relations with others:

> Archbishop Hanna was in spirit and bearing ever the simple, wholehearted, kindly priest of God. He knew no distinction between the socially elect and the humblest waif of the streets. Rich and poor, the learned and unlettered, found the same unfailing courtesy which marked his relationships to all fellow mortals. He was the most approachable of men, and the penitent outcast met him with the same sense of confidence which was felt by the fortunately conditioned of his fellows....He was perfectly oblivious of himself when there was a question of service to others. There was no meanness or pettiness in his character; he was fine gold and sterling worth, and always measured up to the full stature of a Christian gentleman.[38]

Hanna's progressive style as a pastoral minister was also evident in his theological perspective. His extant sermons and writings highlighted traditional themes, but, as one might expect from his experience as a professor of dogmatic theology, he promoted the intellectual life and encouraged theological innovation. His thought, at least thematically, was summarized in a series of sermons preached during Lent 1920 in the cathedral.[39] Hanna was strongly devoted to the Eucharist, as evidenced by his regular attendance at International Eucharistic Congresses. In Chicago in 1926 he stated,

> The Blessed Sacrament is not only our way of thankfulness, of adoration of praise—the Blessed Sacrament is not only our touch of divinity which makes us partakers of the divine nature, not only our source of knowledge and of power, but it

is also our seal of redemption, our pledge of life with God everlasting.[40]

Hanna spoke strongly of the need for Christ as regenerator of the world, against "those who use their position and power in the world for destruction and selfish purposes." In a February 1918 sermon he preached the need for a lived spirit of charity:

> Men are distinguished one from another by the motives that guide and control their lives. The natural man is influenced by selfish aims and his aspirations are for treasure, power, and the comforts of life—things that pass like ships in the night. On the other hand, the man who tries to live the supernatural Christian life finds his motives in the love of God and his neighbor. He is the unselfish character whose deeds and self-sacrifices are made meritorious by the love and grace of God which brings hope and strength and peace to his soul.[41]

Hanna also proclaimed the need to be cautious of the world and place one's confidence in Christ. During the Lenten 1920 series he remarked,

> It is the spirit of the world that has brought disaster into men's way of thinking;...Opposed to this is the spirit of Christ, which makes men feel their dependence upon God the Father and their subjection to Him; which makes men recognize that all authority comes from Him, and that we must obey the law and the authority and the voice of God Himself.[42]

Hanna presented a measured perspective on the benefit of the new apologetic and the role of the theologian, possibly showing the battle scars of his earlier brush with modernism. He claimed that reason "has been unable to sound the fullness and the depth of the wisdom that man needs to guide him unto God." He promoted the proper use of scholarship in support of Church teaching:

> The findings of natural science are used to countenance the established doctrines of Holy Church, and thus historians and

scientists are attempting to destroy many truths which are dearest to Christian hearts. Still, no man can hope for a hearing who has not mastered the principles of higher criticism, who is not adept in their application. There are true principles of higher criticism, and these we must use for the defense of revealed truth, and in using these principles show ourselves stronger, more scholarly, more scientific than those who accept not divine revelation, and who are turning higher criticism against its most essential truths.[43]

Hanna suggested that the work of the theologian required "abundant intelligence," "a reverent spirit...imbued with the persuasion of the sanctity of the truth and with confidence in truth's ultimate victory." In the end, in contrast to his earlier brush with modernism, Hanna took a rather conservative approach, concluding that the theologian's task was not to test the new waters of progressive thought but to support revealed truth with intellectual tools:

> These men [theologians] must go down from the heights into the conflict, they must be able to battle for the rights of the Holy Church, when the secular power would encroach upon such rights, they must be able to discern the true and the false of the philosophy of the day, they must be able to make philosophy the handmaid of the higher knowledge of God in revealed truth, they must use their secular learning in defending a God-given revelation, they must aid in solving the social problems, which are vexing men's minds, and finally they must take what is material in the fine arts and inspire it with a vision that is spiritual, for otherwise the worship of beauty must be harmful to man.

Similarly, the student of theology has the duty "to order and work out the new apologetic. His task is the final one, the gathering into one ordered and united whole the labors of those who have worked in the many fields of research." Such work requires a "depth of intelligence, calmness of spirit, and courage of...conviction."[44]

Hanna's spiritual perspective, while also bearing the mark of his life experience, was more progressive than his theological perspective, which had been stunted by Pius X and *Pascendi Dominici Gregis* in 1907. The archbishop insisted that religion could never be divorced from the issues and events of everyday life but rather must permeate what we do. In a baccalaureate address at Stanford University he remarked, "Without the touch of God in your conscious lives, your service will be of no permanent value."[45] His spirituality was based on a sense of justice and a strong moral ethic. Hanna, who referred to himself as "the custodian of public morals," called for all civic officials to govern with justice. He proclaimed, "The condition of our peace with God is the peace we hold with our fellows upon earth. The way to peace is the way of Christ—unselfishness of the individual and of the nation: pardon for our neighbor, whether he be one or many."[46] He believed that private interests must be secondary to the common good and that personal responsibility must be constantly practiced. His concept of justice and moral ethics combined a self-sacrificing love that resulted in greater service to others with an awareness and perspective that our actions are performed to fulfill God's kingdom in our world.[47]

Hanna's theological and spiritual beliefs shaped his views on significant issues that bridged the church-state gap. Hanna held a very traditional view of the family and of the home environment, proclaiming that the health of the family and the home was an important indicator of the nation's Christian image. He believed the home was under greater attack in contemporary society than in any other time because Americans were allowing wealth to determine how a household was operated. He stated,

> We are living in luxury. History tells us that every nation that allowed luxury and wealth to undermine the fibre of the people disappeared. We can only survive by developing here a race of men and women educated in the right, in truth and honor. That education must teach the glory and sanctity of the home.[48]

Hanna feared that children were finding many activities that pulled them from the home and, therefore, away from the source that kept them headed in the proper direction.[49]

Closely allied with his understanding of the home were his ideas on the sanctity of marriage, which he strongly promoted in the sermon, "Church and the Family":

> If we measure the place and the dignity of an institution by its sacredness, its deep significance for human happiness, the great responsibility which it implies for the future of mankind, then surely marriage must claim reverence and respect of every mind capable of appreciating what is good and true and necessary unto the high development of the race.[50]

He insisted "that the Church must never lag for an instant in its duty of impressing on mothers and fathers their responsibility as home-makers."[51] According to Hanna, no moral danger was so great as the present attitude toward marriage, which seemed to disregard the permanence of marriage. He strongly promoted the indissolubility of marriage as a basic tenet of Christian life, warning that contrary views, leading to fewer children, would devastate future society:

> In Christ's wisdom, this union [marriage] only death can sever, and the history of christian [sic] civilization attests the farsee-ing wisdom of Jesus Christ, for when men and women have reverenced the marriage bond, and in fear and in love of God have reared their children unto a realization of the noble things of life, civilization reached its greatest height; when lax-ity crept in and men no longer considered this sacred union binding until death, there has come corruption and degrada-tion of life's highest goods.[52]

Hanna also held a traditional view on women and their role in soci-ety, suggesting that women should not be wage earners, since work outside the home diverted them from their primary task. He stated, "Old-fashioned motherhood is the career of careers, the biggest task in the world, so much larger than all these little things women are doing today."[53] He objected to women's suffrage on the grounds that involvement with the political process would detract from more important tasks. He stated,

The hand that rocks the cradle is the hand that rules the world. Many are inclined to laugh at that old saying nowadays. But may it not be true? In the highest development of domestic life and in the highest development of women's gifts, would not the mother rule the state without voting, merely by her influence with her sons?[54]

Hanna supported women's Church organizations, such as the National Council of Catholic Women (NCCW), but only because the women's parent body, the National Catholic Welfare Conference (NCWC) for which Hanna served as administrative chairman from 1919 to 1935, refused to support women's groups that promoted ideas contrary to Church policy:

Resolved that the Conference of Bishops through the Department of Laws and Legislation opposes any Federal or State legislation sponsored by the National Women's political organizations or similar bodies, insofar as it may contain provisions contrary to the doctrines and discipline of the Catholic Church in regard to marriage or other Christian social and economic principles.[55]

In a 1924 speech to women at the Bank of Italy, Hanna summarized his views on home, marriage, and women, making the child the center of concern:

I wish there were more old fashioned mothers who would teach honesty, generosity, purity and modesty, the only things after all which help when one gets in a jam in the thick of life's battles. I wish there were more homes which were sanctuaries, centers of recreation and rest, built on better marriage conditions. A child is as his environment, as his home, as his mother, his teachers, the world make him.[56]

While traditional in many basic issues of society, Hanna built significant bridges between the laity and clergy in an era when bishops, priests, and religious were viewed as the apex of the pyramid, the symbolic model of the hierarchical Church. He believed cooperation was necessary between the laity and the clergy, based on "self restraint, brotherly love, [and] self immolation for Christ's sake." Hanna supported lay organizations in the Church and the civic realm for their "labors, sacrifices and generosities" and lamented the fact that few people were aware of these groups' great contributions to church and to state. He was always viewed as "the laymen's friend" because of his constant attention and concern for human welfare. One commentator wrote, "His heart seemed always to go to the layman in such a manner as to bring him to God and man. He was able to seize and throw the doubts of man to give him a new starting point, a larger hope, a nobler faith and a clearer vision of the truth."[57]

Administration of the Archdiocese of San Francisco

The Church in early twentieth-century America has been characterized by the historian Gerald Fogarty, SJ, as having gone through a period of "romanization and modernization" governed by five principal ideas. First, it was an age of consolidation, especially intellectually, in the wake of the condemnation of Americanism and modernism. Second, bishops concentrated time, effort, and resources on their own dioceses, looking inward rather than responding to national Church needs. Third, bishops were often chosen on the basis of friendship and their connection to Roman officials, a trend best seen in the episcopal administrations of Cardinals George Mundelein of Chicago and William Henry O'Connell of Boston, archbishops who by their flamboyant style promoted the concept of *romanitá*. Fourth, bishops were builders and organizers, constructing new parishes and promoting education. Lastly, this was a period when bishops defended the faith but equally pledged their patriotic loyalty to the state.[58]

While James Gaffey has accurately described San Francisco as an archdiocese on the "fringe" of Catholic America, "distinct from the power centers" of the Midwest and the East Coast, Hanna nonetheless made significant contributions to church and state, while gaining the confidence and admiration of those in San

Francisco and beyond.[59] Upon assuming the reins of the archdiocese, Hanna had to set up his own team of assistants. Initially John Cantwell was appointed vicar general; one year later his brother James was made chancellor, upon the death of P. J. Cummings. On December 5, 1917, Hanna consecrated John Cantwell bishop of Los Angeles, leading to the appointment of Patrick J. Ryan as vicar. In 1926 Thomas Millett became Hanna's personal secretary, following a number of others briefly appointed to the position.[60] In general Hanna's administration was a period of chancery centralization.

Hanna vigorously dove into his episcopal duties, emphasizing parishes because of their importance in promoting family life. The new archbishop traveled about his see presiding and preaching at the invitation of pastors, getting to know his priests and the faithful of the archdiocese. His parochial message consistently echoed his ideas about the family. He proclaimed the centrality of the Church in parish life as the home for all the faithful, with the pastor as the ecclesiastical authority who held the enterprise together. He once stated, "The parish is a family, living a spiritual family life under the fatherly guidance of one who has been appointed to guard the regional interests of his children and to guide them unto the fullness of Christian life."[61]

During Hanna's tenure as archbishop, the number of parishes and missions increased from 180 in 1915 to 222 in 1935, peaking at 225 in 1933. During this same period numerous church renovations and additions were made, for a total of 120 parochial foundings or expansions. Much of this effort was guided by a special archdiocesan building committee that Hanna set up in 1923 to help evaluate needs, the purchase of properties, and the allocation of funds for various building projects.[62] Growth, especially outside the city of San Francisco, was extensive from the end of World War I until 1930 when expansion tapered off dramatically, at least partly because of the Great Depression. There is no evidence that this growth was anything other than normal demographic changes caused by the increased number of Catholics. Although Hanna was a great proponent of immigrants (see chapter 6), a concomitant rise in national parishes is not indicated.[63]

Hanna also established certain diocesan policies regarding finances, reception of the sacraments, and prison chaplaincies.

Parish assessments were levied and a system of taxation was implemented on Sunday plate collections, on stipends from sacraments, on Easter and Christmas collections, and on rents from parish facilities.[64] Hanna set a diocesan age policy for the reception of confirmation; in 1924, along with his suffragan bishops, he issued a pastoral letter on marriage. As a demonstration of his pastoral care, Hanna ordered a report on the Church's ministry efforts toward prisoners in the archdiocese. When the document showed that the religious training of Catholic inmates was very low, he investigated ways to address this lacuna in ministry.[65]

As archbishop, Hanna had numerous opportunities for travel. On three occasions he was asked to consecrate new bishops: he journeyed to Los Angeles in 1917 to consecrate his friend John Cantwell; in 1920 he consecrated P. J. Keane as auxiliary in Sacramento; in December 1922 he erected the Diocese of Monterey-Fresno and in June 1931 the Diocese of Reno, both of which were carved from San Francisco.[66] Hanna was often asked to give retreats and to address groups. In the San Francisco region he was invited to speak at baccalaureate services at the University of California, Berkeley, and at Stanford University.[67] In 1922 and 1928 Hanna gave retreats to the priests of the Diocese of Cheyenne, Wyoming. He also preached at the Dedication Mass for Kenrick Seminary in St. Louis, at Solemn Pontifical Vespers in the Baltimore Cathedral on the occasion of Cardinal Gibbons's fiftieth anniversary as a bishop, and at St. Mary's Seminary in Baltimore during its celebration of 140 years of operation. In July 1927 Hanna traveled to Honolulu, Hawaii, to address the Institute of Pacific Relations on "The Religious Background of Pacific Relations." During Hanna's administration he made *ad limina* visits to Rome in 1920, 1924, 1930, and 1932. Additionally, in 1925 Hanna led a Holy Year pilgrimage to Rome, with stops in Ireland, England, France, Switzerland, and numerous cities in Italy.[68]

Hanna demonstrated his devotion to the Eucharist by attending three International Eucharistic Congresses. In 1926 he traveled to Chicago, where he spoke at the twenty-eighth international congress. In September 1928 he attended, as the official representative of the American hierarchy, the twenty-ninth congress in Sydney, Australia, where he preached at the meeting's opening as well as an "occasional sermon" at the dedication of the Sydney Cathedral, St. Mary's. In the spring and summer of 1932, he traveled to Europe to attend the International Eucharistic Congress in Dublin and to conduct an *ad limina* visit to Rome.[69]

In addition to traveling widely, Hanna became well known at home as a prelate who liked to be with his people. On fair weather days the archbishop usually walked from his residence to the chancery, both in the morning and at lunchtime, often encountering people along the way and engaging them in conversation. He once remarked to a reporter, "I like to be with the crowd, to keep close to humanity....Here you see the outward signs of family life." Media personnel in the city commented, "You wonder whether any shepherd is so close to his flock."[70] A prayer published in the *Monitor* crystallizes the love Hanna generated:

> It is fitting also to offer a fervent prayer that in His goodness, God may grant Archbishop Hanna many happy returns of the day and that his presence in San Francisco may continue for years to come as an abiding benediction to his people.[71]

Hanna utilized his great energy, versatility, and skill in the service of others. One friend wrote, "He has subordinated self-interests to the welfare of others, in fact he seems oblivious of self, and intent on doing whatever he can for the improvement and happiness of others."[72] Hanna's contributions to society marked him out from others: "His [Hanna's] manifold diversified activities along charitable, educational and social betterment lines are unquestionably contributing more to the better side of California's life than are those of any other citizen of whatever position or creed."[73]

As early as 1916 and continuing almost nonstop through 1930, the archbishop's skill as a pastoral minister and administrator led to rumors about his possible elevation to the Sacred College of Cardinals. The death in 1918 of Cardinal John Farley of New York fueled speculation that Hanna might be named his replacement. The *San Francisco Examiner* spoke optimistically of the potential honor for Hanna and for the city:

The distinction that comes to Archbishop Hanna himself will be viewed with general gratification by his fellow citizens of San Francisco. He has impressed all those with whom he has come in contact as so much of a man, he has shown such distinguished ability, he has been so active in all sorts of works for the good of the city, the State and the Nation, in works for the people irrespective of creeds that he has won a golden opinion in San Francisco. The people of the city will be proud of Edward J. Hanna as a cardinal, as the people of Baltimore have long taken pride in James Gibbons.[74]

Similar rumors surfaced on several other occasions but especially in 1921, after the death of Cardinal James Gibbons of Baltimore. Three separate groups—the faculty at the Catholic University of America, the Baltimore Archdiocesan Council, and the Sulpicians—suggested that Hanna would be the perfect replacement for Gibbons.[75]

Rumors of Hanna's elevation to the cardinalate continued throughout the 1920s, especially in 1929. That year rumors abounded in Rome that Hanna was to be chosen in the next consistory, prompting a letter from Cardinal Donato Ceretti to John Cantwell in Los Angeles saying that he would be happy "if the announcement made…concerning Archbishop Hanna be true." Yet he feared "that a new hat will not be conferred in America before one of the four will be hanged on the roof of the cathedral."[76] Speculation on Hanna's appointment continued through 1930, but as in all previous cases, nothing came of the rumors.[77]

The Advocate for Education

Hanna steadfastly and passionately supported the education of youth and the promotion of Catholic schools. He once stated, "The education of our children is the most important thing in any community. Children growing in knowledge and power insure the future."[78] Hanna believed that Catholics needed to be well educated and had to support educational institutions to make this goal a reality. He stated,

We must have the liberty to teach our children that we have inherited from our traditions of the past, we must feel that we are welcome within the precincts of the great temples of knowledge and science. We must use every gift we have to uphold stone by stone these living temples dedicated to wisdom, that from these portals may come forth a race of men who know the truth and have the courage to stand undaunted by the truth.[79]

Seeing it as a "bulwark for democracy in America,"[80] Hanna placed all energies and influence behind every effort to promote Catholic education in the United States. He saw public schools as good and as a practical necessity, but he felt secular education fell short:

We may admit the practical necessity of the public schools such as they are, we may pay for their upkeep, we may serve on school boards, we may teach in their halls, we may send our children to their classes, but there is one thing we cannot do, and that is give our approval to the theory that mere secular education can take the place of religion and of those fundamental truths which teach the high purpose of our life.[81]

He saw education as the vehicle to make youth responsible and faith-filled American citizens. In a sermon in 1920, he stated, "There is no adequate system of education equal to the system of the Catholic Church in America, to reach at once the ideals of our American State, the ideals of American citizenship, the ideals of perfect living and thinking."[82] He believed the Catholic school was "a vital necessity," "the framework in which students can learn the moral sanctions of the law." It served as the basic means for "the transmission of the faith to our children."[83]

Hanna also expressed the importance of the Christian educator as the one who planted the American system in youth:

More efficacious than the crash of cannon and the clang of arms will be the Christian teacher at whose feet we can learn the answer to the questions that vex our age; more efficacious

72

than embattled militarism will be the Christian school wherein the children of our great Republic will learn there is a God in heaven whose behests they must know, and before whose judgment seat they must stand.[84]

In a baccalaureate address at the University of California at Berkeley, Hanna described the significance of the vocation of educator:

The teacher has the noblest task ever given to man, the task of molding the soul of the boy or the girl unto knowledge, unto sympathy, unto courage, unto power, unto right ideals of life; the task of molding these souls more and more unto the image of the great God, in whose image they were created.[85]

Hanna often stated that his role was integral to assuring that children received proper education. He clearly stated this belief in a communiqué with Angelo Rossi, mayor of San Francisco, in 1932:

Certain matters committed to your care, however, involve or may involve matters affecting Catholic principles of Christian morals. With respect to such matters, the Archbishop cannot remain indifferent. The education of our youth is one of these matters, whether it be given in the private or parochial systems of our city or in the public schools. Matters of education vitally affect the spiritual and temporal welfare of our people and are matters in which the Archbishop is and must be vitally interested. Therefore, if I believe that the official acts of any civic officer is [sic] detrimental to the best interests of our people in matters of education or in any other matters affecting Catholic principles of Christian morals, I reserve the right to express my criticism or disapproval of such action, either directly or through my official organ or chosen representatives.[86]

Hanna promoted Catholic education on national and local levels. He fully supported the work of the National Catholic Education Association (NCEA)[87] by attending various conventions. He opened the 1918 national meeting, held in San Francisco, with a stirring address, "Religion and Democracy," connecting Catholic educational endeavors to those of the nation as a whole. Additionally, he was invited to lead a national effort of the bishops to prepare a catechism for Catholic children in the United States and served as a member of the Board of Trustees for the Catholic University of America in Washington, DC.[88]

Hanna believed that Catholic education was a necessity because it provided youth with the foundation of the moral law as taught by Christ and because children needed to be formed in the image of Christ in order to move forward in the faith. He wrote, "Without Christian schools for the little ones of the flock, the faith of the next generation will be imperiled."[89] John Mitty, Hanna's successor in San Francisco, beautifully summarized the latter's advocacy of Catholic education: "He loved the school and made it one of the aims of his life to be an advocate and defender of Christian education....He fearlessly defended the doctrine of Catholic education and his sincerity and earnestness always won for him a successful hearing."[90]

From the outset of his tenure as archbishop, Hanna placed a top priority on Christian education. He stated, "Since the time the Pastoral Office in this archdiocese was committed to our charge, nothing has been closer to our heart than the education of our Catholic children."[91] In 1915 Hanna acted on his perceived mandate by establishing the Scholastic Council of the Archdiocese, with Father Ralph Hunt, the first superintendent of schools, as its chair. Under Hunt's direction, the council worked for four years to create a standard program of study in all subjects for grades one through eight. The plan was completed, approved, and implemented in 1922, bringing standardization in reading, language, grammar, composition, spelling, arithmetic, history, and geography. The *Monitor* called the document "an impressive monument to the intelligent interest and unswerving devotion he [Hanna] has manifested in Catholic education and to the whole-hearted support and unfailing inspiration of which he has been the source."[92]

Hanna backed additional initiatives promoting Catholic education. In June 1916 he organized an institute for religious in the educational apostolate "to inaugurate the fuller development of our Catholic school system." The conference, which was well attended, was lauded both in and outside the archdiocese for attempting to improve the quality of educational training.[93] Hanna also supported the efforts of James McHugh, superintendent of Catholic schools, to obtain better textbooks; as a result, by May 1926 a uniform system of textbooks existed in all schools and all grades.[94]

Hanna blessed the efforts of religious communities to start schools in the archdiocese. Many congregations received permission to start educational apostolates, provided the schools were quality institutions.[95] Hanna insisted that academic standards be maintained and that the schools operate in the black; he was prudent in approving new foundations, making sure that need existed and that there was no duplication. Hanna played the overseer to assure that the Catholic schools in his jurisdiction were institutions of which he and the Church could be justly proud.[96]

During his tenure Hanna published an annual report on the status of Catholic education in the archdiocese. While there were some fluctuations, in general the number of schools and the students serviced increased gradually, from 69 schools and 15,791 students in 1915 to 112 schools and 32,000 students in 1935.[97]

Edward Hanna's promotion of Catholic education also included efforts in the academic formation of seminarians. Hanna's experience at St. Bernard's, a leading national seminary, and now as a local ordinary for a major metropolitan region, gave him at least two good reasons to support the archdiocesan seminary of St. Patrick's. First, Hanna's predecessor, Patrick Riordan, received permission from Pope Leo XIII during his 1888 *ad limina* visit to establish a seminary. Riordan raised $300,000 from six prominent San Francisco Catholics and received an eighty-acre plot in Menlo Park (forty miles south of the city) from Kate Doyle Johnson. Second, he engaged the Sulpicians, prominent at St. Joseph's Seminary at Dunwoodie, to open a minor seminary in 1898. In 1904 the major seminary of St. Patrick formally opened its doors.[98]

Hanna brought a particular mindset to his oversight of the seminary. He believed that twentieth-century society needed a body of men with great spiritual insight who could use this knowledge and adapt it to particular conditions of life, and he believed this formation process had to be centered in the seminary. In an address given at St. Bernard's Seminary, he stated, "The seminary then must open the mind, refine it, [and] fill it with knowledge of Christ. The seminary must give to its students mastery over the knowledge they possess and power to apply this knowledge to the world's needs. The seminary must give exactness and...eloquent expression."[99]

The Sulpician presence at St. Patrick's continued during Hanna's administration, but the relationship was not close. Publicly, Hanna supported the faculty and administration of the seminary, professing confidence in the rector, who was responsible for academic and personnel matters. However, James Gaffey, chronicler of St. Patrick's, claims that Hanna had little true interest in the faculty. Rumors abounded that Hanna was thinking of replacing the Sulpicians with his own diocesan men, more on the model of St. Bernard's, which he considered the ideal.[100]

Based on his experience at St. Bernard's, his life as a priest, and his position as archbishop, Hanna developed specific expectations for his seminarians. He believed that candidates for the priesthood should demonstrate cleanliness of life, be willing to sacrifice self, and proclaim the saving message of Jesus. In their training seminarians needed to develop a strong knowledge of their mother tongue, philosophy, and contemporary issues, but above all they had to be good and sound teachers. He described priests as

> master teachers in the school of Christ; it means men who have consecrated themselves without reserve; it means men who ponder by day and by night the life of Christ, and who by law of association have become Christ like. It means men who daily say with St. Paul, "I live, not I, but Christ lives in me."

Since priests were to be exemplary teachers, they had to be educated in the best schools. He concluded, "Neither time nor treasure should be spared in this effort."[101]

Probably because of his own heritage, Hanna had a special affinity toward Irish seminarians, whom he welcomed in abundance to the Archdiocese of San Francisco. While many individuals petitioned for admission to the archdiocese, and he never had problems meeting his quota for clergy, Hanna clearly preferred the Irish, even recruiting them for service.[102] He was in contact with the rectors of several Irish seminaries, seeking candidates for San

Francisco. A typical invitation went to the rector of St. Patrick's College in Thurles: "The Archbishop would be glad to have you prepare for affiliation with the [arch]diocese some students who have completed their second year's philosophy or even their first year's philosophy."[103] Hanna expected that the last two years of training for these Irish candidates would be conducted in a U.S. seminary, stating, "American training for an Irish priest working in this country cannot be over-estimated."[104] Like American candidates, he expected Irish seminarians to pay half their tuition after their ordination.[105] James Gaffey claims that Hanna's fondness for Irish seminarians polarized American and Irish-born seminarians.[106]

Hanna's active recruitment of Irish seminarians for San Francisco did not, however, compromise his high standards for service in the archdiocese. On numerous occasions Hanna complained to various rectors in Irish seminaries about the ill-preparedness and lack of performance of those who had been sent to St. Patrick's. One rector was told, "His Grace would have you inform those same students, especially the first and second year theologians, that unless their respective reports show a marked improvement next year he will be obliged to withdraw his adoption." He often raised the problem of lack of pulpit eloquence. Hanna's secretary Thomas Millett wrote to Nicholas Cooke, rector of St. Patrick's Seminary in Thurles:

> He [Hanna] is very disappointed with the poor attempt made by many of your alumni to read a simple announcement, or the Epistle and Gospel on Sunday, intelligently and intelligibly. Again and again complaints have reached His Grace about our Irish priests regarding this matter, and in particular of one priest, recently ordained in Thurles, who it seems obtained distinction in sacred eloquence.[107]

In a similar vein, Hanna's vicar general, Patrick Ryan, informed Cooke, "It is not a question of strange accent or brogue, which we all have, but rather a matter of slovenly expression or indistinctness and unintelligent reading, and, may I add, often mispronunciation."[108] Although Hanna had a special interest in the seminary, it is the opinion of James Gaffey that the institution did not prosper under his administration. Gaffey claims that St. Patrick's suffered from a lack of educational professionalism during the latter Riordan and early Hanna years. One indicator of this was the apparent "cold indifference" of Hanna to encourage his gifted students to continue their education at the Catholic University of America or similar sites. Another important marker was the inadequate library holdings at St. Patrick's. Instead of providing a fixed budget to purchase books and periodicals, Hanna promised to procure the requisite sources himself, allowing the library "to decline in holdings, especially in the fields of spirituality, Scripture, and Church history." Gaffey concludes, "In his two decades as ordinary in San Francisco (1915–35) he [Hanna] had the most complex and inconsistent relationship with his seminary."[109]

Another significant project associated with the education of seminarians that Hanna supervised was the construction of a new minor seminary, St. Joseph's in Mountain View. Located forty miles south of San Francisco, it was only ten miles from the major seminary, St. Patrick's in Menlo Park. A significant increase in seminarians, from 84 in 1910 to 284 in 1923, forced Hanna to attempt to reduce the overcrowding at St. Patrick's. His initial solution was to shorten the seminary program from six to five years, but the Sulpicians rejected the plan.[110] Therefore, in March 1920 Hanna purchased seven hundred acres of land near some Jesuit-owned property in Mountain View as a site for the new institution.[111]

In order to finance the new institution, the archbishop inaugurated a development drive, the "Catholic Educational Fund." The Archepiscopal Council suggested that Hanna couch his appeal in a more general way, seeking funds for the overall educational and welfare needs of the archdiocese. In January 1922 Hanna called a meeting of all pastors in the archdiocese to discuss his plans for the fund drive. In March Hanna issued a pastoral letter describing his plan and seeking the economic assistance of the faithful.[112] On May 27, 1922, the Catholic Educational Fund was formally initiated, seeking monetary assistance in three areas: (1) to better equip St. Patrick's, (2) to build St. Joseph's, and (3) to purchase a normal school for religious women to prepare them for teaching in college, high school, and elementary education.[113] While the fund drive never achieved its goals,[114] the construction of St. Joseph went forward. Hanna was grateful for those who had contributed. The minor seminary, "the jewel of his accomplishments,"[115] operating under the guidance of the Sulpician fathers, opened its doors in September 1924.[116]

Besides directly promoting Catholic educational institutions and curriculum, Hanna became the primary ecclesiastical official to support or oppose legislative measures that affected Catholic schools. In 1919, for example, Hanna opposed a California State Senate bill that read in part, "It is unlawful to conduct any exercise of a religious nature or to address a public gathering in the State of California, in any other than the English language, *provided however* [emphasis in document] that this sanction shall not be construed to apply to the ritualistic portion of any religious service." It was clear to Hanna that the proposed legislation was aimed at immigrants, many of whom at this time were Catholics from southern and eastern Europe or from Mexico.[117] In 1921, Hanna spoke against an initiative that mandated compulsory education for Native Indians, thus effectively eliminating the opportunity for Catholic education for this ethnic group. Two years later Hanna opposed a series of bills in the California State Assembly that mandated specific courses of study in private schools. He said such initiatives "would have prejudicially affected parochial schools." He continued, "There is no need of such legislation, as no objection has been made to the manner in which private schools in the state were being conducted, or to the courses of study being taught therein."[118]

Throughout the 1920s, Hanna coordinated efforts to bring tax-exempt status to California's parochial schools.[119] He did not deny the obligation of Catholics to support public education, but he wanted people to get their money's worth for their tax contributions:

> Now we Catholics do not believe that we can get anything for nothing. We pay our share of the upkeep of public schools, we relieve the rest of you of part of the taxes by educating some of our own children and even these schools are taxed. No we do not believe that we can get anything for nothing, but we do want our money's worth for what we pay.[120]

In 1925 Hanna promoted a bill that would grant tax-exempt status to all secondary schools accredited to the university and not run for profit.[121] Assembly Bill #27 was passed but because it was a change in the constitution, it required the approval of the voters.[122]

Hanna began an all-out campaign to have Ballot Initiative 11 approved in the 1926 November general election. Besides lobbying Catholics through flyers and sermons on Sunday mornings, Hanna contacted organized labor leaders, Chambers of Commerce, fraternal orders such as the American Legion, and educational leaders, including Herbert Bolton at the University of California, asking for their support. Local newspapers were asked to pledge their support or, if this was not possible, to stay neutral on the issue.[123] However, despite all of Hanna's efforts, the initiative failed.

In 1928, the issue was raised again, but Hanna refused to support it, fearing that it might hurt the Catholic candidate for president, Al Smith.[124] His sentiments were expressed by his chancellor, James Cantwell:

> His grace has given very serious consideration to the question of a campaign for the exemption of private schools from taxation. He feels that this would be a very inopportune time to start such a campaign, especially if Mr. Smith is nominated for President. Besides the time is too short to conduct the campaign that would be necessary....When a serious campaign of this kind is on His Grace feels it would be advisable for all Bishops of the Province to take an active part, and this, as you can see, is impossible this year.[125]

In 1933 Hanna led the battle to secure tax exemption for private nonprofit schools in California. In May the California Legislature overwhelmingly passed a bill introduced by Charles Dempster that would have exempted private nonprofit schools from taxation. Again, because the initiative was a change in the California Constitution, the measure had to be placed before the general voter population. Bishop John Cantwell in Los Angeles wrote to his friend exhorting him once more to lead the fight supporting the initiative:

> Now in this and other matters San Francisco must take the lead. You for so long have spent yourself in many causes, and

have yet asked nothing from the public at large for your own people, and we of the South are your people. You have over the years won such great respect in the State that I am convinced that a campaign for the exemption of schools from taxation could not be defeated. Not only is your influence great in your own diocese, but from one end of California to the other, and if we are so selfish as to capitalize [on] the popularity of our archbishop from the greater good of souls, you will find it, I am sure, in your heart to forgive us.

Cantwell insisted that, win or lose, the battle was worth the effort, since it would make people better Catholics: "The campaign will be a wholesome tonic to unite all of our people and will be for the country at large a practical example of Catholic Action."[126]

Hanna proposed an extensive plan to achieve his long-standing goal of tax exemption for Catholic schools. First he solicited newspaper magnate William Randolph Hearst, asking for the support of his papers, arguing the merits of Catholic education and its complementarity with the American ideal. He wrote to other significant citizens, calling his advocacy "a campaign for freedom of education" and claiming "it is an injustice to penalize us [Catholics] when by our religious schools we are saving the State of California millions of dollars annually."[127]

Hanna organized an energetic and far-reaching campaign, dividing the archdiocese into fourteen districts and placing a priest in charge of each. The priest-managers organized teams of lay people who went door-to-door within an assigned area, explaining the amendment and asking for a "Yes" vote. Wisely, canvassers argued that if private nonprofit schools were forced to close, it would cost the state $20 million up front to build new schools and $10 million annually for the educational expenses for the some one hundred thousand students who presently attend private schools.[128]

The campaign embraced not just Catholics but all voters within the archdiocese. Records were kept and reports submitted to Hanna personally. Hanna's personal support for Ballot Measure #4, which was to be decided in a special June 27 election, combined traditional and progressive ideas, articulating three specific arguments. First, he claimed that it was not fair to tax schools that save the state the expense of educating thousands of children. Second, he argued that the amendment was not initiated by Catholics but by members of other creeds. Lastly, he reminded people that California was the only state in the union that did not exempt private nonprofit schools from taxation.[129] Three days before the vote Hanna gave a public radio address stating:

> As the principle involved in this proposed amendment has already been accepted and embodied in our constitution, and as its extension involves no new principle of government inimical to our welfare and practically no additional cost to you [the public], there can be no valid reason against giving to the children of less than collegiate grade what has already been bestowed upon those of collegiate grade.

He concluded his speech, "Shall we of California, proud as we are of our progressive spirit and our generosity, be an exception to all the other United States in this vital and essential matter?"[130]

Despite the herculean efforts of Hanna and his campaign team, the voters rejected the amendment. Admitting his disappointment but vowing to continue the fight, Hanna wrote to his priests:

> It is a deep source of regret that in the recent election, the citizens of California did not grant private non-profit schools exemption from taxation. To our mind, this was due to a lack of understanding of the fundamental principles involved. We do not consider this election a final settlement of the question. No problem is ever settled until it is settled properly. And we pledge ourselves to continue our efforts until the citizenry of California gives fair settlement that will bring this commonwealth into line with the practically universal tradition of America.[131]

Hanna immediately issued a call for signatories on a petition asking the legislature to consider the tax exemption question.[132] Not until 1951 did California's parochial schools achieve tax-exempt status.[133]

Edward Hanna's significant work in support of education for youth mirrored his own continuing pursuit of the intellectual life, even though his appointment as auxiliary bishop in 1912 had forced him to leave the seminary and the classroom. Hanna was a member of and somewhat active in several academic societies, including the American Irish Historical Society, the Universal Knowledge Foundation, the National Geographic Society, and the American Historical Association. He was especially active in the National Archeological Society, a group he had originally joined in Rochester, lecturing to and acting as chairman of sessions for the San Francisco branch and, in 1926, serving as national president.[134] In addition to his association with academic societies, Hanna often gave scholarly lectures on topics ranging from the Roman catacombs to the philosophy of Roman Catholicism.[135]

The Archbishop and His Clergy

Through his Roman education and over twenty-five years of experience in ministry as both priest and bishop, Hanna had developed specific ideas on the priesthood and its role in Church and society. In a very traditional sense he understood the priest to be "another Christ," living the life of Jesus and doing his work. The area of Christ's ministry that Hanna most heavily gravitated toward was that of teacher, with special emphasis on social education. He saw priests as "teachers of all nations…bringing every soul unto the obedience of Christ."[136] The priest-teacher must courageously describe to the rich the proper use of their wealth, but more important, he must stand on the side of the poor and in solidarity with those who suffer. In an address at St. Bernard's Seminary he stated,

> The work of Christ in our land of plenty is, strange to say, the defense of the poor: poor himself, the priest must know the value of poverty in order to help those who struggle on, and who find life's burden too hard to bear; and this sympathy with the poor will stimulate a desire for the knowledge of the social remedy given in the Gospel and so needed in our time. The work of the Church, in this land, is with the rich who gives us of their treasure for the upbuilding of the Kingdom of God; and the priest must have the courage to tell the rich and powerful

the right use of the wealth of which they are only stewards. The work of the priest in this land is with the outcast and the sinner. He must see in them the image of God and the blood of Christ. The work of the priest, in this land, is in behalf of the thousands who are outside the fold, and to those he must make appeal, not only by his knowledge, but by his dignity, his kindliness, his forgetfulness of self, his immolation on the altar of Christ.[137]

For Hanna, in order to boldly proclaim the veracity of Christ's message, the priestly life of discipleship required a countercultural attitude, which would lead America back to its old path, away from things that pass quickly, away from attitudes that devour others, away from false political ideals and theories of education, away from soul-destroying pleasure, pride, and arrogance. He wrote,

We must live for the truth, and if necessary for the truth we must calmly die. In these days when the world needs Christ's message—as it has never needed it for centuries—we must surrender ourselves unreservedly, irrevocably, to the service of truth; we must sunder all ties; we must have no aspirations beyond the service of Christ, and like the Master, we must be consumed with zeal for the will of the Father—the salvation of man. In a word, we must give all if we would have all.[138]

As local ordinary of a major metropolitan, Hanna needed to engage his priests regularly and develop a good working relationship with them. Through his congenial personality, straightforward approach, integrity, and loyalty, Hanna developed a close relationship with his clergy, articulating his expectations and then demonstrating his support for them. Hanna's expectations centered on personal behavior as well as on responsibility and loyalty to the archbishop. Hanna provided generous financial support for the education of his clergy, but, as stated previously, he expected his priests to return 50 percent of the expense and was perturbed when they ignored this financial responsibility. He was equally adamant in holding pastors accountable for meeting their parishes' financial commitments to the archdiocese.[139] Possibly learning a lesson from the embarrassment of Archbishop Michael Corrigan in New York and his long-running feud with Father Edward McGlynn,[140] Hanna forbade his priests from speaking on political platforms.[141] In accordance with the 1884 Third Plenary Council of Baltimore, Hanna instituted junior clergy exams and closely scrutinized the progress of his young priests.[142]

Hanna also insisted that his priests follow his stated policies and archdiocesan programs. The archbishop's passion for education led him to build St. Joseph's Seminary and then to create the Catholic Educational Fund to support it; priests who did not support this program felt his ire. One admonition to a pastor read:

> Rumors have been confirmed by a parishioner who states that you tried to dissuade him from collecting and giving generously as he felt he could for the educational welfare of the diocese....His Grace feels very sorry that he has to write to you in this manner, and is especially grieved as almost every priest in the diocese has spent every effort to help him in this drive.[143]

Hanna also clearly articulated his policy on funerals and burials: "His grace does not wish his Catholic people to be buried in non-Catholic cemeteries or in non-Catholic mausoleums, and forbids his priests to give services in such places....The Archbishop has tried to provide Catholic cemeteries for his people, and it is no hardship on anyone to patronize them."[144] Hanna also insisted that his priests participate in the Clerical Relief Fund, which supported priests in retirement or in situations that hindered their ability to minister.[145]

Hanna's insistence that his clergy follow the rules of the archdiocese was demonstrated in 1933 when the archbishop and Monsignor John Rogers, pastor of St. Patrick's parish in the city, argued bitterly over the use of parish funds. A review of the parish financial records revealed that Rogers had diverted funds raised for a shelter associated with St. Patrick's to finance parish activities. In an atypically angry letter Hanna spoke of his disappointment and ordered Rogers to turn over to the archdiocese some $58,000. He concluded, "My decision in this matter is now final."[146]

In return for compliance with his policies and the accepting of personal responsibility, Hanna supported his clergy as a loving father figure. He supported their spiritual needs by providing and often attending an annual retreat at St. Patrick's. When making parish assignments, he willingly took specific needs into account, and took particular care that priests not live alone for any length of time. He was more than generous in granting sabbatical leaves and periods of rest for priests, especially if a previous assignment had been particularly difficult. Hanna was also quick to offer economic assistance when it was needed, either for the parish or on a personal level. He defended his priests when they were maligned and took their side in arguments where church and state collided. Clerics who worked hard, mirrored the priestly image of Christ the Teacher, and followed Hanna's policies enjoyed a very harmonious and familial relationship with him.[147]

A mutual love and respect existed between Hanna and his clergy. Their affection for him was clear on several fronts. Many accounts after Hanna's retirement speak of the "reverence and respect and deep attachment your priests have for you"; other reports speak of him as "a kind father." One observer stated, "Hanna was genuinely loved by his priests and people as a warm, fatherly shepherd who was always available and approachable." He was viewed more as a pastor than as an administrator, a man who cared deeply for the church as the people of God.[148] Hanna reciprocated the affection shown to him. On the occasion of his consecration as archbishop Hanna addressed his priests:

> If you could see my thoughts they would tell you what no tongue can tell, of my love for the priests of this diocese. To them I came as a stranger, unknown, untried. Without question they took me to their hearts, and the only joy I feel today in the shadow of the great Cross that is placed upon me is that they rejoice, and the only hope I have of being equal to my task is founded on their unwavering loyalty and their mightily consuming zeal.[149]

Hanna made significant efforts to reach out to his priests and to demonstrate his fatherly care. Every New Year's Day he hosted an open house exclusively for clerics of the archdiocese, serving sandwiches and soft drinks in an environment that fostered fellowship and friendship. In 1932, when welcoming his coadjutor, John J. Mitty, he was able to state, "No priests in this vast land are more responsive to their dignity than my priests, no priests have ever aided a bishop as my priests. No wonder the archbishop loves his priests and no wonder they love him."[150]

Hanna held a special relationship with the Cantwell brothers, John, James, Arthur, and William, Irish born but educated in San Francisco. John, who was Hanna's first vicar, was consecrated bishop of Los Angeles only two years after Hanna's assumption of the archepiscopal see. The two regularly corresponded and Hanna was a frequent visitor, especially when he traveled to Southern California for his various civic activities. James was Hanna's long-time chancellor and advisor. Arthur and William served as local pastors, the former at St. Elizabeth from 1942 to 1970 and the latter at St. Monica from 1929 to 1962.[151]

Hanna's principal concern with the San Francisco clergy did not detract or inhibit a similarly harmonious relationship with various religious in the diocese, numbering some 1200 in June 1915. Hanna expected religious clergy to follow the same guidelines as his diocesan priests; in return, he supported the congregations' efforts and commended them for their work, especially in academic apostolates. Hanna was prudent in his invitations to religious to enter the archdiocese, however, extending them only when he believed local clergy and institutions could not meet the actual or future need.[152]

An American Catholic

Since the Constitutional period of U.S. history, American Catholics have faced the question: Can one be Catholic and American simultaneously? Protestants, citing loyalty to the pope, believed it was virtually impossible for Catholics to be "true" Americans, arguing that split loyalties between Washington and Rome would compromise one's ability to truly adopt the American ethos. Catholics, on the other hand, saw no discontinuity and answered the question in the affirmative. Some nineteenth-century American Catholic figures, most notably the Paulist father Isaac

Hecker, asserted that Roman Catholicism could find no better place to thrive than the United States.

In the twentieth century these same questions were being asked in different ways, with Catholics like Edward Hanna debating issues such as the purpose of the state and the relationship of the Church to democracy. Hanna believed that the state derived its power from God, who thus determined the extent of civil authority: the state was established to promote the common good by respecting and protecting the divine rights of the individual. Thus, there was an absolute need for religion and government to remain closely allied. For Hanna, this goal was accomplished through democracy. In a 1918 speech to the National Catholic Education Association Convention in San Francisco, he proclaimed,

> In a democracy, religion must have the largest place, for only in religion have men learned these mighty, these saving truths; only religion can make men adopt the high and lofty standards; only religion has taught men to place the fulfillment of their hopes, not in the things that pass with this life, but in the possession of the treasures which belong to the life to come.[153]

Religion must be direct and must influence government, so that citizens will understand law as the will of God. While Hanna supported a close connection between religion and government, he claimed that the Church should not interfere in politics unless moral and spiritual matters were involved.[154] He summarized his view of the connection between religion and government in a February 1918 speech in Berkeley:

> We stand here today the champions of religion; we stand here today defenders of our country, her liberties and her weal; and we feel that those two great sentiments—God and Country, Religion and Patriotism—must blend harmoniously if there is to be real conquest, if real victory is to come to us, with justice and peace.[155]

Hanna was proud to be an American, proclaiming that the privileges of citizenship incurred significant responsibilities. In a baccalaureate address at the University of California he told graduates, "Your country has a right to ask from you any sacrifice necessary to uphold her dignity and her honor, any sacrifice that will help her take her rightful place in the galaxy of the nations." In a similar address at Stanford he stated, "Alma Mater sends you forth to battle for God, the battle that justice be meted to your fellowmen, to battle for the ideals of freedom and of government that are our American birthright."[156] He promoted the ideal of service: people needed to seek a higher justice by trying to solve the world's problems.[157]

Responsible citizenship mandated promoting cooperation between church and state. He stated that the Church recognizes "that Democracy can be made efficient and lasting for the Catholic Church." He acknowledged the Catholic principle that citizens are subject to those who command the state but that the state "ought to be the first to appreciate the importance of the Catholic truth for the preservation of the common weal, for it makes men bow to the laws of our rulers as they would to God Himself."[158] Hanna put it succinctly, quoting Cardinal James Gibbons, "This is our watchword—loyalty to God's Church and to our country—this is our religious and political faith."[159]

Hanna believed not only that American Catholics needed to be loyal to the state but that the American nation was responsible to the world at large. Returning from an *ad limina* visit in 1924, Hanna expounded on the devastation still apparent in Europe and reminded Americans, "For the next fifty years [our] country holds the world in the hollow of its hand." He continued, "Never in all history has such power been given to one country. To a single race of men, are we going to be equal to the responsibilities of that power?" For Hanna the answer was clear, "We have a monumental task before us and we shall not be found wanting."[160]

Hanna wore his patriotism on his sleeve, but his support for American efforts in World War I changed over time. When Hanna was asked to support peace efforts during the early stages of the war, he admitted that Christianity is "uncongenial with war," noting the horrible destruction that armed conflict brings, but he also said that peace could not be obtained without honor. He stated that Woodrow Wilson's policy of isolationism needed modification: "Peace with honor is strength; without honor it is weakness. Our peace at any price party would fade away in a situation that required surrender of national honor for the sake of peace." Hanna understood the official reasons for the war, but in the end he suggested that the peace the world needed could be found only through a return to Christ.[161]

When the United States entered the war in 1917, Hanna, like most American Catholics, stood staunchly behind the president. He played a leading role in addressing a letter from the American hierarchy to the president, pledging Catholic loyalty in the war effort. He also called for Catholic organizations to support the Knights of Columbus, who spearheaded the Church's most visible war effort: a series of recreation camps in Europe and the United States.[162] In a speech to the Knights he exclaimed, "We must do everything within reason for our troops who are willing and able to dedicate their lives to the service of their country and to yield themselves if necessary that this country may live....We must forget ourselves entirely for greater issues are at stake." He believed that the president's call to service must be heeded: "The time for words has passed. This is the time for deeds. And we owe not only our allegiance—we owe our active service."[163]

In his position as archbishop of San Francisco, Hanna was very active with the San Francisco Liberty Loan Committee, which encouraged people to support the Liberty Loan program (similar to savings bonds) "to put autocracy down for good and all."[164] Hanna was also a significant asset to the San Francisco chapter of the Irish Relief Commission, which in 1916 sent $17,000 for the relief of Ireland. He also supported the Shamrock Fund, which raised money to support Irish soldiers permanently disabled due to the war. Hanna served as vice president for the Permanent Blind Relief War Fund.[165] Numerous other groups also petitioned Hanna for support or for his time, but his participation in them was minimal.

Hanna also supported the war effort by tending to the spiritual needs of soldiers. He fought for military chaplains to be assigned at Fort Mason and at the Presidio, for large army bases in San Francisco, and for the construction of an adequate chapel at the Presidio, perceiving the present facility as totally inadequate for the personnel assigned to the base.[166] Hanna also pushed hard for more Catholic chaplains to meet the spiritual needs of soldiers.

Besides releasing several of his own priests for military service, Hanna petitioned Senator James Phelan of California to inform the secretary of war, Newton Baker, that the number of Catholic chaplains was far below the quota allowed based on the number of Catholics in uniform.[167]

The end of the war brought new questions to the forefront for American Catholics. The major issue for the archbishop was the same question all others were asking: Should the United States enter the League of Nations? In agreement with many Catholic weeklies,[168] San Francisco's archdiocesan newspaper, the *Monitor*, traced a slow transition from support to utter disdain for the League. In February 1919 the paper extolled President Wilson's efforts, claiming that he would be known as "the greatest benefactor of the human race" if the League succeeded. The paper described the League as " a vital thing...demanded as the basic machinery of a lasting settlement" and "a great triumph for the lofty and clear-minded leaders of peoples." By July, however, the paper was referring to the League as "international burglary," a "gigantic fraud," and the "illegitimate child of justice and the Fourteen Points." In November the paper triumphantly stated, "One blessing for which the American people should be devoutly thankful this Thanksgiving Day...is the rejection of the British League of Nations covenant backed by President Wilson by the vote of the Senate last Wednesday night."[169]

Hanna, like the *Monitor*, initially lent his support to the League but joined national opinion when it turned negative. For Hanna, the real answer consisted of turning toward peace. In an address to the Pacific Coast Peace Conference he stated, "There is little hope of happier conditions until those who sway the destinies of earth put their trust not in the force of arms or the enticement of power, but in justice and mercy and love which ever comes in the vision of peace."[170]

Hanna also called for American action to deal with the devastation that the war had caused in Europe, where he spent three months in 1920 as part of his periodic *ad limina* visit. The pope told Hanna that he felt the United States needed to take a greater role in bringing stability to the area. The destruction Hanna himself observed led him to proclaim that the United States had not met its responsibilities in the region. He wrote, "After all is said and done, we must admit we have not quite lived up to the program: We have not kept faith with our mighty ideals. This is the reason for the condition in Europe today."[171]

Hanna responded to the need through energetic participation in varied relief agencies. Hanna was an active member of the Northern California State Committee for European Relief Council, headed locally by the San Francisco businessman Frederick Koster and nationally by the future president Herbert Hoover. The latter petitioned Hanna in his role as NCWC administrative chief (see chapters 7, 8, and 9) for a national collection in Catholic parishes to aid the starving children in Europe.[172] In a similar vein, Hanna, as a member of the executive committee, supported the Armenian and Syrian Relief Committee of San Francisco.[173] However, Hanna was prudent enough to realize that too many relief efforts simultaneously would dilute assistance to the poor. Thus, he gave priority to certain causes, most notably that of Ireland, while remaining sensitive to the refugee issue at large.[174]

Given his ancestry, Hanna's support for varied Irish causes and relief programs was quite natural. In line with the *Monitor*, which proclaimed the cause of Irish home rule as irrefutable,[175] Hanna strongly supported Ireland's drive for freedom. He suggested that the United States owed a debt to Ireland based on its millions of immigrants, as well as the heritage and the religion it had bestowed on the New World. In a speech Hanna proclaimed, "Let the word go out of this meeting and similar ones to those in whose hands rest the destinies of nations that they will realize and acknowledge the justice of the Irish cause and bring about the reality of the dream for centuries of all the Irish people."[176] Hanna also welcomed Irish freedom fighter and later president Eamon de Valera, who came to San Francisco in 1919, 1927, and 1930. Supporting de Valera's efforts, Hanna addressed an Irish freedom rally at the San Francisco Civic Auditorium:

> If we are in tune to this ideal [liberty and freedom], if we stand for the things that have been voiced abroad by our President, if we stand by this mighty charter of our liberties, then we must do all that in our power is to aid battling Erin, that she may be

a nation once again....Oh, let this thought fill our hearts, and let us with all the power we have strive that Erin may indeed be free, and her children may go forth to do for the world the mightiest work that has been done through all ages.[177]

Besides calling for Irish independence, Hanna also supported the Emerald Isle and its people through membership and participation in various Irish nationalist groups. Hanna was honorary national vice president and president for the San Francisco branch of the Irish Relief Commission, which collected funds to relieve the destitute in Ireland. Hanna called for action:

It is evident that Ireland is facing a crisis and for help she can look only to us. Surely we cannot look upon her distress with indifference....Our sympathy and our aid have gone out generously to every suffering people in the catastrophe of humanity; we cannot close our hearts on our own.[178]

Hanna was also associated with the American Commission on Irish Independence, the northern California branch of the American Committee for Relief in Ireland, and the Irish Freedom Fund Committee of San Francisco. The archbishop was asked on numerous occasions to speak, and he often accepted such invitations as those issued by the Ancient Order of Hibernians.[179]

The 1924 Holy Name Parade

The decade of the 1920s was a time for muscular Catholicism to shine brightly. The resurrection of the Ku Klux Klan in 1915 and its emergence as the most virulent anti-Catholic organization of the century brought a Catholic backlash. In her seminal study of the 1920s, the historian Lynn Dumenil demonstrates how Catholic militancy and organized activism were manifested most strongly in public demonstrations of Catholic faith. She comments: "Public parades and rallies in which Catholics sought to display their numerical strength and their patriotism at the same time became commonplace." Dumenil continues, "In the 1920s this type of demonstration not only multiplied but also became more overtly linked to countering anti-Catholicism." The most famous example of this idea occurred on September 21, 1924, when one hundred thousand members of the Holy Name Society marched in Washington, DC, carrying papal banners and American flags. At the end of the march, society members were addressed by President Calvin Coolidge and Cardinal William O'Connell of Boston.[180]

Hanna's American spirit and his desire to fight anti-Catholicism came together in 1924 under the ostensible guise of his return to San Francisco from a periodic *ad limina* visit with the pope. The *Monitor* reported that a grand parade, under the auspices of the Holy Name Society and with representatives from every parish in the archdiocese, would be held on October 5. The paper stated that the parade was to honor Hanna's return, to observe the 650th anniversary of the Holy Name Society and its 70th anniversary on the West Coast, and to celebrate the feast of St. Francis. But while stating these reasons, the paper was also running parallel stories of the Klan and the parade. Dumenil concludes concerning San Francisco's Holy Name Parade: "The accounts of the event subtly but unmistakably made it clear that it was intended as a symbolic show of strength against anti-Catholicism generally, and the Klan specifically."[181]

Despite a constant downpour of rain eighty thousand people marched down Market Street "to assert Catholic citizens' rights to participate in public life."[182] Another ten thousand lined the street to watch the spectacular, including the principal reviewers, Hanna; Mayor James Rolph; Edward F. Dunne, former governor of Illinois and principal speaker; and Dr. J. Franklin Smith, archdiocesan president of the Holy Name Society. As the parade concluded at the Civic Center, a service was held at which Dunne congratulated the society's members for "acting along the ideals of good citizenship always advocated by the Catholic Church."[183] Hanna, who was described as "bristling with energy, looking the picture of health and with his general, kindly smile much in evidence," spoke with great pride and authority to those assembled:

In these days of hatred and strife, we must make them [Catholic opponents] learn that they are children of Our Father, cemented into one great and loving family by the blood of Christ, that out of brotherly love may come peace.

These great truths are our Catholic profession, putting these truths into practice is our great purpose, and to emphasize them as never before, is the meaning of this mighty throng of Catholic men who make up the great church of San Francisco.[184]

The power and influence of the parade was captured by one local reporter: "Undaunted by the rain, which had continued since early morning, the thousands of marchers proclaimed to the world that they, like the early Christians, would let nothing interfere with their plans in the carrying out of an ideal. While the men and boys marched, their clothes soaked and dripping and their skin chilled by a cold wind, the wives and mothers stood on the sidelines, which had been blocked off by the public department, and cheered the modern crusaders time and again."[185]

Conclusion

Edward Hanna, arriving in San Francisco in December 1912, hit the ministerial trail running. As auxiliary to Patrick Riordan, he conducted typical duties such as presiding at confirmations and at the dedications of new churches. He also became almost immediately involved with the civic affairs of the city, a ministry that characterized his tenure as local ordinary. Once he was made archbishop, he set up his administration and immediately began to make significant inroads in areas that were dear to his heart. An active promoter of education on all levels, Hanna fully supported his archdiocesan schools, both in their construction and as their advocate for tax exemption. Additionally, he supervised the construction of St. Joseph's Seminary as the feeder school to the archdiocesan seminary, St. Patrick's. Hanna also fostered his special relationship with the local clergy, and became known as the most beloved archbishop in the city's history. As a man of his time, he fully supported America's efforts in World War I but took the nation to task for disregarding the destruction wrought by the war in eastern Europe. Hanna's episcopal career in San Francisco was marked by a genuine love of church and nation. Through his untiring efforts as advocate for others he truly became an archbishop for all the people.

Chapter 4

AN ARCHBISHOP
FOR THE PEOPLE

As archbishop of San Francisco, Edward Hanna actively sought to serve the Church, which he understood to be God's people,[1] and the state, for he realized that both of these great institutions were integral to people's daily lives. Although as local ordinary of the largest archepiscopal see west of the Mississippi Hanna associated with the rich and powerful in both church and state, he was also an archbishop for all people; he affiliated with and was an advocate for the poor, marginalized, and forgotten in society. In his twenty-three-year episcopal career Hanna joined and often led groups, agencies, and organizations that sought to aid the average person in the community. He especially attempted to assist youth, particularly orphans and others abandoned by society. Long before it was fashionable Hanna was also a major proponent of ecumenism, freely associating with Protestants and championing Jewish-Christian relations.

Municipal Affairs in San Francisco

San Francisco in the 1920s has been characterized differently by various historians, describing both a city reveling in the financial prosperity of the decade but simultaneously suffering through a significant transition in municipal politics. The historian Tom Cole has written of the period:

> Following the war, San Francisco shared in the frantic prosperity of the 1920s. The city was used to the giddy highs of good fortune and the frenzy of a stock exchange drunk on ever

rising values, and it joined in on the national frolic of the Roaring Twenties.[2]

The hollow prosperity of the decade was, however, tempered by some significant shifts in political winds and factions in party loyalties. Historians William Issel and Robert Cherny refer to this decade as "the factious and personality-oriented politics of the 1920s." Polarization between rich and poor sections of the city became much more defined. Simultaneous events converged to create this situation. The most prominent was the virtual disappearance of political parties and the emergence of several factions organized around powerful political leaders, most of whom were republicans. These republicans, who composed some 80 percent of the electorate by 1930, were split between conservatives such as William Crocker, Herbert Fleishhacker, and M. H. de Young and progressives led by Hiram Johnson, A. P. Giannini, and John Francis Neylan. The business community also flexed its muscle through its private establishment of the San Francisco Bureau of Governmental Research (BGR), which "emerged as a major force representing the business community." Between 1916 and 1930 the BGR sought to reform San Francisco's municipal government, which it saw as illogical in its organization, along the more beneficial lines of a business corporation.[3]

Advocate for the Poor—Civic Efforts

From his earliest days in San Francisco, Hanna made a profound and lasting impression on those he met. People experienced the archbishop as "a just and broad minded man" in opinion and interests, affable, diplomatic, dignified, and one who always fought hard for the underdog.[4] Shortly after his arrival in the city, the archdiocesan weekly, the *Monitor*, reported, "Bishop Hanna is a man in whose presence you cannot pass an hour without coming away improved in mind and refreshed in spirit. He is interested in everything, but most of all in humanity and that, in particular, on the side which brings us nearest to our Maker."[5] Hanna was known to be "an indefatigable worker...with a perpetual and inexhaustible supply of energy."[6] He possessed a genius for garnering respect from all sides and avenues of society and parlayed this ability to his advantage over many years in his work with civic and Church groups that assisted average citizens in their everyday needs. Upon his death in 1944, the San Francisco *Call-Bulletin* wrote: "This kindly and earnest man of religion had a genius and an instinct for human understanding, an amazing capacity for commanding the attention of the community, and an inspiring capacity for winning the respect of the community."[7] From the very outset, it was also noted that Hanna's versatility and general appeal provided him access to people that others did not have. This, in turn, allowed him to understand better human welfare and gave him the capacity to do something positive to enhance it.

Hanna garnered widespread respect among church, state, and religious officials, but he also received numerous letters from ordinary people who had experienced his pastoral touch. One typical note read, "Words could not express my gratitude for your kindness to me, by sending me the twenty dollars when I was in need of it." He was regularly congratulated for his public spirit and community service, which were "constant and helpful."[8] Herbert Fleishhacker, who worked with Hanna on the Commission of Immigration and Housing of California, stated upon the archbishop's death, "His humanity was so great that it extended to every creed besides his own."[9]

Because of his reputation, Hanna was much sought out by civic groups to support their projects and issues. People spoke of his "manifest interest in charities," adding that his "participation in the affairs of the community was constant and helpful." People were deeply appreciative of the active way Hanna got involved, holding nothing back when he believed in the validity and worthiness of a cause.[10] For example, Hanna contributed significant time and effort to the Legal Aid Society of San Francisco, which was formed through the efforts of the Commission of Immigration and Housing of California, shortly after its foundation in 1913, to correct the widespread and severe exploitation of immigrants.[11] O. K. Cushing, president of the Associated Charities of San Francisco, and a prominent San Francisco attorney, was elected the society's first president. Hanna was appointed honorary vice president, but his involvement was much greater than the title implied: he permitted a member of his staff, Miss E. F. McCarthy, to serve as the agency's secretary and provided personal and archdiocesan funds when other sources of revenue ran dry. He once stated, "The work must not fail. Go on and the money will be forthcoming."[12]

Numerous other civic organizations received Hanna's attention and assistance, especially agencies involved with emergency medical and monetary assistance and aid to local government. The archbishop's service for several years as a member of the Board of Directors for the American Red Cross's San Francisco chapter was appreciated:

> During the Red Cross campaign for membership you gave us a great deal of encouragement and assistance in putting us in touch with a large number of people in San Francisco, and in behalf of the San Francisco Chapter of the American Red Cross I wish to express to you our appreciation of your good work.[13]

Hanna was active in a similar capacity with the Society for the Prevention of Tuberculosis and served on the board of the Alcohol Education Association of America, headquartered in Pasadena, California.[14] In the Travelers' Aid Society of California, he served as vice president and as a member of the organization's executive committee, speaking in support of the organization and keeping its assistance to the immigrant population in the public eye. Mayor James Rolph frequently asked Hanna to help him get legislation passed, especially bond issues. Hanna's position as head of the city's largest religious denomination was undoubtedly a factor in these requests, but the perception that his backing was much more than ceremonial made him an even more valuable ally.[15]

Municipal organizations in San Francisco also enjoyed Hanna's attention and assistance. Throughout his tenure in the city Hanna was involved in some capacity with the San Francisco Community Chest, serving as vice president and board member. He lauded the organization's efforts to improve orphanages and institutions for the indigent poor and encouraged his city residents to open their wallets as well as their hearts:

Let us resolve today as citizens of a great city, spiritually and commercially, to give generously of our finances and to be just as generous with our moral support to the Community Chest. Truly this will be a going out of hearts of the people to those who have fallen out of the common way of life.[16]

Hanna was even more personally invested in the Associated Charities of San Francisco, making a personal contribution of $1,000 to free it from debt. He encouraged others to assist the work of the Associated Charities:

The Associated Charities is indeed the common concern of every citizen, for it is the great non-sectarian, child-caring and relief organization which is responsible for those destitute persons who have no other definite place to go for relief. As such, its survival is the anxious concern of each and every one in the community....San Francisco should not fail in her duty to the afflicted who are dependent upon her through the Associated Charities. We must all unite in the support of this community welfare organization.[17]

Hanna was a director of the San Francisco Community Service Recreation League, a member of the National Public Safety Committee (San Francisco branch), and a member of the "Citizen's Committee of One Thousand," which was founded to push for passage of school and hospital bond issues.[18]

Hanna's advocacy for the poor extended beyond the boundaries of San Francisco and the archdiocese. Throughout the 1920s, he presided at general sessions of the California State Conference of Social Agencies, and recruited priests and religious of the archdiocese to attend local meetings. In the 1930s Hanna joined the National Citizens Committee of the Welfare and Relief Mobilization, headquartered in Washington, DC.[19]

Catholic organizations that assisted the poor also received significant attention from the archbishop. Nationally he served as the supreme director of the Affiliated Catholic Charities and spoke frequently at various meetings of the National Conference of Catholic Charities.[20] On the local level he introduced the Society for the

Propagation of the Faith into the archdiocese in January 1925,[21] energetically supported the Knights of Columbus (an organization with which he was closely allied from his days in Rochester), and assisted the Catholic Truth Society. He served as honorary chair of the St. Vincent de Paul Society,[22] and encouraged his pastors to support its work. Writing on Hanna's behalf, his vicar general and secretary, James Cantwell, stated, "The Most Reverend Archbishop asks you to kindly help Mr. [James] Fennell in the great work of charity which he is undertaking, and strive to bring the organization within your parish up to the ideals of the great Founder of the Society."[23] Fennell, president of the society's San Francisco chapter, responded to Hanna, "The St. Vincent de Paul Society is well aware of your generous activity in all Catholic charities."[24]

Hanna was a great supporter of two youth-oriented groups in San Francisco. He had a special affinity to the St. Francis Welfare League, which was founded in 1912, "to provide for the entertainment and spiritual advancement of young people, by organizing and conducting noon-day clubs in mercantile and manufacturing establishments, evening classes and mothers' clubs." Hanna served as general director of the league in 1920 and was a regular speaker throughout the decade.[25] Hanna also supported the work of the League of Cross Cadets, a very popular temperance organization that used paramilitary drill. He served as honorary chairman, making certain that a chaplain was assigned to the group.[26]

Hanna held great respect for young adults as evidenced through his promotion of youth organizations both inside and outside the Church. For the Young Men's Institute (YMI), founded in San Francisco in 1883,[27] Hanna consistently attended meetings, presided at its annual communion breakfast, served as honorary grand chaplain, and recruited enthusiastically. Personal letters were sent to pastors stating,

> In order to keep up the high standard of past years, His Grace asks you to take a personal interest in the present drive for membership [for the YMI], and see that the candidates are practical Catholics and good citizens, and give evidence in their lives of the motto of the Y.M.I., *Pro Deo et Pro Patria*.[28]

Hanna even-handedly supported the YMI's sister organization, the Young Ladies' Institute (YLI), attending meetings and praising the group's support of the good works of the archdiocese.[29] The archbishop was concerned that the dignity of the women involved with the YLI be maintained. When the local paper ran pictures of YLI members in swimming suits, James Cantwell, writing on Hanna's behalf, suggested a more dignified approach:

> His Grace does not feel that a Catholic organization established for the social and spiritual welfare if its members should have become an athletic club. The Archbishop has no objection to the YLI availing themselves of the facilities for recreation at the YMI Hall, or of any contests held there, but he feels that the dignity of the Young Ladies' Institute, and the standard and high ideals for which they are coming are very much lowered when individual members lend themselves to the world idea of the present day.[30]

The Siena Club, founded in 1913 along the lines of the Newman Club by a group of Catholic students attending San Francisco Normal School, also enjoyed Hanna's support. He almost immediately developed into the group's spiritual head, presiding at the annual communion breakfast and giving a yearly retreat to its members.[31]

Advocate for Children

While Edward Hanna was a friend of the poor and the marginalized, children held a particular place in his heart. His description of the child illustrates his concern for them and the potential he saw in them:

> The child is the most precious thing the world holds. In his mind and in his will he reflects the glory of God—God's might, God's intelligence, God's power. As he grows unto the fullness of manhood, as he grasps the deep meaning and purpose of life

so will be the future of this land you love [,] this land for which
our fathers fought verily with life's blood.[32]

Hanna considered it a privilege to do anything he could for God's
children. He promoted all efforts toward the training and education of youth, viewing them as the future of society.[33] During
Advent 1920 he preached a series of sermons centered around the
basic theme of children.[34]

Girls' and boys' organizations of all stripes found a friend and
advocate in Archbishop Hanna. He financially supported the
California Home for Girls and served as honorary president of the
California Society for Befriending Girls from 1920 to 1924.[35]
Hanna was even more active and committed to organizations for
boys, a fact that was noted by prominent local citizens.[36] Upon his
appointment as local ordinary he became a board member of the
San Francisco Working Boys Club and served as the organization's
president in 1916. He assisted the club financially and advised the
group in its efforts to incorporate.[37] He was also an active member
and, in 1918, general director of the Boys Welfare Society of
California.[38] Hanna served as honorary vice chairman for Boys
Week in October 1920 and supported the drive to raise money for
a new home for wayward boys.[39] In February 1922 he called a meeting of local groups to see how they could help orphaned and abandoned boys, and he chided the nation's men for their failure to
adequately train boys:

> This is the only country in the world where men will not teach
> boys! The future of our country lies in its boys; yet we can't
> find men who will turn from the struggle for self in order to
> develop and mold the growing mind into a greater unity of
> Americanism—to develop wisdom and leadership in the com-
> ing generations.[40]

Hanna was especially active in supporting the fledgling Boy
Scouts of America program. One scout official noted, "Your
[Hanna's] belief in the Boy Scout Movement, as expressed during
your addresses on a number of occasions, has been a source of
encouragement and inspiration to those of us who are directly

responsible for its promotion." The president of the San Francisco Council of the Boys Scouts of America lauded Hanna for his support:

> The evidence of your interest in the work we are striving to do for the development of boyhood in San Francisco [is] a source of great encouragement to the hundreds of men who are giving voluntarily of their time and energies in the supervision and training of 5000 boy scouts.[41]

Hanna asked his clergy to "enthusiastically support" the scout movement "to keep our boys under Catholic influence, and instill into them religious and patriotic ideals."[42]

Hanna's advocacy for child welfare and his participation in youth assistance agencies continued throughout his tenure as archbishop. From his early years in the city, Hanna participated actively in the Little Children's Aid Society, an endeavor of the Associated Charities of San Francisco, which secured foster homes for children displaced from their blood families. Hanna spoke at many meetings of the society and gave his full support to its endeavors.[43] The Children's Home Society of California, the California Society of Crippled Children, and the Children's Theater Association of San Francisco all petitioned the archbishop for his support.[44] Hanna was a major advocate to the establishment of National Child Health Day. With an eye to the future he commented:

> I pledge you our active cooperation in national Child Health day and I can think of nothing more beneficial to the whole nation than placing before our people, once in the year, the importance of caring for the physical as well as spiritual wellbeing of our children. Upon their right development depends the future of the coming generation.[45]

Destitute and orphaned children found a special friend and advocate in Edward Hanna, who provided support for various orphan asylums in the archdiocese. In 1917 he became greatly concerned over reports about sanitation and other health problems in certain state-run facilities.[46] Hanna's vicar general, John Cantwell, wrote to one concerned religious sister, "We are, as

Catholics, anxious in every way to co-operate with the State in bringing the institutions that receive money from the State to such conditions as our means will allow and that reasonable people expect."[47] Hanna personally supervised archdiocesan efforts to assist orphans. In 1916 he successfully solicited funds for badly needed repairs at the St. Francis Orphan Asylum, a facility that was slated for closure.[48] Hanna also served as president of St. Vincent's Orphan Asylum in San Rafael in 1919, personally supervising—as much as was possible with his other episcopal duties—the home's operation. In 1924 he directed his chancellor, James Cantwell, "to raise money" for the extensive repairs and improvements the facility needed.[49]

Hanna's advocacy for destitute youth also extended to handicapped children. He made an overt effort to identify deaf and mute children and provide them with adequate religious instruction through the efforts of the Sisters of the Holy Family. He financially supported St. Joseph's Home for Deaf Mutes in Oakland, first using personal and diocesan funds, then seeking permission from James Rolph in 1920 to hold a "Tag Day" fundraiser.[50] Hanna additionally served as the chairman of the Board of Directors of Youth's Directory, a free home for destitute children in San Francisco, and as "grand director" of the Catholic Humane Bureau, an agency that provided for abandoned and neglected children.[51]

Advocate for the Poor

Because Edward Hanna made friends easily, moved among the people with great ease and joy, and was always willing to assist a person in need,[52] the people of San Francisco, Catholics and non-Catholics alike, petitioned for his assistance, believing that he would listen and respond favorably. A typical plea from a woman in need read, "I beg to be excused for writing to you. I have herd [sic] you were such a kind, charitable Father to the poor. I thought I would write to you [for] I am a poor afflicted woman." Hanna was asked to find jobs, provide money to bury the dead, and financially assist families who could not make ends meet. On many occasions he personally responded to such requests, sending money, assisting with job placements, or promising archdiocesan support of just causes, such as obtaining compensation for victims of industrial accidents and giving the dead a proper Christian burial.[53] Hanna also promoted agencies that assisted the physically handicapped and supported state legislation to alleviate their suffering. It is clear that people found Hanna approachable; the hierarchical "ivory-palace" image of an archbishop was not Hanna's style nor his personality.[54]

Another measure of Hanna's advocacy of the poor was his concern for the rights of prisoners. In October 1915, shortly after his appointment as local ordinary, Hanna participated in a conference of the American Prison Association held in Oakland. He served as an advocate for the rights of inmates with the California Prison Commission, supporting parole for inmates who had been model prisoners, and becoming involved in cases where irregularities in the evidence and trial had led to highly questionable verdicts and sentences. Hanna took up the cause of inmates at San Quentin and Folsom prisons in a special way. His secretary, James Cantwell, often wrote on the archbishop's behalf, questioning the parole hearing rulings on several prisoners and in the case of one man, Alexander Hagan, speaking of the injustice of his eighteen-year sentence. Hanna's plea for Hagan went national through Michael Williams, who was editor of the NCWC *Bulletin* at the time.[55]

Hanna's outreach to the marginalized also extended to African Americans, and he recognized the Church's need to minister to this population. Because of his "great interest in the colored members of the Church" he was asked to support the application of blacks to membership in the Knights of Columbus. Hanna actively recruited members of the Society of the Divine Word (SVD) to minister to the black community of San Francisco.[56] Additionally, Hanna supported the efforts of the Sisters of the Helpers of the Holy Souls, who established a mission to black Catholics on O'Farrell Street, dedicated to St. Benedict the Moor.[57]

On an institutional level, Hanna also aided the poor through his support of Catholic charities in the archdiocese. In the wake of the 1906 earthquake and fire, Archbishop Riordan authorized the first permanent Catholic charities agency, The Catholic Settlement and Humane Society. During Hanna's administration, Catholic charities expanded significantly so that by 1932 some twenty different agencies were operating in four areas: child welfare, family welfare, protection of girls, and social action. Hanna's coadjutor and successor, John Mitty, beginning in the early 1930s, sent priests to gain advanced degrees in various disciplines to prepare them for leadership in social service work.[58]

Hanna's advocacy for the poor and marginalized led him to support the Cemetery Protective Association, which opposed measures in the 1920s to reclaim cemetery lands in the city. When Yerba Buena Cemetery, located in the present-day Civic Center of San Francisco area, was abandoned in 1860, four separate cemeteries were eventually established to replace it: Old Fellows, Masonic, Laurel Hill, and Calvary. As early as the 1880s, partly due to the opening of Holy Cross Cemetery in Colma, the cemeteries were criticized as ill-kept and havens for crime and juvenile delinquents. In 1913, local residents became more vocal in their campaign to remove the cemeteries, calling them "menaces to health, eyesores, and obstacles to community progress."[59]

Hanna was drawn into this dispute in 1915, when the Cemetery Protective Association asked him to speak against state legislation that would remove the cemeteries from local control, as a first step toward their abolition. Hanna's attorney, Garret McEnerney, wrote to him, "If consistent with your views we should like you to oppose Senate Bill twelve twenty relating to cemeteries as we consider it a very mischievous measure and violative of the religious sentiments and traditions of many people." Hanna, replied to the state senate, "I hope it will be consistent with your sense of public duty to oppose the measure."[60]

Although the state measure failed, its supporters were ready for a protracted battle. In 1921 and 1923 the state legislature passed the Morris Acts (I and II), which gave cemetery officials the right, with certain restrictions, to remove bodies and devote the land to new purposes. Almost immediately, the San Francisco Board of Supervisors passed an ordinance ordering the removal of bodies from three city cemeteries—Masonic, Odd Fellows, and Laurel Hill. Supporters of the initiative claimed that city cemeteries interfered with new transportation needs, that the land was needed for municipal expansion, and local residents were unhappy with the ill-kept facilities.[61] The laws were contested in the courts and in 1923 the Morris Act was invalidated by the California Supreme Court.

In 1924, despite the high court's decision, the San Francisco Board of Supervisors proposed an initiative, similar to that of 1921, adding Calvary, a Catholic cemetery, to the list of facilities to be closed. Hanna's office "served notice...the he [Hanna] intend[ed] to fight the ordinance,...bringing the matter if necessary to the notice of San Francisco [voters], and finally to the courts."[62] Archdiocesan officials told the supervisors that the removal of fifty-four thousand bodies from Calvary would cost $3.5 million, and with the county only reimbursing $2,500 per lot (448 lots), the archdiocese would be forced to pay $2.4 million. The chancery appealed, "A great injustice will be done to thousands of our citizens represented by the Archbishop." Despite Hanna's opposition the Board of Supervisors passed the measure in May.[63]

Hanna almost immediately opposed the new law, re-forming the Cemetery Protective Association and arguing for a citywide referendum against the law. As a compromise, Mayor James Rolph suggested combining all the cemeteries into a single proposal rather than writing separate proposals for each cemetery. This idea actually unified the opponents of the supervisors' initiative and, therefore, helped their cause. Hanna backed the "compromise," stating that it would eliminate turf wars between various cemetery factions. However, those who favored the removal of the cemeteries, led by the Civic League of Improvement, knew that the archbishop's major fear was financial, and therefore rejected the mayor's proposal, suggesting, "If the Archbishop is faced with serious financial loss, then the people could leave the Calvary Cemetery until a later time and order the removal of the others."[64]

The re-formed Cemetery Protective Association was sufficiently influential to place the question before the voters of San Francisco. Proposition 43 on the November ballot asked for repeal of the Board of Supervisors' May initiative. Supporters of the ballot measure countered the arguments of those who had pressured the supervisors to pass the law, stating that the cemeteries were not a hindrance to municipal transportation or expansion needs, and adding that removing bodies at city expense would not be cost effective.[65] Backers of the proposition also argued that "the distress of survivors of those buried there, and…the apprehension of future plot owners" must be a serious consideration.[66]

As voting day neared, Hanna became increasingly proactive. He wrote a letter supporting Proposition 43, and had it read at all Masses celebrated on Sunday, October 12, 1924:

> I would exhort our faithful people and all right-minded citizens, regardless of creed, to make certain that no injustice is put upon us to whom the city of San Francisco owes so much. I feel sure that no one who hears the appeal [of the supervisors] can refuse to acknowledge its injustice, and I am sure also that with justice on our side we must, in the end, be victorious.[67]

He claimed that the economic burden the supervisor's decision would place on the Catholic community was "an injustice so gross that one wonders how such injustice could be possible in a city where the citizens are so fair-minded, where the citizens are so just." Hanna acknowledged that Calvary was "not in good condition" but he promised to put it in order, "no matter what the cost," if what he labeled "the persecution of more than 40 years" against the cemeteries ceased.[68]

The passage of Proposition 43 prompted Hanna to thank and congratulate his allies in the fight. One typical letter to a local pastor stated:

> In great thankfulness my heart goes out to you and to the people of your parish for the hearty and the loyal support given us in our battle to maintain intact the sacred ground where be the bodies of our loved ones. We felt we were champions of a cause at once just and holy, and the people of San Francisco by their magnificent support have shown that we were not mistaken.[69]

Hanna was hopeful that the election had "settled the question for all time."[70]

Hanna continued to argue against the removal of Calvary Cemetery until his retirement in 1935. In 1937 the archdiocese finally dropped its opposition to the planned removal, prompting the San Francisco Board of Supervisors to pass an ordinance, which was ratified by the voters, requiring the removal of Laurel Hill and Calvary cemeteries. Beginning in 1939 some fifty-five thousand bodies were removed from Calvary, most to be reinterred in Holy Cross Cemetery in Colma, south of the city.[71]

Edward Hanna as Ecumenist

Ecumenical dialogue in the early twentieth century was basically the purview of Protestants, with Catholics lagging far behind and making little significant progress until the Second Vatican Council (1962–1965) and the publication of *Unitatis redintegratio* and *Nostra aetate*. Internationally, the World Council of Churches (WCC) was organized at Amsterdam in 1948 through the union of two ecumenical movements, Life and Work and Faith and Order.[72] The WCC defined itself in this formative meeting as "a fellowship of churches which accept the Lord Jesus Christ as God and Savior." Domestically the Federal Council of Churches was formed in 1908, with twenty-eight communities, including all mainline churches except Roman Catholic. In 1950 the National Council of the Churches of Christ in the USA (NCCC-USA) united twelve interdenominational agencies, including the Federal Council of Churches.[73]

While Roman Catholicism's institutional reaction to the ecumenical movement was virtually nonexistent, Edward Hanna was open to other religions and views, even as a youth. In his high school he expressed "a broad view of...membership in the Church." His friendship with Walter Rauschenbusch, an ardent Baptist, was unusual in a time when Catholics tended to associate only with one another.[74] Hanna felt that ecumenism grew from the need to follow one's conscience:

> For man will ever stand judged because he too followed the commands of an enlightened conscience, and the very foundation of the liberties our Fathers bequeathed unto their children, the only hope of peace and of harmony amid the varied differences in our mingling of races and creed, must ever be in

allowing our neighbor to worship God, to fashion his moral
life according to the dictates of his conscience.[75]

Hanna's ecumenism took many forms. He was active and
"very interested" in Better Understanding, a group of religious
leaders in San Francisco that promoted dialogue by seeking themes
common to various religions and denominations. He was an elected
board member and vice president of the North American Board for
the Study of Religion in Higher Education, an interfaith board of
Jews, Protestants, and Catholics.[76] Hanna was often asked to support ecumenical initiatives; for example, the California Sunday
School Board of Religious Education asked him to support legislation in the state senate granting release time from public schools
for religious education. The cochairmen of the National
Conference of Jews and Christians, Newton Baker, Carlton Hayes,
and Roger Strauss, invited him to give the opening address at their
March 1932 conference. Hanna was also a well-known supporter of
the Week of Prayer for Christian Unity.[77]

Hanna was viewed by his clergymen peers as open to varied
religious traditions. One account of Hanna's ecumenical bent stated:

> The archbishop accentuated the liberal trend of his church-
> manship by the leading part he has taken in the great modern
> movement for uniting all religious backers in a common cause
> against the forces of disruption, moral anarchy and authentic
> iconoclasm.[78]

He was lauded for an approach that "contributed to better understanding of all men, a ministry that brings men together and helps
them understand each other better and love each other more."
Many people referred to Hanna as the archbishop of San Francisco,
rather than the Catholic archbishop, suggesting that he "provided
a type of spiritual fatherhood to all the city's residents, regardless of
their faith."[79]

While Hanna's ecumenical efforts embraced many Protestant
faiths, his interfaith work with Jews was extraordinary, especially
for the time in which he lived. From the outset of his time in San
Francisco, he viewed Catholics and Jews as joined by the fact that

both religions included many immigrants and were, therefore, ostracized by many in American society. He complimented the Jews of the city for their "active part in every good work" and their "wholehearted response to every appeal for relief of the unfortunate and needy, regardless of race or creed."[80] He supported the efforts of the Jewish National Welfare Fund, stating, "I am heart and soul with you in your campaign to raise money for the support of your splendid agencies."[81]

In May 1930 Hanna contributed $500 for the establishment of a Jewish Community Center in the city. He lauded the Jews for their significant contributions to society at large, stating, "The greatest contributions made to the cultural life of our city come largely from the Jews. If you turn to those institutions that assist those who have fallen by the wayside and require help, you find that the noblest contributions come from the Jews."[82]

In 1931 the Jewish community in the United States awarded Hanna the American Hebrew Medal. The award was presented annually "to that American man or woman who, during the year, has achieved most in the promotion of better understanding between Christians and Jews in our country." The first recipient of the award was former secretary of war Newton Baker, for his work as Protestant chairman of the National Conference of Jews and Christians. Hanna was unanimously voted the second recipient.[83] Rabbi Isaac Reichart, in announcing the award, stated, "No man has succeeded so well as he in winning the love and admiration of all classes of his fellow citizens."[84] Hanna responded graciously: "To be selected by your great group because I have loved my brother brings happiness and joy to my heart. For all that you have done and said my heart goes out to you in gratitude and appreciation as well as love."[85]

Hanna received congratulatory letters from leaders of church and state throughout the country. Speaking for the Protestant community, Newton Baker stated of Hanna, "That we delight in acclaiming him a warrior in the fight against prejudice gives us pride and pleasure and, I trust, gives him the satisfaction which ought to come to so great a man from the admiration and affection of his friends." California Governor James Rolph described the award as "a fitting tribute to our archbishop."[86]

The medal was awarded at a gala dinner held in New York's Hotel Pennsylvania on November 19, 1931, with many prominent figures in religion and politics in attendance. Hanna was praised for his "fights against racial prejudice" and his achievements in promoting the "brotherhood of man."[87] In a congratulatory note read at the banquet, President Herbert Hoover stated, "This distinguished prelate has done much to promote that comity, resulting from better understanding which forwards the objective this award has in view." In his acceptance speech, Hanna demonstrated his American Catholic roots, extolling shared freedoms and the inherent dignity of the human person:

> The cloud that appears on the horizon no bigger than a man's hand is indeed threatening. We shall need every spiritual resource if in the days to come we emerge victorious. The charter of our freedom is based upon the dignity of man, upon the willingness to sacrifice every personal advantage that our liberties may not perish from the earth. We who gather here believe in man's dignity. "Thou hast made him a little less than the angels." We believe that the law is the voice of Jehovah speaking unto us. And through the years of hard trials we have learned to sacrifice all things for the things we hold dear.[88]

The Beloved Archbishop of San Francisco

During his life Hanna was recognized for his significant contributions to church and state. The archbishop received numerous and regular invitations to speak with varied civic groups, in San Francisco and beyond. His ecumenical approach to all matters also generated many requests to speak to varied religious associations and meetings. Hanna also received numerous awards for his service. In 1931, besides being the recipient of the American Hebrew Medal, Hanna was also awarded an honorary doctorate of laws from the University of California at Berkeley. In reading the citation on that occasion, the university president, Dr. Robert Sproul, called Hanna "a friend to mankind."[89] Two years later the University of Rochester offered Hanna a similar degree, but he declined because he was unable to attend the commencement exercises. In 1934 Hanna was one of eight citizens of San Francisco awarded the Nicaraguan Presidential Medal of Merit, for his efforts in 1931 to raise funds and secure relief after a severe earthquake devastated that country.[90]

Edward Hanna, an archbishop for the people, was universally loved and esteemed. Historian Jeffrey Burns's comment, "Hanna became the most beloved archbishop in the history of San Francisco," is verified by the facts of his life and the many honors he received for his outstanding contributions to civic and Church communities.[91] Hanna was the "ideal citizen" interested in the welfare of the community, willing to contribute to the relief of the afflicted, maintaining a sense of justice and fair play toward all.[92] One comment captures Hanna's universal appeal:

> As an outstanding citizen and leader we regard our Archbishop as second to none. Whenever the cause of the working man is to be championed, there is our archbishop in the vanguard. When the poor need a friend, again His Grace is at the beck and call. When our statesmen want advice to whom do they unhesitatingly go? To Archbishop Hanna, who is ever ready to listen to them and to assist them by his wise and sage counsel.[93]

Hanna's reputation rested on a philosophy of self-sacrifice that followed the pattern of Christ. He did not allow his position in the Church to impede or cloud his vision of that pattern and he practiced a humble type of service, seeking to be the true shepherd that the role of bishop demanded. The equanimity with which he treated people was noted by a contemporary reporter:

> His Grace, Most Rev. Edward J. Hanna...one of the first prelates of the land and a great Thomistic scholar, is at heart a simple man....His great humanity has caused him to be likened to gentle St. Francis himself. He built no wall between himself and the people. The toil-stained laborer, the bent scrubwoman, the shopgirl, the woman of society, the wealthy businessman, all he received in his office with the same cheery

smile and the word of kindness when they came to him with their troubles. [94]

After his death, a similar tribute was made to Hanna:

> All we know is that a well worn path led to his door and that up that path came people of all ranks and classes, of all creeds and colors. Came Catholics and Protestants, Jews and Gentiles, priests and laymen, bankers and beggars, saints and sinners, the successes of life and the failures. No one was too lofty or too poor to approach the Archbishop. And to each he gave the same captivating smile of welcome. Each left with gratitude in his heart and a blessing on his soul.[95]

Conclusion

Edward Hanna, citizen of the world, truly was the archbishop of San Francisco in its broadest context. Beloved by all, rich and poor, American and immigrant, Catholic and non-Catholic, Hanna was able to bridge many groups in his support for people of all classes, faiths, and nationalities. Through his active support of civic and Church organizations he became a true advocate for the poor and marginalized in society. In particular he supported all causes that aimed to alleviate the suffering of youth, especially groups and organizations that assisted boys, whom he saw as the future of society. Young adults were another of his favorite causes. Hanna was a strong advocate of ecumenism, most notably in his work with the Jews in San Francisco, which resulted in his being awarded the 1931 Hebrew Medal. Hanna was the Catholic archbishop of San Francisco, but he was undoubtedly just as much the archbishop of all the people.

Chapter 5

EDWARD HANNA AND LABOR IN SAN FRANCISCO, 1915–1930

As an archbishop for all people, Edward Hanna was unwavering in his support of varied groups, in both church and state. His advocacy for education, immigrants, agencies assisting the poor, and children's aid societies was simply a continuation of his work as a priest in Rochester. In a similar way, Hanna brought a preexisting sense of justice and fair-mindedness to labor and capital issues in San Francisco. Beginning in 1914 with his election as head of a local commission to investigate local unemployment, Hanna brought this wisdom to bear on the critical issue of labor, working with city officials and leaders of labor and capital alike.

Catholicism and Labor in the United States

President Warren Harding's 1921 edict of a "return to normalcy" heralded the shift in post–World War I America away from the group consciousness of the Progressive Era toward a new emphasis on individual gain. The Roaring Twenties began with Americans attaining greater prosperity and control of their own economic future, while the vigor of the Social Gospel movement that had accompanied progressivism was replaced by a false sense of security. One casualty of this shift of national consciousness was organized labor, which saw many of its gains in the first twenty years of the century reversed. While numbers of workers and their compensation rose—and, consequently, labor's expectations—the power of unions themselves began to wane. The stock market crash of October 1929 and the Great Depression that followed created tension and fueled clashes between organized labor and employers.

American Catholics found themselves on both sides of the labor-capital debate. The secretive nature of unions in the nineteenth century led to their condemnation by the church hierarchy. At the Second Plenary Council of Baltimore (1866) the bishops stated their opinion:

> Care must be taken lest workingmen's societies under the pretext of mutual assistance and protection, should commit any of the evils of condemned societies; and lest the members should be induced by the artifices of designing men to break the laws of justice, by withholding labor to which they are rightfully bound, or by otherwise unlawfully violating the rights of their employers.[1]

This stance began to moderate when Cardinal James Gibbons of Baltimore supported the Knights of Labor, which was headed by Terrence Powderly and was heavily Catholic in membership, against the action of Archbishop Elzear Taschereau of Quebec, who sought the union's condemnation.[2] The publication in 1891 of Pope Leo XIII's encyclical *Rerum novarum*, which promoted organized labor and collective bargaining, shifted Catholic social thought to support of labor unions. The pre–World War I era thus found Catholics in alliance with Progressive-Era Social Gospel proponents and similar minds who supported workers' rights.[3]

Labor in San Francisco

The historian Michael Kazin in *Barons of Labor* describes how labor was the dominating influence in the city during the latter half of the nineteenth century and first half of the twentieth century. Kazin presents four reasons for this significant control by organized labor. First, since San Francisco was the primary urban center of the West Coast and rather isolated geographically, employers had difficulty finding strikebreakers, thus giving crafts and laborers an advantage. Second, the city's economic base of shipping and manufacturing made it problematic for business to forge a unified front against organized labor. Third, the ethnic homogeneity of the Caucasian population and the absence in neighborhoods of more than one national group gave class identities more salience than ethnicity. Lastly, after World War I, organized labor in San Francisco faced a business elite that was fragmented ideologically as it was divided by profit-making pursuits. Kazin concludes, "For the first twenty years of this [twentieth] century, the West's largest city was a conspicuous exception to the national pattern [of weak unions]. Beginning in the late 1890s, San Francisco workers built the strongest labor movement that existed in any American metropolis."[4] The Workingmen's Party under Denis Kearney and its successor, the Union Labor Party headed by Patrick H. McCarthy, gained power by aligning with political forces in the city. As the twentieth century dawned, the machine politics of San Francisco's municipal government, as illustrated by the career of Abraham "Boss" Ruef, realized its dependence upon unionism in the city.[5] The period of 1900 to 1915 can accurately be labeled the "Golden Age" of San Francisco labor. The power of the Union Labor Party was bolstered by support from Father Peter Yorke,[6] who championed the cause of organized labor throughout the first decade of the new century. Yorke was the champion of organized labor during the 1901 Teamsters and Waterfront strike and the 1907 Carmen's strike. These strikes and others between 1900 and 1910 led to the institution of the closed shop throughout the city. The coalition between municipal government and unionism made labor king in Progressive-Era San Francisco.

Business and church institutions played major roles in the San Francisco culture, thus influencing labor from the late Progressive Era until the Great Depression. The historian William Issel argues that organized business, which was closely allied with the municipal government, was instrumental in the promotion of the American Plan (open shop), an idea that obviously clashed significantly with supporters of organized labor. He concludes because of this, "Resentment and suspicion of business power marked the city's history throughout the 1920s."[7] Catholicism, which had been "an active component of the state's political and social life from the onset of its existence under American auspices,"[8] also held a significant amount of influence with labor and support for it. Issel claims, "Although previously neglected by historians, the religious foundation for San Francisco political culture was also important, particularly the role of Roman Catholic [social] teachings." He goes on to say that the Church's emphasis on the dignity of workers "predisposed San Franciscans to be sympathetic to claims of white working-class residents for equity in the workplace and equality in the councils of government."[9]

The election of James Rolph to a long tenure as mayor of San Francisco[10] created conditions that challenged the general acceptance organized labor had previously enjoyed. Unlike most recent mayors, Rolph had no particular interest in organized labor. Initially his administration's policies seldom clashed with organized labor's needs or demands, but neither did they result in mayoral action on labor's behalf. Not until 1916 would problems necessitate action from Rolph or his administration.

Hanna's Views on the Labor Question

Edward Hanna's experience in Rochester, his sense of justice, and his understanding of Catholicism's response to the "social question" shaped his mindset on the labor-capital issue in San Francisco. His philosophy favored neither side, but rather promoted a sense of mutual responsibility, which "insisted upon the rights of all citizens to participate in governance."[11] He often stated that workers must be respected, afforded proper dignity, and given a living wage that would allow them to marry and start families, with reasonable provisions for future needs, relaxation, and possible sickness. On the other hand, respecting these rights gave an employer the right to expect faithful service from workers.[12]

Hanna, as one might expect, called the labor-capital issue "a moral and religious matter," suggesting that the ultimate solution to any conflict was Christ:

When both labor and capital attain a deeper understanding of the obligations they owe to the moral law, to Christ and His teachings of brotherly love, and to the people as a whole and to each other, then, and not until then, will come the solution of the great industrial problems of the day.[13]

In a speech, "The Church and the Industrial Conflict," Hanna suggested that his policy of mutual responsibility would satisfy the common good:

> The rights of the community are paramount, and must not be allowed to suffer from an internecine feud between the employer and employee. The latter must be granted this moral right to organize and bargain collectively for a living wage, as well as to cooperate to a certain extent in the management of production for the public good. The worker must not forget his moral obligation to render faithful service for adequate wages, and should take an interest in the government of his union so as to prevent unscrupulous radical leaders from ruling and wrecking the organizations.[14]

The 1916 Labor Arbitration Effort in San Francisco

On July 22, 1916, the calm of the labor scene and the city of San Francisco in general was shattered. The city had marked this date as "Preparedness Day" with a planned parade to demonstrate solidarity with America's general preparation for possible international conflict, World War I having started two years earlier in Europe. Just as the parade, led by Mayor Rolph, was beginning a bomb exploded near the corner of Steuart and Market streets, killing nine and injuring forty more. Organized labor had opposed the parade, believing that preoccupation with war preparations was an excuse to squelch unionism in the name of patriotism. Thus, two known labor radicals, Tom Mooney and Warren K. Billings, were soon arrested, tried, and convicted, although evidence in the case was lacking. The men were convenient scapegoats as Rolph was under severe pressure to find and punish those responsible.[15]

The relative calm on San Francisco's labor front was shattered by a series of citywide strikes. The first and most serious strike, directed toward the maritime industry, began on June 1, when the International Longshoreman's Association (ILA) walked out on the Waterfront Employers' Union (WEU), seeking a 35 percent increase in wages to 55 cents per hour with $1.00 per hour for overtime. A July strike by culinary workers, to increase wages and lower the working hours for members of the union, prompted a general lockout of employees by the San Francisco Restaurant Association (SFRA) on August 1. In July, the Structural Iron Workers called another strike, this one seeking an eight-hour day, one less than the normal workday in the local steel industry.[16]

Capital seized the strikes of 1916 as an excuse to renew its battle against organized labor. Angered by the ILA's breach of contract with the WEU,[17] Frederick Koster, president of the San Francisco Chamber of Commerce, called a meeting for the "Merchants of San Francisco."

> An intolerable situation exists on the waterfront. Intimidation prevents merchants from receiving or delivering goods from or to the docks. You are all urged to attend a meeting of merchants on the Floor of the Chamber of Commerce, Merchants' Exchange Building on *MONDAY, JULY 10th at 3 P.M.* where the situation will be discussed. Law and order must be maintained in San Francisco. *YOU ARE URGED TO BE AT THIS MEETING WITHOUT FAIL.* If you have the interest of San Francisco at heart you will be there. This is a matter of urgent duty and should cancel any other business engagements.[18]

Koster made it clear to the hundreds of merchants who attended the meeting that the Chamber of Commerce would no longer tolerate the disrespect for order the unions were showing in the tripartite strike. In his speech Koster called lawless unionism "an industrial and political disease...the baleful influence of which no one is immune."[19] Although Koster repeatedly stated that he was not out to destroy unions, his actions contradicted his words. An outcome of the meeting was the creation of a five-merchant committee committed to the following goals: (1) maintenance of law and order in the city, (2) the right of business to employ either union or nonunion labor, and (3) the scrupulous maintenance of work contracts. The committee, with Koster as chairman, became known as the Law and Order Committee[20] and rapidly gained strength within the business community.

Labor and capital were diametrically opposed in their attitudes toward the Law and Order Committee. Big business and local merchants by their tacit consent supported the actions of the committee, which represented the most significant move in years to mobilize antiunion forces. What is more, capital and the Law and Order Committee both supported the open shop. One local paper described the common view:

> Nothing not intrinsically right or just is demanded [in the fight for the open shop]; nothing less will be accepted. War unremitting, consistent, legitimate will be waged against conditions which have hampered and penalized business, destroyed confidence, driven forth industry, and shamed us in our hearts and therefore the world.[21]

The business community supported the committee's action as a wing of the Chamber of Commerce. A typical response came from William Sproule of the Southern Pacific Company,

> The Chamber is not the champion of any class or group against any other class or group, but insists on the right of every man to work here and to live peacefully among us, sure of the equal protection of the law for every one [sic] and equal obligation to obey the law.[22]

Predictably, labor opposed the Law and Order Committee, viewing it, in contrast to employers, as synonymous with the Chamber of Commerce.[23] The *Labor Clarion*, a publication of the San Francisco Labor Council, stated in reference to the committee, "Some of the members of the Chamber of Commerce helped to keep the population of San Francisco and the bay districts highly amused during the past week by their ludicrous antics and boastings."[24] The major critique came from the *Leader*, edited by the aforementioned Father Yorke, who referred to Koster as an

"obscure person…intoxicated with the exuberance of his own ver-
bosity [who] aspires to be the Czar of San Francisco."[25] In an even
more heated editorial, Yorke spoke of the destruction of unionism
by capital:

> While the captains and kings of commerce and industry, rec-
> ognizing the broad principle of unionism as an effort to better
> the great majority of the common brotherhood of men, you,
> newly promoted corporals of the hospital squad of hucksters,
> lacking the vision to see and the soul to comprehend, would
> dethrone humanity for the temporary triumph of your own
> paltry ambition.[26]

The impact of the Law and Order Committee in San
Francisco was significant. The committee threatened restaurateurs
who operated under the closed shop with boycotts, provided funds
to hire scabs and strikebreakers to help the WEU in its ongoing
battle with the ILA, and, most significantly, threw its full support
behind the refusal of ten San Francisco steel products companies to
meet union demands for an eight-hour workday.[27] Michael Kazin
summarizes the efficacy of the committee: "Less than six months
after its formation, the Law and Order Committee had dealt
unions a more sweeping blow than fifteen years of cruel open-shop
language and tactics achieved."[28]

The three-strike summer of 1916 created problems for commerce as well as for the construction and maritime industries. The
Monitor, which seldom commented on local labor unrest, proposed
a solution to the hostilities: "The differences between employers
and employees should be settled by some body or commission of
big men of unimpeachable character and integrity."[29] In the same
issue the paper backed the closed-shop policy of the unions: "The
individual employer who treats his employees fairly may oppose the
position of the closed shop with a show of Constitutional justice,
but he is trying to turn back the hands of the clock."[30]

Because of threatened violence in the culinary and steel
strikes, Mayor Rolph heeded the *Monitor*'s advice and called for a
board to arbitrate the dispute:

> As Mayor of San Francisco, and to prevent such industrial warfare, I request the Chamber of Commerce to appoint five representatives of the employers, and the Presidents of the three central labor bodies, namely the San Francisco Labor Council, the Building Trades Council, and the Waterfront Workers' Federation, jointly to appoint five representatives of the employees; the ten representatives of the employers and employees so chosen to be members of a general Arbitration Board to be composed of fifteen members, of which the other five members shall be the Most Reverend Archbishop Edward J. Hanna, and four clergymen of various denominations, to be selected by the Archbishop.[31]

The appointment of Hanna to the board was not as unusual as it might first appear. In addition to commanding the respect of Roman Catholics, the largest religious denomination in the city, he enjoyed widespread appeal throughout the religious, business, and labor communities. Koster had invited him to join the Law and Order Committee (an offer that Hanna refused); labor, through the preponderance of Irish Catholics in their ranks, also saw him as a friend. The historians William Issel and Robert Cherny have labeled Hanna one of the "big five" in San Francisco public life in the 1920s and 1930s.[32] It was noted almost from his first days in the city that Hanna possessed the special gifts needed to work in such delicate matters:

> The Bishop is known in his old home city as one who on many and varied occasions has acted as an arbiter. His quick wit, his thorough understanding of humanity, and his great sympathy with his fellow men have enabled him repeatedly to exercise a healthful influence in the community where he had cast his lot. It is well for San Francisco to possess such a leader and it is of even greater importance that his fellow citizens have so quickly recognized his worth.[33]

Mayor Rolph put it well in his letter convoking the arbitration board: "There is no other member of the community who possesses in such a unique degree, the confidence of all classes."[34]

Hanna, for his part, was appreciative for the appointment and willing to serve: "I am grateful beyond my power to tell—I am ever willing to be of service....You can use me as you see fit."[35]

Reactions to the idea of an arbitration board were generally positive. A typical response came in a private letter to the mayor: "In re: Suggested Arbitration Board. Yours is the only sane, sensible suggestion for the settlement of industrial controversies which, to my mind, has yet been made by any man of affairs, or any man in authority in connection with the existent local labor situation."[36] All three of the umbrella union organizations approved the mayor's plan. Letters from P. H. McCarthy (Building Trades Council), E. Ellison (Waterfront Workers), and James A. O'Connelly (San Francisco Labor Council) were received in the mayor's office on or before August 16. McCarthy's letter was typical in spirit: "We further beg to advise that, after a thorough discussion of the subject, the Building Trades Council, by unanimous vote, approved of the plan presented by you, and authorized the President of the Council to act in conformity with your request."[37]

Despite the good intentions of the mayor and the support of labor, the arbitration board never materialized. The Law and Order Committee, acting for the Chamber of Commerce, refused to send representatives to the board because nonunion labor would not be represented in the hearings. Thus, Rolph had no choice but to drop his endeavor. The *Leader* commented on this chain of events: "Sixteen years ago the Merchants' Association forced the Draymen of San Francisco to break their agreement with the teamsters....It is evident that the Chamber of Commerce is following in the footsteps of the Merchants' Association."[38]

With the arbitration board defunct before it had materialized, the strikes dragged on. The Law and Order Committee met on August 17, with Hanna present, to try and find some solution to the dispute, but the meeting accomplished little, and it appeared that both sides were ready for a fight to the finish.

Following the failure of the meeting, the Law and Order Committee tried to enlist local clergy to help end the dispute, hoping to neutralize the bad press the committee had received when it failed to cooperate in the arbitration board. Representatives of six local churches, Methodist Episcopal, Temple Emmanuel El,

Central Methodist Church, First Unitarian Church, First Presbyterian, and First Baptist, came to an August 22 meeting sponsored by the Law and Order Committee. Grace Cathedral and the Protestant Episcopal Church did not attend and did not explain their absence; Hanna was "unable to attend."[39] The representatives, unimpressed by the committee's presentation, refused to sign a statement supporting the Law and Order Committee; thus, the committee lost the support of an important segment of the San Francisco community that would have helped improve its image. The *Leader* editorialized about the failed conference:

> The net result of the conference is to show that the Law and Order Committee is a syndicate of selfish gentlemen whose care for law and order is confined to the laws and order that suit their own interests and whose industrial interests are, on their own admission, incompatible with the law and order which every decent citizen desires.[40]

The attitude toward labor of the two principal "impartial" figures in the 1916 strike situation shows a proclivity for unionism and the rights of workers. Archbishop Hanna made no secret about his support for labor. In a letter to Koster he wrote, "I will spare no pains to assist the rightly organized forces of labor to make battles against their greatest foes...."[41] He also spelled out his opinion about unionism in his Labor Day address of September 4, 1916, delivered at the request of organized labor in Golden Gate Park. In speaking of the progress of labor over the previous fifty years, Hanna stated, "These are labor's triumphs, and in large measure these victories are due to unionism more than to aught else."[42] Hanna also commended unions for their ability to produce good leaders to foster their cause: "That labor organizations have in fifty years been able to rear a race of men out of their own ranks who have brought labor's cause to the present high standing in the esteem of the community seems to me little short of wonderful."[43] Hanna concluded his Labor Day address by praising those who had supported labor's cause. He stated, "Our hearts go out to the men who have done so much to better the conditions of the laborers' life—may they grow and wax strong."[44]

Like Hanna, Mayor Rolph advocated labor's cause. In writing to Frederick Koster following the latter's announcement of his July 10 meeting in which the Law and Order Committee was formed, the mayor stated,

> While conceding the ability and importance and numbers of those who contend for the "open-shop," my faith has always been in Organized Labor!
>
> It is my professed conviction that the union makes for the moral uplift of the country as a whole and places the prosperity of all on a firm basis.[45]

At the same Labor Day rally, Mayor Rolph also lauded the efforts of organized labor. Referring to the present struggle he stated, "In San Francisco, at this moment, a strong effort is being made in certain quarters to destroy Organized Union Labor. I prophesy the failure of this movement."[46] He further warned the enemies of labor that they would need to take a new tack: "Capital and labor cannot fully understand each other until they think in the same terms, and it would be well for the opponents of labor to think in terms of humanity."[47]

Labor tensions continued through the end of 1916, except for the ILA strike, which ended on July 17, when the dock workers went back to work as negotiations continued. On August 20 a compromise was hammered out: employers recognized the closed shop and raised wages to 55 cents per hour for straight time and 82.5 cents for overtime.[48]

The resolution of the culinary strike was a complete victory for capital, thanks to an antipicketing ordinance passed in the November 1916 general election, largely as a result of pressure from the Law and Order Committee. Picketing of restaurants dwindled rapidly under the threat of fifty-day jail terms. On December 25, 1916, the San Francisco. Labor Council admitted defeat and called off the strike. Workers returned to their jobs under the same conditions as before the strike.

The resolution to the steel strike was more advantageous for labor. During the course of the dispute, Dyer Brothers, one of six holdout steel firms, had been granted a contract to help build a new

128

wing of the San Francisco Hospital on Potrero Street. Supported by the Law and Order Committee, Dyer insisted on the nine-hour workday, automatically limiting the work to scab and strike-breaker personnel. As a result, hospital construction fell far behind schedule. Additionally, special guards hired by the Law and Order Committee to protect scab workers were proving a nuisance to regular police and local residents. Mayor Rolph, frustrated from his continual battle with the Law and Order Committee, ordered Dyer released from the contract; the project was completed by San Francisco Public Works. The Law and Order Committee could no longer support the six companies that continued to hold out against the eight-hour day. By January 1917, with their source of financial support gone, all six companies capitulated to the union's demands. Olaf Tveitmoe, secretary of the Building Trades Council (BTC), expressed labor's gratitude to Rolph in a letter to the mayor,

> It gives us profound pleasure to convey the sincere expression of appreciation and gratitude of the Building Trades Council of San Francisco…whereby your Honor caused the enforcement of the municipal safety ordinances and the State planking law on the construction of the San Francisco Hospital.[49]

The 1916 strikes left bad feelings on both sides. The Chipman Report, an analysis of complaints made during the struggle, denounced both labor and capital for their extremism, claiming that although management and labor shared the blame for the unrest, the bulk of the responsibility lay with the employers.[50] One clear result of the strikes was the evolution of attitudes on both sides. Employers were able to begin to call for the open shop; workers argued for the eight-hour day. This evolution would continue as the struggle between labor and capital entered the 1920s.

The 1921 and 1922 Wage Arbitration Boards

America's involvement in World War I brought industrial peace to San Francisco, with plenty of work under conditions acceptable to both workers and employers. The scarcity of workers and the wartime need for industrial peace stressed by the federal government minimized the activity of both unions and the Law and Order Committee, now called the Industrial Relations Committee of the Chamber of Commerce.

The country's return to a peacetime economy brought immediate problems: returning soldiers put jobs at a premium, and unemployment was high. The inflation that struck Europe so severely occurred in the United States as well. The *Monitor* called for the government to control prices:

> After all the State owes more than political freedom to its people. It should afford them moral and economic freedom. To avoid the dread consequences of revolution, the State must organize itself not only for political purposes but also for social justice and the service of its creators.[51]

Throughout the country, tough economic times would lead to renewed industrial unrest, with unions and management clashing over the long-standing issues of wages, hours, and the right to organize.

In San Francisco, the pro-labor attitudes that survived from the Progressive Era, including those of the Church, began to dissolve in the face of labor's unrealistic demands that wartime salaries be maintained, an impossibility under postwar conditions. The local economy could no longer support the economic buildup created by the war. Shipbuilding contracts were cut; worker layoffs followed. Other industries suffered similar problems. The *Monitor* chided labor for its refusal to moderate its demands:

> Since the need of speeding up production has ceased and foreign competition must be met, it stands to reason that the shipworkers should not kill the goose that lays the golden egg and cause our shipyards to be closed and America to lose the chance of gaining maritime supremacy in the world...by making unreasonable and unjust demands upon the government and the owners.[52]

In 1919 and 1920 plasterers, hodcarriers, painters, and metal roofers all went on strike for an increase in wages; a general walk-out of all building crafts seemed imminent. The situation elicited a suggestion from the *Monitor* about how to settle the disagreement:

> When capital gets through telling us what is wrong with labor, and labor rehearses the crimes of capital, we have a very sorry picture. They are both wrong and the wrongest thing about them is that one only sees a capital "C" and the other a capital "L."...If they both come down from the mountains of ologies and isms they might lose their class conscious viewpoint and strike the valleys of common sense. Christianity is waiting for them there.[53]

In a sermon delivered at St. Mary's Cathedral Archbishop Hanna also voiced disappointment in the local labor situation. Referencing *Rerum novarum*,[54] Hanna stated,

> The industrial question in the opinion of some is merely an economic question, whereas in point of fact it is, first of all, a moral and religious matter and for that reason its settlement is to be sought mainly in the moral law and in the pronouncement of religion.

Although Hanna acknowledged the right of workers to organize and to receive "honorable compensation," his main concern was how best to foster public welfare, and he saw collective bargaining as the answer to the city's labor problems:

> The public, too, would share in the advantage of a larger and steadier production. Industry would be carried on as a great co-operative enterprise for the common weal [*sic*] and not as a contest between two parties for the production of a restricted output.[55]

Hanna's mediated position was also expressed to Father John Burke, general secretary of the National Catholic Welfare Conference, with whom he would work closely for almost twenty years:

> The Encyl[ical] *[Rerum novarum]* of Pope Leo [XIII], and the
> letter of the Bishops both uphold the forming of labor organ-
> izations as well as the doctrine of collective bargaining. And
> *personally* [Hanna's emphasis] I feel that "open-shop" will jeop-
> ardize these things, but no Catholic group has pronounced
> authoritatively against the so-called "American Plan," and I
> can see even a thinking man could favor both "unions" and the
> "collective bargain."[56]

This less-favorable position toward labor, illustrated by the statements of Hanna and *Monitor* editor Joseph Duggan, was appearing simultaneously in other parts of the country as well. In the Midwest, Chicago's *New World* demonstrated this shift: "The present time is thought to be a particularly good one to put into practice the theory of the Open-shop. It has always been a high contention that every man was entitled to work whether or not he carried a union card."[57] In the East, the *Brooklyn Tablet* commented, "The country from coast to coast wearies of strikes....The idea of arbitration is lifting into a widening popularity."[58]

With no reasonable alternative available, Vice Mayor Ralph McLeran (acting on behalf of James Rolph) formed an impartial wage arbitration board in an attempt to end industrial unrest. In October 1920 McLeran assigned selection of the board to Atholl McBean, president of the Chamber of Commerce. McBean formed a three-man panel to arbitrate and set basic wages for seventeen crafts within the city. The members of the board were Archbishop Hanna (chairman), Max Sloss, a retired justice of the California State Supreme Court, currently acting as an investment banker, and George L. Bell, an independent personnel consultant who belonged to the Industrial Association of California.

Archbishop Hanna was a logical choice as chairman because he was qualified to analyze the positions of both sides of the labor-capital issue and judge fairly. Hanna's role on the board was signif-icant for other reasons. American Catholicism was just beginning to gain acceptance in mainstream American life. The multiple waves of anti-Catholicism that had persisted in the nineteenth cen-tury were yielding to increased respect and social status, and the resurgence of the Ku Klux Klan and its vehement anti-Catholicism was widely denounced.[59] Given the tumultuous history of Irish Catholics in San Francisco's labor disputes, it is noteworthy that the Catholic archbishop would be asked to chair a board that would determine the economic fate of so many of his people.

On January 18, 1921, the BTC and the Builders Exchange signed an agreement to settle disputes through arbitration, specifically to submit

> all disputes as to hours, wages and working conditions in building trades where there are no disputes now, as well as in those where there are, when and as such disputes arise between signatory parties and the decision of the Board shall be accepted as final and carried out by all parties.[60]

It was hoped that the board would provide "a permanent method of settling amicably and in a reasonable manner labor disputes in this city affecting building trades."[61]

Following the signing of the January 18 agreement, the board met to begin its hearings. The Builders Exchange was represented before the board by John S. Partridge, a mayoral candidate in 1905 and an established corporate lawyer. The BTC was represented by Ira B. Cross, economist and professor at the University of California at Berkeley. Cross's arguments before the board relied heavily on statistics compiled by the federal government, showing that the cost of living for a typical family of four in the United States had risen some 85 percent to $3,300 per year between 1914 and 1920, whereas wages for San Francisco laborers had risen only some fifty cents per hour, an average increase of 75 percent. Cross told the board that the current wage in San Francisco

> discourages efficiency and personal initiative, leads to inferiority in quality of product, engenders and fosters social strife and discord, retards natural progress, hampers all efforts of sincere social and religious advance, discourages fraternal associations among working men.
>
> Unless conditions are changed in the building trades, to say nothing of conditions existing in other trades, we stand to see dark days ahead for our country and its institutions.[62]

In his arguments, Partridge invoked the "natural law" of a capitalist economy, asserting that World War I had thrown the normal flow of the free market out of balance and that workers had acquired the bad habit of demanding more pay regardless of the health of the industry. Partridge stated,

> The emphasis…belongs to service; that is, what does the workman exchange for his compensation; and upon the general law of Supply and Demand, untrammeled by artificial interference…redounding in the long run to the lasting benefit of the workman himself.[63]

Partridge also ridiculed Cross's description of labor as being in the depths of despair and poverty. He stated, "The steady men who make up the great bulk of the artisans live more than decently, acquire homes and educate their children.…By and large their rank as citizens is equal to any class or occupation in the city."[64]

Each of the fifteen trades involved in the arbitration case submitted a report to the board, providing salary histories from 1914 to 1920, data on the cost of materials and equipment used in their particular trade, information on union personnel, and a recommendation for union wages. A typical recommendation was submitted by the Reinforcing Iron Workers:

> Therefore we respectfully request:
> (1) That the wages of the men be fixed at $7.50 per day.…
> (3) That the other matters complained of above be taken into consideration by your Honorable Board and such evidence to support our statements be presented as you may desire and that you make your recommendations accordingly.[65]

On March 31, 1921, the board announced its decision: a complete victory for the Builders Exchange, with a 7.5 percent reduction in wages for nineteen crafts, four more than the fifteen initially targeted by the board, effective April 11, to remain in effect for six months, subject to change based on the cost of living. The decision of the board to cut wages was guided by three principles: (1) Wages for the next six months could not be predicted based on estimates or rumors of present or future fluctuations in the cost of living.

(2) It was desired to establish acceptance of regularly published government findings on wages and cost of living as a permanent principle in the industry as it is only by periodic findings of such a recognized authority that the advantages in one period can be made to balance the disadvantages of another. (3) Cost of living figures and their comparison to wages were of limited value; the more relevant comparison was to the most recent wage increase or decrease.[66] The board agreed that it would continue to deliberate on the questions and make necessary adjustments in the future.

Because of Hanna's former strident advocacy for workers' rights, labor was taken aback by the board's decision. When the award was announced the BTC immediately petitioned the board to reconsider its decision, arguing that the board had no jurisdiction to award a decrease in wages. P. H. McCarthy wrote, "The award is for that reason null and void and not binding on the parties."[67] The board, citing the January 18 agreement between the BTC and the Builders Exchange to abide by the board's decision, responded, "After full consideration and hearing of their [BTC] petition, the members of the Board of Arbitration are unanimously of the opinion that the award should not be withdrawn or reconsidered."[68]

The BTC decided to strike as a last resort, and thus the employer lockout McCarthy had feared became a reality. To aid the lockout, the Chamber of Commerce re-formed the Industrial Relations Committee (the old Law and Order Committee) and publicized the fact that the BTC had reneged on its agreement to abide by the wage board's decision. Archbishop Hanna quickly joined the committee to show solidarity with the Chamber of Commerce.

With his support almost totally eroded, McCarthy had little choice but to capitulate and order the BTC back to work. The union chief wrote to Charles Gompertz, president of the Builders Exchange:

> Feeling it a solemn duty to inform the public of the precise position of the Building Trades Council in the present controversy, the Building Trades Council hereby accepts the award of the Board of Arbitration hereby rendered.
>
> The Building Trades Council hereby accepts the full jurisdiction of the Arbitration Board...and reaffirms said

agreement [January 18] including the right to make further revisions in hours, wages and working conditions.[69]

The combination of the board's decision, the lockout, and McCarthy's capitulation was the death knell for the closed shop in San Francisco. Although the board made no decisions concerning unionism per se, the reduction in wages made a powerful statement about the new parity between organized labor and capital. No longer could labor demand union membership as a prerequisite for employment. The *Monitor*, quoting from the *New York Freeman*, commented, "But if the labor unions were to undertake the abolition of monopoly leaving trade-union issues to be taken care of after that piece of work had been accomplished it might confidently expect to find a substantial body of support."[70] McCarthy's twenty-five-year reign as president of the BTC ended with his resignation; capital had gained a strong foothold in its climb to equality with organized labor.

The board's decision, followed by implementation of the lowered wages, produced numerous critical letters. The Varnishers and Polishers Local Union No. 134 wrote, "We have been discriminated against."[71] The International Union of Elevator Constructors was most bewildered by its wage reduction, since it had not petitioned for redress in the first place, having made an agreement with the Builders Exchange in November 1920 for a specified wage. In a letter to the board, elevator constructor's president Edward McGee stated,

> We are at a loss to understand how your Board became possessed of the idea that there was any right or authority vested in you to abrogate the aforementioned agreement, and attempt to cut the wages of Elevator Constructors.
>
> We, therefore, beg to very respectfully request that your Board set aside its decision, which is undoubtedly the result of a misunderstanding, and we further beg to advise that we cannot and will not allow the wages of the Elevator Constructors of San Francisco to be cut by anyone in violation of the understanding and agreement reached by and between the officers of the Elevator Manufacturers' Association [member of Builders' Exchange] and the officers of the International Union of Elevator Constructors.[72]

Despite this plea (and apparent error) the board insisted that its decision stand and that wage continuity remain in effect for all trades mentioned in the award.[73]

Since the board decision fixed pay rates for six months, a new board had to be formed to revisit the issue beginning in the fall of 1921. Thus on October 1 the Industrial Association of San Francisco, an umbrella organization for employers in the city, called for nominations for members of the board, seeking men of unquestioned integrity who had no association with either side, so that they could represent the community at large. Hanna was again asked to chair the panel, but two new members joined him, Henry Brandenstein and C. F. Michaels (a former member of the Law and Order Committee), both prominent citizens of San Francisco.[74]

The board, which met almost daily for two months, was charged with listening to both sides and rendering a judgment on the issue of wages. Rather than being considered an arbitration panel, the board was described in its document of incorporation as being responsible for the "establishment of proper differentials in wages paid to the various crafts which will involve readjustments rather than general flat increases or decreases." The board was to have no jurisdiction over working conditions, hours, or questions of production.[75]

On December 22 the board's report was made public. Wage reductions, ranging from 10 cents to 2 dollars per day, were ordered for 31 of 48 crafts, with stonecutters receiving the largest pay cut. The standards were effective January 1 to December 31, 1922. Hanna, speaking for the board, stated, "We have endeavored to give consideration to every phase of the problem and to be absolutely fair to all interested." As would be expected, the Building Trades Council, speaking for crafts, responded to the decision with disdain, stating that the board had no authority to adjust wages.[76]

In June 1922, the board reconvened to prepare for a new round of arbitration. Hanna, who continued to chair the board, decided that each craft would be allowed to petition the board individually, rather than having one representative speak for all unions seeking wage enhancements, as had been done in the past. The board planned to meet in November.

Before the board actually met, letters arrived from several labor advocates seeking redress. A typical plea came from the general contractors of the city:

> The General Contractors of San Francisco are desirous that a wage scale be fixed for the local building trades workmen that shall enable the average industrious mechanic to support his family in accordance with normal social requirements and also to lay by a reasonable surplus each year.[77]

The board also received the newly completed "General Report on the Cost of Living in San Francisco," which showed that the cost of living in the city had risen 23.6 percent between 1914 and 1921, while wages had climbed 35 percent.[78] Fearing a repeat of the board's action of March and December 1921, the BTC wrote to Hanna, Brandenstein, and Michaels: "As a result of our investigations we find that the merchants and citizens generally are of the opinion that peace and prosperity can best be conserved in San Francisco by not attempting any wage changes at this time."[79]

The board met on November 17, 21, 22, and 27. In his opening address, Hanna set the tone for the board's work:

> It seems to be the lot of the two gentlemen who are with me, and the Archbishop's lot to undertake anew a task that is both delicate and difficult; delicate because it concerns the wages of men on which their standard of living and upon which their lives and the lives of those that they love depend; delicate also because it touches those who employ labor; delicate also because it touches the community. No man has ever attempted to adjust the wages of men that did not find himself faced with perhaps the most difficult task in life. I may be wrong (I often am), but it seems to me that a wage board such as faces you to-day [sic] will be the best guaranty to the men that they will have adequate consideration and justice, that the kindliness of thought will prevail, and that our aim will be to maintain a standard that will award a decent living.[80]

Hanna's attitude here is certainly different from that of his Labor Day speech of 1916, but it is consistent with his St. Mary's homily emphasizing collective bargaining, and it is representative of the shift in Catholic opinion in general, which put labor and capital on an equal footing.[81]

During the hearings the board took testimony from fifty-eight trades seeking increased wages and/or adjustment of working hours. A typical comment was received from M. W. F. McAllister of the elevator workers:

> We realize the fact that the cost of living is high and we feel we are justified in asking $9 a day. Certainly we don't know what Mr. Fessenden or the Spencer Elevator people propose to give us, but we feel we are justified in asking.[82]

The board received proposed wages for trades from W. H. George, new president of the Builders Exchange. Hanna stated in reply to the obvious insinuation by the Builders Exchange of what was a proper wage, "If new conditions of any kind whatsoever have arisen since our last award, it is upon the basis of these new conditions [that] we wish to fix the wages of the future."[83]

Despite testimony from fifty-eight trades and numerous representatives of management, the board decided to delay their decision. Although the extant record is not clear, it seems that the board was hesitant to change the status quo because the city and surrounding communities were struggling with a serious molders' union dispute. As a delaying tactic, the board adjourned, promising to reconvene in early 1923, when, it was hoped, the molders' dispute would be settled.[84] The delay would also give the board more time to gather and review evidence and render a fair decision.

As soon as the board was formed, Hanna began receiving reports detailing the city's economic situation. One bulletin, from the General Contractors of San Francisco, showed that while the cost of living in June 1922 was only 3 percent higher in San Francisco than the national average, wages in some trades were as much as 30 percent higher than the national average for that trade.[85] Another study showed that the projected cost of living in January 1923 would be at the same level as September 1921.[86] A third report stated, "Business will be better in 1923 than it was in 1922, without, however, resulting in a period of inflation."[87]

The board also received a series of letters from the Builders Exchange claiming that maintaining wages at their present levels was necessary for the good of industry nationwide. A typical letter concerning the sprinkler fitters illustrates this stance:

> Any raising of this rate over $7.20 per day at the present time here in San Francisco would have a bad effect on the industry all over the country as the uniform scale all over the country for sprinkler fitters is $7.20 per day of eight hours.[88]

Even more revealing were letters sent to Hanna from private citizens and unions describing the needs of the union members. Writing on behalf of asbestos workers, Edward Dwyer stated,

> The men of this craft are not satisfied with the present scale of $7.00 per day….Since your last award the cost of living has not reduced but advance [sic] and because of this fact and the scarcity of skilled asbestos workers I respectfully request your Board place the wages of asbestos workers back to where they rightly belong at $7.85 per day.[89]

A similar note of dissatisfaction with the board's former award was voiced by the Cement Finishers' Union: "The wage scale set by your Honorable Board for 1922 is entirely too low and Finishers having families to support find it impossible to properly care for them on the amount of money they earn on the scale set in 1922."[90]

After reviewing the data, the board published its findings on January 1, 1923, stating that a general raise for all trades was not practicable nor necessary, based on current economic conditions in San Francisco. Eight trades received wage increases: bricklayers, bridge engineers, and reinforced concrete housesmiths were awarded a one dollar per day raise; hodcarriers, cement finishers, glass workers, roofers, and tile setters were awarded a fifty cents per day pay hike. All other trades retained the wages set in 1921. The basis for the changes was testimony received and the prevailing economic conditions. The board set eight hours per day and five and one-half days per week as normative.[91] Again speaking for the board, Hanna explained the rationale behind the award: "We are striving to establish a new principle. It is no secret that in some cases the workers have been getting more than the wage board scale, and we want it accepted openly that superior workmen deserve higher pay."[92]

Wage Arbitration Boards, 1926–1933

Despite the crafts' disappointment at the board's decision, labor-capital relations were relatively calm for almost four years. However, in October 1926 the Industrial Association appointed a third impartial wage panel to review pay rates in the city. Hanna continued to anchor the board as chair, with Judge Max Sloss and Selah Chamberlain joining him. Upon its appointment the board issued a statement of its purpose:

> The present board, under the same chairmanship, has undertaken to hear all interested parties that an adjustment may be reached enabling our city to continue its wonderful building program with profit to all concerned in it. This board represents the public interest and trusts that the personnel serving on it guarantees its impartiality.[93]

The board's creation drew immediate, loud, and sustained complaints from the various labor organizations, who feared it would continue the downward spiral begun in 1921. Speaking for union leaders, the BTC and SFLC wrote to the board:

> We submit that your board has no moral or legal right that is greater than the rights of the United States Government, and inasmuch as the wage scales promulgated by your board have been used as a medium of depriving workingmen of the wages that they are really entitled to...we respectfully request that your board cease its interference with the constitutional right of the building trades workmen by attempting to be parties to a system that dictates their wages.[94]

William Stanton and John O'Connell, president and secretary of the SFLC respectively, protested that the board, which had been formed without their knowledge or approval, had no right to exist. They suggested, "We believe that wages and working conditions can and should be arranged by agreement in conference between employers and workmen who are directly affected."[95] In an effort to gain Hanna's attention, they continued:

> Such a condition [the board's formation] is not only un-American but outrageous. It is in direct conflict with the recommendations of the various church federations and in our opinion is diametrically opposed to the lasting principle annunciated [sic] by Pope Leo XIII [in *Rerum novarum*].[96]

Despite these objections, the board continued to meet; Hanna tersely explained, "the Board agreed that it was a wise plan to continue with the sessions."[97] On December 9, 1926, the board announced its decision. Pay increases for forty-three trades, ranging from 50 cents to 1 dollar per day, would be effective January 1 to December 31, 1927. Albert Boynton, managing director of the Industrial Association, praised the board's work and also justified its existence: "The decision of the board is *prima facie* evidence itself of the validity, equity and justice of the impartial method of settling wage schedules in an industry so vital to San Francisco's progress and prosperity."[98] Despite the favorable decision of the board toward workers, *Labor Clarion* continued its vehement opposition to the board's existence:

> The truth of the whole matter is that the Industrial Association does not represent anyone except its own very limited membership, and most of its members cannot, by any stretch of imagination, be mistaken for employers in the real sense of the word. Yet this organization would arrogantly set itself up as absolute dictator of industrial conditions in a great American city and say to employers and workers alike: "You cannot sit down at the conference table and agree among yourselves upon wages and working conditions because we have decreed otherwise."[99]

The wages set by the 1926 board were maintained for two years, then in November 1928 a fourth Impartial Wage Board was formed by the Industrial Association. Once again Archbishop Hanna was appointed chair and was joined by two new men, Harrison S. Robinson, an Oakland attorney, and Henry J. Brunnier, a structural engineer and president of the California State Automobile Association. On naming the board, Frederick Koster, president of the Industrial Association, stated:

> The character and public records of the men who have accepted service on the new board are sufficient guarantees of a square deal to employes [sic], employers, and to all individuals and groups concerned in the maintenance of fair wages and proper working conditions in San Francisco's most important industry.[100]

As before, the BTC continued its argument that the board had no right to exist. Appealing to Hanna directly, the Building Trades Council representatives stated,

> We respectfully call to the attention of Your Grace the fact that the building trades men whose wages and working conditions are to be set by this Industrial Association wage board have no voice in the selection of the personnel of the wage board, and therefore deny the right of such board to sit in judgement upon matters which so vitally affect the lives of workmen as do their wages and working conditions.[101]

The board met for five listening sessions between December 5 and 14. On December 5, Hanna met with representatives from the BTC who were concerned about the archbishop's leadership of the board. Hanna told them that he would never serve on another board and would resign immediately if testimony proved that workers were being paid less than the 1926 award levels. Labor leaders claimed that the December sessions amply proved that workers were not receiving the full amount of the board's previous reward, prompting their request for his resignation.[102]

Despite this request the board continued to meet under Hanna's leadership, publishing its award at the end of the month. Effective on April 1, 1929, pay raises from 25 cents to 1 dollar per day were ordered for twelve trades and reductions of 50 cents per day for four others. The board made no decision on a request for a five-day week; the standard five-and-one-half-hour day at eight hours per day was maintained.[103] Hanna commented on the board's work:

> Considering the interests and necessities of all the groups involved in the building trades industry here, the new schedules are as fair as [is] humanly possible to make them. We are confident that all owners, builders and contracting groups will observe them meticulously in their own behalf and in behalf of labor and the welfare of the community.[104]

Later, sounding somewhat self-congratulatory, Hanna stated, "Here in San Francisco the men who preside over labor destinies have always recognized the dignity of labor, and have championed descent [sic] wages and decent living."[105]

Hanna's involvement with the city's Industrial Association and the wage arbitration ended with the fourth wage board, but his active interest in labor continued, especially through the inspiration received through the 1931 publication of *Quadragesimo anno*.[106] As described in chapter 11, Hanna was a strike negotiator, both for the state of California and for the nation in 1933 and 1934. In May 1933 Hanna hosted the Catholic Conference on Industrial Problems. He explained, "It [the conference] attempts to bring together employers, workers, economists and students of social problems to consider problems of industry. It is a great medium for education and has been so considered and accepted any place the conference has held sessions."[107] Hanna strongly encouraged his clergy to attend the sessions, "not only to become better acquainted with the teachings of the Church in these problems, but also to show the laity that we are all deeply interested in this teaching of the Pope and are anxious to fulfill his wishes."[108] The sessions on May 9 and 10 were attended by seven bishops and featured several prominent speakers, including Raymond McGowan, director of the NCWC's Social Action Department, Father Robert Lucey of Los Angeles (later archbishop of San Antonio), Will J. French, member of the Industrial Accident Commission, and Frank C. MacDonald, California State labor commissioner. In an opening address to the conference, Hanna asked those assembled to "have the courage to follow out needed changes in the social order no matter what the consequences."[109]

Conclusion

Attitudes toward organized labor in San Francisco underwent a major shift during the period of 1916 to 1923. "Progressivism undone" accurately describes how society shifted from strident advocacy of unions to a more neutral position where labor and capital were seen on an equal plane. The exalted position of labor was tamed as employers began to gain equal standing with union leaders.

Catholic opinion concerning labor also shifted during this time. From an institutional viewpoint the work of Archbishop Hanna illustrates this shift. Moving from a position promoting organized labor as the friend of worker and society, Hanna, through his chairmanship of a series of wage arbitration boards, shifted to a more neutral attitude toward labor and capital. Acting on a secular board did not divorce Hanna from his Catholicism. The attitudes expressed by the archdiocesan newspaper, the *Monitor*, are consistent with the shift made by Hanna. Catholic opinion, while promoting the common good in society, continued to advocate for the rights of workers to organize, just compensation (including the minimum wage), and reasonable work hours. The evolution of Hanna's thought on this issue demonstrates the even-handed approach he brought to all arbitration situations. As with his many other ventures in the secular public field, Hanna remained the archbishop of all the people of San Francisco.

Chapter 6

An Advocate for Immigrants

Edward Hanna's penchant to seek out the lost and lonely and to become an advocate for the disadvantaged was remarkably demonstrated through his work with immigrants in San Francisco. As he had done earlier as a priest in Rochester, Hanna worked to alleviate the plight of the immigrant poor, but as archbishop he was able to work on several levels and in many domains to assist them. Hanna never forgot that as a first-generation American he was closely tied to these men and women, who, like his own parents, sought to better their lives by coming to America. Beginning almost immediately after his arrival, Hanna worked in San Francisco and in particular with the state government to assist immigrants who sought to assimilate. Hanna was not blind to the problems that immigration generated in the nation, and he unabashedly raised concerns when he felt it necessary, but in the end, he was a friend to immigrants and an advocate for their cause.

Immigration in California, 1850–1915

Beginning in 1848, when gold was discovered at Sutter's Mill, California began to change from a sleepy territory inhabited largely by Native Indians and Californios (descendants of the region's eighteenth-century Spanish settlers) into a land of opportunity. The discovery of gold at Sutter's Mill near Sacramento in 1848 made California the land of promise and San Francisco a boom city almost overnight. The arrival in the region of fortune hunters, workers, and, later, businessmen and their families and the almost instantaneous natural attraction of the region contributed to California's admittance as the thirty-first state of the Union in September 1850.

Among the many immigrants included in this rapid influx, the Chinese were numerous and highly visible. By August 1852 there were eighteen thousand Chinese males in the state, but the construction of the transcontinental railroad, beginning in 1862, prompted an even greater infusion of these people. By 1880 the Chinese population in the United States was 105,000, most of whom were in California.[1]

Nativism reared its ugly head in California when the Chinese explosion reached its apex. In 1877 Denis Kearney, an Irish immigrant living in San Francisco, led the charge against the Chinese by organizing the Workingmen's Party and campaigning to remove the Chinese from local jobs. Kearney's fiery speeches generated a media blitz against the Chinese. In 1882 the attorney and journalist Burnette Haskell, editor of the San Francisco weekly *Truth*, challenged the presence of the Chinese: "Query, which is best, to allow unlimited importation of the cheapest labor; then to educate that labor up to its duty, and so in the end to civilize the world all at once; or to shut the door against degraded and uneducated men in every land, then educate in each land for itself and win the battle country by country?"[2] Later that same year the Chinese Exclusion Act abolished the immigration of Chinese laborers to the United States for ten years. After an extension in 1892, the ban was made permanent in 1902.

In June 1886, one month after the infamous Haymarket bomb blast in Chicago, a new nativist group, the American Party, arrived in California. Claiming that immigrants were largely responsible for the recent crippling wave of strikes and riots nationwide, its leaders demanded immigration restriction, stricter naturalization laws, and a ban on alien ownership of real estate. The short-lived party failed to expand beyond California but its agenda poisoned the minds of many Californians against immigrants.[3]

Efforts to exclude the Chinese actually made life better for other immigrants in California. Even though Burnette Haskell railed against the "hordes of ignorant, barbarous, incompetent, incapable, intractable slaves from the Mediterranean,"[4] Irish,

Italian, Spanish, Portuguese, Mexican, and Filipino workers continued to settle in the state. The historian Moses Rischin says that nativist attitudes toward all nonwhites, combined with the longstanding Catholic tradition of the state (which antedated Protestant migrations), made the general reception of European immigrants to California "remarkably benign." He continues, "Without doubt the relatively advantageous lot of all European immigrants in California was attributable in part at least, to the low esteem in which all non-whites were held."[5] In line with national trends, most of California's immigrants were urban dwellers, but the state's rich agricultural industry also attracted many migrant workers. In 1914, Italian, Spanish, and Portuguese workers made up almost 16 percent of those residing in California's labor camps. After the turn of the century but especially after World War I, Mexicans began to arrive in great numbers, totaling 32.5 percent of workers in the camps by 1933.[6] The historian Carey McWilliams comments about this situation, "The single most distinctive fact about the culture of California has been the perpetually high proportion of newly arrived residents among the inhabitants."[7]

Edward Hanna and Immigration in California

Hanna's pastoral presence in San Francisco, like his ministry on the East Coast, placed high priority on the rights and concerns of immigrants, while praising the immigrants' courage in facing the pain of dislocation from family, friends, and home environment. Looking at the history of the United States, Hanna acknowledged the contributions that immigrants had made, concluding, "There is no man as necessary, as important or interesting as the immigrant. In him are all the possibilities of the mighty future of this mighty land."[8]

Hanna firmly believed that the United States was responsible for providing immigrants with housing, education, and Americanization efforts, among other things. Hanna's views were based on his sense of justice, the social teaching of the church, and the pragmatic belief that society in general would profit from aid to immigrants. Conversely, if immigrants were neglected, they could create much havoc in society. In April 1913, while still auxiliary bishop, Hanna summarized his views in an address to a YMCA-sponsored conference on immigration: "See that they [immigrants] are properly housed in the city and camps; that you follow up their interests in school and State; see that they are prepared for citizenship. Try to see that these men may have power to vote in five years."[9]

Hanna also believed that the Church had responsibilities toward immigrants. Like the state, the Church was to aid the immigrants' efforts to gain citizenship by fostering in them the qualities of justice, honesty, and sincerity, which were, in Hanna's mind, almost universal in America's foreign-born population. The archbishop believed that the Church had not done enough for these people: "The Church has tried, but the problem is such an extensive one. It involves the question of industry, social economy and endless others."[10]

Because of his support of the rights of immigrants, Hanna was constantly asked to speak to groups with similar attitudes. Hanna was a featured presenter at the Immigration Work Conference in March 1915 as well as at the Third Pacific Coast Immigration Congress in August, which also featured Ira B. Cross, professor of economics at the University of California, Berkeley; Rabbi Martin A. Meyer; Simon Lubin, president of the California Commission of Immigration and Housing; and U.S. senator Walter S. Davis of Washington.[11] Hanna also gave a speech entitled "The Immigrant and Tuberculosis" to the California Association for the Study and Prevention of Tuberculosis and, in September 1927, an address entitled "Some Immigrant Problems Peculiar to California" to the National Conference of Catholic Charities convention in Los Angeles.[12]

Hanna's experience in Rochester combined with his personal preference to create a particular interest in San Francisco's Italian community. He gave his "hearty approval" to the Italian-language newspaper *L'Unione*, seeing it especially as a counter to secular papers that were often highly anticlerical.[13] Concerned about the "leakage" of Catholics from the Church, Hanna worked vigorously to provide Italian clergy to minister to the immigrants. Salesian and Franciscan religious staffed major institutions, including the principal Italian parish, Saints Peter and Paul in Washington Square.

Hanna was delighted when Franciscan sisters opened a new school in North Beach for Italian youth. The archbishop even intervened with the Italian consul in San Francisco in an effort to exempt native Italian clergy from being recalled to serve in the Italian army during World War I.[14]

While Hanna ministered to the needs of Italian immigrants, he always maintained a level of prudence, demanding that the Italian community follow the basic guidelines used by all other ethnic groups in the archdiocese; he gave no blank checks to Italian priests. When clergy needs were met, requests for incardination were rejected. Additionally, Hanna encouraged Italians to receive the sacraments in their home territorial parishes rather than flocking to San Francisco as many attempted to do.[15]

The archbishop also assisted his Italian parishioners in peripheral ways, speaking before groups and soliciting their support of the Italian community. Additionally, he contributed $1,000 from his own resources to the University of California at Berkeley to create an endowed chair in Italian culture.[16]

Hanna supported his priests under unusual experiences as well. For example, between January 30, 1926, and January 9, 1927, Saints Peter and Paul Church was bombed on four occasions. None of the blasts caused serious damage and there were no injuries, but the multiple attempts were unnerving to all, especially the Salesians who administered the parish. The administrator, Father Oreste Trinchieri, received calls from Hanna and offers of assistance, but no help was considered needed.[17]

Hanna's significant efforts on behalf of the local Italian community were recognized in 1922 when he was awarded the "Commander of the Crown of Italy." Hanna was honored, along with Mayor James Rolph and Dr. David P. Barrows, president of the University of California, "because of his personal knowledge of the needs of the former subjects in Italy." The citation continued, "The archbishop has helped tremendously the immigrants who have come here, intending to become American citizens."[18] In accepting the award, Hanna spoke of Italy and Italians as "a land and people I have always loved and admired."[19] Hanna's efforts on behalf of Italians were also reported to the Vatican by the California secretary of state:

> Permit me to state that I attribute almost entirely the advancement of the Italian settlers and Italian community in our State to the cultured guidance of...His Grace, [the] Most Reverend Edward J. Hanna, Archbishop of San Francisco....His continual work for the care and guidance of your fellow Italian people appeals to me as wonderful for we are confronted with the great problem of coalescing people of every Race and Nationality beneath the sovereignty of the Flag of the United States of America.[20]

The situation in Italy, especially the rise of Mussolini, evoked an initial response from Hanna that emphasized the positive value of Italy's return to law and order. He commented, "If we take the lesson of Italy to heart, then we will have a nation which will make for better and greater citizenry."[21] Hanna's observations from his 1920 and 1924 *ad limina* visits to Italy had convinced him that the nation understood the value of law and order, so it is not surprising that his early reactions to Mussolini concentrated more on the good he did for Italy than on his ideology or Machiavellian mode of operation, an emphasis that was common among many Roman-educated American prelates.[22] In 1924, for example, Cardinals William O'Connell of Boston and Patrick Hayes of New York, citing significant improvement in the state of the Italian nation since their last visits, voiced their approval of Mussolini.[23] In a speech to the Downtown Association Hanna stated,

> One does not have to be in sympathy with the particular type of government that Signor Mussolini represents to appreciate what he has done for Italy. Any fair-minded man must say, "this man has done well!" It remains to be seen if the price tag has been too high.[24]

In 1929, commenting on the Lateran Treaty that "saved Italy and Europe," Hanna was still favorable to Mussolini. However, by 1931, perceiving the true nature of fascism, Hanna had reversed course, perceiving Mussolini's "dreams of an absolute state" as contrary to "our fathers love of liberty" and inconsistent with justice and Christian ethics.[25]

While not as extensive as his work with Italians Hanna did reach out to other specific immigrant groups. He provided support "for the development of Japanese work in California."[26] Outreach to Chinese immigrants was started by Paulist father Ignatius Stark in 1903. Assisted by Sisters of the Helpers of the Holy Souls, the mission grew so much that by August 1921 a permanent Chinese school and social center, under the direction of Charles Bradley, CSP, was in operation. Hanna assisted the mission by writing to the Maryknoll community seeking a priest to minister to Chinese Catholics. Still, their relative fewer numbers compared with other groups made them less significant in Hanna's mind.[27] Hanna's association with eastern Europeans centered on his work with Polish and Russian immigrants in the archdiocese. Poles were grateful to Hanna for the concern he showed toward their country during the war. Hanna expressed direct interest in Russian immigrants, believing that many could be converted to Roman Catholicism.[28]

The special interest Hanna felt for the Italian community did not extend to Spanish-speaking immigrants. As will be described in detail in chapter 9, Hanna, in his capacity as administrative chairman of the NCWC, was very concerned about the political and religious situation in Mexico, beginning as early as 1916 and continuing until his retirement in 1935. He was also worried about the proselytization efforts of Protestants toward Spanish-speaking peoples. In 1915 he conducted a census of the Spanish-speaking population, then used it to determine the need for national churches. Yet it is also clear that Hanna was rather cautious in granting permission for clergy to enter the archdiocese, as he was with any group. The primary criterion was always, Is the need present? Writing for Hanna, John Cantwell informed one priest seeking to minister in San Francisco, "We have one church here for Mexicans and Spanish and I am fully convinced there is no neglect in looking after the welfare of the Mexican and Spanish people."[29]

The archbishop's attitude toward Mexican immigrants to California in the 1920s was, however, in striking contrast to his general support of immigrants. In 1926 a national law was proposed to eliminate visa restrictions and a head tax on Mexicans working in the United States. In his role as president of the California Commission of Immigration and Housing, Hanna opposed the initiative, stating that if it passed, those working the fields would become a significant burden on private charities and public welfare agencies and it would swell the Mexican population, thereby reducing the percentage of white population. He also feared that the law would bring into the country people who would not be assimilable.[30]

In a letter to the California delegation of the United States Congress supporting his position, Hanna argued that Mexican immigrants would drain charities, fill the jails, harm the health of the local community, create problems in labor camps, and require special attention in the schools because of their low mentality.[31] Hanna supported his claims with statistics: while the Los Angeles population was 7 percent Mexican, 28 percent of regional charity funds went to this same group. Additionally, he claimed that 50 percent of Los Angeles's city benefits and 25 percent of the total general hospital budget (including 75 percent of its maternity funds) went to Mexicans.[32] Hanna told the delegation that the commission found that Mexicans "are Indians and very seldom become naturalized. They know little of sanitation, are very low mentally and are generally unhealthy. Their children, however, who are born here are citizens and have all the rights and privileges as such." Hanna felt Mexicans were a danger because "they diminish the percentage of our white population."[33] Hanna's attitude was sufficiently well known that he was asked by the California Joint Immigration Committee to support immigrant restriction legislation.[34]

Hanna's views were highly controversial, both in his own day and in retrospect. The historian Don Mitchell claims that Hanna's comments "drew considerable ire from Mexican-Americans and their supporters."[35] One extant letter that rebutted each of Hanna's arguments stated:

> If you, yourself, Honorable Sir, have not been able to withdraw, in spite of your Christian charity from these racial prejudices, accruing charges against Mexicans and asking that it be made difficult their entering California, what may be expected of one not possessing the exquisite culture of your Highness nor the Christian spirit to which a high apostolic mission commended obliges?[36]

Historians have also criticized Hanna's views toward Mexican immigrants. Moises Sandoval is generally critical of bishops and clergy for their apparent disregard for nonmainstream Catholics, especially Hispanics, but he claims that Hanna was "openly hostile" to Mexicans in California. Similarly Manuel Gamio reacts negatively to Hanna's attitude and comments.[37]

Although Hanna's sharp critique of Mexican immigrants was unquestionably different from his attitude toward other groups, it was consistent with the high value he placed on assimilation and contribution to the common good. Hanna's negative reaction to the proposed 1926 law does not appear to be based on a dislike of Hispanic peoples, but rather on the fear that they would be a drain on the public and private resources that should be available to all. Hanna supported immigrants and the marginalized on the basis that with assistance they would become productive citizens. Hanna's comments were harsh, but, in the context of the day, in his overall support of immigrants, and in his strong belief in Americanization, his attitude is to some extent understandable.

It must be noted as well that Hanna strongly supported several efforts to aid Mexicans, both nationally and locally. As administrative chairman of the NCWC, Hanna was attentive to the political and religious situation in Mexico, beginning as early as 1916 and continuing until his retirement in 1935. During the Cristero Rebellion Hanna offered sanctuary in the archdiocese to Carmelite nuns and Mexican Sisters of Perpetual Adoration.[38]

The California Commission of Immigration and Housing

On June 12, 1913, the California state legislature created the California Commission of Immigration and Housing in response to the state's need to deal with numerous immigration-related issues. The act empowered Governor Hiram Johnson to appoint a five-person commission "to research the condition, welfare, and industrial opportunities of all immigrants arriving and being within the State." The original five members, Hanna, Simon Lubin, Mary Gibson, Arthur Fleming, and Paul Scharrenberg, were charged with "protecting immigrants from exploitation in the early stages, by guiding and aiding them in adaptation to American standards of living and by encouraging their education in the English language, and particularly in the duties of citizenship."[39] According to the historian Christina Ziegler-McPherson, the commission members served "out of a commitment to social reform" and "shared a vision of an active welfare state that was designed to protect those seen as less capable of taking care of themselves such as newly-arrived foreigners, women, children, the elderly, and disabled workers."[40] The commission, which recognized the need for greater attention to immigrants,[41] met for the first time on October 3. Simon Lubin, a native Californian who had studied immigration at Harvard, was unanimously elected president; Hanna was similarly selected as vice president and appointed with Paul Scharrenberg to the commission's auditing team.[42] Johnson, in a letter to Lubin, was very positive on the commission's potential:

> I think there is great work ahead for this particular Commission and that it may be possible for the State of California by virtue of its efforts, to avoid the distress and the horrors of the great problems of congestion of population that now confronts our eastern brethren.[43]

From the outset Hanna acted as a stabilizing force on the commission. So that the group's work could proceed smoothly, he forced commission members to resolve personal grievances in "face-to-face" confrontations and insisted that partisan politics be kept out of deliberations.[44] Ziegler-McPherson calls Hanna "the moderator and peace-maker of the Commission." She continues, "As a religious figure Hanna carried that respect with him into the Commission, and he was often the one to resolve disputes among members."[45] In response to an inquiry by Lubin on what political stance the commission should take, the bishop stated,

> To me…the answer to your question is amazingly simple—I do not see how you as an individual can do ought [sic] else than throw yourself whole-heartedly into Governor Johnson's campaign.…It is just as clear to me that the Commission as such

has no right to take sides in the campaign. It ought to serve the State, not the individual, it ought to serve the interests of the whole people, not the interests of a political party, it ought to shape its politics with no particular reference to any particular administration and then to trust to the work it actually accomplishes for the approval of the people. And the approval of the people will compel any political party to continue our work—any other course would seem to be unjustified and not in keeping with the highest purposes.[46]

Hanna's philosophy became the commission's policy.

The backgrounds of Lubin and Hanna instantly gave the commission both local and state acceptance and status. Hanna's reputation as a well-organized intellectual and a champion for immigrants was at least partially responsible for his selection as a charter member of the commission. Lubin, who had long supported the concept of inculturation, believed the immigrants' varied cultures brought special gifts to American society. He professed respect for cultural differences: "[T]he right kind of assimilation [is] not a one-sided affair; we only impart and the other receives; but a mutual give-and-take." He argued that forcing an immigrant to disavow his native culture was misguided, for if you "get him to make fun of his national customs and ideals, you make him a very bitter, disconnected and reckless person and by no means a desirable citizen."[47]

Led by Lubin and Hanna, the commission started its work in early 1914, dividing its duties into four departments: Americanization, bureau of complaints, labor camp inspections, and housing. Besides being head of the complaints section, Hanna oversaw efforts to protect immigrants against fraud in the public transportation systems and publicized the commission's work.

Commission members believed they should immediately address two problems, neither of which had been analyzed or standardized in the state: immigrant welfare and housing. Their first step was to conduct six preliminary surveys regarding the nature and extent of the problems and to obtain recommendations on their resolution. The hearings dealt with (1) the tenement house situation in San Francisco, (2) lodging and cheap hotels in San

Francisco, (3) naturalization of aliens, (4) education of immigrants, (5) the alien and the administration of civil and criminal law, and (6) the immigrant and transportation. Hanna regularly attended commission meetings[48] as the body moved around the state in an effort to establish a baseline for the commission's future work.

Its first report to the governor indicted the state for its lack of immigrant programs, its negligence in rooting out injustice, and its apparent indifference toward crimes perpetrated against immigrants. The commission's survey of tenements revealed that San Francisco was one of the few large metropolitan areas in the country with no home inspection system. The housing problem was labeled "as dangerous and demanding an immediate thorough-going program." The commission estimated that thirty-five to forty thousand immigrants lived in temporary lodging and cheap hotels in San Francisco under inadequate hygienic conditions. Thus, the commission recommended the establishment of rigid health standards, with a licensing and inspection system to ensure compliance.

Corruption and abuse in naturalization procedures were also uncovered by the commission surveys. Citizenship classes were often conducted by "private and doubtful sources" who preyed on innocent immigrants seeking to learn enough English and civic knowledge to become naturalized. Because illiteracy was also found to be common among immigrants, the report suggested that the commission work with the State Board of Education to solve the educational deficiencies of both child and adult immigrants. The final two surveys revealed the corruption and inequities that immigrants confronted within the legal and the transportation systems. The commission found that many judges, rather than being impartial, were actually hostile to immigrant cases and demonstrated little if any patience with aliens, "who of necessity know nothing of American laws, city ordinances, and legal traditions." Finally, the survey revealed that immigrants were handicapped by counsels "appointed in a hasty and perfunctory manner" by judges. The report lamented, "It is well known that many of these appointed counsels are selected from the hangers-on and 'shysters.'" Immigrants were found to be the pawns of transportation providers who routinely overcharged and often gouged clients, creating fictitious charges for transport of belongings. Such was the case from the time immigrant-laden vessels docked at Ellis Island to the arrival of these aliens in California.[49]

The Commission of Immigration and Housing of California conducted its work under the banner of Americanization, thus reflecting national attitudes. Four major tenets to the commission's Americanization program can be identified: (1) the United States has the right to determine under what conditions immigrants will be accepted, but when they are admitted, the state has obligations to them; (2) Removal of natural handicaps of language, ignorance of American laws, and customs must be a priority; (3) Immigrants must be educated toward American citizenship; (4) Immigrants must enjoy the same rights and freedoms as all other citizens.[50] These goals demonstrated that the commission's concept of Americanization involved much more than flag-waving and patriotic slogans or merely teaching English to foreigners. Rather, Americanization for the commission was

> an interchange of the best in all the world's national traits: our democracy and freedom and commercial and material skill, in return for whatever they have that has stood the test of centuries. We can build consciously and deliberately a nation that shall unite the best of all cultures, ancient and modern—a result no other nation can attain.[51]

Commission members believed that nativists and restrictionists who expressed fears about the quality of immigrants coming to America's shores should review the existing immigrant policy to determine whether revision was necessary. The report argued that if immigrants were treated well and afforded equal and fair opportunities, then future immigrants, knowing they could also expect fairness, would be more likely to contribute positively. If, on the other hand, immigrants did not receive justice or opportunity, future immigrants would learn of the situation and be more problematic when they arrived. Ziegler-McPherson describes the commission's Americanization program as "paternalistic in its belief that immigrants were at a disadvantage in American society."[52]

Hanna supported Americanization efforts, emphasizing the benefits immigrants brought to America. He responded to Simon

Lubin's query on what kind of Americanization policy the commission should follow:

> I feel that these strangers can bring elements to our civilization that are invaluable—a bit of Psychology *[sic]* and a bit of experience ought to teach our people that if we attempt to destroy absolutely the good and the moral[e] of these immigrants already here, and then strive to give them the "American spirit" we shall have a rebellion, etc.—We have a great field ahead of us, and I always feel that our greatest task will be to educate our ignorant Americans.[53]

Once again, Hanna's stance became the agency's standard.

Creating a home-teacher program for immigrant mothers was the commission's first initiative to promote Americanization. The commission as a whole followed Hanna's lead[54] claiming that the dominant cultural construction of the home was a good blueprint for Americanization. The commission had learned that although immigrant men were exposed to American ways and the English language through their daily work, and immigrant children were similarly exposed through school, women had no such opportunities. Thus, the commission recommended a home education program that would send visiting teachers to immigrant homes to instruct mothers and preschool-age children in the need for school attendance and preparation, sanitation techniques, and English. Additionally, home teachers gave instruction in buying and cooking foods, proper use of clothing, and the fundamental principles of the American system of government, including the rights and duties of citizenship. The Home Teachers Act of 1915 formally instituted the commission's recommendations.[55]

The Americanization program next addressed the deplorable conditions in many immigrant homes, which had been discovered during the commission's statewide hearings. The State Federation of Women's Clubs, under the direction of the commission, formed an immigration committee to address problems of sanitation, especially in urban tenements. A 1923 report on housing, sponsored by the commission, concluded, "Something must be done, for unless housing conditions...are improved there will be no improvement in our civilization."[56]

Inspection of labor camps, where immigrant men were common workers, was the third prong of the commission's overall Americanization plan.[57] Its first report to Governor Hiram Johnson stated that unsanitary conditions and neglect were the norm for rural labor camps. In the initial survey period the commission members, with assistance from the volunteer corps in the commission's satellite offices, inspected 308 camps housing over 9,300 workers; only 42 were judged satisfactory. Passage of the Labor Camp Sanitation Act of 1915 was a major step toward regulation and standardization of better camp conditions. The *Fresno Republican* praised the commission: "A monumental work has been done in placing the labor camps in California in a sanitary condition and to generally supervise the welfare of a migratory group of workers who, prior to 1913, were helpless against social and economic errors."[58] In its first nine years of operation the commission was responsible for the inspection of 12,570 camps housing over 465,000 men, women, and children. The efforts of the commission in general brought significant improvements to the camps. The historian Cletus Daniel has concluded, "The Commission established a reputation as a friend and protector of the migratory worker."[59]

From the outset, the complaint department of the commission, which was the responsibility of Hanna, was one of the most active. The department's original purpose was to furnish statistical data to help establish programs for immigrant aid and legislative reform and to protect immigrants from exploitation. During the commission's initial year, when the six surveys were being conducted, notices printed in twelve languages were posted in the regional offices, asking immigrants who believed themselves to be "wronged or defrauded" to inform the main office. The department responded in three stages: receiving and diagnosing the problems, addressing the complaint either directly or through a cooperating agency, and then seeking to prevent future difficulties by attacking root causes through legislation and reshaping public opinion. Careful study of complaints led commission members to conclude that most problems immigrants experienced were also experienced by native-born citizens but that the level of abuse in the areas of housing, court and police dishonesty, illiteracy, and poor education was greater for immigrants than for others. The commission, therefore, proposed legislation to eliminate discrimination and to remove barriers that prevented immigrants from obtaining justice. Removing handicaps, the commission contended, "gives to the immigrant the chance to work his way toward a contented life here. It also saves our country from the 'menace of the immigrant,' so feared by many who now oppose immigration."[60]

Hanna's ability to guide and stabilize the commission went beyond the complaint department and Americanization effort. In 1919 the commission's housing department issued the "Report on Large Landholdings in Southern California," an exposé of California's land monopoly and a call to dismantle the system. The commission's stinging report prompted the State Board of Control—which was responsible for public lands and called the document "radical propaganda"—to block its publication by the State Printing Office. Informed of the impasse, Hanna traveled to Sacramento, smoothed the waters, and the report was printed.[61]

After nine years of operation the commission could proudly claim many accomplishments. It was instrumental in the passage of many acts, including the Labor Camp Sanitation Act (originally enacted in 1913 but strengthened in 1915, 1919, and 1921), the Tenement House and Home Teacher Acts (1915), and the Hotel and Lodging Act (1917). The commission promoted the creation of the State Land Bureau (1917) and issued regulations for private employment agencies (initiated in 1913 and amended in 1915). The commission could be most proud of its work to advance the education of immigrants. Besides the Home Teachers Act, the commission helped launch the first normal schools for teachers in California and wrote a manual for home teachers and a primer for immigrant women.[62]

The commission's sense of accomplishment gave way to shock when Governor Friend W. Richardson's proposed 1924 fiscal budget eliminated the commission. Richardson, believing that its duties were being duplicated by other state agencies, recommended "that the functions of this Commission be transferred to the state bureau of statistics."[63] The commission met privately in February 1923 to formulate a response. Because Hanna had recently led the charge to save the

National Catholic Welfare Council from a combined internal and external campaign to destroy it[64] (see chapter 7), he was chosen to direct the commission's response. A strongly worded statement signed by all members of the commission briefed the governor on the commission's accomplishments and warned that to transfer its work to another agency would jeopardize its many successes. Moreover, the letter reminded the governor that since the commission members had served without even per diem pay, and since the bureau of statistics budget would have to be increased to cover the extra work it would now carry, disbanding the commission would not save any money, invalidating the supposition upon which the commission believed the governor had made his proposal.[65]

In a separate but related move, Paul Scharrenberg, who attacked Richardson's plan, was summarily dismissed by the governor under the pretext that he had used "his prestige as a state official to influence legislation." Lubin immediately sprang to his colleague's defense, threatening to resign if Scharrenberg was not reinstated. In October 1923, Richardson fired Lubin as well. The two vacant positions were filled by G. B. Ocheltree, a Berkeley businessman and president of the Berkeley Chamber of Commerce, and George F. Haller, president of the San Francisco Labor Council.[66]

The local press supported the commission's fight for its existence. One representative newspaper, the *Fresno Republican*, commented, "The state commission on immigration and housing has been a valuable arm of the state to prevent abuses where hundreds of thousands of men are employed. Will it be profitable even to the big taxpayers of California to substitute labor deficiency or strikes for the cost this division has been to the public treasury?" Reprinting the entire text of the commission's response to the governor, the *Sacramento Bee* also praised the commission's work as "essential" to the welfare of the state.[67] The *San Francisco Call* lauded the commission for its work, calling it "a sacred refuge, an infallible source of guidance and aid [for the immigrant] in difficulty."[68]

The commission's crisis was resolved in rather short order. Hanna and San Francisco capitalist Herbert Fleishhacker met with Richardson, who, on February 8, 1923, less than a week after the governor's proposed budget was published, rescinded his plan to eliminate the commission but reduced its annual budget to

$125,000. Both Hanna and Fleishhacker "were instrumental" in convincing the governor to change his mind on the matter. Hanna's role in the "rescue" of the commission from extinction gained him even greater respect within the agency. Described as "thoroughly familiar with the immigration question in California," Hanna was elected president of the commission after Lubin's ouster in November 1923, and he held the post until he retired in 1935.[69]

The commission continued to operate under Hanna's leadership for the next twelve years. However, the federal policy of legislated immigration restriction, which was reenergized in 1917[70] and reached its culmination in the 1924 Johnson-Reed National Origins Act, and the onset of the Great Depression minimized the commission's effectiveness and slowed the growth of California's immigrant population. Additionally, reorganization of parts of California's governmental structure in 1927 deprived the commission of its independent status, effectively eliminating its power to significantly aid immigrants.[71]

In spite of its dwindling strength, the commission was respected as a friend and protector of the immigrant, using "sympathy, understanding, and a genuine love of service" to assist its foreign supplicants. In a congratulatory note sent for the archbishop's silver episcopal anniversary, A. E. Monteith, chief of the Division of Immigration and Housing for California, noted Hanna's accomplishments in particular:

> The memory of your generous effort and your lofty ambition for the work of this Division is still an active voice in the humanitarian work of the organization as when your activity helped to guide its destiny. The thought uppermost in the minds and hearts of the Commission and its personnel to-day [sic], as when you left it, is to carry on and perpetuate the splendid and far-reaching work of their one-time beloved friend and leader.[72]

Conclusion

The post–World War I period in America was a time of heightened concern for national security, as the nation returned to its isolationist roots. The Red Scare of 1919 and the postwar return of massive numbers of immigrants generated anxiety and restrictive policies. As a product and supporter of the American way, Edward Hanna was concerned about the problems involved in immigration, but for the most part he used his authority to support and protect immigrants. Although he had a special interest in Italian immigrants, through his work on the California Commission of Immigration and Housing he brought education, better housing, and justice to immigrants from many nations, while insisting that they assimilate into their adopted country. Criticized for his opposition to legislation that favored Mexicans, his overall support for the immigrant was consistent with his lifelong advocacy of the underdog. Edward Hanna was always an archbishop for the people, in San Francisco and beyond.

Chapter 7

HEAD OF THE NATIONAL CHURCH—THE NCWC AND DOMESTIC ISSUES

Archbishop Hanna's significant efforts in the realms of church and state established him as the leading churchman of the city of San Francisco. Because he truly understood his call to serve society in a collective sense, his utility and expertise spread beyond municipal limits. Thus, almost from the outset of his tenure, he began to serve the state of California, first as a charter vice president and then, beginning in 1923, as president of the California Commission of Immigration and Housing. During its later stages, Hanna's work with the state would lead him to participate in numerous agencies, commissions, and organizations.

In 1919, Hanna's fame spread nationally, through his leadership of the National Catholic Welfare Council (NCWC), formed in 1917 as the Catholic response to the problems created by World War I. During his long tenure (1919–1935) as chairman of the Administrative Committee of the NCWC, Hanna guided America's bishops as they responded to domestic and international issues involving every constituency of society. Hanna's unique position gave him a voice in virtually every issue of church and state that arose during the interwar years. Assisted by John Burke, CSP, the conference's general secretary, Hanna assumed this leadership position in spite of the logistical problems caused by his geographic distance from NCWC headquarters in Washington, DC.

The National Catholic Welfare Conference: Formation and Purpose

The problems created by World War I led the American Catholic hierarchy to meet collectively for the first time since 1884.[1] In June 1917, two months after America's entry into the European war, Paulist priest and *Catholic World* editor John J. Burke, Catholic University sociology professor William Kerby, Paulist Lewis O'Hern (who was responsible for assigning Catholic chaplains during the war), and the former secretary of labor Charles O'Neill met in Washington, DC, to formulate an official Catholic response to the war.[2] As spokesman, Burke consulted with Cardinal James Gibbons of Baltimore, who approved an August meeting. Representatives from sixty-eight dioceses and twenty-seven Catholic societies met at the Catholic University of America and formed the National Catholic War Council, "to study, coordinate, unify and put in operation all Catholic activities incidental to the war."[3] An executive committee, chaired by Cardinal George Mundelein of Chicago, was formed in December 1917 to oversee the work of the council.

After the war ended Burke and Gibbons led a campaign to establish a permanent bishops' council. The issue of prohibition and the threat of federalization of education necessitated a united Catholic response that only an episcopal conference could provide.[4] Thus, on September 24, 1919, ninety-five prelates from eighty-seven of the country's one hundred dioceses came together at the Catholic University; the result was the formation of the National Catholic Welfare Council ("Conference" after 1922). Five departments were created: education, legislation, social action, lay organizations, and press and publicity, each headed by a bishop. John Burke was appointed general secretary and Archbishop Hanna was elected to chair the Administrative Committee, which was formed to manage the nascent body.[5] He described the committee's task: "The Executive Department has to deal directly with the United States Government and its numerous departments on matters that affect Catholic interests."[6]

The Administrative Committee met four times in its first year in an effort to organize, determine its role, and set a course for the

NCWC's overall approach and agenda.[7] The NCWC was uniquely positioned to provide the Catholic viewpoint and lobby the national Congress on issues that affected the Church in the United States and by extension the whole world. One trend that the bishops immediately recognized as unhealthy was the growth of government bureaucracy. Burke claimed this tendency "would eventually sovietize our form of government." The council members, speaking less bluntly, realized that federal assistance and direction was at times helpful and even necessary but that extreme bureaucracy was antithetical to everything American:

> The forward-looking forces in our national life must resolutely stand against further encroachments on individual and state liberty. The press, home, school, and the Church have no greater enemy at the present time than the paternalistic and bureaucratic government which certain self-seeking elements are attempting to foist upon us.[8]

Varied ecclesiologies, the emergence of the Church from the papal condemnations of Americanism and modernism, and the fact that the American bishops had not met as a body since the Third Plenary Council of Baltimore in 1884 created much dissension within the Church, which was reflected in the NCWC. Because the NCWC was a voluntary organization, several bishops felt no need to cooperate with it, and this attitude generated many internal disagreements and much wrangling for control. The first major obstacle facing the NCWC was ignorance about its purpose and authority, particularly in terms of how it differed from the War Council of 1917.[9] In 1921 their authority was challenged by the Knights of Columbus, who proclaimed to the secular press that they were the official mind of the American Catholic hierarchy. In a report to Hanna, Burke warned "The result of their attitude and activity in this direction, if not curtailed, is going to be disastrous for the Catholic cause." He continued, "Much of our time is lost to the promotion of Catholic interests, because it must be expanded in explaining and showing that the K of C pronouncement is not the official mind of the Church in the United States."[10] Besides the Knights, Catholic newspapers, having little knowledge of the council's activity and purpose, often sabotaged its efforts by proclaiming ideas that contradicted council pronouncements. Hanna admitted his difficulty in controlling even the San Francisco *Monitor*, writing to Burke: "One of my difficulties here has been the supervision of just such matters, and with the burden of many things some of them always escape and return to make me ashamed."[11]

The NCWC also suffered from poor internal communication. Various departments sent out unauthorized communiqués, often embarrassing the Administrative Committee. Hanna angrily complained to Burke about an official statement issued by the social action department as "the Catholic teaching" on the hotly debated labor topic of the open shop: "No committee has justification in sending out an important pronouncement and failing to inform you. Courtesy to me (if not to you) demands this much."[12] Burke admitted to Hanna that there were no standard methods for issuing pronouncements: "My pleasure has always been that the Executive Committee here, made up of representatives of the different departments, should be acquainted with the programs and pronouncements of every department."[13]

Realizing that his role as administrative chair of the council was critical for its efficacy as the official Catholic voice in the United States, Hanna linked the work of the NCWC to the mission of Christ:

> Our plan is the uniting of all of our forces together that we may work nationally: our plan is the putting of our ideals into our national life, which we have not done sufficiently in the past: the putting together before our people the great truths that will save our civilization....And may we, united in one great noble body, with the ideals of Jesus Christ before us and the ideals of our mighty country beckoning us on, help us to bring back this big old world to the love and brotherhood which ought to be ours, to that fullness of life, liberty and freedom that is the American ideal: and above all, to that dream that fills all hearts today, the dream of peace and of unity and of love.[14]

Because Hanna believed the council should be permanent, he realized the importance of safeguarding its operations. The NCWC was required to supplement the work of the bishops and to assist and guide local ordinaries on numerous issues.[15] With an eye to the future, Hanna summarized the present need for the NCWC:

> The work already done, and the evident work to be done, demand not only the building of the National Catholic Welfare organization, but the continued security of it. Any doubt with regard to the necessity of such a Council and its operating Departments cannot be entertained now in the face of the great Federal problems that will affect the well-being of the entire Catholic Church in the United States. The forces against us are centralizing their efforts on Federal legislation and unless we meet those efforts at the beginning the whole body of the Church in this country will suffer harm. Education, marriage and family, child welfare, health, hospitals, the aged and the feeble-minded are all eventually affected by Federal legislation or by National movements laboring to standardize such work. At the present time this standardization is inspired solely by secular motives and aims.[16]

Pleased with the initial accomplishments of the NCWC, Hanna congratulated Burke and the council for gathering forces to work for Christian education and social welfare along Catholic lines. He was proud of the organization's high standards, "It must bring joy to your heart to know and feel that your work is…forming public opinion in accordance with our high ideals."[17]

Others echoed Hanna in noting the NCWC's importance and potential. Burke informed Hanna that the council's work was gaining esteem, "even with non-Catholics." Cooperation with the council's objectives and "great patriotic and religious work" was recommended.[18] From America's heartland, the *Indiana Catholic and Record* praised the council's efforts:

> It [NCWC] has made possible the fullest realization of the Holy Father's desire for Catholic Action and has brought together the various forces through which action may be accomplished. It has done more than anything else to banish the spirit of parochialism and to bring us to a realization that

the Church in this country as elsewhere is universal, having always the same objectives and the same ideals.[19]

Commonweal noted that the NCWC was the one organization in the American Church commanding sufficient respect to promote the social order. Pope Pius XI wrote the American cardinals extolling the NCWC, "This organization is not only useful but also necessary for you."[20]

The Early Years, 1919–1923

From its beginning, financial problems plagued the NCWC, stunting its ability to completely fulfill its role. To obtain operating funds, the council assigned each diocese an annual assessment, based on its size and perceived ability to contribute. Hanna wrote appeals to his fellow prelates asking them to meet their financial commitments to the organization, but he was often snubbed. Extant records reveal many dioceses, including Boston; Springfield, Illinois; Alton, Illinois; Peoria; Louisville; Davenport, Iowa; Philadelphia; St. Joseph, Missouri; Sioux Falls, South Dakota; and Tucson, were habitually delinquent in their annual payments.[21] Hanna lamented the fact that a source of "permanent and adequate funds" was not available, and he appealed to his fellow bishops for support:

> The support and continuation of the work which these reports cover are made possible only through your generous support. The interests of the Church were never so jeopardized as they are today, not so much by anti-Catholic attack[s] as by well-supported and well-financed endeavors to undermine the foundations of our Christian civilization. These departments are at daily work and indeed the Executive Department at Washington is today handicapped by lack of assistance.[22]

The NCWC Administrative Committee continued to struggle financially for its first fifteen years of operation. John Burke described his own frustrations to Hanna:

> I am at times worried about the funds and I do hope they will
> come in as promised and that the importance of this work is
> realized by the bishops because the more I see of it, the more
> I realize that the national welfare of the Church is protected
> and how many things are stopped at the root, so to speak,
> which, if we were not here, would grow [and] develop into
> matters of controversy and perhaps handicap the action of the
> Church very seriously.[23]

Internal reports in the council's first few years show that the episcopal chairmen were asked to speak to their fellow bishops about
failing to meet their assessments. Hanna was forced to "administer the work as economically as possible" by reducing activities.[24]
Throughout the 1920s and 1930s Burke wrote to Hanna about the
unsatisfactory state of the NCWC's financial affairs. During this
period lay employee salaries were often cut, at times as much as 20
percent. When the pinch became even more severe, workers were
reduced to half pay for specific amounts of time. The onset of the
Great Depression in the 1930s also forced severe budget cuts and
layoffs.[25]

Financial problems notwithstanding, the NCWC addressed
pertinent issues, the first being disarmament and peace after World
War I. Although the National Catholic War Council, like the
majority of American Catholics, supported President Woodrow
Wilson and U.S. participation in the war with "sincere loyalty and
patriotism toward our country,"[26] the end of the world conflict
brought a call for disarmament. The Church Peace Union,
founded by Andrew Carnegie, pressed Burke to enlist the NCWC
in a joint declaration to President Warren Harding on the need for
disarmament, but Burke responded that the NCWC would issue its
own statement.[27] While the general tenor of the nation was toward
disarmament, the *Monitor* warned that such efforts would go
nowhere without a change in human understanding toward peace
and warned that the United States must not be taken in by empty
rhetoric.[28]

In April 1921, the NCWC Administrative Committee initiated its call for disarmament by requesting the formation of an
international conference on arms limitations:

> While, therefore, we must leave the immediate question of disarmament to our national legislators, we should take active means to bring about, for the purposes of general disarmament, a meeting of the representatives of all the leading nations of the world. America should sound such a call and we should do all in our power to make it known that such is the will of the American people....A congress of nations, called at Washington by the American Government, backed by popular interest and appeal, will secure undoubtedly practical, effective measures for the promotion of enduring world peace. Thus shall America once again show her leadership on the path of civilization.[29]

Hanna met with President Harding, gave him a copy of the NCWC statement, and expressed the American Church's concern about the world's precarious peace. When Harding called for a naval disarmament conference that same spring, Hanna could proudly boast, "We may say that [our] pronouncement was a most effective instrument in having called the World Conference on the Limitations of Armaments to be held here in November next [1921]."[30]

The NCWC and the Vatican immediately issued statements supporting the proposed conference. The Administrative Committee again emphasized America's important leadership role:

> We should take active means to bring about, for the purpose of general disarmament, a meeting of the representatives of all the leading nations of the world. America should sound a call and we should do all in our power to make it known that such is the will of the American people.[31]

Pope Benedict XV fully backed Harding's initiative and designated November 11, the opening date of the conference, a day of special prayer for peace. Hanna heartily agreed, adding his voice to the call for prayer, which was held throughout the archdiocese.[32]

The World Conference on the Limitation of Armaments, with representatives from the United States, Britain, Italy, Japan, and France, met in Washington, DC, in November 1921 and proposed limiting the size of certain naval vessels for a period of fifteen years. In a statement issued on February 11, 1922, the NCWC's Administrative Committee praised the results of the conference, stating that its reasons for supporting the conference "have been substantially vindicated." The bishops concluded, "We trust that the practical results will not fall short of the expectations of our peace-loving people."[33]

While the Administrative Committee was seeking disarmament, Hanna was advocating a more general message of peace. He acknowledged the NCWC's role in promoting peace, but advocated personal commitment as well: "We should individually and through organizations earnestly study to preserve the peace of the world. Our dealings, our thoughts, our aims should be in the path of peace. Peace should be our goal."[34] Hanna maintained this position throughout his tenure as Administrative Committee chairman. In 1932, on behalf of the committee, he wrote to the Union Catholique d'Etudes Internationales, meeting in Geneva, voicing the "hope and abiding prayer that the nations of the world may take effective measures to throw off the heavy burden of armament and thus promote among all peoples a spirit of peace and fraternal charity."[35]

The Suppression of the NCWC, 1922–1923

In early 1922 the NCWC's financial and internal crises came to a head. On January 22 Pope Benedict XV died, and on February 6 his successor, Pius XI, was elected. Less than two months later, on March 22, in a stunning announcement, the apostolic delegate, Cardinal John Bonzano, informed the Administrative Committee that the Consistorial Congregation had ordered the NCWC suppressed.[36] Dumbfounded, the Administrative Committee asked for an explanation.[37] In the meantime, rumors circulated. While conservative Conde Pallen pointed toward John Ryan and his "radical social ideas,"[38] the most common culprits were either the Knights of Columbus, which had been criticized by the NCWC for usurping its authority, and Cardinals William O'Connell and Dennis Dougherty, who had been openly hostile to the council. The two powerful archbishops had regularly stated that the council was not a valid organ for Catholic opinion; it is more likely that these two men resented the power they felt they had lost when the NCWC was created.[39]

Although under a cloud, NCWC operations continued somberly. Austin Dowling expressed the attitude of many:

> The Welfare Council cannot be saved. We shouldn't try to. Rightly or wrongly Rome has spoken definitely, authoritatively, crushingly. Not to submit would justify our accusers. I grant it could have been saved had we known in time, had we had a Roman protector. But the process of recreation will be tedious, exposed to many obstacles and without the sincere backing of the largest Sees in the country.[40]

Hanna told Burke to keep things going in Washington while he got the Administrative Committee moving.

Peter Muldoon, episcopal chairman of the social action department, urged Hanna to call a meeting of the Administrative Committee as soon as possible. Since pressing duties in San Francisco kept Hanna at home until mid-April, he ordered Muldoon to hold an emergency session in Cleveland. The Administrative Committee (less Hanna) met on April 6 and quickly agreed to petition the Consistorial Congregation asking that the February 25 decree not be published in *Acta Apostolicae Sedis*. They argued that publication would: (1) disrupt ongoing NCWC projects; (2) cause grave consternation for Catholics, especially when the secular press republished the order; and (3) provide an opportunity for church enemies in the United States to push their agenda, especially regarding the federalization of education (see chapter 9).[41] It was also decided that a delegation, headed by Bishop Joseph Schrembs, episcopal chairman of the department of lay organizations, be sent to Rome to respond to the suppression decree. The bishops were somewhat heartened when Cardinal Peter Gasparri, prefect of the Apostolic Chamber, telegraphed Schrembs, "Holy Father received telegram. Decree will not be published in Acta. Fuller information will shortly be given by [the] Apostolic Delegate."[42]

In late April the Administrative Committee petitioned the Consistorial Congregation to review the suppression decree. The

American bishops expressed great surprise and concern that the congregation apparently felt that the NCWC was an example of the American hierarchy's disloyalty to Rome, protesting that the Roman order had come without consultation and had given the NCWC no chance to defend itself. In part the petition read,

> We protest…Holy Father that the accusation [of disloyalty] is false, and without any foundation, either as regards ourselves or as regards our brethren of the American Hierarchy. We declare also our conviction that the National Catholic Welfare Council has been grossly misrepresented to the Holy See.[43]

The Administrative Committee also described the severe consequences that a suppression order would bring to the Church in the United States. With the petition for redress of the February 25 suppression order, the Administrative Committee enclosed a thirty-nine-page report detailing the origins, organization, purposes, and principal works of the NCWC. A cover letter stated:

> It is our fervent hope and prayer that the plain exposition of the aims and the work of the National Catholic Welfare Council demonstrate that it is useful and necessary for the welfare of the Church in the United States; and not only this, but that the work is one whole, a living body, all of whose members work together for the common good…none of which could be cut off without inflicting serious mutilation.[44]

In a bid for additional support, Hanna wrote to rank-and-file American bishops asking them to sign the Administrative Committee's petition. He explained, "We feel it is most important for the welfare of the Church that we show unanimity of judgment in the matter of these petitions." Seventy-nine of one hundred local ordinaries endorsed the measure.[45] On April 26 the Administrative Committee met with the trustees of the Catholic University of America, who went on record requesting that the suppression decree be suspended.[46]

While the NCWC Administrative Committee's delegation (Bishop Joseph Schrembs, Archbishop Henry Moeller, and Father

James Hugh Ryan) presented its petition in Rome, domestic thoughts turned to identifying the motivation behind the suppression order. Most signs pointed to a cabal between Dougherty and O'Connell. The historian Douglas Slawson comments, "Supported by Dougherty, O'Connell planned to smash the NCWC. Although both had theoretical reasons for wrecking it, O'Connell had the added motives of personal pique and ambition."[47] On his way to Rome, Schrembs encountered Archbishop Bonaventura Cerretti, papal nunio to France and former secretary of the Congregation of Ecclesiastical Affairs, who told him "Dougherty as well as O'Connell is at the bottom of affairs." O'Connell told Muldoon that he had been out of the country for two months and knew nothing about the matter.[48] Despite O'Connell's claim of total ignorance, Bishop Louis Walsh of Portland, Maine, wrote bluntly to Hanna, "I can only say that the 'archplotter' of our Hierarchy seems bent on undermining our work and our NCWC....The Boston swan intends to rule or ruin."[49] Years after the affair, Burke, writing to Hanna's successor, John Mitty, offered his explanation for the suppression:

> The old charge that the NCWC would be an *imperium in imperio* carries no longer any weight with anybody. It was the fear that the NCWC might take up ecclesiastical matters and be used as a preliminary to a plenary council, or take the place of a plenary council, that led some to oppose its establishment.[50]

While the bishops bickered about assigning blame, the Administrative Committee delegation made its appeal to the Vatican hierarchy. In Paris, Schrembs learned that the suppression order had been orchestrated by Cardinal Gaetano de Lai, whom O'Connell and Dougherty had convinced that the NCWC's existence violated canon law. In fact, many members of the congregation and Pius XI himself knew little or nothing about the matter. Thus, when Ryan and Moeller met with the pope on May 30, he assured them that the decree was an error and would be rectified. Ignoring de Lai's intractability, the pope ordered the Consistorial Congregation to revisit the case in a June 22 plenary session.

During the interim Schrembs personally lobbied the members of the congregation.[51]

At the end of the plenary session the Consistorial Congregation published a decree removing the February 25 suppression. In part the decree read, "The Sacred Consistorial Congregation, acting on new data, has decided that nothing is to be changed concerning the National Catholic Welfare Council." The document provided a nine-point instruction on how the next NCWC meeting, which was scheduled for September 22, should be conducted.[52] Schrembs cabled Burke, who passed the information on to Hanna: "Prepare program [for] bishops' meeting [in] September. Official notice will be cabled next week. Hard struggle [but] complete victory. Pope blesses bishops and Welfare Council." An elated Hanna responded to Burke's cable: "Words cannot express the joy I feel but greater is the joy I experience because your work and the work of your assistants has received the highest approval we can hope for on earth."[53]

Hanna sent a flurry of letters thanking those who had helped reverse the suppression. He thanked Schrembs for his work that "won for the Hierarchy and the Church in the United States a decision which promotes its welfare, not only for the present, but for all of its future history." Hanna also thanked Burke for his "devoted service."[54] Early in 1923 he wrote to the Consistorial Congregation, speaking of the American bishops' gratitude for withdrawing the decree and concluded, "The National Catholic Welfare Council is more necessary than ever before."[55]

The final episode associated with the attempted suppression of the NCWC was the organization's consequent name change. In their June 22 decree, the Consistorial Congregation suggested a name change away from "Council" to satisfy those who believed this word created the misunderstanding that the nascent body had organizational ties to Rome. After some wrangling, at their September 1923 regular meeting, the bishops agreed to substitute "Conference" for "Council."[56]

Domestic Issues, 1919–1935

Throughout his tenure as chairman, Hanna and the Administrative Committee grappled with the drive to change federal laws so that birth control information could be distributed through the United States mail system. In 1876 a federal statute was enacted that declared unmailable all articles, drugs, medicines, instruments, and other related items for preventing conception, as well as all books, pamphlets, and other printed material on the subject. In 1897 another statute forbade importing similar materials and printed matter. In 1909 the sale, free distribution, or exhibiting of any article, instrument, or medicine for the prevention of conception was also banned.[57] After World War I the American Birth Control League, led by its president, Margaret Sanger, and the Voluntary Parenthood League of New York City lobbied intensively to change this national policy against birth control materials. In 1921 the first American Birth Control Conference convened in New York "heralding Margaret [Sanger's] bid for bourgeois approbation."[58]

American Catholicism's rejection of birth control grew with time in the twentieth century. The historian Leslie Woodcock Tentler has shown that parish clergy rarely spoke on the subject prior to World War I. By the 1920s, however, anti–birth control literature sponsored by the Church began to appear. Additionally, the subject began to be addressed in Sunday sermons but generally in veiled language. Contraception was strongly denounced in annual parish missions. She writes, "By the 1920s, every religious order that preached missions routinely inveighed against contraception in the course of its standard sermon program."[59]

Hanna and the Administrative Committee responded quickly to the perceived threat to America's moral fabric. Lauding the efforts of the NCWC and exhibiting an attitude consistent with most Christian clergy of the day, Hanna wrote:

> This is a radical birth control movement. It knows no moral standards. It recognizes no God. Its only concern is economics. It has no respect for men as natural and splendid creatures, it makes him lower than the animal....We may say with confidence that the only force which has prevented their success is

the National Catholic Welfare Council. We have watched their every move, we have blocked their designs in national conventions.[60]

The Administrative Committee also forcefully denounced the birth control lobby and reasserted Catholic teaching on the issue:

> The activity of the advocates of birth control is an affront to all genuine Christians, and to all persons who cherish the elementary principles and sentiments of morality. We protest against this unholy movement, and we take the occasion to reassert the teaching of the Catholic Church. The Church condemns all positive devices and methods of birth control as necessarily immoral, because they are perversions of nature and violations of the moral law. Moreover, they lead inevitably to weakening of character, degradation of conjugal relations, decline of population and degeneracy of national life. As a remedy for social and economic ills, birth control is not only mistaken and futile, but tends to direct attention from genuine methods of social betterment.[61]

Burke agreed with Hanna and the Administrative Committee, but warned that "It will need intelligent and unified action on the part of Catholics to block legislation in this line."[62]

The Voluntary Parenthood League and the NCWC Administrative Committee sparred almost constantly over the birth control controversy. In a 1922 pamphlet, "A Friendly Word with Catholics concerning Birth Control," the Parenthood League criticized Catholic opposition to the free distribution of birth control materials, accusing the Church of attacking the basic American right of freedom. The league argued that although Catholics might personally have no use for the subject information, they had no right to interfere with the freedom of conduct of millions of other Americans. Since Catholics demanded freedom from persecution and suppression, they owed the same freedom to those who held different opinions.[63] Ignoring their argument, Hanna simply responded, "They seek to undermine the moral principles that have always guided our people.... Their propaganda is most insidious and is receiving many supporters. It would be deplorable if federal law even negatively recognized it."[64]

In the 1920s the National Committee on Federal Legislation for Birth Control (known as the National Committee), a coalition of the Birth Control League and Voluntary Parenthood League, got several initiatives introduced into Congress, all aimed at eliminating federal restrictions on the public handling of birth control materials. The NCWC was the only organized body opposing the bills, calling them "a terrible menace to public morality."[65] As part of its campaign, the NCWC in 1925 published a series of eleven information sheets on the "Question of Birth Control."[66] One pamphlet condemned birth control because "it isolates sex passion from the normal controls and correctives and counter checks placed upon it by nature and the God of nature....It reaps the pleasure of sex while evading the normally consequent sacrifices and responsibilities."[67] The Administrative Committee also began building its own coalition through Burke's efforts and in communication with Hanna. Burke reported writing to 174 non-Catholic organizations asking them to help build a team opposed to the birth control lobby. By April 1926, eight-four groups had accepted Burke's invitation.[68]

As the decade continued, the NCWC's efforts to neutralize the birth control lobby broadened. The council sent representatives to various international conferences on world population and eugenics, presenting the Catholic view on the conference topics. Hanna realized that the National Committee's lobby was concentrating on the state level, after several failures on the federal level. Realizing that success in one state could have a domino effect, Hanna wrote, "We beg, therefore, a corresponding watchfulness in the different states, and encouragement and guidance for our Catholic lay organizations to oppose any and every attempt."[69] To counter the state lobbying efforts, Hanna ordered the printing and wide distribution of three pamphlets, "Birth Control," "Feeble-Mindedness," and "Sterilization."[70]

Catholic opposition to the birth control lobby did not sway Sanger from believing that some compromise could be worked out. In January 1926 she met with officials from the NCWC, including John Burke, seeking some common ground. Sanger's biographer,

Ellen Chesler, however, states that she was somewhat naïve about the veracity and strength of Catholic opposition:

> Viewing birth control as a threat to the power of the church and its prelates, and not to their deepest moral principles, she [Sanger] let herself believe too quickly that Catholic opposition to contraception would in time be subject to compromise.

The NCWC told Sanger that it was its task to assure that no legislation passed that did not conform to the tenets of Catholic doctrine.[71]

The NCWC's campaign against the birth control lobby continued into the 1930s, but the conference's rigid policy had to be modified somewhat. Hanna continued to condemn "this iniquitous practice" and maintained that the NCWC must hold the line against any substantive changes in the penal code, but a stronger coalition would result if birth control was classified not as "obscene" but as "forbidden and harmful," like narcotics. He reported, "By holding to our original position we may lose all. By offering to give our opposition to the removal of the word 'obscene' and to accept a classification for this matter under narcotics, we might save something."[72]

Specific birth control initiatives in the 1930s were opposed by the NCWC Administrative Committee. In 1931 two bills, the Jones Maternity Bill and the Gillette Birth Control Bill, both of which dealt with the distribution of birth control literature, came before Congress. Although the NCWC was successful in thwarting them both, their task was complicated by the fact that some part of their 1920s coalition favored each bill. Like Hanna a year earlier, Burke began to believe that some modification in the NCWC's stand would be needed "to keep the code as rigorous as possible."[73] In 1932 additional initiatives were introduced in Washington. The Cutting Bill, which changed censorship language, was opposed by the NCWC because its language was "too loose." Two other measures, the Hatfield and Hancock Birth Prevention Bills, both actively supported by Margaret Sanger, died in committee,[74] as did the Hastings Bill in 1935.[75]

The NCWC's staunch opposition to the moral issue of birth control was not matched with equal support for the ongoing labor-capital struggle and the rights of organized labor. While Hanna, as seen previously, defended the rights of workers, the NCWC showed no great fervor on the organized labor question. Even the Social Action Department (SAD), headed by John Ryan, manifested little effort in this realm. Because of Ryan, the SAD did support the proposed child labor amendment to the Constitution, but as the historian David O'Brien writes, "Ryan was never excited by the labor movement as were many of his fellow Catholics."[76] This lack of initiative was noted by the labor priest and social activist Peter Dietz in a complaint to Hanna: "You were so good to me at Washington and you gave me so much heart, promising me help as well as backing. Is there a special reason for the general silence? If so would you be kind enough to tell me?"[77]

During Hanna's administration, the NCWC's principal labor efforts were in response to the Great Depression and the massive unemployment that it created. The Administrative Committee issued a series of statements, suggesting reasons for the crisis and offering possible solutions. A statement issued in November 1930 suggested, "Unemployment is not due to a lack of intelligence nor any more to ignorance. It is due to a lack of good will. It is due to a neglect of Christ." The bishops said that more was necessary than alms or even work:

> Our country needs, now and permanently, such a change of heart or will, intelligently and with determination, to organize and distribute our work and wealth that no one need lack for any long time the security of being able to earn an adequate living for himself and for those dependent upon him.[78]

Hanna was "delighted" with the statement, telling Burke, "The most important note in dealing with the matter of unemployment...is always prevention for the future."[79]

The government's feeble initial response to the Depression triggered pressure for federal intervention. In 1931 some fifty bills granting federal monies for unemployment relief were introduced in Congress. After reviewing the earlier NCWC statements in vain,

Burke sought Hanna's advice on the proper response to the federal initiatives. In his annual report, Hanna said the NCWC's response must be guided by two principles: (1) federal aid, since it eventually means federal control and domination, should be limited as strictly as possible; however, (2) given the present conditions, federal emergency measures to relieve the immediate distress and suffering should be supported.[80] Based on that rationale, the NCWC called upon Congress to: (1) mandate a living wage for the family, (2) demand wages that provide employment to the greatest extent possible, and (3) avoid unjust and inequitable wage reductions. The NCWC also recommended a conference in which employers, their associations, unions, and the government could fully discuss options.[81] In 1933 the Administrative Committee called for action, stating that these proposals were insufficient to promote "the innate dignity of man" and to redress the trampling of human rights.[82]

Family, Human Rights, and Federalization

The period between the two world wars saw a severe family crisis in American society. Ernest W. Burgess and Ernst Groves, two of the most prominent family sociologists of the period, believed that in the wake of World War I families experienced a period of dislocation that would eventually pass, as the basic unit of human society righted itself. However, a concern over increases in divorce rates and juvenile delinquency and over a growing tolerance toward the aforementioned artificial contraception and other forms of family planning resulted in the formation of many groups that aimed to aid families. The National Conference on Family Relations, founded in 1938, and its organ, the *Journal of Marriage and Family Living*, became the leading secular platform for discussing family issues. The National Conference on Family Life, often referred to as the White House Conference on Family Life, which met in Washington, DC, in 1948, was seen by many as the high point of the family crisis movement.

American Catholics disagreed with sociological mainliners like Burgess and Groves, who tacitly approved of divorce and spoke of children as "by-products" of marriage; their ideas contradicted

Catholic teaching on the indissolubility of marriage and on the procreation and education of children as the primary reason for marriage. Additionally, sociologists claimed personal happiness was the goal of marital bliss, violating Catholic teaching that marriage was social and not a personal sacrament.[83] The historian Jeffrey Burns, a leading authority on the American Church's response to the family crisis, outlines four responses made by American Catholics to this situation: (1) the national bureaucratic approach, (2) the personalist sacramental approach, (3) the internal educational approach, and (4) the specialized environmental approach.[84]

Developed along a time continuum, each of the four approaches offered something unique in its method. The national bureaucratic approach, centered about the Family Life Bureau (FLB), founded in 1931 as an agency of the social action department of the National Catholic Welfare Conference (NCWC), emphasized education. Operating from a supradiocesan perspective, the FLB made policy and gave recommendations on actions, but did not perform the tasks itself. The personalist sacramental approach taught that family renewal, centered in the personalist philosophy and ideas of such giants as Emmanuel Mounier, Dorothy Day, and Paul Hanly Furfey, must be achieved through personal change, not legislation or organizational or institutional reconstruction. The internal educational approach, manifest in the Cana Conference and its associated marriage counseling centers, sought family restoration through the improvement of marriage. Lastly, the specialized environmental approach was centered about the Christian Family Movement (CFM), a Catholic Action organization that used the "observe, judge, act" approach to transform the environment in which the family lived. While Cana sought to fix the family from the inside, CFM attempted to remedy the problems from the outside.[85]

The national bureaucratic approach, manifested in the FLB, was the one principal effort of the institutional Church to rectify the family crisis. Father Edgar Schmiedeler, OSB, founder of the FLB, believed the American family was a victim of a dual revolution in industry and philosophy. The Industrial Revolution had transformed a rural agrarian culture into an urban machine culture.[86] Accompanying this shift was the philosophical movement to an individualistic and rationalistic philosophy. The priest viewed the medieval world as the "Golden Age" of the family—rural agrarianism reigned and fixed duties and responsibilities were understood and practiced. The Industrial Revolution had undercut this ideal situation. Schmiedeler described the problem:

> That our family life is showing alarming symptoms of disease and unmistakable signs of decay is apparent to all who care to see....There is every reason, therefore, to speak of conserving the family. It is high time for action on behalf of the home. Such action to be really effective will have to seek the causes of the family's troubles and apply the remedies there.[87]

The American hierarchy supported Schmiedeler's work and issued the 1949 statement "The Christian Family," calling the family crisis a "present danger more fearsome than the atomic bomb."[88]

The family crisis was also acknowledged by the American hierarchy, as is witnessed by the bishops' support of the Family Life Bureau and the work of Schmiedeler. In 1933 the bishops linked the decline of home life with birth control: "The destruction or serious impairment of home life has brought about a menacing decline in the birthrate and has helped to promote the godless, selfish, and inhuman propaganda of birth prevention."[89]

Another effort to protect the family was an NCWC campaign against indecent movies throughout the 1920s and culminating in 1933. The bishops sent a representative to a national committee associated with the National Association of Motion Picture Producers and Distributors that established a preview system providing suggestions and critique for films. Hanna reported, "We may say that through our representatives much has been done to change the policy of this industry...and bring its standards nearer, at least, to Christian principles." He could proudly boast in 1922, "Our most influential work has been in endeavors to raise the standard of moving pictures."[90] The crowning achievement of the bishops' efforts to bring the Catholic view to films was the establishment in 1933 of the Legion of Decency.[91]

In contrast to its success in addressing the immoral content of films, the NCWC and the American Catholic Church accomplished little to help African Americans in their struggle for rights and freedom. Many fine monographs and essays have detailed the failures of the Church to respond promptly and adequately to the needs of black Catholics,[92] yet in the immediate post–World War I period there were calls for justice and more attention to blacks. The *Monitor* called for fair and equitable treatment for blacks, suggesting false priorities as the source of their neglect: "A great deal of our sympathy for the subject races and downtrodden peoples of Europe and elsewhere could be better expended in behalf of our black population in America."[93] The NCWC's efforts to aid black Catholics were limited to educational programs, and Hanna admitted the problem could be traced to the Church rather than to individuals. In 1929 he called for more efforts toward a black apostolate: "We think that greater consideration, more thoughtful appreciation and more definite steps toward meeting the first demands of the Catholic Negro for representation ought to be given."[94]

While addressing the needs of various Catholic constituencies, the NCWC issued warnings against creeping federalization, especially with the election of Franklin Delano Roosevelt in 1932 and the prompt articulation of his New Deal. Hanna, writing for the hierarchy, congratulated Roosevelt and pledged support but worried that the country's recent redistribution of wealth was making the federal government the overseer of all fiscal affairs.[95] Burke, expressing similar sentiments, suggested to Hanna, "The whole situation—while it seems to be too big, too complex for everyone—merits the most thoughtful consideration by the Administrative Committee."[96]

Hanna and the NCWC— A Contemporary Appraisal

The formation and first critical years of the NCWC received praise from many quarters. After the 1922 suppression controversy, the Vatican became very supportive of the NCWC, calling it a "well-deserving association." Hanna was personally congratulated for the conference's "work accomplished" aiding the "general welfare of the Church and the faithful."[97] The Vatican secretary of state, Eugenio Pacelli (future Pope Pius XII), lauded the NCWC:

"It's most consoling to the Holy Father to realize that the Bishops of the United States are very zealous in all various phases of Catholic Action and that the results of their deliberations and labors are most fruitful."[98]

Many noted Hanna's significant contribution to the work of the NCWC. A tribute written after his death placed his work with the NCWC in perspective:

> Though he had been brilliant as a student, highly capable as an orator, effective as a seminary professor, indefatigable as a parish priest, respected, beloved, and eminently successful as the Archbishop of a great Archdiocese, it was in his connection with the National Catholic Welfare Conference that he reached his full development and exerted the admirable influence of his personality over the widest area.[99]

Conclusion

As an archbishop for all people, Edward Hanna could not limit his domain to the city of San Francisco. Thus, when in 1919 the American Catholic bishops sought to make their nascent National Catholic War Council a permanent organization representing Catholic opinion, the bishops called on Hanna to lead their new organization, the National Catholic Welfare Council. Leadership of such a fledgling organization was not easy, especially when its own members sought to undermine its existence, but under Hanna's guidance the NCWC responded effectively to numerous domestic issues between 1919 and 1935. Guided by fundamental principles that avoided centralization and federal control, the NCWC delayed or defeated national legislative measures that contradicted the hierarchy's policies and/or Catholic teaching. Yet, the story of the NCWC and its domestic agenda is incomplete, for the conference's work with its two most significant American issues—immigration and education—must still be told. It is to these issues that we now turn.

Chapter 8

THE NCWC
AND IMMIGRATION

During its first fifteen years, NCWC addressed many domestic issues that affected the daily lives of American Catholics. While disarmament, unemployment, and birth control were important, the Bishops' Conference placed its major emphasis on two even more significant domestic issues: immigration and the attempt to federalize the American educational system (chapter 9). Hanna and the NCWC championed the rights of immigrants and opposed the harsh immigrant restriction acts of the 1920s, which targeted immigrants from southern, central, and eastern Europe, many of whom were Catholic. Hanna's work in this area echoed his leadership role with the California Commission of Immigration and Housing as well as his advocacy of immigrant rights as a pastoral minister and priest professor in Rochester. His sense of fair play and justice mandated that he use his position as administrative chairman to protect immigrants' rights and to lobby against restrictive legislation that was debated and eventually made law in the period from 1921 to 1924. Hanna's leadership was instrumental in bringing some light to brighten the darkness of the nativist attack against immigrants.

Immigrants and Immigration Restriction, 1850–1920

During the Progressive Era, the United States renewed and strengthened its nativist attitude. The *New Republic* articulated this fresh vision: "Freedom of immigration from one country to another appears to be one of the elements in nineteenth-century liberalism that is fated to disappear. The responsibility of the state for the welfare of its individual members is progressively increasing. The democracy of today...cannot permit...social ills to be aggravated by excessive immigration." Madison Grant in *The Passing of the Great Race* (1916) also used racist concepts to justify the belief in immigration restriction that was sweeping the nation.[1]

Opinions differ regarding the catalyst that triggered the period's widespread belief in tougher immigrant restrictions. Traditionally historians have traced the source of restrictive attitudes to nativists and their hostility to immigrants from southern and eastern Europe, areas that dominated U.S. immigration after 1900. Another factor was the more generalized fear that immigrants would take jobs from native-born citizens, especially after World War I. Even Samuel Gompers, chief of the American Federation of Labor (AF of L) and a traditional supporter of immigrants, began to push for restriction. Anti-Catholicism was another factor, although it was less severe and less prevalent than in earlier periods. The historian Robert Divine suggests that support of additional restriction was prompted more by the transformation of American political and economic life than by the ethnic makeup of the new immigrants. Technological advancements and the migration of African Americans to northern industrial cities reduced the need for immigrant labor. After World War I, America's world status demanded a greater degree of unity and conformity, leading to more intense nationalism and increased fears of immigrants. The war fatally weakened the historic confidence in the capacity of American society to assimilate all who came to its shores; the "melting pot" theory began to evaporate. At this same time the traditional nineteenth-century prejudice based on color expanded to include prejudice against distinctive cultural and social patterns. A burgeoning group that included prominent figures such as Henry Cabot Lodge and Francis Walker praised the Anglo-Saxon race and condemned the "lesser breeds" from southern Europe.[2]

The postwar period brought with it political efforts to stop immigration. In March 1919 Republicans took control of the House of Representatives and Albert Johnson of Washington, a vehement nativist, was made chairman of the House Committee on

Immigration and Naturalization. Johnson's committee, described by John Higham as "a sensitive barometer to the trend of [national] opinion [concerning immigrants]," gained allies in its restriction fight. In addition to Madison Grant, Harry H. Laughlin, a leading eugenicist, and John B. Trevor, a patrician New York lawyer, joined the battle. The fate of aliens was sealed in President Calvin Coolidge's first annual message to Congress:

> New arrivals should be limited to our capacity to absorb them into ranks of good citizenship. America must be American. For this purpose, it is necessary to continue a policy of restricted immigration....I am convinced that our present economic and social conditions warrant a limitation of those to be admitted.[3]

In contrast to prevailing trends in the nation, Roman Catholics at all church levels traditionally supported the cause of immigrants. The hierarchy was especially active on behalf of aliens, supporting national parishes and immigrant aid societies. However, the bishops also endorsed Americanization in general. The historian Gerald Fogarty, SJ, describes New York bishop John Hughes, an Irish immigrant himself, as "a militant defender of immigrants' rights." Yet, Fogarty continues, "For him [Hughes] the immigrant was to be urbanized and Americanized, and that meant, in part, to be patriotic."[4] For John Ireland, another Irish immigrant and a leading Americanizer, the United States was the perfect place for Catholicism. He, along with John Lancaster Spalding, bishop of Peoria, started the Irish Colonization Society in 1879, in an effort to settle immigrants into rural areas. In 1910 Archbishop John J. Glennon of St. Louis became the first general director of the Catholic Colonization Society of the United States, which gave immigrants spiritual guidance as well as assistance in getting settled. Hanna's support of Italian immigrants in San Francisco was duplicated by Archbishop Michael Corrigan and Cardinal John Farley in New York and by Archbishop James E. Quigley in Chicago.[5]

Immigrant aid societies served specified ethnic groups as well as the general Catholic immigrant population. Virtually every European country had one or more societies for emigrant welfare, the most famous being the St. Raphael's Society for German immigrants.

Several societies aided specific groups in port cities, including the Mission of Our Lady of the Rosary for the Protection of Irish Immigrant Girls, Leo House for German immigrants, the Belgian Bureau, and the St. Raphael's Italian Emigrant Society. The American Federation of Catholic Societies, founded in 1901, attempted to centralize national efforts to aid immigrants; the St. Vincent de Paul Society worked principally in port cities to curb exploitation of immigrants; and the Catholic Church Extension Society, founded in 1905 by Francis Clement Kelley, aided rural immigrants. The Catholic Church also sponsored settlement houses, which had previously been sponsored only by Protestants, but Catholics were slow to recognize their value.[6] Despite the efforts of the hierarchy, the presence of many aid societies, and the work of many religious communities, Richard Linkh has concluded, "Until 1917,...while some considerable efforts were made, Catholics by and large did not see immigration as a key problem for the Church to concern itself with, and those efforts that were made were for the most part haphazard, disorganized, and characterized by a duplication of effort."[7]

While Catholics did not view unlimited immigration as a blessing, they frequently took issue with the national trend toward immigration restriction, fearing that it was motivated by anti-Catholic nativism or suspect theories such as Social Darwinism. Catholics sought to refute restrictionist arguments point by point. Rather than taking jobs from natives, Catholics argued, immigrants pushed American-born workers to higher and better-paying jobs; the claimed overabundance of workers was a misperception. Catholics such as James Gillis, CSP, editor of the *Catholic World*, also argued that to close America's doors was to deny its role as "a refuge for the oppressed."[8] Catholics generally opposed the 1917 literacy law, although a significant minority insisted that self-preservation required some immigrant restriction. Louis Budenz in *Central Blatt and Social Justice* wrote that Catholic opposition to restriction was "far from wise." Arthur Preuss, editor of the *Fortnightly Review*, believed that the Church could not care for the flood of immigrants. Chicago's *New World*, Portland, Oregon's *Catholic Sentinel*, and the San Francisco *Monitor* all advocated some form of immigrant restriction.[9]

The NCWC and Immigration

The NCWC, which declared itself from its foundation a primary advocate for Catholic immigrants, focused the Catholic effort to aid immigrants to the United States.

> The great purpose of Catholic immigrant aid under the auspices of the National Catholic Welfare Conference...is to safeguard the faith of the Catholic immigrants and to assist them in becoming desirable residents of this country by helping them to a knowledge of its language, its laws and its ideals, and to aid them in any difficulties which they may encounter.[10]

Hanna believed the conference could effectively correct social ills and show Catholics of every nationality the opportunities extended to, and the duties expected of, prospective citizens. As administrative chairman he understood his special responsibility for "the care of the immigrant."[11]

The NCWC's Bureau of Immigration, established "for the purpose of rendering assistance to immigrants arriving in the United States," was created on December 20, 1920. The bureau was organized under the executive department and thus came directly under the supervision of Burke and Hanna, both of whom saw it as the vehicle to initiate a national plan to aid Catholic immigrants.[12] Hanna was especially pleased that the U.S. government almost immediately recognized the bureau as a national immigrant organization.[13] Bruce Mohler, a former deputy commissioner of the Red Cross in Poland, was appointed by Burke, with the approval of Hanna, to head the bureau. A national office was set up in Washington, DC, with satellite offices in New York, Ellis Island, Philadelphia, and El Paso.[14]

While all the regional offices were active, the work conducted on Ellis Island was especially noteworthy. Four representatives of the Bureau of Immigration arranged for regular religious services, prepared immigrants for marriage, reunited families, provided instructions for naturalization, prepared visa applications, and dispensed employment information.[15] The bureau's work on Ellis Island was lauded by the U.S. commissioner of immigration, who commented, "Your organization [the Bureau of Immigration] may well be proud of the untiring efforts it has made in giving to the Catholic immigrants that which is so necessary to their happiness."[16]

The historian Douglas Slawson has divided the bureau's efforts into four categories. First, the bureau set up European branch offices at the points of embarkation. Next, it coordinated the work of Catholic immigrant aid organizations in ports of entry. Third, it attempted to safeguard newcomers from exploitation as they traveled inland. Last, it helped to Americanize aliens.[17] Besides these services the bureau followed the progress of immigrants once they reached their final destinations. The bureau worked with local diocesan officials so that the immigrant could "establish himself,...keep intact his Catholic faith and practice, and learn to become a loyal American citizen." The historian Richard Linkh states that by 1924 "Catholic immigrant welfare work had become a highly efficient and well coordinated effort."[18]

A quick reversal in the temporary lull in immigrant arrivals after the war brought with it an even more virulent call for restriction. Fear of inundation by aliens combined with a renewed feeling of nationalism to produce a mandate for legislation on restrictions. The result of this drive was the Immigration Act of 1921, which reduced annual immigration for any particular ethnic group to 3 percent of its population based on the 1910 census.[19] The law, described by John Higham as "a makeshift designed to hold the gate while a permanent plan was worked out," was applicable for fourteen months.[20] In May 1922, however, Congress extended the life of the initiative for another two years. Although it was designed as a stopgap measure, Higham describes it as "in the long run the most important turning-point in American immigration policy."[21]

Surprisingly, Catholic opposition to the 1921 law was almost nonexistent. The NCWC made no official proclamation about the law before or after its passage. Perhaps it appeared that, since the 1910 census was used as a base line, no overt attempt was being made to discriminate against any particular nationality or religion. However, it is equally likely that because the NCWC Bureau of Immigration had just been established, it was simply not equipped to mount a significant campaign against the initiative.[22]

The 1921 law was only the warm-up to the main event, the Johnson-Reed National Origins Act. Signed by President Calvin Coolidge on May 26, 1924, the new law consisted of two plans. For three years the quota set up by the 1921 law was reduced to 2 percent, with the qualifying census set back to 1890. This rather artificial means of setting quotas was to be followed by a hard quota of slightly over 150,000 immigrants per year, with numbers to be distributed based on percentages of ethnic peoples in the nation in 1920. Proposed by Senator David Reed and New York Congressman John B. Trevor, the system was designed to preserve America's racial status quo, a goal that the original plan approached only crudely and indirectly. A report, "Restriction of Immigration," prepared for the House Committee on Immigration and Naturalization, summarized the objective of the initiative's sponsors: "It is hoped to guarantee, as best we can, at this late date, racial homogeneity in the United States."[23] The resultant quotas would be beneficial to the British but detrimental to other northern Europeans. Trevor prophetically proclaimed, "The passage of the Immigration Act of 1924 marks the close of an epoch in the history of the United States."[24]

In 1923, when it became clear that legislation was being considered to target immigrants from southern and eastern Europe, Catholic opposition was nationwide. Archbishop Michael Curley of Baltimore attacked the proposal as "conceived in an anti-Catholic spirit." Bruce Mohler, who saw the act as a "deplorable departure from our enduring heritage as a nation," commented, "The message of our country to the world will not be one of good will and equal justice for all, but of discrimination, of difference, and dislike." Wisely, however, Mohler used as his primary argument the claim that the law would impede the Americanization of southern and eastern Europeans already present in the United States.[25] Douglas Slawson summarized the feelings of many at the time, calling the 1924 law "a patently discriminatory piece of legislation."[26]

At Hanna's suggestion the Bureau of Immigration led the opposition to the 1924 initiative when it was introduced into Congress.[27] For the first few months of 1924 the bureau totally focused on the bill and how it could be modified or defeated. Burke and Mohler agreed that the initiative would severely reduce immigration from southern and eastern Europe. Hanna suggested that Mohler write a brief to Congress, setting out all the NCWC's objections and suggesting modifications to the bill.[28]

Mohler submitted his brief to Albert Johnson, chairman of the House Committee on Immigration and Naturalization, on January 7.[29] The document argued that the bill was un-American in its flavor:

> We protest against the principle and purpose underlying this Bill which excludes immigrants from certain countries and favors admission of immigrants from other countries. Such a policy is a distinct and deplorable departure from our enduring tradition as a nation. Our fundamental tradition as a nation is fair treatment to all nations. The proposed Bill involves an evident discrimination and a substantial injustice to certain particular nations. No reason of statesmanship can be advanced in its defense. Nothing can cloak the arbitrary unfairness in selecting the 1890 census as against that of 1910 as a basis for establishing the immigration quotas. The process is purely mechanical, designed for an ulterior purpose which cannot but result in arousing against us the enmity of other nations.

The brief agreed that "restriction in immigration should be enforced" but argued that fitness for citizenship based on economic grounds was more just than the arbitrary and clearly discriminatory use of the 1890 census. The brief also argued that the bill would jeopardize the Americanization of immigrants already in America, since the bill labeled certain people as "undesirable aliens" and, therefore, in theory inassimilable.[30]

After outlining the bureau's general objections to the bill, the brief recommended several specific changes. First, a nonquota class was suggested for aliens who were family members of citizens and declarants. Such a provision "will alleviate many of the hardships and tragedies" faced by immigrant families. Next, the brief asked for the elimination of the requirement that "ministers of religion" had to serve continuously for at least four years prior to their arrival in the United States. The document also protested the classification as immigrants of those aliens who were returning from a visit abroad, recommending that they be labeled nonimmigrants. Next, it recommended that the 1910 or 1920 census be used as a basis for the quotas. Fifth, it protested the minimum quota of two hundred for any nationality as insufficient and recommended raising it to five hundred. Last, the brief asked that the bill be modified to prevent an unscrupulous consul to use up a country's quota by assigning places in the quota to nonquota immigrants.[31]

The bureau's strategy of targeting specifics of the proposal paid off and the initiative was significantly modified. The experience level of service for ministers was reduced from four to two years, and a nonquota class was added to the bill.[32] Hanna expressed the satisfaction of the bureau and the NCWC as a whole: "We succeeded in having some exceptions made to the sweeping exclusion laws."[33]

Rather than ending the debate on restriction, enactment of the 1924 immigration law ignited a new controversy over the national origins section of the law, scheduled to take effect in 1927. In the original debate on the measure, Senator Reed's national origins plan received little attention; the selection of the 1890 census as the baseline was the principal issue of contention. However, when 1927 rolled around and implementation was imminent, controversy erupted. The main issue of contention was the distribution of immigrants from European countries, not the quantity, since only slightly more would be admitted under the 1890 census quota compared with the national origins plan.[34] However, the composition of the national origins quota differed considerably from the 1890 plan, with a pronounced change in the countries of northwestern Europe. Great Britain would gain the most, receiving nearly 50 percent of the total under the national origins arrangement, as opposed to 25 percent under the old plan. Germany, the Irish Free State, Norway, Sweden, and Denmark, on the other hand, suffered dramatic reductions. Several ethnic organizations, including the Steuben Society, the Sons of Norway, and the American Irish Historical Society, protested vigorously against the concept of national origins. On the opposite side, the Sons of the American Revolution and the Junior Order of United American Mechanics led the charge for national origins.[35] Despite the debate, the original plan was ultimately implemented, two years late, on July 1, 1929.

While the national origins debate raged, the NCWC and its Bureau of Immigration regrouped before entering its next immigration battle. Initially Hanna was not optimistic about the immediate future: "Federal laws will most probably be amended in the next Congress with a further restriction of immigrants."[36] Nevertheless the bureau continued to use its influence to advocate for Catholic immigrants.[37] In 1927, when the national origins debate was ignited, the bureau aggressively challenged the plan. Even after the system was instituted, Mohler was confident that it would ultimately fail or be repealed.[38]

One of the Bureau of Immigration's strongest and most consistent campaigns during Hanna's tenure as administrative chairman was its advocacy for religious and priests seeking nonquota visas. Hanna remarked that the 1921 immigration law made no provision for the admission of Catholic priests born in foreign countries, but concluded, "We secured a change that would admit our priests and our religious sisters."[39] Beginning in 1924, the bureau accelerated its battle to gain admission of more religious and priests. In addition to lowering the time of experience for "ministers of religion" from four to two years, the Department of Labor agreed that for Catholic clergy the two years' experience would henceforth begin at the time of ordination to the diaconate.[40] Foreign seminarians educated in the United States circumvented the law by taking two years of graduate courses after ordination while they ministered, a formula that permitted them to stay in America after their education visas had expired.[41]

Securing admission for religious women was more difficult and less successful than for priests. The only exemption from quota under which sisters could qualify was as "professors in colleges, academies, seminaries and universities."[42] In 1927 Burke reported that the bureau had lobbied Congress for two years "to have the law amended so that Catholic sisters would be admitted." Although the talks were cordial, Burke commented, "nothing definite has been accomplished." Burke informed Hanna that religious superiors who wished to get more sisters admitted under nonquota status should send their members as "professors" regardless of the level of school they planned to teach.[43] Despite all the bureau's efforts,

Mohler reported, "The serious problem with regard to the admission of religious sisters still exists."[44]

The bureau's efforts on behalf of religious and priests continued into the 1930s, when their emphasis shifted to individual applications for admission, deluging the Washington, DC, office with requests for assistance in securing visas, fighting deportations, and assistance in naturalization efforts. Between July 1, 1932, and June 30, 1933, the Washington office assisted 684 priests, bishops, sisters, brothers, and seminarians on an individual basis. Ironically, anxiety about immigration actually worked to the advantage of priests and religious seeking entry to America, since they were not perceived as likely to need public assistance and were therefore often admitted in place of other applicants.[45]

During the postwar and Depression era the Bureau of Immigration also worked tirelessly to reunite families separated by quota laws, calling the issue "the greatest need now existing relative to immigration legislation."[46] In 1925 the bureau supported an initiative granting nonquota status to wives and children under eighteen of aliens who had entered prior to July 1, 1924. Defeat of the measure only strengthened the bureau's efforts: Hanna authorized a letter to the American bishops, asking them to send letters and telegrams supporting a 1928 initiative to reunite immigrant families. The bureau's efforts paid off in late 1932 when the State Department issued special instructions to American consuls ordering them to review all cases where relatives of citizens and resident aliens had been refused visas on the grounds that they were "likely to become a public charge." These instructions immediately liberalized policy toward immigrant relatives: by 1934 less than 2 percent of all relatives who applied for admission were denied visas. Statistics in the period from 1932 to 1934 reveal that relatives made up nearly 60 percent of the total number of immigrants.[47]

The onset of the Great Depression in 1929 led all parties to see the need for immigration restriction. Restrictionists urged Congress to reduce quotas by as much as 90 percent, while others favored strict enforcement of the existing laws. Since the first option might have become permanent while the second could easily be terminated once economic conditions improved, the latter policy was adopted. On September 9, 1930, President Herbert Hoover directed the Department of State to immediately interpret the provision of the 1917 literacy law that prohibited the admission of persons likely to become a public charge to mean that all immigrants should be excluded except for prosperous European immigrants.[48] This decision, which "remained the basic American immigration policy throughout the depression," was effective: within five months, less than 10 percent of the monthly immigrant quota was being admitted. Hoover accepted the policy "as the best means of restricting immigration during the economic crisis."[49] While 1931 was the apex of the restrictionist campaign, some legislators continued to push for a more stringent immigrant policy well into the decade. Texas Representative Martin Dies, known for his House un-American Activities Committee, was especially virulent in a March 1934 essay in *National Republic:*

> Necessity compels us to adopt and develop a strong nationalistic spirit and policy. We must ignore the tears of sobbing sentimentalists and internationalists, and we must permanently close, lock, and bar the gates of our country to new immigrant waves and then throw the keys away.[50]

The bureau argued that Hoover's policy "was fraught with disastrous consequences to many worthy persons, both in this country and abroad," and that it would separate many more families than the previous policy. The bureau realized that every tightening of the immigration process had brought additional suffering to large numbers of people. John A. Ryan, chairman of the NCWC's social action department, criticized the exclusion policy in general:

> Our policy of partial exclusion carried out against other peoples is neither charitable nor necessary nor wise. The alarming decline in our rate of population increase in the last decade demands the cessation of this policy of rigid restriction....The conclusion seems inevitable that the present restriction of immigration is definitely unjustified and immoral.[51]

The Roosevelt administration brought renewed hope to the Bureau of Immigration. In 1933 the NCWC annual report praised the New Deal policy for granting immediate relief to thousands of aliens whose status had been jeopardized by Hoover's strict interpretation of the 1917 literacy act.[52] Secretary of Labor Frances Perkins was credited with engineering this new more lenient policy. The 1933 report concluded:

> It is the first time since our NCWC Bureau was established that we can look forward to a really humane administration of the immigration laws with due consideration given to social justice for the alien and the welfare of his dependent family. If these policies can be continued there will be wonderful opportunities for our Bureau to assist in correcting the many existing evils in this field.[53]

During Roosevelt's first term the bureau successfully lobbied for granting postulants and candidates for religious communities "visitor" status and nonquota visas. Reduced visa restrictions resulted in the reunion of immigrant families. Additionally, the bureau helped defeat the Dies initiative of 1935, which advocated the total abolition of immigration.

Conclusion

Believing in the need for a vehicle to assist Catholic immigrants in the United States, Edward Hanna used his influence and position as chairman of the NCWC to establish the Bureau of Immigration. Led by Bruce Mohler and reporting directly to Hanna and NCWC general secretary John Burke, the bureau effectively coordinated the efforts of Catholic aid societies, worked with officials at points of embarkation to aid prospective immigrants, and helped Americanize the new arrivals. Hanna led the opposition to the 1924 Johnson-Reed National Origins Act, seeing its restrictions as directed especially toward Catholics. The NCWC succeeded in limiting the sweeping exclusions originally mandated by the bill, particularly those placed on priests and religious, and those that separated immigrant families. Hanna represented the Catholic point of view on immigration policy at the same time that he effected changes to the policy that were advantageous to Catholics. The anti-Catholic animus that drove the immigrant restriction effort was also found in the drive to federalize education in the United States. It is to Hanna's and the NCWC's efforts on this major front that we must now turn.

Archbishop Patrick Riordan,
Hanna's mentor, c. 1910.

Edward J. Hanna's portrait as
bishop, c. 1920.

The 1924 Holy Name Parade: Archbishop Hanna, Mayor Rolph,
and other dignitaries.

Archbishop Hanna
with seminarians at
St. Patrick Seminary,
Menlo Park, c. 1930.

Archbishop Hanna receives
the Hebrew Medal, 1931.

Archbishop Hanna
receives an honorary
degree from the
University of
California, Berkeley,
1931.

Mayor
Angelo Rossi,
Archbishop Hanna,
Archbishop Mitty,
Governor
James Rolph upon
Mitty's arrival in
San Francisco,
1932.

Rossi, Mitty,
Hanna, and Rolph
in motorcade, 1932.

Rossi, Hanna,
Rolph, and Mitty,
1932.

Archbishops
Hanna and Mitty at
outdoor Mass in
Golden Gate Park, c. 1934.

Archbishops Hanna
and Mitty aboard a
ship,
c. 1934.

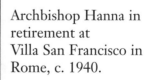

Archbishop Hanna in
retirement at
Villa San Francisco in
Rome, c. 1940.

Archbishop Hanna
in retirement at
Villa San Francisco
with two Franciscans,
c. 1940.

Archbishop Mitty
blesses Hanna's
body on its return
to San Francisco,
1947.

Memorial Mass
as Hanna's body
returns to
San Francisco,
1947.

THE NCWC AND THE DRIVE TO FEDERALIZE EDUCATION

As discussed in several previous contexts, Edward Hanna was a strong promoter of education on all levels. Because he had enjoyed an excellent education, from elementary school through his seminary training, he continuously promoted formal learning as both a teacher and a Catholic cleric and prelate. A product of the public schools, Hanna nonetheless championed Catholic education while he was archbishop of San Francisco. Locally he supported educational drives and initiatives, construction of schools, and the work of the National Catholic Education Association (NCEA); on a national level, through the NCWC Administrative Committee he resisted attempts to federalize the public school system. The conference argued that federalization was inconsistent with the Constitution and the concept of subsidiarity; wisely, they avoided accusations of anti-Catholic bias, as well as the argument that federalization would jeopardize Catholic schools. Hanna's leadership, direct and indirect, was instrumental in the NCWC's efforts to stave off federal control of national education throughout his tenure as administrative chairman.

Catholic Education in the United States in the Nineteenth Century

The American Catholic school system was established because the bishops believed it was needed so that parents could meet their obligation and right to educate their children, a belief they publicized through a series of provincial and plenary councils.[1] Additionally, the hierarchy promoted Catholic education as a partial antidote to the perceived and real anti-Catholicism that was so pervasive in the nineteenth century. At the First Provincial Council of Baltimore in 1829 the bishops' pastoral letter stated, "We judge it absolutely necessary that schools be established, in which the young may be taught the principles of faith and morality, while being instructed in letters."[2] John England, bishop of Charleston and author of the pastoral written to the laity, additionally stressed the need for parents to "attend to the education of your child; teaching him first to seek the kingdom of God and His justice."[3]

Throughout the nineteenth century the hierarchy supported Catholic schools. The Second Provincial Council of Baltimore (1833) appointed two committees, one to search for anti-Catholic material in common school texts and the second, consisting of the presidents of Georgetown, St. Mary's Seminary (Baltimore), and Mount St. Mary's (Emmitsburg, Maryland), to supervise the preparation of suitable textbooks. The Fourth (1840) and Fifth (1843) Provincial Councils warned parents against common schools where the King James Version of the Bible was used,[4] arguing that use of the King James Bible was sectarian and thus un-American:

> We have seen with serious alarm, efforts made to poison the fountains of public education, by giving it a *sectarian* [emphasis mine] hue, and accustoming children to the use of a version of the Bible made under *sectarian* [emphasis mine] bias, and placing in their hands books of various kinds replete with offensive and dangerous matter. This is plainly opposed to the free genius of our civil institutions.[5]

By the time of the First Plenary Council in 1852, the bishops had abandoned the idea that common schools could be made more nonsectarian. Instead, they recommended establishing Catholic schools and asked parents to "make every sacrifice which may be necessary for this object." At the 1866 Second Plenary Council the bishops in Title IX of their pastoral, "The Instruction and Pious Education of Youth," proclaimed the Church's right to establish schools and the need for youth to receive a Catholic education.

Reversing priorities from their statement of 1829 the bishops declared,

> The best, nay the only remedy that remains, in order to meet the very grave evils seems to lie in this, that in every diocese schools—each close to the church—should be erected, in which the Catholic youth may be instructed in letters and the noble arts as well as in religion and sound morals.[6]

Appropriately, what turned out to be the Catholic hierarchy's final general meeting in the nineteenth century also produced the most comprehensive statement on the need for Catholic education. The catalyst for the bishops' decrees at the 1884 Third Plenary Council of Baltimore was found in an interchange of letters between James McMaster, editor of *Freeman's Journal*, and the Holy See. In 1874 McMaster presented a "Memorandum" to the Congregation of the Propagation of the Faith *(Propaganda Fide)* describing the dangers that American public schools posed to Catholic children. After evaluating a questionnaire sent to the American hierarchy,[7] the papacy sent the American bishops a document, "The Instruction of 1875." The Instruction (1) spoke of dangers which existed in public schools, (2) mandated Catholic schools be constructed, (3) declared Catholic children should go to these schools, and (4) stated that absolution should be refused to parents who denied the opportunity to send their children to Catholic schools.[8]

The "Instruction of 1875" was the basis for Title XI, "Education of Catholic Youth," of the 1884 Plenary Council decree, which mandated that within two years each parish establish a school and that priests support this effort. Additionally, the decree provided details on teachers, methods of study, and administration. Title XI, however, did not address the issue of refusing absolution to parents who did not send their children to parochial schools.[9]

Background to the Federalization Conflict

The Progressive Era (1900–1919), with its emphasis on institutional reform, coupled with America's participation in World War I, was a transition period for the nation. According to the historian Alan Dawley in *Struggles for Justice*,[10] during this period the roles of American government, business, and the individual changed from what they had been in the nineteenth century. Governmental presence and influence expanded greatly, in the form of industry regulation and enlarged executive powers, as demonstrated by Theodore Roosevelt's "New Nationalism" and Woodrow Wilson's "New Freedom." Many business monopolies were dissolved while organized labor gained a stronger voice in its struggle with employers and owners. Belief in personal conversion and reform shifted to greater emphasis on the needs of society as demonstrated in the Social Gospel movement and a renewed Catholic social policy triggered by Pope Leo XIII's 1891 encyclical, *Rerum novarum*.[11]

Increased governmental control and a renewed spirit of nationalism encouraged a serious review of the nation's educational problems, which conscription helped to identify. An illiteracy rate of 12.5 percent among Caucasian immigrant draftees led to further investigation. Teacher education and training were found to be poor; most educators had received schooling only three to four years beyond the primary grades. The physical disrepair of school buildings and consistently low teacher salaries were two additional signs of problems.[12] Inefficiency on state and local levels, as perceived by the National Education Association (NEA), led to a call for even greater governmental control and centralization in order to solve the problems.

While the United States in general experienced postwar disillusionment, American Catholics became optimistic as they struggled to separate themselves from the antireligious culture surrounding them.[13] The perception that secularism had alienated American culture provided an opportunity for the Church to come to the forefront. Catholicism's certitude and moral direction, demonstrated by the neo-Scholastic natural law tradition that Leo XIII mandated for seminary training in *Aeterni patris* (1879),

seemed a cure for America's spiritual malaise. The Church's leadership role was challenged in the 1920s by the revival of the Ku
Klux Klan, whose Imperial Wizard, Hiram Wesley Evans, promoted the image of America as white, native, and Protestant. Evans
camouflaged his vituperation against Catholics as objections to the
Church as institution: "The real objection to Romanism in
America is not that it is a religion—which is no objection at all—
but that it is a church in politics; an organized, disciplined, powerful rival to every political government."[14] The age-old argument
that Catholics could not be good Americans because of their loyalty to the pope was renewed by the supporters of the 100–percent
Americanism standard.[15] Anti-Catholic animus, Catholic notions of
separatism, and the bishops' long-standing support for education
prompted the Church to attempt to protect Catholic schools
against the perceived threat of federalization throughout the 1920s.

The First Skirmish—Smith-Towner

The first legislative attempt to create a Federal Department of
Education, introduced in October 1918 by Senator Hoke Smith (D-
Georgia), set the standard for subsequent bills and was the model
against which the institutional Church argued.[16] The Smith bill was
a response to lobbying efforts of the NEA, which demanded federal
leadership and money to rectify the problems in the American public school system. NEA support for the measure was the natural
outgrowth of a late nineteenth-century coalition of education
administrators, college presidents, and business leaders who wanted
to expand, centralize, and standardize public education and put it in
the hands of "enlightened experts" and "cosmopolitan elites."[17]

The main provisions of the bill were the creation of a
Department of Education, with a secretary in the presidential cabinet, and an annual $100 million appropriation to the states to meet
various educational needs: $7.5 million to help abolish illiteracy,
$7.5 million to teach immigrants to read and write English (monies
to be divided based on the numbers of immigrants), $20 million for
building recreational and medical facilities, $15 million for extend-
ing state facilities for continuing education for teachers, and $50

million for the physical improvement of public schools. In order for a state to receive the latter stipend, it had to enact not only a compulsory school attendance law of a term equal to or greater than twenty-four weeks, but also a law mandating English as the basic (though not "official") language of instruction for "public, private and parochial" schools.[18]

Catholic opposition to the Smith bill stressed the traditional right of parental choice in education and, in line with its separatist stance, rejected the government's new-found desire for centralization of power at the expense of the states. The National Catholic Education Association (NCEA)[19] voiced a generic but typical complaint: "The establishment of Federal Control of Education offers no advantages, so far as can be perceived, for Catholic educational interests, while…it involves some very distinct dangers."[20]

Cardinal William O'Connell of Boston spoke for the majority of Catholic opponents of the bill, arguing that the concept of federalization originated in European secularism and state socialism, which aimed to dethrone religion from its rightful place of honor in society. Fearing that the positive reforms of the Progressive Era would be destroyed by rising statism, he commented, "We are not far, even in a democracy, from the old pagan idea that the State is a god and that for it the individual exists."[21] O'Connell proposed a renewed recognition of the individual and the family as basic units of society. The state should act only when the common good demands it and private initiative proves inadequate, and O'Connell insisted that neither condition existed in the American educational system. While the Smith bill died in committee without any official response from the National Catholic War Council, the initiative was important because its precepts would be repackaged and rearranged throughout the ensuing decade in an attempt to create a Federal Department of Education.

The first revision of the Smith bill was introduced early in the new year with the lame-duck Sixty-fifth Congress. On January 30, 1919, Representative Horace Mann Towner (R-Iowa) submitted a bill that aimed to: (1) remove illiteracy, (2) Americanize immigrants, (3) equalize educational opportunities, and (4) promote health education. The Smith bill's "centralist spirit" was softened by cutting assistant secretaries from three to one, eliminating the solicitor position from the Justice Department, and fine-tuning details regarding appropriating funds to the states. In February, Smith introduced a companion bill in the Senate. In order to court Catholics, who operated many schools in the vernacular language of the people, he dropped the earlier bill's requirement of a compulsory attendance law in order to receive federal funds and removed the word "parochial" from types of schools required to have English as the primary language of instruction.[22]

While it was being discussed in the House and Senate education committees over the next two years, the Smith-Towner bill was amended in many ways, but modifications intended to appease Catholics were mostly cosmetic. Exclusion clauses on state appropriations were removed but without altering the constitutional provisions eliminating the use of public money for private schools. All nuances of the words were mere rhetoric to Catholic ears; the basic elements of the legislation—creation of a Department of Education and federal appropriations to the states—remained the stumbling blocks.

Catholic opposition to Smith-Towner was more widespread and more broadly based than Catholic opposition to the Smith bill had been. The NCWC, in its inaugural meeting in September 1919, formulated the opposition strategy that persisted throughout the decade. The bishops would attack all initiatives on the basis that federalization was unconstitutional because it appropriated states' rights to a federal department, which had no legal right to exercise such power. Privately, however, as noted by the historian Lynn Dumenil, the bishops felt that federalization was a threat to Catholic education.[23] Bishop Louis Walsh of Portland, Maine, was typical in stating that the bishops must oppose Smith-Towner, "as it would give the death blow to our schools."[24]

Publicly the NCWC and other Catholic organizations attacked the Smith-Towner bill on its constitutionality.[25] John Burke believed the hierarchy should keep a low profile, argue only legal points, and reject the temptation to bring religion into the debate. This policy of opposition was threatened when the Knights of Columbus, appearing to speak in an official Church capacity, attacked Smith-Towner as a threat to parochial schools. Burke wrote an angry letter asking Hanna to silence the Knights with ecclesiastical sanctions, concluding, "The result of their [Knights'] attitude in this direction, if not curtailed, is going to be disastrous for the Catholic cause."[26]

The Catholic press supported the NCWC's constitutionality argument. Paul Blakely, editor of the Jesuit weekly *America*, commented,

> The real intent of the Smith[-Towner] Bill is to transfer authority over the schools from the States to the Federal Government. This transfer cannot be effected without the bait of a Federal grant. What the Federal Government subsidizes, the Federal Government controls, root and branch, lock, stock and barrel. To say that the Federal Government can distribute money among the States for education, or for any purpose, without controlling that purpose is to qualify for the care of the alienist.[27]

The *Monitor* linked the Church's public and private fears,

> The danger in the future is that zealous sectarians will endeavor to centralize the education system under an autocratic head at Washington, and the next step will be to attempt to close the Catholic schools as was done by the atheist government of France.[28]

One of the NCWC's own organs published supporting arguments from that segment of the public sector that feared centralization in education. Quoting C. W. Eliot, the president emeritus of Harvard, one source commented that the elimination of private schools "would strike a fatal blow at traditional American liberty."[29]

The NCWC frequently proposed alternative legislation to deflect attention away from federalization initiatives rather than as true alternatives. As a substitute for Smith-Towner, the NCWC recommended a federal agency or commission that would investigate educational problems of national scope and significance, with states using their own resources to meet their needs.[30] The bishops' intent was merely to deflect attention away from Smith-Towner, rather than present a true proposal. Similar tactics were used throughout the protracted fight for federalization.

The Battle Escalates: Sterling-Towner

The death in committee of Smith-Towner at the end of the Sixty-sixth Congress in February 1921 sent proponents of federalization back to the drawing board. On April 21 Towner introduced a revision of Smith-Towner, while Thomas Sterling (R-South Dakota) submitted a companion proposal in the Senate. Proponents of the Sterling-Towner bill attempted to include provisions that would preserve state control of education. For instance, they proposed a National Council on Education "to consult and advise with the secretary of education on subjects relating to the promotion and development of education in the United States."[31] This body, to be chaired by the Secretary of Education, would include the principal educational authorities in each state, so, in theory, the states would have a voice on all aspects of the administration of the Department of Education.

The effect of federalization on parochial schools, which Hanna and Burke had tried to avoid, was nearly broached when the Scottish-Rite Masons, much of whose literature was anti-Catholic, publicly backed the Sterling-Towner initiative with a $125,000 contribution to support lobbying efforts. Robert Robinson, grand master of the Masons of New York State, described Sterling-Towner as "a proposed national program for the equalization of opportunities."[32] Realizing the importance of keeping religion out of the debate, Burke wrote to Hanna, "It is most advisable to see to it that our opponents are not allowed to make a religious issue out of this question."[33]

Burke maintained that silence was the best way to curb the Masonic rhetoric and to avoid the religious question, but in private he continued to invoke the issue of legality while calling for broader-based support:

This [Sterling-Towner Bill] ought to be opposed on grounds of Americanism, because it is against the whole idea of the

American government; and in the opposition it would be good always to have non-Catholics with us, so as to avoid the charge that it is a purely religious movement.[34]

Burke's tactic of silence was logical given the anti-Catholic fervor of the time, and he did not have to go far for broad-based support: the National Tax Association, the American Association of Bankers, and the U.S. Chamber of Commerce all opposed Sterling-Towner in particular and federalization in general.[35]

Although he did not perceive the situation as immediately critical, Burke recommended that the NCWC "act now wisely and effectively" by preparing a pamphlet against federalization, highlighting the views of non-Catholics.[36] Burke telegraphed Hanna, suggesting that he "get prominent men [in] your locality, Protestant[s] preferred [to] telegraph their opinions."[37]

As with the Smith-Towner initiative, the Catholic press attacked Sterling-Towner on legal grounds. Arguing against support provided by both the Masons and the NEA, *America* commented,

> A department which is administered by a political appointee, which fixes educational standards for the schools, which withholds money when these standards are not met, which requires annual reports from the States, and which regulates the annual disbursement of more than $100,000,000 necessarily destroys the school control reserved by the Constitution to the States, for it substitutes control by a group of politicians and bureaucrats in Washington. No smoke-screen, even when raised by the united efforts of 100 National Education Association lecturers operating simultaneously, can obscure that potent fact.

As an alternative, the magazine suggested establishing a National Council on Education under the Department of the Interior, which would help the federal government eliminate illiteracy and other national education problems.[38]

Catholic opposition to Sterling-Towner received an unexpected boost when President Harding suddenly proposed a plan to reorganize the federal government. The proposal, although never fully mapped out, deflected attention from the proposal to create another federal department. Douglas Slawson, a historian of the NCWC, describes the importance of the planned federal shake-up: "The whole reorganization scheme would prove a godsend to the NCWC by providing a viable alternative to the Sterling-Towner Bill."[39] General opposition to federalization was increasing: the Association of American Manufacturers and the National Farmers Association joined other groups in public statements against the establishment of an education department. Additionally, prominent educators, including Nicholas Murray Butler, president of Columbia University, Abbott Lawrence Lowell, president of Harvard, and James P. Angell, president of Yale, voiced their opposition to the proposal.[40]

The Oregon School Case

From late 1922 until June 1925, the focus of the struggle for governmental control of education shifted from the federal government to the states. Bills to ban or curtail Catholic education had been initiated in Michigan, Nebraska, Texas, and Iowa, but it was successful legislation in Oregon that attracted national attention. Sponsored by Scottish-Rite Masons and supported by the Knights of Pythias, the Federation of Patriotic Societies, the Oregon Good Government League, the Loyal Orange Lodges, and the Ku Klux Klan, the Oregon School Law of 1922 mandated public school education for children (with few exceptions) between the ages of 8 and 16. During the course of the fall campaign "it became quite evident that the proposed legislation was directly and principally aimed at Roman Catholic parochial schools and institutional systems."[41] The initiative passed on November 7 and was to take effect January 1, 1926.[42]

Both secular and Church venues reacted swiftly against this overtly anti-Catholic law, but for different reasons. The *Oregon Voter* called the new law "a disgrace to the state. It inflicts a hideous wrong…a wrong so cruel that only the flames of prejudice could have permitted it to be passed." The *Monitor* described the initiative as "a direct and vicious attack upon the fundamental liberty in

State and Nation of education, parental rights, and rights of children and property rights."[43] The initiative labeled Catholic schools as un-American, which was a complete misrepresentation of educational institutions where obedience to the Constitution and patriotism were taught as religious as well as civic duties.[44] The bishops of the province of Oregon City, led by Archbishop Alexander Christie, met on November 22 and agreed to (1) have the constitutionality of the law tested immediately and (2) seek the assistance of the NCWC to coordinate this effort and raise the necessary legal funds.[45] Christie appealed to Hanna for financial assistance:

> The conduct of the campaign [prior to passage] has exhausted our resources. Without assistance we would not be able to take the steps necessary to protect the rights of our sorely aggrieved people. Surely the bishops of this country will not stand by inactive while the faith is being strangled in our innocent children. Our case today will be theirs tomorrow.[46]

Hanna called an emergency meeting of the Administrative Committee at Loyola University in Chicago for January 11–12, 1923, to discuss the proper response. Christie, disappointed that the NCWC had not been able to prevent the bill from passing,[47] sent the committee his views on what should be done. In response Hanna appointed a subcommittee of Archbishop Dowling and Bishop Edmund Gibbons of Albany to study the case and make recommendations for securing funds.[48] An agreement between the NCWC and Christie detailed how the campaign would be run. The NCWC agreed to provide $100,000 for finances, $40,000 of which was to go for existing debts. Additionally, the Administrative Committee would confer with Christie on the assignment of counsel, as they would on all other decisions in the case. Now that the NCWC was controlling the opposition efforts, any monies received from outside sources were to be returned.[49]

As with the federalization initiatives, the bishops agreed to take a secular tack in opposing the new law in the courts. Six points of assault were recommended: (1) The law violates the rights of liberty and property guaranteed by the Fourteenth Amendment. (2) It materially damages and would ultimately destroy the private primary school system, a useful and legitimate business. (3) It interferes with parental rights over children. (4) It interferes with the occupation of teaching. (5) The invasion of the above rights is in excess of state power. (6) It violates Article I, Section 10 of the U.S. Constitution on contracts, virtually destroying the chartered right of existing societies to conduct schools.[50]

As chairman of the Administrative Committee, Hanna felt obliged to inform Rome of the details of the case. He reported to the Consistorial Congregation that the Oregon bill had passed, that the fight to repeal it would be waged through the NCWC, and that a united Catholic front was being presented to secure "the rights and liberty of Catholic education."[51]

When Hanna went to Portland to speak with Christie and to plan the repeal campaign, their first order of business was the assignment of counsel. The two prelates decided that Judge John Kavanaugh, Christie's friend and attorney, would argue the case at its initial level, in the Federal Court of Appeals; William Guthrie, a New York attorney, would argue the case on the national higher level, with Garret McEnerney, Hanna's personal attorney, as his associate.[52] After consultation with these lawyers, Hanna assured the Administrative Committee that the defense could be financed for no more than $15,000.[53]

The internal battle associated with financing the court battle proved almost as troublesome for Hanna as the law itself. While the NCWC had agreed to finance the fight, the Knights of Columbus, seeking recognition, were willing and, more important, able to assist. The fledgling NCWC was still limping along financially, while the Knights were well established and financially sound. Nevertheless, Muldoon warned Hanna to stay clear of the Knights and their interference: "You no doubt noticed that the K[nights] of C[olumbus] have announced that they are to finance Oregon. If they persist in this matter it will be most unfortunate and will surely cause complications."[54] Muldoon advised Hanna to write the Knights and decline assistance, informing them that the NCWC was to maintain control. However, in the interim Christie accepted $10,000 from the fraternal organization, prompting Hanna to respond, "I was afraid of a mess from the beginning and I was not far out."[55] The historian Christopher Kauffman has suggested that, despite Hanna's complaint, since Christie had no money from the NCWC at this time, "it is evident that the K[nights] of C[olumbus] subsidy was crucial in preparing the brief for the case."[56]

The Oregon case was adjudicated in Oregon and Washington, DC. On July 10, 1923, Hill Military Academy (associated with the Protestant Episcopal Church) filed suit, and on August 22, 1923, the Society of the Sisters of the Holy Names of Jesus and Mary also filed suit; they claimed that the Oregon law was a violation of the due process clause of the Fourteenth Amendment. The Catholic cause in Oregon had been strengthened when on June 4 the U.S. Supreme Court struck down restrictive education laws in Iowa and Nebraska. On March 31, 1924, the Federal Court of Appeals struck down the 1922 Oregon School Law. Judge Kavanaugh thanked Hanna for his support and that of the NCWC:

> The service which the [National] Catholic Welfare Council has rendered directly to Oregon is beyond praise. As the head of the Administrative Council, you should feel greatly pleased that you have been able to execute such a service for all the people of this country.[57]

Hanna reported to the Administrative Committee that the case would probably go to the Supreme Court in 1925.[58]

The battle in the Supreme Court was contested on March 16 and 17, 1925. In *Pierce v. the Society of Sisters*, Guthrie and McEnerney, facing off against former governor and U.S. senator George Chamberlain of Oregon, successfully argued that the basis for the Oregon law was bigotry against religious groups and thus violated the First Amendment. On June 1, 1925, the Supreme Court unanimously overturned the Oregon law. Immediately Hanna reported to Gasparri that the Supreme Court decision "has made safe for all time the right of the Catholic school to exist and to function."[59] The next day Burke wrote to Hanna congratulating him on his efforts:

> I wish to send you my heartiest congratulations on the splendid result of your labors in carrying the [Oregon] case to the Supreme Court. It secures for all times the rights of Catholic

Education in this country, and on several other points the decision of the court both reflects and guarantees the Catholic position on fundamental matters. Your leadership in the work will be a source of gratification to all the Catholics of the country.[60]

Elated, Hanna described the victory as a blow against federalization:

> The decision has safeguarded forever and in all places in America our parochial schools. We feel, too, that it has lessened somewhat the heretofore unhappy possibilities that lurk in the endeavor to federalize education....News of the decision has gone round the world and cheered and encouraged the Catholics of other nations fighting for the right of Catholic schools and Catholic education.[61]

Final Drive: Curtis-Reed

Although it was early in the decade, the last major drive to establish a Federal Department of Education began in the last session of the Sixty-seventh Congress when, after Sterling-Towner failed to reach the House floor for debate, Sterling and his new partner, Representative Daniel Reed (R-New York), introduced the same bill as before, changing only its sponsorship. Olive M. Jones, NEA president, immediately supported the new initiative, appealing to basic American ideals:

> With the introduction of the education bill, the Nation's teachers served notice that they intended to stand unitedly in defense of the American principle of equal opportunity for all children, regardless of birth, wealth, or class; that they realize that on the defense of the American ideal of education depends the defense of the American ideal of democracy.[62]

James Hugh Ryan, secretary of the NCWC education department, led the Catholic opposition by arguing on several fronts, one of them new. The now-familiar arguments on constitutional grounds and on the principle that centralization would destroy local initiative were joined by the new contention that the increased taxes needed to fund the proposed department made education a political issue. He wrote,

> In these [present] circumstances it would be foolhardy to change the whole direction of American education away from the features of local initiative and control, which have always characterized it, into channels in which the Government must assume a monopoly of the educational resources of the nation.[63]

Alternatives to Sterling-Reed came from different fronts. Ryan proposed a National Education Commission to assess the educational needs of the nation, suggested ways to correct defects discovered, and offered a new federal agency to administer all educational work assigned to the federal government by the Constitution.[64] A second alternative, introduced in March 1924 by Massachusetts Representative Frederick Dallinger, chairman of the House Committee on Education, in an effort to appease Catholic opposition, expanded the previously proposed Bureau of Education to include responsibilities assigned to the federal government under Sterling-Reed: illiteracy, immigrant education, physical and health education, and teacher preparation. Dallinger substituted a commissioner of education for a department secretary, who would create a National Council on Education, consisting of educators from across the country, to advise the commission.[65] While Burke as usual recommended silence, the Administrative Committee privately favored the Dallinger bill "for co-ordinating all educational work of the Government in the enlarged bureau of education."[66] Again, both bills died in committee.

The final significant federalization initiative of the decade consisted of a companion bill introduced by Republican Senator Charles Curtis and Representative Reed in December 1925. The bill maintained the idea of a department with a secretary but dropped the concept of state appropriations and substituted a $1.5 million fund for operational expenses.

The NCWC's response to Curtis-Reed was colored by significant events of the previous summer. The NCWC Administrative

Committee had initially been lulled into complacency by the Supreme Court decision invalidating the Oregon School Law, since its opinion had been couched in terms of familiar Catholic principles:

> The fundamental theory of liberty upon which all governments in this Union repose excludes any general power of the State to standardize its children by forcing them to accept instruction from public teachers only. The child is not the mere creature of the State; those who nurture him and direct his destiny have the right, coupled with the high duty, to recognize and prepare him for additional obligations.[67]

In its annual fall meeting the NCWC Administrative Committee admitted that the Oregon decision, for all practical purposes, guaranteed the future survival of Catholic schools, "the lack of which heretofore was our chief anxiety." Nevertheless, the bishops remained cautious and recommended that the NCWC maintain silence, neither supporting nor rejecting Curtis-Reed.

The NCWC was forced to abandon its passive stance when, on January 2, 1926, an essay published in *America*, "An Alarm and Warning," implied that the NCWC, by virtue of its silence, supported Curtis-Reed. Burke immediately contacted Hanna, describing the "outrageous wrong" done by *America* and requesting permission to mount a public campaign, "as effective as possible," against the bill. Hanna responded by wire, "In [these] circumstances I favor definite protest."[68]

The campaign promptly launched by Burke outdistanced all the NCWC's previous attempts to defeat federalization of education. With Hanna's help, Burke arranged to have a total of forty-five witnesses, consisting of non-Catholics as well as members of the National Council of Catholic Men (NCCM) and the National Council of Catholic Women (NCCW), testify before the House Education Committee. For three days, beginning on February 24, they presented arguments based on three premises: (1) The U.S. Constitution gave no authority to establish a Federal Department of Education. (2) Education was a function of local government and institutions. (3) The historical record precluded education as a federal function. Confident of victory, Burke reported to the hierarchy, "We feel that an effective impression was made upon the members of the Committee by the protests presented."[69]

In spite of his confidence, Burke left nothing to chance, proposing an alternative measure in addition to arguing against the bill. On March 11, at Burke's behest, Senator Lawrence Phipps (R-Colorado), chairman of the Senate Committee on Education and Labor, introduced legislation similar to the old Dallinger bill, creating a Bureau of Education to sponsor research and disseminate information on educational issues. The bureau, funded by an annual appropriation of $250,000 (against Curtis-Reed's $1.5 million), would not be accountable to Congress for expenditures and would thus avoid congressional control of research projects. The bill retained the Federal Council on Education and National Council on Education proposed in the Dallinger bill.

Archbishop Dowling, NCWC education department episcopal chairman, initially favored the Phipps initiative. The Administrative Committee agreed, perceiving "nothing unreasonable in its provisions." *America* had reservations about the bill, but concluded that all initiatives were superfluous: "The most powerful argument against the establishment of a Federal Department of Education is that it is unnecessary. The States can care well enough for their educational needs."[70]

Both the Curtis-Reed and Phipps initiatives died in committee in March 1927; in December a revised bill was sponsored by the same people. The new Curtis-Reed, which provided a National Council on Education as an advisory body to the department secretary, met stiff opposition from James Ryan of the NCWC Education Committee:

> Central Control means bureaucracy, red tape, national standards of education and the beginning of the end of educational liberty and educational advance. Federal domination of education would make the school the football of national politics. It would be difficult to imagine anything more disastrous to true educational progress than to involve the public school in the squabbles of conflicting political parties on a national scale.[71]

Hearings on the revised Curtis-Reed initiative began in February 1928. As with the February 1926 hearings, Burke mounted an attack supported by well-respected educators, including Homer Albers, dean of the law school at Boston University; Harry Pratt Jordan, president emeritus at the University of Chicago; and Frank J. Goodnow, president of Johns Hopkins University.[72] Members of both the House and Senate challenged the Catholic opposition, claiming that every effort had been made to purge the bill of centralization The real reason for Church opposition to federalization— the fear of possible injury to the Catholic school system—long known to Catholics was now apparent to all. Douglas Slawson has captured the essence of the struggle: "Both sides acted out of fear: Catholics feared what bigots might do to their schools, and nativists feared what the Church might do to their country. Against such time honored fear, logic and reason were useless. These fears had to run their course."[73] Catholic opposition to the federalization of education, in the form of NCWC action, continued throughout the 1930s and 1940s. The Administrative Committee in its annual meetings continued to voice opposition to "a federal department of education." When in April 1953 the Department of Health, Education, and Welfare was established, under the direction of Oveta Culp Hobby, Administrative Committee chairman, Archbishop Karl Alter of Cincinnati, wrote to President Dwight Eisenhower requesting that someone familiar with Catholic education be appointed to the Advisory Committee on Education created under the new department. The request received no action. Catholic defense of its schools never wavered.[74]

Conclusion

Throughout the 1920s the NCWC perceived that one of American Catholicism's greatest institutions, its educational system, was threatened by ongoing efforts to federalize the nation's school system. Wisely and carefully the Bishops' Conference, under Hanna's direction, fought numerous federal initiatives, not by suggesting that they would damage Catholic schools but rather by claiming that such a move was inconsistent with the federal

Constitution, a violation of states' rights, and an infringement of the principle of subsidiarity. The NCWC's efforts were successful to the extent that all legislative efforts during Hanna's tenure died before reaching Congress. Hanna's brilliant strategy of fighting federalization with secular arguments damped the fires of anti-Catholicism during a period when, as evidenced by the Oregon school initiative of 1922, the Klan and other anti-Catholic groups continued their attack on the Church and its institutions.

During the interwar years the NCWC championed the Catholic domestic agenda, but it was simultaneously alert to global issues affecting the Catholic community. It is, therefore, necessary to describe the NCWC's significant efforts to promote Catholicism on the international scene.

Chapter 10

THE NCWC
AND THE INTERNATIONAL
COMMUNITY

Established in the wake of World War I as a national organization for the American Catholic hierarchy, the NCWC looked first at domestic issues that directly or indirectly affected the Church. Immigration, education, unemployment, and birth control were issues addressed in significant ways almost from the outset. Because the United States had emerged from the war as one of the leaders of Western society, international issues with implications for Catholicism also came to the attention of the American bishops and thus to the NCWC. The gradual evaporation of America's long-standing isolationist posture became part of the Church's new role as well. The bishops discussed many complex questions in their semi-annual meetings, but two questions were most significant to Hanna and the Administrative Committee: the situation and recognition of Russia and, most prominently, religious persecution in Mexico.

The NCWC and Russia

The Bolshevik Revolution of 1917 and the rise of Communism under Vladimir Lenin completely changed the relationship between Russia and the rest of the world, including the United States. The threat posed by Communism, with its political and economic ideologies antithetical to American democracy and laissez-faire capitalism, was strongly felt in the United States, especially after World War I. American citizens feared that the Bolshevist influence, which was rapidly spreading in Europe, demanded vigilance to prevent it from penetrating America as well.[1] In 1919 this fear generated the infamous "Red Scare," led by U.S. attorney general A. Mitchell Palmer and future FBI director J. Edgar Hoover. Placed on high alert, Americans often saw the Communist menace around every corner. The *Monitor* expressed the view of many: "The Real Communist who would establish the Soviet in America by violence must be brought to bay and taught that free America will not stand for the methods that have ruined rich and poor alike in Russia."[2]

Despite calls for moderation from many quarters, raids by Justice Department personnel in the fall and winter of 1919 and 1920 targeted radical groups in general, and Industrial Workers of the World (IWW known best as the "Wobblies") and other Bolshevist-leaning organizations in particular. The historian Richard Gid Powers has summarized the situation: "Hoover's raids were so outrageous by any standards of deceiving and legality that they mobilized lawyers, clergymen, and civil libertarians to demand a halt to the antiradical campaign."[3]

Catholics responded to the American preoccupation with Communism in several ways. First, they viewed Communism as a threat to America's economic system and therefore supported American workers rather than critiquing socialism or promoting capitalism. The *Monitor* editorialized,

> If the United States wishes to prevent the spread of Bolshevism among the working classes, it must speedily find ways and means of destroying the economic foundations of poverty and executing world wide agreements regarding wages, length of working hours...[and] physical needs of workers and their families.[4]

Second, although Americans in general were anxious about the terrorism and mayhem created by the Russian Revolution, American Catholics were more concerned with the injustice and religious persecution that was normative in the new regime. In April 1923 Archbishop Hanna and Bishop Peter Muldoon, representing the NCWC Administrative Committee, asked President Warren Harding to join in protesting death sentences that Soviet authorities had pronounced against Archbishop John Zepliak and

Monsignor Constantine Butchkavitch.[5] The American Catholic concern and support for Christianity in Soviet Russia was best expressed in an NCWC resolution adopted in September 1924:

> We view with pain and deep anxiety the extremely sad plight of the Christian communities of Russia. To them today, in the throes of a religious persecution surpassing in studied cruelty the fearful sufferings of the early Christians, we extend our heartfelt sympathy.
>
> Speaking in the name of twenty millions of Catholics of this republic, and supported, we are sure, in this, our action, by the liberty-loving Christian millions of America, we condemn the wholly unjust attitude of the present Russian government, opposed as it is to the fundamental principles of justice and repugnant to the best sentiments of all Christian people. We furthermore declare that we are ready to aid in every way possible our suffering brethren, bishops, priests, and the people of Russia.[6]

The U.S. relationship to the Soviet Union took a significant leap forward with the election of Franklin Delano Roosevelt as president. In early November 1933 the new administration began formal negotiations with Maxim Litvinoff, the Soviet commissar for foreign affairs, to reestablish the diplomatic relations between the United States and the Soviet Union that had been severed during the Wilson administration. Ostensibly Roosevelt made the move to increase Soviet-American trade, thereby invigorating the stagnant economy, and to forge a coalition between England, the United States, and the Soviet Union that would halt Japan's aggression against China.[7]

Hanna and Burke began discussing the NCWC's responses to the possibility of America's recognition of the Soviet Union. Burke suggested that some statement be made since "a great number of Catholics, and some of our own Catholic journals, will cry out against it [recognition of the Soviet Union]."[8] After considerable thought and some discussion with "capable people," Hanna cautiously responded to Burke:

I would say nothing unless forced by circumstance to take a stand in the matter. If forced to give any expression of our opinion, I would say that "at this time it is *inopportune* [emphasis Hanna] for the Conference to deal with the question." I appreciate more than I dare write your difficulty, but I feel that at present we ought not to go further. What the future will demand, we can meet when a new situation is presented.[9]

Burke persisted, telling Hanna that several bishops had contacted him suggesting that during the April 1933 meeting, the Administrative Committee discuss a possible NCWC response to the issue of recognizing the Soviet Union.[10]

As a result of their discussions, Burke and Hanna sent a letter to the local ordinaries in several dioceses,[11] posing three questions: (1) Would recognition of the USSR by the United States adversely affect social, religious, and moral life in America? (2) Based on your answer to question one, should the hierarchy publicly oppose recognition of Soviet Russia? (3) What is your opinion on issuing a joint pastoral statement against Communism? Extant responses almost unanimously opposed making a public statement. The response of Cardinal Dennis Dougherty of Philadelphia was typical: "This [a public statement] might bring humiliation and contempt on the Church, if recognition by the U.S. took place." As a substitute, Dougherty suggested that Catholic Democratic senators be encouraged to notify Roosevelt of their disapproval of recognition.[12] Archbishop John McNicholas of Cincinnati, the only respondent to support a public statement, added that if it was decided to not issue a statement, Hanna should decry America's recognition of atheistic governments. He wrote,

Can we let such an opportunity pass without taking advantage of it to teach at least our Catholic people and all who believe in God and in a supernatural religion, an important lesson? If all the laboring and trade classes of this country are united in protest because of labor conditions in Russia, should we not care for an infinitely greater reason to speak our mind? Such a statement from Archbishop Hanna ought to get wide publicity, and would, I think, make a favorable impression on all right-thinking people, particularly on the laboring and trade classes.[13]

At its April 1933 meeting the Administrative Committee decided not to issue a public statement, even though all its members were opposed to recognition.[14]

The institutional Church's official silence did not curtail public debate in either secular or Church circles. American opinion ran strongly in favor (5 to 1) of recognizing the Soviet Union, with supporters acknowledging the problems associated with the Soviet form of government but claiming that the economic benefits, especially with the United States mired in economic depression, outweighed the disadvantages. Supporters also noted that many leading nations, including England, France, Germany, Greece, Italy, and Japan, had already extended recognition.[15]

Catholics, drawing on their long-standing criticism of Soviet atheism, wrote in opposition of recognition and described its potential negative ramifications. Their major concern was religious persecution in Russia, which had closed churches and made the open practice of Christianity virtually impossible. The NCWC Administrative Committee declared that if recognition was granted to the Soviets, it did not mean that the nation sympathized with "the religious and moral institutions and teaching of the Government in question." *Commonweal* complained that recognition would bestow international prestige to the Soviets' practices of atheism and totalitarianism. Many Catholics suggested that recognition be contingent on the Soviets' agreeing to extend their citizens greater freedom of religious practice. However, Wilfrid Parsons, SJ, stated the common belief that the Soviets could not be trusted, especially in matters such as religious tolerance.[16]

Catholic commentator and Paulist priest James Gillis's sharply critical attitude toward recognition is typical of most Catholics' arguments. He did not believe that Russian trade would stimulate the American economy and wondered where the Soviets would obtain the money to buy American goods. Moreover, he felt that to do business with "a crafty, unprincipled, conscienceless, murderous group" would compromise American principles. Like Parsons, Gillis did not trust the Soviets; they had no basic reason to be truthful. Surprisingly, however, when recognition was extended on November 16,[17] he made no public statement against the move.[18]

The only protest from the American bishops regarding the proposed recognition was sent through official government channels. Burke told the assistant secretary of state, William Phillips, that recognition would be a grave mistake, would injure American institutions, and would be "interpreted by millions of our citizens and by many citizens of other nations as at least a toleration of this irreligion and immorality."[19] But when recognition was actually granted in November 1933, the NCWC produced no extant response.

The Mexican Situation, 1916–1929

Mexico, a nation steeped in Catholicism from the sixteenth-century Spanish conquest, yet one whose church-state relationship had been shaky since its nationalist period in the early nineteenth century, began a slow but systematic suppression of all Catholic institutions during the administration of President Benito Juarez (1861–1872). Laws were passed to seize the Church's wealth and to suppress Catholics' civil rights.[20] A period of relative peace under Porfirio Diaz ended in 1915, when President Venustiano Carranza began curtailing freedom of religious public assembly and instituted a rabidly anti-Catholic educational policy. Despite the instability, President Woodrow Wilson granted diplomatic recognition to the Carranza government on October 27, 1915.[21] In addition to the poor relationship between church and state, America's ire against Mexico grew due to the unprovoked murder in Chihuahua of sixteen Americans in January 1916.[22] The murders prompted Hanna to decry this tragedy and call for more generic assistance in Mexico:

> I feel we must protect not only the lives and property of our citizens, but in the light of our Pan-American situation, we must protest in Mexico the interest of other nations and must aid the seemingly helpless Mexicans to establish that condition in their unfortunate country which would make for the restoration and maintenance of orderly government within their boundaries.[23]

The Church's status in Mexico further declined in February 1917, when President Venustiano Carranza promulgated the Queretaro Constitution, establishing state sovereignty over natural resources and religion, critical areas that Mexico's revolutionaries felt had previously put the country at the mercy of outside influences.[24] The historian Douglas Slawson has commented about the Queretaro Constitution: "In effect, the Constitution denied the Church any legal personality and gave the government the patronato exercised by the kings of Spain."[25] The Catholic press pointed out that American support for Carranza was exacerbating the problem. The *Monitor* commented, "The work of the Catholic Church in Mexico for the last four hundred years has been almost completely ruined by Mr. Wilson's policy of backing Carranza, and the economic and social life of the nation has been destroyed by the enemies of religion and morality."[26]

The end of Juarez's presidency and the ascendancy of Alvaro Obregon (1920–1924) began a period of relative calm between church and state, but the peace was shattered in 1924 with the election of President Plutarco Elias Calles. Owing a debt to the revolutionary factions who had helped him gain office, he demanded implementation of Article 27 of the Queretaro Constitution, which nationalized all lands and thus deprived the Church of many of its economic assets. In February 1925 Calles ordered closer scrutiny of the clergy's activities and exiled apostolic delegate Archbishop Ernesto Filippi. When his replacement, Serafino Cimino, was forced to seek medical attention in the United States two months later, he was denied reentry and resigned a few months later.[27] As chairman of the NCWC Administrative Committee, Hanna arranged for Charles Phillips, a professor of literature at Notre Dame, to go to Mexico, investigate conditions, and report to the bishops. Phillips related that the Mexican bishops wanted their plight made known but that public demonstrations against the Mexican regime would only make matters worse. Hanna reported in his annual report that the Mexican hierarchy was following a policy of passive resistance.[28]

In 1926, with the situation growing only more severe, the Mexican primate, Archbishop José Mora y del Rio, asked American Catholics to begin protesting on behalf of the Mexican Church. In response, Burke suggested diametrically opposed strategies. First, citing the Mexican bishops' fears, he warned that formal protests would trigger negative publicity against the American and Mexican Churches. Conversely, Burke described the situation as "very critical" and recommended that the Administrative Committee formulate some policy of action in its regular April meeting.[29] The Administrative Committee decided to become actively involved, following a four-step procedure. (1) The bishops would ask to speak to President Coolidge personally and present a letter of formal protest. (2) The NCWC would issue a statement on the situation to American Catholics. (3) The NCWC would establish a national committee to publicize the Mexican situation. (4) The National Councils of Catholic Men and Women (NCCM and NCCW) would organize protest rallies.[30] In a formal statement the Administrative Committee declared,

> We call upon our Catholic people not only to interest themselves as a body, but to hold meetings with their non-Catholic brethren that will voice the protest of the public; that will call upon our own government to use its good offices to see that justice is restored and that religious and educational liberty are enjoyed by the people of Mexico.[31]

The April meeting also produced an official statement, "Mexican Injustice to the Church," which described the history of the recent conflict and the reasons for the bishops' collective protest. The bishops continued to maintain, despite Secretary of State Frank Kellogg's statement to the contrary, that American recognition of Mexico's government in 1915 and in 1923—recognition was suspended between 1920 and 1923—was made in conjunction with a request for religious liberty. The bishops stated:

> We are amply justified, and not only justified, but as is every American, obligated, to call upon our government therefore that its original request upon which recognition of Mexico was granted, be lived up to by the government of Mexico....No American can view with indifference the active propaganda of principles that are subversive to our own government; that

will, if persisted in, embitter our relations with the whole of Latin America. Where religious justice is violated, there can be no political, no civic peace.

The statement ended by encouraging Catholics to meet, protest, and call upon the American government to act.[32]

Acting on the four-prong plan, Hanna, on behalf of the Administrative Committee, promptly wrote to President Coolidge. He reminded the president that recognition of the Mexican government was predicated on its support of religious freedom and that the rigid and long-term enforcement of the 1917 Constitution would completely destroy organized religion in Mexico. He insisted that the United States must act immediately to safeguard innocent and persecuted peoples. Speaking as both churchman and citizen, he concluded:

> As representatives of the Catholic Church in the United States, we cannot fail to make known to you our indignation and horror at these acts of religious persecution of the Calles Government. As American citizens believing in the principle of religious freedom, we shall continue to raise our voices in protest until the intolerable conditions which exist in our Sister Republic have been remedied.[33]

As a follow-up to his letter, Hanna joined Burke and Peter Muldoon, (representing the Administrative Committee) in a personal visit to Coolidge on April 16.[34] The bishops suggested that the Administrative Committee publish a letter expressing indignation at the Mexican government's violation of Catholics' religious and civil rights. Coolidge said he had no objection to such a protest if Frank Kellogg agreed. Unfortunately, Kellogg took issue with one of the committee's initial premises, namely that in 1915 the Mexican provisional government had promised to guarantee religious education and freedom to all in return for recognition from the United States. Kellogg said that if the NCWC published the letter, he would be forced to write a rebuttal pointing out the error. The State Department stood by its belief that because Mexico's religious program was an internal matter, the United States had no right to protest until the rights of American citizens were violated.[35] Frustrated by the lack of support, the Administrative Committee refrained from publishing their letter but described "the distress and anxiety we feel, because...the growing danger to our country and to international good will upon this hemisphere, caused by the present conduct of the Government of Mexico in its studied violation of fundamental human rights." The letter continued, "We wish to present with every emphasis our grave anxiety concerning the conditions consequent upon the present conduct of the Mexican Government in its persecution of religion."[36]

In late spring 1926 actions on both sides of the border made the situation even more critical. First, Calles published a patently anti-Catholic pamphlet, "The Church Problem in Mexico," for distribution in the United States. Hanna protested to Kellogg, who in turn spoke with the Mexican ambassador to the United States, Manuel Tellez, who promised to withdraw the document.[37] Meanwhile the NCWC Administrative Committee also became more proactive, encouraging Catholics to petition the American government for action in Mexico as a departure from the current noninterference policy. The NCCW and NCCM joined forces to found the "National Committee for Protecting Religious Rights in Mexico."[38] Burke continued to work with Kellogg, attempting to balance the interests of the Church and the U.S. government. Kellogg agreed to present the protests of all Americans, of whatever religion, through official channels. The two men also worked on a letter of protest from the NCWC that was released on May 18.[39]

That month, tensions escalated when the Mexican government made plans to expel the Archbishop George Caruana, the Apostolic Delegate to Mexico and a naturalized American citizen. Calles's rationale was that Caruana had entered the Mexico with false immigration papers and had violated the constitution by functioning as a clergyman. Despite protests from Kellogg and the American ambassador to Mexico, James Sheffield, Caruana left on May 16.[40] In a statement issued in Hanna's name, Burke immediately denounced the action:

> The order of deportation which...has been issued by [the] present Mexican government against Archbishop Caruana,

Apostolic Delegate to Mexico, is an affront not only to his position as a high church dinatary [sic] but also to his rights as an American citizen. The Mexican government in deporting Archbishop Caruana shows its contempt for both religion and civil rights of our own country. Every reason assigned by [the] present government for the deportation is without warrant. Our own government has not been inactive in the matter and we trust that efforts will be effective in protecting the rights of our citizens.[41]

Hanna also wrote to the secretary of state, Frank Kellogg, protesting on behalf of the U.S. bishops:

In the name of the archbishops and bishops of the Catholic Church in the United States, I must solemnly protest against the deportation from Mexico of the Apostolic Delegate. He is an American citizen employed in a peaceful mission in behalf of religion and of order and I can only hope that our government will see that at least the rights of our citizenship remain inviolate.[42]

Hanna commented on the situation as an individual and as the NCWC Administrative Committee chairman. He lashed out at the Mexican president in the San Francisco press: "What President Calles calls law and authority is odious tyranny. Refusal to endure such tyranny is the first line of defense for justice and liberty."[43] When the Mexican government responded with a program of misinformation about Caruana, Hanna appealed to the secretary of state:

Does not this abuse of the courtesies of diplomatic relations require such actions as will at least put an end to the Mexican Government using its officials in this country as agents of all the falsehoods and misrepresentations which it chooses to issue?[44]

Burke thanked Hanna for his protest, saying that it "made a very deep impression and may result in something more drastic and effective."[45]

Hanna also generated support in the Archdiocese of San Francisco for the Mexican Church. In response to the call from Pope Pius XI for prayers for the Mexican Church on August 1, the Feast of St. Peter in Chains, Hanna directed his priests to lead prayers in their parishes. He concluded with an appeal to the Americanist side of his personality and ministry: "I need not tell you that the last manifestations of hatred against the Church not only outrages [sic] every inborn right of men, but the particular form the persecution has taken attacks the liberties for which our Fathers in this country have always battled even at the price of blood."[46]

The situation in Mexico grew more tense beginning on July 2 when Calles published a decree more severe than the Queretaro Constitution. The order outlawed religious education in primary schools, banned monastic orders, and forbade a person from taking religious vows. The National League for the Defense of Religious Liberty (Liga Nacional) responded initially by suggesting a boycott of religious services by clerics hoping that such action would lead the laity to pressure the government to pull back from its harsh stance. The ploy backfired, however, as churches were ordered closed. In December the Liga took up arms in resistance under the banner of "Viva el Cristo Rey."[47]

The Mexican situation was the dominant issue of discussion at the bishops' annual meeting in September. Hanna told the committee of his protest letter to Coolidge[48] and reported that initially most Americans had sympathized with the Mexican government, but that efforts had been successful in changing the minds of many. Rene Capistran Garza, a Mexican layman, attorney, and one of the leaders of the Liga Nacional, told the committee that the United States would stop supporting the Mexican government if there was grassroots support for the policy change,[49] and suggested a letter sympathizing with the Mexican Church as a strategy for garnering such support. The Administrative Committee, after listening to a detailed report by John Burke, proposed: (1) that the NCWC write a letter sympathizing with the Mexican bishops and condemning the actions of the Mexican government, (2) that the NCWC lodge a formal protest with the president of the United States "against the conduct of Mexican Government officials in this country" as well as against the expulsion of the apostolic delegate, (3) that a general collection be taken for the Church in Mexico, and (4) that the NCCW and NCCM reveal the facts of the situation and thus neutralize Protestant propaganda and popular misinformation.[50]

The bishops promptly acted on their September 1926 proposals, issuing the recommended letter, which spoke of the Mexican Church's "magnificent fight against a tyrannical government," before the meeting had even adjourned.[51] In November Hanna protested again to Frank Kellogg, sending press statements and other materials circulated by the Mexican consuls criticizing members of the American hierarchy and defending the Mexican government's tactics.[52]

The bishops' most important action following the September meeting was a Pastoral Letter on Mexico issued on December 12:[53]

> If we as American bishops had no other reason for issuing this Pastoral than to show our deep sympathy with the suffering people of Mexico in the persecution now raging in that country, it would be justified; but there are other reasons, carrying even greater weight and urgency, that make of this act a duty. They are found in the fact that Mexico is our neighbor—...a republic which it was intended should be modeled on lines similar to ours, and a nation with a Christian population whose devotion to the Catholic Church makes [sic] a special call upon the charity of the faithful everywhere, but more especially those of the United States.[54]

The document was divided into two sections. The first part compared the constitutions and statutes of the United States and Mexico, arguing that Mexican law violated basic human rights and attempted to destroy religious freedom, whereas the U.S. Constitution guarded both. The bishops wrote:

> The power of the State, coming from God, may be bestowed by the people, but when thus bestowed, it does not and cannot include what is not within the competency of the State to accept. Had God ordained the role of the State over the soul and conscience, he would have given the State the means to direct conscience and control the operations of the soul, since

he gives means to an end. The sanctuary of the soul and of conscience the State cannot invade. It is precisely this that the Government of Mexico seeks to do.[55]

The second part of the pastoral letter summarized the many Catholic contributions to Mexico, including the evangelization of native peoples, educational institutions, service to the poor, and social outreach. The document concluded by emphasizing the debt that the Mexican government owed the Church.

The Mexican situation continued with little change into 1927. The Vatican acknowledged the efforts of the NCWC on behalf of the Mexican Church. Cardinal Donato Sbarretti, prefect for the Sacred Congregation of the Council, praised Hanna for petitioning Coolidge and correcting much false information that was circulating in public forums.[56] More important, Pope Pius XI wrote Cardinal William O'Connell in Boston (who, recall, had been instrumental in the 1922 attempt to suppress the NCWC and must have been made extremely uncomfortable by the pope's letter), extolling the conference's efforts toward Mexico: "Quite recently we learned with pleasure from Our Apostolic Delegate at Washington how zealously the organization known as the National Catholic Welfare Conference has hitherto striven to defend and in every possible way succor the Church in Mexico which has been sorely tried."[57] On the other hand, Hanna, in a letter to Burke, rather uncharacteristically questioned the NCWC's efficacy in the Mexican affair: "May I say that when there is a question of our influence in behalf of our own high ideals, we seldom have sufficient power to make public opinion." He added that Vatican support meant little if the Administrative Committee could not unite all forces to battle for Mexico's spiritual existence.[58]

By September Hanna was attacking the Calles regime more forcefully, even as it faced opposition from forces supportive of the Church within Mexico. In response to the Cristero Rebellion, Calles exiled Mexico's bishops[59] so systematically that by May 1927 over half of them were gone.[60] In response Hanna accused Calles of "cruelty and ruthlessness," claiming that he was unable to deal with the Cristeros and their "armed movement in defense of liberty and justice," which had spread throughout Mexico. Contrary to reality,

Calles argued that the faith had not been destroyed in Mexico, but Hanna challenged the former's claims, "which are strangely at variance with facts of common knowledge."[61]

By September 1927 Burke was characterizing the Mexican situation as "critical." Acting on behalf of the Administrative Committee, Burke met with President Coolidge in November 1927, requesting a formal protest against the Calles government and its treatment of Catholics, especially clergy. Fearful that such a move might escalate the situation to war, Coolidge told Burke, "I do not want war with Mexico. I am certain the people of the United States would be and are decidedly against war with Mexico and anything that would lead to war."[62]

Burke's meeting with Coolidge was the first event in an extended international diplomatic effort centered around him. Burke's training as a priest did not equip him particularly well to negotiate a resolution to the Mexican crisis, although the historian Douglas Slawson has called Burke a "reluctant diplomat" but one who served "with tact and skill."[63] In December 1927 Burke met twice with the under secretary of state Robert Olds who, speaking on behalf of the new American ambassador to Mexico, Dwight Morrow, recommended that Burke go to Mexico and speak with Calles about the whole affair. Burke was reluctant to proceed without Administrative Committee approval and indicated that he felt Calles should make the first move.[64]

In January 1928 Burke embarked on the diplomatic route that would temporarily resolve the Mexican crisis. On January 3, Hanna called an emergency Administrative Committee meeting, but only Edmund Gibbons of Albany and John Murray of St. Paul could attend. The two bishops went to the apostolic delegate, Archbishop Pietro Fumasoni-Biondi, who recommended that they cooperate with the U.S. State Department; at this point, Burke accepted Olds's earlier invitation to diplomacy. On January 17 and 18 Burke met with Ambassador Morrow in Havana to discuss the situation. While the two men disagreed on who should initiate contact, in the end they decided that Burke would go to Mexico and seek a conference with Calles.[65] While in Havana, Burke also spoke with the exiled archbishop of Yucatan, Martin Tritschler, and the aged primate, Archbishop Mora y del Rio, who told him that although

Calles was "determined to root out the Catholic Church in Mexico," Burke might well achieve "useful results" because Calles was receptive to outsiders.[66]

Morrow met with Calles and told him that Burke was willing to speak with him. A meeting was arranged for mid-February 1928 but information leaks led to its cancellation. The cancellation gave Burke time to seek advice from Hanna, but the archbishop only replied, "I have no particular directions to give you, and I feel that I can trust not only your good judgment, but also the judgment of the Apostolic Delegate, in all that concerns the delicate matters in Mexico."[67] Finally, on April 4, Burke and Calles met in Veracruz. Calles launched into a tirade about the Church, even though Burke initially asked only that the exiled Mexican bishops be let back into the country. The two men exchanged letters outlining conditions for settlement and future desires.[68]

Burke went to Albuquerque, New Mexico, to deliver to Fumasoni-Biondi copies of the two letters. He also met with the exiled Mexican bishops in early May 1928 to discuss their feelings about a settlement. One of the terms they requested was restoration of public worship, which Burke, Fumasoni-Biondi, and Olds included in a carefully worded letter to Calles, describing the terms and assuming compliance. When Morrow read the letter, however, he said Calles would never accept such terms in letter form and suggested that Burke return to Mexico to present the terms to Calles in person. Thus on May 17 the general secretary and archbishop Leopoldo Ruiz y Flores again met with Calles, who gave up very little but agreed to restore public worship. Burke believed general progress was better than insisting on more specifics.[69]

Updating Hanna on developments, Burke explained that essentially he was trying to negate the laws of registration of clergy, which had been destroying public worship by removing religious liberty. In June, Burke was not too optimistic, stating, "The outlook at present is not encouraging."[70] Hanna, however, congratulated Burke on his zeal and accomplishments and voiced hope for a more permanent settlement.[71]

The Mexican situation took another quick turn on July 17, 1928, when Alvaro Obregon, elected on July 1 to succeed Calles, was assassinated by a fanatical Catholic. Hanna immediately condemned the act: "The assassination of [the] President-elect of Mexico[,] Alvaro Obregon[,] will be deplored by the whole civilized world. It is an outrage against every law of God and man. My utter condemnation of it and all connected with it cannot be made too emphatic."[72] Calles blamed the murder on the Church, and *Osservatore Romano* published articles vilifying him. Negotiations remained stalled for the rest of the summer and well into the fall.[73]

The inauguration of Emilio Portes Gil on November 30, 1928, as the provisional president was the first step in a resolution of the crisis. On May 1, 1929, Portes Gil announced that the government would not persecute the Church and that Catholic clergy were free to resume worship at will, provided they respected the law. In an attempt to finalize matters, Rome appointed Archbishop Leopoldo Ruiz y Flores as apostolic delegate to Mexico. On June 12 Ruiz y Flores and Portes Gil met and, with the assistance of Ambassador Morrow, hammered out a five-point plan to resolve the conflict: (1) The government never intended to destroy the Church; (2) the government would register only priests appointed by the bishops; (3) religious instruction of children could take place in churches; (4) the government would periodically confer with the primate about application of the law; and (5) clergy had the right to apply for modification of the constitution. For a week both men sought advice from counselors, and on June 21 the resolution was officially signed.[74] Ruiz y Flores commented, "I entertain the hope that the resumption of religious services may lead the Mexican people, animated by a spirit of mutual good will, to cooperate in all moral efforts made for the benefit of all the people of our fatherland."[75]

Reaction to the settlement was guarded but positive. Burke took little credit for his efforts, instead giving his honest assessment of the deal:

> The present adjustment does not by any means give that liberty to the Church to which she is by every right entitled; nevertheless it does acknowledge the corporate right of the Church and the authority of the Bishop of the diocese. The Bishops, therefore, may return with dignity and the right of the Church to exercise its spiritual functions is recognized.[76]

Pietro Fumasoni-Biondi was more optimistic in his assessment: "Needless to say, I am most grateful to hear of the solution of the religious conflict in Mexico. A continuation of the mutual good will and cooperation which have effected the settlement will mean an era of peace and prosperity for the Mexican nation."[77] Hanna later conveyed the gratitude of the Mexican Church to the NCWC for its efforts. Archbishop Ruiz y Flores of Michoacan-Morelia wrote, "May God bless all bishops, clergy, and people of the United States who were kind sympathizers in the days of trial."[78]

The Mexican Situation, 1930–1935

The new decade was supposed to bring restoration of the Mexican Church, but numerous institutional forces prevented the Church from reaching the goals promised in the hope-filled June 1929 settlement. In the first part of 1931 the Mexican apostolic delegate, Archbishop Ruiz y Flores, formally requested economic assistance from the NCWC in rebuilding the Mexican Church. Specifically, Ruiz y Flores wanted an endowment of $1 million, to be generated and administered by the American hierarchy, to establish the Mexican Catholic Social Welfare Foundation. Hanna told the Administrative Committee that economic conditions in the United States made it difficult to grant such a request, especially because the bishops had already agreed to support the Catholic University of America's development drive to raise $20 million. Although the NCWC could not financially support the Mexican Church, it helped develop social action ministries in the country.[79]

The end of the Cristero Rebellion in 1929 had given Mexican government officials time to return to their old ways. Many of the rebel leaders were arrested and executed. Next, the functions of the clergy were again restricted by local officials. In the fall of 1932 Archbishop Ruiz y Flores was expelled. Initially the NCWC Administrative Committee decided "it was inadvisable to have any public protest" because the situation in Mexico was too complicated. By the fall of 1932, however, the American bishops decided they had to make a statement of some kind. Bishop Francis Kelley of Oklahoma City presented the bishops a draft resolution, but it was decided that Burke's judgment on the issue should prevail.[80] After consulting with the exiled apostolic delegate, Burke agreed that a statement be issued,[81] and on January 12, 1933, the American hierarchy went on record as opposing the renewed persecution of the Church in Mexico. Hanna, speaking for the bishops, signed the letter, which read in part:

> The right of religious liberty, of freedom of worship, is native to the thought of our country. We feel, therefore, we are justified in asking all our fellow citizens actively to interest themselves in the restoration in Mexico of religious freedom for its citizens.[82]

The Administrative Committee continued to monitor the situation, hoping that once again cooperation with the American government would produce a final and permanent resolution to the problem.[83]

The renewed persecution in Mexico started just as Franklin Delano Roosevelt was entering the White House. Almost immediately after his inauguration, in addition to his alphabet soup of New Deal programs, Roosevelt committed the nation to a Good Neighbor Policy, which spoke of respect for the sanctity of America's agreements with other nations and included a refusal to interfere in their affairs, thus obviating action to stop persecution of Catholics in Mexico.[84] Meanwhile by 1934 thirteen Mexican states had closed all or nearly all of their churches.

The persecution of the Church in Mexico produced the "most severe strain"[85] in Roosevelt's generally harmonious relationship with American Catholics. The Six-Year Plan announced by Mexican president Lazaro Cardenas in 1934 pledged to amend the national constitution to ban all but state-run schools, which would teach the socialistic and anticlerical ideas upon which the Mexican Revolution was based. Religious education was to be excluded from all primary and secondary schools. Clerics were declared "professionals" and placed under the watchful eye of the government.

This state of affairs, repugnant to American Catholics, was greatly exacerbated when Josephus Daniels, the U.S. ambassador, gave a speech in Mexico City on July 26, 1934, apparently endorsing the proposed secularization of education in Mexico. Daniels became the scapegoat in a wide-ranging diatribe by prominent Catholics, including *Commonweal, America*, radio commentator Charles Coughlin, Francis Kelley, and the NCWC, who all denounced Daniels's statement and demanded his ouster.[86] Catholic journals called for a boycott of Mexican products, promoted an antitourism drive, and challenged Roosevelt to speak out against the tyranny of the Mexican government, which held the Church prisoner.[87]

Efforts to resolve the crisis continued despite the tension. In the summer of 1934 Archbishop Amleto Cicognani, apostolic delegate to the United States, asked Burke to submit a plan for action in Mexico. After being endorsed by the Vatican, the plan was returned to Burke with the request that he work with Roosevelt to implement it.[88]

Meanwhile, on November 15, 1934, the NCWC issued a pamphlet, "Tyranny in Mexico," portraying the crisis as a renewal of the persecution that began in the 1920s and outlining all the ongoing abuses perpetuated by the Mexican government against the Church. The bishops stated:

> We protest with our whole heart and soul against this anti-Christian tyranny, and again call upon all the faithful in our country in their power by word and by act to make the fact of such tyranny known....As American citizens we present our plea that justice may be done, that all our fellow Americans may make themselves advocates of that common justice of man, which is the security of every man and every nation.[89]

In addition to the committee's statement, Hanna himself issued a pastoral letter on December 5 asking that the archdiocese celebrate December 12, the Feast of Our Lady of Guadalupe, as a special day of prayer for the persecuted Church in Mexico.[90]

American involvement in the Mexican Church crisis took a major step forward in January 1935, when the Knights of Columbus entered the fray uninvited and without consulting the NCWC, as they had done with the Oregon school case a decade earlier. The Knights' Supreme Board of Directors, led by Supreme Knight Martin Carmody, adopted a resolution calling on President

Roosevelt "to make representations to the government of Mexico" that unless the persecution was "ended forthwith, further recognition of the Mexican Government will be withdrawn and diplomatic relations...will be severed."[91] On July 17, 1935, Roosevelt publicly endorsed those who were making "it clear that the American people and the Government believe in the freedom of religious worship, not only in the United States, but also in other nations."[92] Meanwhile the Knights lobbied Catholic senators to introduce a resolution in Congress noting the atrocities in Mexico and calling for an investigation by the Foreign Relations Committee. William Borah, the ranking Republican on the Foreign Relations Committee and normally an isolationist, introduced the initiative to the Senate in February 1935. Burke informed Hanna of these events and asked for advice about how the Administrative Committee should respond.[93]

The Borah Resolution called for a U.S. protest against the antireligious practices of Mexican government officials and the condemnation of "the cruelties and brutalities" presently perpetrated against the profession and practice of religious belief. Additionally, the resolution suggested hearings before the Foreign Relations Committee to obtain evidence that would inform America's response to the situation.[94] Burke again petitioned Hanna for advice, but John Mitty, Hanna's coadjutor archbishop (see chapter 12), replied that Hanna was under medical treatment after an accident and could not respond. He suggested that Burke's judgment would be accepted by Hanna.[95]

Americans lined up on both sides of the Borah Resolution. Michael Curley, archbishop of Baltimore, the Knights, and Archbishop Ruiz y Flores, the Mexican apostolic delegate in exile, formed a coalition to support the measure. The Administrative Committee was noncommittal. Opponents included the *New York Times*, which stated in an editorial entitled, "A Dangerous Resolution":

> If there is to be a Catholic revolution in Mexico, it will be the work of the natives and the American Government has no more to do with it than with the religious disturbances in Germany or in Spain. It would be a fine place to exhibit the

American principle which Mr. Borah and other Senators have been expounding for weeks, which is to have nothing to do with the burning questions of other countries.[96]

Meanwhile, Burke continued working behind the scenes with Roosevelt to ease tensions in Mexico.[97]

When the Borah Resolution became stalled in Congress, Catholics divided on the issue even more strongly. Burke, believing that he would be subpoenaed by the Foreign Relations Committee, sought advice from the bishops. While many were sympathetic to the resolution, none suggested an outright endorsement, which amounted to the Administrative Committee's rejecting the measure, although in a private rather than in a public forum. Curley was irate and threatened to repudiate the committee, even though Hanna had personally informed him that the bishops when polled had provided no support for measure.[98] The Baltimore ordinary might have been placated if he had known that the Administrative Committee was working on its own plan to resolve the Mexican crisis and that its rejection of Borah was based on a desire to control the Knights rather than on disagreement with the resolution's principles.[99] Finally in May 1935 the Administrative Committee issued a public statement revealing its ongoing work with the Roosevelt administration to formulate a response to the Mexican situation.

Despite the death of the Borah Resolution in committee and the absence of an American response to the situation in Mexico, tensions between the Church and the Mexican government began to ease in November 1935. Gradually more and more churches were opened and clergy allowed to function. Teachers were told to remove antireligious rhetoric from their curriculum; exiled bishops began to return. In August 1937 the Vatican appointed a new apostolic delegate, Luis Maria Martinez, the archbishop of Mexico City.[100]

Conclusion

The NCWC, formed in the wake of World War I, could not directly influence American international policy; however, the Administrative Committee voiced Catholic opinion on several significant international issues, and provided a forum for discussing and attempting to resolve several conflicts. Fearful that recognition of the Soviet Union was tantamount to recognition of godlessness, the Administrative Committee spoke for American Catholics in rejecting Roosevelt's recognition efforts. In Mexico, the Administrative Committee, and in particular the diplomacy of John Burke, restored the Church to a position of acceptance, redressing grievances perpetrated by an oppressive government that sought to eliminate all religious influence in the country. Hanna's influence in these matters was sometimes tangential and at other times direct. While Burke served as the chief negotiator, he did not act without the advice and consent of Hanna. As chairman of the Administrative Committee Hanna always guided the collective opinion and actions of the American hierarchy. In the international arena, he found new ways to be an archbishop for all people.

Chapter 11

SERVANT OF THE STATE IN THE 1930S

Edward Hanna's significant contribution as servant of both church and state highlighted his tenure as archbishop of San Francisco. Even before his appointment as local ordinary, his experience and reputation from civic work in Rochester led to his selection as a founding member and vice president of the California Commission of Immigration and Housing (CCIH) and his prompt involvement with local labor and unemployment. As his ecclesiastical duties increased, especially as administrative chairman of the National Catholic Welfare Conference (NCWC), Hanna's civic work diminished somewhat, although throughout the 1920s he continued to contribute significantly to wage arbitration boards in the city, to the CCIH, and to numerous humanitarian organizations. In the last four years of his service as archbishop, Hanna became more active in the civic sector on both state and national levels. Because of his experience and distinction, as well as his reputation for fairness and compassion, Hanna was asked to help rectify problems created by the Great Depression and to resolve labor disputes in California's cotton industry and in ports from Seattle to San Diego.

The Depression, Franklin Roosevelt, and American Catholics

Several issues were of dominant national interest in the 1920s. One was immigration restriction, as embodied in the passage of the 1917 literacy test, and the Johnson (1921) and Johnson-Reed (1924) acts. Another was prohibition, which divided the nation into "wets" and "drys" when the Eighteenth Amendment was ratified in January 1919 and the Volstead Act was passed in October of the same year. Implementation of the law was impossible: government enforcement agencies found it virtually impossible to prevent the small-scale production of alcohol. By the mid-1920s the failure of prohibition was obvious to all, with the possible exception of the Women's Christian Temperance Union (WCTU), which had worked long and hard for its passage. In February 1933 Congress passed the Twenty-first Amendment, repealing America's "experiment." On December 5 the measure was ratified by Utah, the thirty-sixth and decisive state.

The decade was also a period of heightened religious tension. The clash between fundamentalism and modernism was most explicitly played out in the summer of 1925 at the infamous "Scopes Monkey Trial." William Jennings Bryan, champion of the fundamentalists, and Clarence Darrow, defender of the modernists, locked horns over the teaching of Darwin's theory of evolution in Tennessee's public schools. While John Scopes, a high school biology teacher, was convicted of violating the Tennessee statute, the trial virtually destroyed the credibility of the fundamentalist position for most Americans.[1] The face of anti-Catholicism once again appeared, through the reemergence of the Ku Klux Klan, which, under the direction of Hiram Wesley Evans, preached the nineteenth-century creed of Protestant, white, rural, and American. Short-lived but ferocious, the Klan was shamed into obscurity when one of its "generals," D. C. Stephenson, was convicted of manslaughter in the death of a young woman with whom he was involved in a scandalous affair.[2]

Prohibition, immigration, religious fundamentalism, and the perceived euphoria of the 1920s in which these issues arose, were eclipsed almost overnight in October 1929, when a series of severe market drops on the New York Stock Exchange transformed American economic prosperity to misery. On October 21 the market dipped sharply but recovered. Over the next week the market continued to fall, with the steepest decline occurring on October 29, "Black Tuesday." By mid-November stock prices had plummeted by 40 percent. Between 1929 and 1932 unemployment rose from 3.1 percent to 24 percent; in the same period over five thousand banks closed with a cumulative loss to investors of over $2.3 billion. Production of goods and services declined 51 percent by 1932 from their 1929 high.[3]

President Herbert Hoover, personally wealthy but reputed to be a man of compassion as well as a good organizer, believed answers to America's greatest financial disaster would be found in individualism. Like many other Americans, Hoover initially saw the crash as a temporary downturn; he never understood the basic weakness of the nation's financial base. He asked for a spirit of voluntarism to right America's economic ship, and was unable to change course when his methods did not work. He remained antistatist, unconvinced of the need for federal aid as part of the solution. Eventually Hoover was branded as an insensitive reactionary. Paulist priest and commentator on America James Gillis summarized what many thought:

> Alas, poor President Hoover. Never since Washington have people expected more of a man elected to lead them, and never has any chief executive proved so disappointing. But one thing all good Americans desire—a leader worthy of the name, to direct us in these distressing circumstances. May heaven send us such a one.[4]

President Franklin Delano Roosevelt, inaugurated on March 4, 1933, was the man the American people chose to lead them from the darkness of the Depression to a new day; the New Deal was his plan of action. After World War I, trends toward management, bureaucracy, and "bigness" were everywhere in American society, a product of the mergers and vastly extended companies from the 1920s boon period. To manage this bigness, Roosevelt chose the New Deal, "a descendant of Progressive reform," as his tool. The historian David Shannon has called the New Deal "a complex set of compromises" generated by outside pressures, which Roosevelt molded into a workable program.[5] Roosevelt fervently believed that the federal government could combat the Depression and relieve those most sorely injured by it, and, to promote the general welfare, he was willing to compromise and modify the independence that had traditionally existed between government and private enterprise. He was no opponent of capitalism but felt that the current emergency demanded innovative steps that might have been undesirable in normal economic times.

Roosevelt viewed his election as a mandate from the American people for immediate action. Within the first one hundred days of his presidency the initial phase of the New Deal, based on recovery, became the law of the land and attacked the Depression on three different fronts: agriculture, unemployment, and business and labor.[6]

At the heart of the New Deal was the National Industrial Recovery Act (NIRA) of June 16, 1933, and its creation, the National Recovery Administration (NRA). Written to stimulate both business and labor, the NIRA satisfied employers' demands for government support of trade association agreements that would stabilize production and prevent price slashing, while protecting workers' wages, hours, and the right to bargain collectively. In an attempt to increase buying power as rapidly as prices and wages, a $3.3 billion public works appropriation was appended to the act to "prime the pump" of the economy.[7]

The nation, thrilled that Roosevelt and his New Deal seemed to be stemming the tide of the Depression and effecting recovery, embarked on a honeymoon period with its new president. The Blue Eagle poster (which stated "We Do Our Part") appeared in shop windows across the nation, indicating the shop owners' support of the NRA. Catholics were enthusiastic about Roosevelt, and they rejoiced in the two Catholics he had chosen for cabinet positions.[8] Leading Catholic intellectuals advocated social positions akin to that of the resident, enhancing his popularity with the rank and file of the Church. The New Deal was well received by Catholics, who saw it as based on Catholic social teaching,[9] which held the government responsible for meeting the needs of the unemployed and other marginalized members of society. Thus, when Roosevelt launched his campaign to curtail the power of Wall Street and regulate the economy, the hierarchy initially supported his efforts both personally and institutionally. Cardinals Patrick Hayes (New York), William O'Connell (Boston), and George Mundelein (Chicago), Archbishop Hanna, and Bishop Karl Alter (Toledo) were all in the Roosevelt camp. The best-known organizations, including the

National Council of Catholic Men (NCCM), the National Council of Catholic Women (NCCW), and the National Catholic Welfare Conference (NCWC), strongly supported the NRA.[10]

John A. Ryan and Francis Haas perfectly illustrated Catholic support for Roosevelt's policies, especially the NRA and the agencies it generated. Ryan, labeled the "Right Reverend New Dealer" by his nemesis, Charles Coughlin, equated Roosevelt's economic policy with social justice. He served as a member of the Industrial Appeals Board of the NRA and promoted the president's New Deal through his work with the social action department of the NCWC as well as through his teaching and writings. His biographer, Francis Broderick, says, however, that Ryan's influence over the president should not be overestimated, since the two men met on only four occasions and corresponded a mere half-dozen times during their government service.[11] The Milwaukee cleric Francis Haas, who was closely associated with Roosevelt's labor policies, argued for a just wage and the importance of cooperation and harmony among industry, labor, and government. During the life of the NRA Haas served on the Labor Advisory Board and its successor, the National Labor Board.[12]

The California State Unemployment Commission

California was hit so hard by the Great Depression that the state government was forced to act. On January 23, 1931, the California Legislature established the State Unemployment Commission, comprising five members appointed by the governor and holding office at his pleasure. The initiative was signed into law by Governor James Rolph on February 3.[13] The commission was considered "immediately necessary in view of the present business depression and unemployment situation…which has thrown large numbers of the citizens of the State out of employment…threatening the peace and well being of the people of the State generally."[14] The commission was authorized to conduct surveys and studies, to investigate the effect and extent of the Depression and the nature and causes of unemployment, and to recommend legislation that would bring relief and would mitigate similar problems in the future.[15]

On August 25, 1931, Governor Rolph appointed the commission's members. Archbishop Hanna once again was asked to serve as chairman. Other members were Rheba Crawford Splivalo of San Francisco, director of the State Department of Social Welfare, Henry J. Bauer, a Los Angeles attorney, O. K. Cushing, a San Francisco attorney, and Will J. French, director of the State Department of Industrial Relations. On September 21 the commission appointed Dr. Louis Bloch, a statistician for the Division of Labor Statistics and Law Enforcement of the State Department of Industrial Relations, its secretary and director of surveys. Hanna was grateful to serve, believing that a moral revival was necessary "to organize the wealth and power of the country in such a way that no one need go hungry.[16] He warned Rolph, however, against inflated expectations: "I hope that you appreciate the great difficulty of the work you have entrusted to our care, and I know in your great kindness of heart you will not expect too much of those whom you have so singularly honored."[17]

From the beginning Hanna urged the commission toward its mandated goals. A staff of economists and investigators was engaged (1) to study the causes and effects of unemployment; (2) to study problems associated with emergency unemployment relief; (3) to study methods of employment stabilization; (4) to design public works programs during the business depression; (5) to review needs for unemployment insurance and compensation; (6) to study the need for a state economic council; (7) to identify the need for public and private employment agencies; and (8) to study the possibility of a shorter work week.[18]

Statistics compiled at the commission's behest illustrated the gravity of the state's economic problems and where corrections might be initiated. In June 1932 unemployment was estimated at seven hundred thousand, 28 percent of the state's work force, but its distribution was very uneven. Los Angeles County's unemployment alone was 344,000, 49.2 percent of the total. Manufacturing workers were especially hard hit, with employment dropping 41 percent between 1929 and 1932. Payroll fell by an even more precipitous 53 percent during the same period. Between 1929 and 1932 California experienced forty-nine bank failures, and exports fell by 53.6 percent.[19] The commission concluded that the major cause of the economic problems was the disproportionate distribution of the returns from production, which was producing vast discrepancies between savings and spending. In other words, many workers were being deprived of the ability to purchase the goods they produced. The commission's final report stated, "This baneful cause of unemployment is present in our entire economic system and can not [sic] be said to be confined to any one State in the Union."[20]

The first few meetings of the commission were devoted mainly to organizational matters. At the first meeting, held on September 3, 1931, at Hanna's residence in San Francisco, a series of hearings was planned, to gauge the pulse of the various constituencies in the state. On September 15 the commission again met, establishing rules for future meetings and sketching the contours of the body's overall mission.[21] In October, Hanna wrote to Rolph telling him that the commission believed families should be its top priority. On November 13 the commission recommended that the governor appoint a special committee to explore the establishment of state camps for single unemployed men. Rolph acted on the suggestion only three days later, appointing a State Labor Camp Committee.[22] In December 1931 Hanna wrote a more extensive progress report to Rolph on the commission's work, indicating that the main problem handicapping the commission was the employers' refusal to share the available work among all workers:

> That "the best cure for unemployment is employment" is a truism which cannot be over-emphasized. The workers of California have been willing to share their work opportunity with their less than fortunate brethren with a spirit of alacrity which betokens the finest kind of altruism and citizenship. Those employers of labor in our state, who have not as yet given the most careful consideration to the possibilities of affording more employment by shortening work periods, should be awakened to the responsibilities which devolve upon them as employers and citizens who can and should do everything within their power to alleviate the distress of the unemployed.[23]

In April and May 1932, the commission conducted eight hearings, in Los Angeles, San Diego, San Francisco, Oakland, Fresno, and Sacramento. Business and commercial organizations, labor groups, members of the legislature, and state and county officials were invited to give public (oral or written) testimony to the commission. Over 150 individuals and seventy-four organizations submitted testimony and about one thousand attended the sessions[24] General topics raised at the hearings included the causes and effects of unemployment, methods of unemployment relief, techniques of employment stabilization, need for unemployment insurance, and the establishment of public and private employment agencies. Topics specific to the state raised at the hearings included the need for a permanent state economic council, the function of state labor camps, and the care of transient and other migratory workers, especially those in the agricultural industry.[25] While corrective measures were offered, the emphasis was on preventive actions, with state and municipal governments urged to find constructive programs aimed at solving problems before they occurred. Preventive measures suggested during the hearings included emergency unemployment relief (state aid), creation of unemployment insurance, mandated reductions in daily work hours, establishment of a state bureau of industrial training, extension of the operation of state labor camps, and automatic adjustment of the minimum wage based on increases in the cost of living.[26]

The commission's report to Governor Rolph followed the basic recommendations arising from the hearings and stressed the importance of mandating a reduction in the numbers of hours one could work. The commission recommended that all public works be placed on a five-day, six-hour-per-day work week "in order that employment may be given to as many employees as possible."[27] Hanna himself had earlier suggested an even more stringent program of work-hour restrictions, without reducing hourly wage rates, that would include all industrial, commercial, and professional enterprises.[28]

The commission's report also suggested that to meet immediate needs, the state provide $20 million in loans to counties and municipalities for unemployment relief. The report proposed that a State Department of Industrial Relations be created to oversee public works projects and to encourage businesses to maximize employment by spreading tasks among workers as much as possible. The commission recommended legislating a system of compulsory unemployment reserves (insurance) to be supported by contributions from employers and employees. Finally, the commission recommended that its successor, a state economic council, be created to continue studying and interpreting unemployment problems.[29]

The California State Emergency Relief Commission

Like the Unemployment Commission, the California State Emergency Relief Commission was created to help residents of California recover from the Depression. In March 1933 Governor Rolph, acting on the recommendation of the Unemployment Commission, appointed a State Emergency Relief Administration (SERA) of eleven members. When President Roosevelt signed the Federal Emergency Relief Act as part of his New Deal legislation on May 12, the California state agency was incorporated into the federal program, with R. C. Branion as its director.[30] Its purpose was to distribute and administer all county, state, and federal relief funds in California. Moreover,

> [the] SERA aims to keep those helped at their trade or profession so they will not lose their efficiency but will be ready to assume their place in private employment when normal times return. Above all, by having its clients work for what they receive, SERA seeks to preserve the workers' self respect.[31]

Following the recommendation of the Unemployment Commission, the SERA adopted the philosophy of work relief as opposed to direct relief.[32]

The work provided by the SERA resembled the wide-ranging tasks sponsored by the Federal Works Progress Administration (WPA). The SERA sponsored jobs such as dental hygienics and traffic surveys, literary research and news writing, preservation of books, artistic decoration of buildings, and photographic services.[33]

SERA jobs were approved by the state and funded using federal monies that were parceled out on the county level.

While the SERA distributed relief funds, the Emergency Relief Commission reviewed applications and made recommendations for awards. Thirteen commission members were appointed (eleven actually served) by Governor Rolph between March 30 and June 10, 1933, and Hanna was asked to serve as chair.[34] Accepting his appointment, Hanna wrote to Rolph, "I thought after I finished your Unemployment Commission that I might be free from the task of carrying out its recommendations. However, I gladly accept the further burden you place upon me, and I will do all in my power to aid you in carrying out its provisions."[35]

Hanna dove into his new responsibilities with his customary energy. He communicated with Harry Hopkins, Federal Emergency Relief administrator, who "placed responsibility upon the California Emergency Relief Commission for the administration of Federal funds made available...[and] full authority to make allocations out of such monies to counties or political subdivisions."[36] By November Hanna's commission was ready to allocate funds, but no counties had yet officially submitted requests.[37] When the requests finally arrived, the commission made every effort to apply uniform standards for relief awards throughout the state.[38]

Hanna's tenure as chairman of the Emergency Relief Commission was short. On August 1, 1934, he wrote to Governor Frank Merriam, "Owing to my ecclesiastical duties and my position on the National Longshoremen's Arbitration Board, I ask to be relieved immediately of the position of Chairman of the State Emergency Relief Commission. I feel I am not able to give the matter the attention it deserves."[39] Hanna also turned his attention to the growing problems present in California's Civilian Conservation Corps (CCC) camps. He stated that the religious welfare of the men in these camps was "a serious matter of concern to me as Archbishop" and asked local pastors to visit the camps weekly and provide a monthly report on "the religious condition of the men."[40]

The California Planning Board

As the 1930s progressed Hanna continued to serve the state of California, but now in a capacity not directly related to the Great Depression. In July 1933 the National Planning Board, an agency of the Federal Public Works Administration, was established. In a move similar to the formation of the SERA, Governor Rolph in January 1934 formed the State Planning Board to map out public works and conservation programs, partly funded by federal emergency relief monies, and to develop a long-term development plan for California.[41] Hanna was appointed vice chairman, but his main contribution was as chairman of the Committee on Legislation, one of the board's eleven advisory committees.[42]

The board met regularly every two weeks, alternating between northern and southern California sites. Hanna attended meetings, but his role appears to have been minimal. In March 1935 he told Governor Merriam and John C. Austin, chairman of the State Planning Board, that he wished to retire "due to the infirmities of advancing years." Austin was grateful to Hanna, even though his tenure was short: "I want to thank you for the kind and considerate treatment that I have received at your hands while acting as Chairman of the Board."[43]

The 1933 Cotton Strike

Edward Hanna ended his service to the state doing what he had begun with in Rochester: settling labor disputes. Rolph called on him once more when a violent and widespread strike hit California's cotton industry in 1933. The scope and details of this conflict are beyond the realm of this work,[44] but Hanna's role in it is an integral part of his life story.

The heavy losses that farmers experienced in the Great Depression were passed on to agricultural workers in the form of reduced wages. Between 1929 and 1932 California farm incomes fell considerably, but cotton workers' wages fell even more severely during the same period: from $1.50 per 100 pounds picked to 40 cents per 100 pounds, their lowest level since 1910. To make matters worse, farm workers averaged only 5.9 months of work per year. California's cotton growers were finding it difficult to keep disgruntled workers happy, especially as they began to realize that mobility made them valuable and that they could move on if conditions and wages in one location were unsatisfactory.[45]

In 1933, California was a hotbed of agricultural strikes, with thirty-one actions idling forty-eight thousand workers; in comparison, the rest of the United States that year experienced thirty farm strikes involving only eight thousand workers. Pea pickers in Alameda and Santa Clara counties in April, cherry pickers in Santa Clara, sugar beet pickers in Oxnard, peach pickers in the Central Valley in August, and grape harvesters in Lodi in September all went on strike before the bloody confrontation in October between cotton pickers and owners throughout the San Joaquin Valley.[46] The imminence of the cotton strike was obvious, but, according to the historian Cletus Daniel, Governor Rolph, when pressured by both sides, "chose the path of political expediency and did nothing."[47] The conflict that arose "has lived on in the writing of numerous historians, social scientists, social critics, and novelists to a degree unsurpassed by any other agricultural revolt of the period."[48]

The California cotton strike of 1933 pitted two rival groups against each other in a violent and at times deadly battle. The workers were represented by the Canning and Agricultural Workers Industrial Union (CAWIU), considered militant by some and thought to be associated with Communists by others. Local newspapers warned that the imminent strike was the beginning of a Communist conspiracy to overthrow the government and confiscate private property in the Valley.[49] CAWIU leaders met with workers and hammered out a set of demands: one dollar per one hundred pounds picked, no discrimination on the basis of sex or race, hiring through union locals, and living quarters provided free. Growers were offering sixty cents per one hundred pounds picked. The stage was set for a strike scheduled to begin on October 4.

When both sides refused to budge, the strike began, with Corcoran as its hub and extending one hundred miles north and south and forty miles east and west, encompassing Tulare, Kern, Kings, and Madera counties.[50] Strikers patrolled the hundred-mile perimeter, looking for fields being picked and encouraging workers to stop. They blocked highways, stopping the delivery of scales to weigh products. Growers responded by harassing workers, attempting to lure them onto private property so they could be arrested; they also hired strike breakers. Regular workers were warned that if they did not return to work on the owners' terms they would be evicted; many suffered this fate. The growers also tried to get the four-acre Corcoran camp disbanded, asking the Board of Health to condemn it as unsanitary. However, needed improvements were made and thus the strikers remained. By October 9, some twelve thousand workers were on the picket line.[51] The historian Don Mitchell has commented, "Peaceful means had proved inadequate to the task of breaking the main base of workers' power during the strike."[52]

The first attempt to settle the strike was through mediation. Rabbi Irving Reichart, a friend of Hanna's and director of mediation for the State National Recovery Administration (NRA) Board, implored Rolph "to end the threat against Constitutional government in California" and order mediation.[53] Rolph appointed California State Labor Commissioner Frank MacDonald to lead the mediation effort, but growers immediately refused this option, declaring "they preferred to handle the situation in their own way."[54] The growers felt Rolph was against them: "Why should we mediate with Governor Rolph's agents? Every one of them is on the side of the strikers. They can't see our side at all. All they want is to get something for the strikers. We can't and will not buck that combination."[55]

On October 10 the strike turned deadly, rendering prophetic the October 9 *San Francisco Examiner*'s description of the valley as a "smoldering volcano." In two separate incidents three workers were killed by growers. Two pickers died and fourteen were seriously injured at Pixley, fifteen miles north of Tulare. In Arvin, sixty miles south, a third worker died from gunshots.[56] Public outrage demanded action when initially no one was arrested for the obvious crimes.

Pressured on both sides, Rolph called for both mediation and an end to the violence, stating, "Unless the parties submit their disputes to arbitration and abide by the results of the arbitration I will have to take some other definite stand." Rolph met with both sides and asked that each side provide a representative to serve on a mediation board with a third member of his choosing.[57] Ordering emergency food relief for workers at the Corcoran camp, he optimistically predicted the strike would end in twenty-four hours.

As tensions rose, George Creel, local administrator of the NRA in California since August, threatened federal intervention unless both sides accepted a three-man fact-finding commission, to be appointed by Rolph, which would investigate the strike and propose a settlement. The governor once again turned to Hanna, asking his trusted friend to chair the commission, along with Professor Ira B. Cross at the University of California at Berkeley and Dr. Tully Knoles, president of the College of the Pacific.[58] The growers and the union reluctantly agreed to the commission, but the union insisted that workers would not return to the fields without an acceptable settlement.[59]

The commission met at Visalia on October 19 and 20, hearing from the growers on the first day and workers on the second. Hanna stated at the outset,

> This commission was appointed by the Governor and we come only to help you. We want to get the facts of this case and come to an agreeable settlement. I want to emphasize that we are here to seek facts and not hear disputes. Out of the facts we ought to be able to find a settlement.[60]

The commission found itself under attack almost from the outset. Growers challenged the board's impartiality and stated that no compromise on wages could be made since sixty cents per one hundred pounds was a fair wage. After listening to both sides, the commission then interviewed George Creel, who opined that seventy-five cents per one hundred pounds was the most that growers could pay and maintain their livelihood.[61]

The commission's report, published on October 23, stated, "Without question the civil rights of the strikers have been violated." It continued, arguing that workers needed the kind of protection described in the laws of the state and the federal constitutions. The committee recommended, probably as a result of Creel's influence, that the standard pay rate be raised to seventy-five cents per one hundred pounds.[62] While tensions remained high and neither side was fully satisfied, workers returned to the fields on October 27, with the higher wage in place.[63]

The 1934 West Coast Dock Strike

Edward Hanna's leadership in the arbitration of labor disputes reached its apex at the twilight of his episcopal career, when a 1934 dock strike idled West Coast ports from Seattle to San Diego. From the perspective of San Francisco, the docks were a critical part of the local economy. The historian Kevin Starr has described San Francisco's working environment in 1934: "Male, volatile, close to a frontier life of men in groups, working San Francisco coalesced along the waterfront." The waterfront "drove the economic engine of San Francisco."[64]

The roots of the 1934 longshoremen's strike led back to June 13, 1933, when President Franklin Roosevelt signed the National Industrial Relations Act (NIRA). Section 7a of the NIRA encouraged the International Longshoremen's Association (ILA)—which had often sought a return to the San Francisco waterfront since its action in the union dock strike of 1916 (see chapter 5)—to once again seek recognition on the docks. The new law allowed the ILA to re-form its local organization, eventually becoming the union of choice on the Embarcadero by 1934. Back in business, the ILA soon began to press the Waterfront Employers' Union (WEU) for higher wages and shorter working hours. In December 1933 the WEU voluntarily offered a pay raise (75 to 85 cents per hour) to all dock workers in the ILA. However, the ILA was not content with the WEU's concession, and in January 1934, through the efforts of George Creel, the ILA requested a meeting with the WEU to press its demands. The WEU refused, claiming that the ILA did not represent all dock workers.

Tensions began to escalate in February, when the ILA convention pressed for wage and hour changes along the entire West Coast. On February 25 the convention voted for a proposed wage of $1.00 per hour and six hours per day for the union. The shortened hours were seen as desirable because they would result in employment for out-of-work union members. Another key issue was the union's demand to control the hiring halls. On March 7, 1934, the convention called for a strike vote unless employers met their demands by March 17. When the deadline came and went, the San Francisco ILA voted to walk out on March 23.

Because of the gravity of the situation along the entire West Coast, on March 21, George Creel asked President Roosevelt to intervene. The next day Roosevelt appointed a special commission to investigate the grievances and, it was hoped, to settle the dispute and avoid the strike. The commission members were Henry F. Grady, chairman of the San Francisco Regional Board and dean of the College of Commerce at the University of California at Berkeley, Dr. J. L. Leonard, Regional Labor Board chief in Los Angeles and professor at the University of Southern California, and Judge C. A. Reynolds, Regional Labor Board head in Seattle. In response to the formation of the commission William J. Lewis, San Francisco district president of the ILA, postponed the strike.

The presidential commission met between March 28 and April 1, and although the board's recommendations (never published) were accepted by the ILA, the employers represented by the WEU rejected them. The commission disbanded with little to show for its efforts. Similarly, a San Francisco mediation board, meeting on April 24, failed to work out a solution. On April 30 the ILA designated May 9 as the strike date, and at 8:00 PM on that day twelve thousand longshoremen from San Diego to Seattle walked off the job.

The longshoremen leader was Alfred Renton (Harry) Bridges, a thirty-four-year-old Australian immigrant. Often accused of being a Communist by his opponents, Bridges nonetheless held the respect and loyalty of San Francisco's waterfront workers. The historian Robert Cherny claims that Bridges "became a leading—and uncompromising—figure in the strike" and "personified militant, left wing unionism on the Pacific Coast."[65] By May 19 local papers listed Bridges as the strike leader.

The strike continued through May and June, with no settlement in sight. The walkout generated many sympathetic actions, and the Sailors Union of the Pacific, the Pacific Coast Marine Firemen, and the Marine Cooks and Stewards Association of the Pacific Coast joined the ILA strike. By mid-May, 34,700 maritime and waterfront workers along the whole West Coast were on strike. With West Coast shipping at a standstill, losses began extending to businesses dependent on moving their products along the water- ways. This situation led the governors of California, Oregon, and Washington on May 15 to request federal assistance. Roosevelt responded by the creation of a three-man panel, the National Longshoremen Labor Board (NLB), to settle the dispute once workers had returned to their jobs. The board was headed by Archbishop Hanna, who was joined by Edward F. McGrady, assis- tant secretary of labor, and O. K. Cushing, a prominent San Francisco attorney who had worked with Hanna previously on boards. The June 26 telegram appointing Hanna stated: "You are hereby appointed Chairman of the National Longshoremen Labor Board [NLB] under the joint resolution of June Nineteenth, pub- lic resolution forty-four of the Seventy-Third Congress. This appointment is effective immediately."[66] Hanna responded, "Honored by your confidence. I will do all in my power to carry out your mandate."[67] The archbishop immediately offered to the striking parties his philosophy to reach a resolution:

> When both labor and capital attain a deeper understanding of the obligations they owe to the moral law, to Christ and his teachings of brotherly love, and the people as a whole and to each other, then and not until then will come some solution of the grave industrial problems of the day.[68]

Hanna's reputation made both sides confident of a settlement. One writer stated, "This is the man who has gained national promi- nence by his work for the betterment of labor conditions in San Francisco."[69] The *San Francisco News* predicted Hanna's participa- tion would be "the crowning achievement…of a lifetime devoted to the service of human relationships."[70]

Under Hanna's lead the local Church made its voice heard on this untenable situation. Historians William Issel and James Collins have characterized the latter years of Hanna's administration as a time when the Church "promoted the legitimacy of moderate and conservative labor organizations while condemning extremists of the labor left and the business right."[71] The *Monitor* articulated this vision in a June 9 front-page editorial: "The rights of the ship-owners over their ships do not give them the right to impoverish the whole community; nor do the rights of the striking workers include the right to pursue their aims regardless of the consequences to the third party in the dispute, namely the people who are directly involved, but who depend upon cargoes for their livelihoods and sustenance." The editorial concluded, "These rights are obscured because of the *laissez-faire* extremists on the one hand and the Communist fanatics on the other." The *Monitor* encouraged Catholic employers in maritime operations to read and follow the precepts of the social encyclicals, especially with respect to issues of capital and labor.[72]

Disgruntled workers were not content to stand idly by and wait for bureaucrats and union officials to find a solution. As Issel and Collins point out: "The 1932–1934 period was marked by increased militancy among San Francisco workers, with the high point of activism coming during 'the July days' of the coast-wide waterfront strike." Hanna personally interceded, speaking with the economist Sam Kagel and unionist E. B. O'Grady in a futile effort to end the violence.[73]

On June 16, in an attempt to resolve the strike, Mayor Angelo Rossi called a meeting of representatives from all sides. One notable absentee was Harry Bridges or any representative from the local strike committee, although the ILA was represented by its international president, Joseph Ryan from New York. The agreement brokered was rejected by the local ILA as Ryan surrendered two of the union's most significant demands, the closed shop and control of the hiring halls. Ryan's blunder in not speaking with the local strike committee or Bridges only strengthened the latter's position within the union membership.[74]

With no resolution immediately forthcoming, violence ensued. On July 2, the Industrial Association, which had taken over the employers' fight from the WEU, Hanna, and Rossi, asked Governor Frank Morrison (James Rolph had died from a massive heart attack on June 2) for assistance (with the National Guard if necessary) to open the port that had been closed since the May 9 strike. The next day violence erupted on the docks to counter the Industrial Association's collective effort. On July 5, which became known as "Bloody Thursday," two died and over seventy others were injured from flying projectiles.[75] In response, the governor sent 4,600 guardsmen, who arrived by July 16.

Meanwhile, the NLB arbitration board met for the first time, between July 9 and 11, 1934, at the San Francisco Federal Court Building. The longshoremen insisted on five points: (1) They would receive satisfactory guarantees before returning to the docks; (2) all strikebreakers would be discharged; (3) there would be no employment discrimination against strike participants; (4) pending decision of the NLB, temporary hiring halls would be established, jointly controlled by unions and employers; and (5) any pay increase recommended by the board would be retroactive to the day workers returned.[76] Historians of the strike note that from the outset the NLB faced two severe problems. First, the board members knew little about the situation and the nature of the maritime industry. One labor leader at the time wrote, "Their minds had no more practical application to the subject than would a group of bricklayers called to judge the merits of a medical controversy."[77] The other problem was that the dockworkers had convinced the San Francisco Labor Council (SFLC) to consolidate all striking unions into one General Strike Committee for the entire West Coast, thus strengthening the union position. Bridges knew that he could not defeat the guardsmen sent by the governor, but he could organize a general strike, although this was risky as it could create a backlash against the union. Thus, Bridges and the SFLC told the NLB that a general strike for the majority of San Francisco workers had been set for July 16.[78]

Hanna wasted no time seeking solutions to the board's problems and to avert the general strike. On July 14 in a statewide radio address, he asked both sides to cooperate with the NLB in finding ways to avoid the citywide general strike. In line with the June 9 *Monitor* editorial, he invoked established principles of social and individual justice, based on the papal encyclicals *Rerum novarum* (1891) and *Quadragesimo anno* (1931) as the foundation on which a settlement could be built. He added that preserving the rights of both sides must become a priority in designing the settlement. He summarized his argument by describing the efficacy of arbitration:

> I desire to make an earnest appeal to all parties concerned to
> let reason rule and to exhaust every effort possible to reach a
> peaceful and just conclusion....The Board feels that settlement
> can be arrived at only by arbitration. In view of the situation
> which has been precipitated by the failure to reach an agree-
> ment, it is the duty of every party to this controversy, to them-
> selves, to their families, to the public, and to their government
> to make every effort humanly possible to adjust differences.[79]

When union leaders and employers could not work out a settlement, the dreaded general strike began on July 16, as scheduled.
The action lasted until July 19, when the General Strike
Committee, over the objections of Harry Bridges, voted to end the
action and submit the entire dispute to the NLB for arbitration.
Simultaneously, on July 20, John Francis Neylan, legal advisor to
the publisher William Randolph Hearst and, more important, a
prominent Catholic lawyer and friend of Hanna's, hosted a meeting of the WEU, the Industrial Association, and the SFLC. He told
the assembled representatives that arbitration was the only rational
solution to the strike. Neylan ultimately succeeded: on July 25 all
unions agreed to arbitrate their disputes before the Presidential
Board. The general strike in San Francisco and the West Coast
dock strike ended on July 30, with workers returning the next day,
after eighty-three days off work.[80] The Masters, Mates and Pilots
West Coast local no. 90 in San Francisco promulgated the return-
to-work order: "We are pleased to notify you at this time that all
licensed personnel on the West Coast have been directed to return
to their respective positions on Tuesday July 31 at 6AM and that
the strike now in force will terminate as of that date and time."[81]
Both labor and management agreed to submit future conflicts to
the Labor Board, and to elect San Francisco union representatives
who would meet with employers for collective bargaining. The
ILA, through its mouthpiece, the Union of Masters, Mates and
Pilots, stated, "We wish to assure you that we intend to cooperate
fully with your Board during the period of readjustment."[82] The
workers' final stipulation in the return-to-work order was that
employees not be required to work more than fifteen hours continuously nor more than forty-eight hours in any week.

Hanna's influence and his experience on the impartial wage boards in San Francisco during the period of 1921 to 1928 helped bring the strike to a close. His reputation for fairness and sensitivity made him a natural choice in the arbitration of what is so dear to all workers, namely, wages and working hours. An account published five days after the strike settlement aptly summarized the respect he enjoyed:

> It was a crisis that called for the leadership of Edward J. Hanna, the man, not the prelate. It was his famed sense of fair play, his well known passion to help faltering mankind, that brought him as an arbitrator into this strike. The fact that he was also a shining disciple of the Prince of Peace was quite incidental. And yet it was to be expected that in taking up his role as mediator, he should turn to the law laid down by the teachings of his calling and apply it to the case in point.[83]

The National Longshoremen's Board convened from August 8 to September 25, 1934, meeting twelve times in San Francisco, then moving to Portland on August 29, working in Seattle September 10–12, and in Los Angeles September 17–19, and returning to San Francisco for its final meeting on September 24.[84] Hanna asked that all parties depend on the board to provide justice in finding a resolution.[85]

The *San Francisco Examiner* pointed to Hanna's "competency, experience and standing as a well respected participant in civic affairs" as his principal qualifications for his position on the NLB. Hanna was described as a "champion of the underdog" with "warm sympathy…for those who toil." He was even more noteworthy for his belief in justice and fairness for all.[86] This nonpartisan attitude was clear when he stated:

> The enumeration of the foregoing principles which I believe to be just and in accordance with American and Christian ideals, clarify the entire problem. If the parties to this dispute are willing to accept these principles, I am willing to proceed as a member....I have always and now believe in the fundamental

principles of democracy, in a ruling of reason, and in the principles of christian *[sic]* charity.[87]

Time, however, was taking its toll on Hanna. One historian has noted that while he was "a very fine man" some contemporaries observed that "he'd aged a bit...he wasn't as fully alive to the situation as he would have been some years before."[88]

During the seven weeks of testimony, the board determined that employers had discriminated against longshoremen for their union activity but that current wages paid to longshoremen were the highest ever paid to the trade on the West Coast, even during the days of greater prosperity before the Depression.

Hanna was keenly interested in the issues of wages, the presence of hazardous working conditions, hours of work (especially consecutive hours without a break for meals), and hiring and firing criteria used on the docks.[89] But he identified control of the hiring halls as the pivotal issue raised during the hearings outside San Francisco. He proposed that the ILA assume exclusive control of the halls, arguing that they would run smoothly so long as the association maintained high standards of worker competence. However, he felt employees should be able to arbitrate regarding those standards.[90] He summarized his nonpartisan stance:

> I stand squarely for the right of all workers in any business or industry to associate themselves into unions to better themselves individually, in body, mind and property. I believe that the membership of each union should be represented by duly authorized agents and that the members of such a union should abide by the decisions and acts of such duly authorized representatives. I believe that each union should make it a matter of solemn obligation on its part and on the part of its individual members, that each give an honest day's work for an honest day's pay and that the union itself should conscientiously penalize any attempt of a member to give less.[91]

The award granted by the board on October 12 was a compromise that seemed to satisfy both sides. First, the NLB declared that labor's call for reduced hours was unreasonable. The formal award statement said, "The demand for a six-hour day and a thirty-hour week averaged over a period of four weeks is not a reasonable or satisfactory method of adjusting and solving the problem of labor reserve."[92] On the other hand, addressing Hanna's concern about consecutive hours of work without food, the board suggested time and a half over normal wages for anyone working more than five straight hours without food. The award set wages at $1.00 per hour with $1.50 per hour for overtime. Straight time was defined as 8:00 AM to midnight, with all work between midnight and 8:00 AM and all meal hours and holidays considered overtime periods. Working hours were set at seven hours per day with thirty-five hours per week being normal.[93] The NLB hoped peace would now reign:

> We earnestly recommend that the employers and workers who are parties to the arbitration agreement endeavor to compose their differences in accordance to what we conceive to be principles of natural justice which come down to us as part of the eternal law, and without the proper application of which there can be no lasting industrial peace.[94]

The end of the strike and the NLB award brought Hanna many accolades. Mayor Angelo Rossi congratulated Hanna for his work, which brought "satisfaction to your Board, as…to us."[95] One local businessman expressed the feelings of many when he thanked Hanna for his work: "The people of California owe you a great debt for your fine performance of a very difficult task."[96] Hanna's role was seen as a shining example of New Deal Catholic activism while reaffirming "his reputation as an impartial arbiter and moderate labor advocate."[97] When the board disbanded upon the completion of its work, President Roosevelt wrote to Hanna, "May I take the occasion to express to you my sincere appreciation for assuming the burdens of a very difficult situation at a most crucial time and for your splendid achievement in promoting peace." He was also praised by Secretary of Labor Frances Perkins, and a local paper claimed, "This was his [Hanna's] most important task in the long list of his achievements for peace."[98]

Conclusion

Ever vigilant to the needs of the civic community, Edward Hanna always placed himself at the service of those needs. While continuing his duties as local ordinary and as administrative chairman of the NCWC, he took on additional tasks as chairman of the California Unemployment Commission and State Emergency Relief Commission and as a member of the State Planning Board. He led statewide and national efforts to end two significant strikes that had crippled agriculture in California and shut down shipping on the nation's West Coast. Governor Rolph chose his close friend Hanna for the state board, and Roosevelt chose him for the National Longshoreman's Board, because of his acceptance in the local community, his sense of justice, and his vast experience. In both cases Hanna was able to effect fair solutions that promoted the common good, capping his long and distinguished career in the public sector through service to workers and their families. His efforts were consistent with his personal ethic and the continuing endeavor of social Catholicism in the twentieth century.

Chapter 12

THE FINAL YEARS— RETIREMENT AND DEATH

Since the time of his ordination at the Cathedral of St. John Lateran in Rome in 1885, Edward Hanna had faithfully served church and state as educator, priest, commission chairman, mediator, and archbishop. Gifted with an apparently endless supply of energy, Hanna promptly accepted all invitations to minister in the realms of the sacred and the secular. His positive attitude, sense of fair play and decency, expertise, work ethic, and affability made him an archbishop for the people. Hanna seemed unconcerned about the trappings of authority—including the cardinalship he never attained. He commuted daily to the chancery by streetcar and on foot, happily chatting with people along the way. As the 1930s dawned, weariness and physical problems made Hanna realize that it would be prudent to end his tenure as archbishop. In his final years he assumed the role of an old warrior, tired from many battles waged and won, retiring in dignity and enjoying the gratitude of both Church and nation.

San Francisco in the 1930s

The Great Depression, even with its significant economic ramifications, could not dampen San Francisco's spirit as the city pressed forward in grand ways to celebrate its past accomplishments and future prospects. The historian Tom Cole has commented: "Despite the Depression, there was little hesitant or unsure about San Francisco in the 1930s. It was a time when the city not only enjoyed itself as usual, but bravely launched some of its most ambitious building projects."[1] During the decade, Joe DiMaggio and other significant baseball greats played for the San Francisco Seals at the city's stadium at Bryant and 16th streets, providing entertainment and escape from personal woes. Many swam at the Sutro Baths on the coast or the Crystal Plunge. In 1933 Coit Tower, erected on Telegraph Hill through a benefaction of $100,000 from Lillie Coit, was dedicated in honor of the city's courageous firefighters. One year later the Alcatraz Island, a military outpost, was converted into a federal prison, housing at various times in its thirty years of operation such notables as Al Capone and Robert Stroud, better known as the "Birdman of Alcatraz."[2]

The decade of the 1930s also saw the construction of the city's two most famous and utilized bridges, the Bay Bridge, connecting San Francisco with Oakland, and the Golden Gate, bridging the city with Marin County. These engineering marvels were two of the longest and costliest bridges ever constructed. The Bay Bridge, built under the watchful eye of Chief Engineer Charles H. Purcell, opened on November 12, 1936, after more than three years of construction. It spanned 8.5 miles across the bay in two separate sections with Yerba Buena Island as the connection point. When built, the Golden Gate was the longest single span suspension bridge in the world; it opened on May 27, 1934, after four and a half years of construction. Chief Engineer Joseph Baerman Strauss took great pride when over 250,000 people walked the span at its opening. Celebrating the construction of these two great bridges, the city made plans to host another world's fair, along the lines of the highly successful Panama Pacific International Exposition of 1915. Beginning in 1934, therefore, Treasure Island, adjacent to Yerba Buena Island was constructed to host the Golden Gate International Exposition, which welcomed visitors from February 19 to October 29, 1939.[3]

A Coadjutor in San Francisco

As his twenty years of service began to take their toll on him, Hanna asked the Vatican for a coadjutor to assist him with his labors. The *Monitor* reported that Hanna sought assistance "because of the growth of the work and the demands made upon his time by his extra diocesan activities as chairman of the Administrative Committee of the National Catholic Welfare Conference."[4] Thus, on January 29, 1932, at the request of Hanna himself, John J. Mitty, bishop of Salt Lake City, Utah, was named coadjutor archbishop of San Francisco, "with the right of succession to our venerable brother Edward Joseph Hanna, Archbishop of the Metropolitan Church of San Francisco in California, with all the faculties and powers pertaining by law to such coadjutors."[5]

Mitty was born in New York City in 1884 and educated at St. John's Seminary in Dunwoodie for service in the Archdiocese of New York. After ordination in 1906, he earned a baccalaureate in theology from the Catholic University of America (1907) and a doctorate of sacred theology from the Lateran Seminary in Rome (1908). He taught at St. Joseph's for eight years and then served as an army chaplain during World War I. After the war he served in parochial ministry until appointed bishop of Salt Lake on June 21, 1926. Archbishop Hanna preached at his installation Mass on October 7.[6]

As metropolitan for the region encompassing Salt Lake, Hanna had associated regularly with Mitty, and they shared mutual trust and respect, although they practiced different leadership styles. Mitty periodically invited Hanna to Salt Lake for special events. For instance, Mitty expressed his enthusiasm over Hanna's impending visit, in October 1931, to dedicate a school hall in Salt Lake: "Your presence would add immeasurably to the importance of these functions and I am most anxious for you to attend them."[7] Mitty not only invited Hanna to preach at his silver jubilee celebration, but made a point of scheduling the event when Hanna was free: "I would not have it without your presence, so I am asking you to settle on some Sunday and let me know what date you have selected."[8]

Mitty's appointment was greeted with general enthusiasm. Hanna himself sent a congratulatory telegram: "My joy and gratitude are beyond my power to tell. We will welcome you whole heartedly to San Francisco and we pray upon you every blessing and every grace for the new task that confronts you." Hanna went on to express how fortunate the archdiocese was to obtain Mitty. He stated, "His presence here will make my own work lighter and no part of the Church's work will be neglected."[9] John Burke was happy that Mitty would lighten Hanna's workload. The hierarchy and general population also applauded the selection. One typical letter read in part: "Permit me to express my admiration for the happy choice that was made for your coadjutorship. I am sure you will find much satisfaction and pleasure in the attitude and services of Bishop Mitty."[10]

For his part, Mitty welcomed the opportunity to work with Hanna in San Francisco. Immediately after his appointment, he sent a telegram to Hanna:

> My appointment as your coadjutor announced. Delighted beyond expression. Heartfelt thanks for confidence shown me. Pledge my hearty loyalty and devotion. Shall strive to [the] utmost to cooperate in all your labors for upbuilding of Christ's kingdom. Fervently pray that our years together may be many and blessed.[11]

The sermons preached by Hanna and Mitty at the latter's installation demonstrated their mutual affection and hope for the future. Hanna welcomed Mitty and added, "We pray upon him every best gift and every perfect gift for his work around the city of St. Francis." Mitty extolled Hanna for his past support and pledged his loyalty and assistance:

> From my very arrival in the Inter-Mountain country as Bishop of Salt Lake, Archbishop Hanna has been to me a father and a friend; he has helped me over the hard places, has given me encouragement and assistance, and has always been a real father and guide to me. To be selected to stand by his side, to hold up his arms in the great work he is doing both for the Church and the State is a source of happiness and gratification to me, and I pledge to him my wholehearted, whole-souled cooperation and loyalty and devotion in the work of this great archdiocese.[12]

Retirement: San Francisco and Rome

Throughout his ministerial life, Edward Hanna demonstrated physical vigor and a sharp mind. The impression he made on Pope

Leo XIII in his 1886 disputation, his scholarship as a professor of dogmatics at St. Bernard's Seminary, and his numerous administrative tasks on behalf of church and state as archbishop were clear indications of his mental acumen. There is no extant data that he was ever seriously ill or missed functions due to injury or sickness.

However, in October 1932, after Mitty's arrival and adjustment period, Hanna became so ill that, at the urging of James Cantwell, Bishop John Cantwell in Los Angeles told Hanna to rest for a month.[13] In another indication of the seriousness of Hanna's illness Mitty wrote Burke and suggested he encourage Hanna to forego the annual bishops' meeting in November. By mid-November Hanna's secretary, Thomas Millett, reported that the archbishop had been under the care of physicians for one month. Hanna received a series of hypodermic injections for pain that at times was extreme. At Thanksgiving 1932 Mitty wrote Burke: "He [Hanna] is still a sick man and it will be some time before he will be able to get back to work again. He has shown a great deal of patience though he has been suffering extreme pain."[14] By December Hanna's health had improved so much that Mitty reported to Burke, "You will be very happy to learn that Archbishop Hanna has improved tremendously. The pain has practically left him and after some x-rays the doctors are fully satisfied that the trouble is gall trouble and nothing more."[15] Just prior to Christmas, Hanna's doctors told him he could return to work after the New Year. In mid-January Mitty provided Burke another update: "He [Hanna] seems to be himself in every way and to have fully recovered from his sickness. He has gotten his weight back, [and] looks and feels his normal self."[16]

In January 1935 Hanna was again hospitalized after a "slight accident which...[was] not serious." The nature and cause of Hanna's infirmity is not clear, but in March Mitty informed Hanna's brother James that the archbishop had fallen, was hospitalized for several weeks, and then "went south" to recuperate. He was then back in normal health.[17]

In a decision that may have included these recent illnesses but that certainly included the factors of age and fatigue, Edward Hanna retired as the archbishop of San Francisco on March 5, 1935. On March 27 he traveled east, then sailed from New York to Rome, where he was appointed archbishop of the titular see of

Gortyna; John Mitty immediately assumed the reins as local ordinary.[18] In a statement released at the time, Hanna explained his actions:

> Realizing the ever-growing responsibilities of my office as archbishop of San Francisco and conscious of the burden of my years, I asked the Holy See three years ago to send me the bishop of Salt Lake to help me in the government of this great archdiocese. In asking that he be sent with the title of coadjutor archbishop with the right of succession I was looking forward to the time when I could resign my office into his hands....After a quarter of a century of service to the archdiocese I feel I may rightly claim a release from active responsibilities and for my remaining days in retirement, a blessed quiet and peace.

He spoke of many "cherished memories" and his "unbounded gratitude" to the priests, religious, and laity, "who have ever given me their loyal, generous, and affective support."[19] Mitty's statement upon Hanna's retirement was filled with gratitude for the work he had accomplished:

> His great activity was not confined to Church affairs. He was vitally interested in civic matters and his own community as well as State and Nation made frequent calls upon his services. He gave himself generously and unsparingly, especially to the problems that concerned the welfare of the working people. His sympathetic understanding and eloquent tongue were ever at the service of every good cause, and citizens of all denominations looked to him with admiration and confidence. In his retirement from active work, the community loses an able self-sacrificing citizen.

Mitty also remarked upon the virtues that helped Hanna draw together groups and factions normally divided by differing interests and traditions: "His name has been synonymous with kindness, gentleness, and courtesy and will be held in loving benediction by thousands of friends and admirers who will follow him with every wish for joy and happiness."[20]

The announcement of Hanna's retirement generated an outpouring of sentiment from the constituencies that had been touched by his service and pastoral care. Mayor Angelo Rossi, who had frequently clashed with Hanna over tax exemption for Catholic schools, nonetheless thanked him for his significant service to the city's poor and for his work of "moral uplift of the city," concluding, "He will remain in the hearts of our people as a dearly beloved and foremost citizen." Governor Frank Merriam of California, who had taken office when Rolph died in 1934, lauded Hanna's concern for workingmen and his leadership in "many human and spiritual movements that have become well established trends in modern life."[21] The Industrial Association of San Francisco described Hanna's work with the city's wage arbitration boards as a great legacy: "You have impressed in the history of the progress of industrial relations in this city the seal of your wisdom, broad tolerance, and undaunted leadership." Parishioners and citizens were grateful for Hanna's support of many municipal and Church organizations. One typical letter read, "You have always been so thoughtful of us, your children, and no obstacle seemed too great for you to surmount when thinking of our welfare."[22] The city's Jewish community acknowledged Hanna's ecumenical outreach: "The atmosphere of cordiality and good will that exists in San Francisco among men and women of all denominations has been strengthened on many occasions by your constant efforts on behalf of interdenominational brotherhood."[23] A stirring tribute to Hanna was published as an editorial in the *Los Angeles Times:*

> Not only in the religious life of his [arch]diocese, but in the civic affairs of San Francisco, Archbishop Hanna has for many years been a compelling influence for good. He is an orator blessed with the fluent eloquence inherited from his Irish ancestors. He is a loyal and zealous churchman filled with a broad sympathy for all humanity and his many contributions to the growth and progress of the northern metropolitan have left their marks on the history page of San Francisco.[24]

When Hanna retired as archbishop, he also resigned from many groups and organizations, most notably the NCWC Administrative Committee. Hanna wrote to John Burke asking him to present the bishops with his resignation, which was due to "the growing infirmities of age and by my desire to retire from active work." He thanked the bishops for their confidence in him:

> From the very origin of the NCWC, the bishops of the country have honored me by allowing me to serve them and the Church as Chairman of the Administrative Committee. I am grateful beyond words for the honor and the privilege they have bestowed upon me, and it is with the deepest regret that I now seek to be relieved of this work.[25]

The Administrative Committee, in turn, thanked Hanna for his significant service: "For your diligent zeal, your unfailing presence at all our meetings, your willingness to serve, we in the name of the general meeting, which instructed us to do so, extend our gratitude and our appreciation."[26]

The hierarchy also praised Hanna for the significant mark he had made on the American Church. Besides accolades from his close associates in the NCWC, gratitude was expressed by prelates he had nourished and guided as young clerics. Ralph Hayes, bishop of Helena, Montana, said:

> Many of us will cherish as long as we live the keen and kindly interest you have always manifested in young priests and bishops. It has meant much to us to receive your hearty greeting, to be strengthened by your words of encouragement, and to be the recipients of your advice born of wisdom and experience. It has meant much more to us to have had the example of your saintly life.[27]

Bishop John Cantwell of Los Angeles, Hanna's longtime friend, praised his more public contributions to church and state:

> He has been not only a great churchman, but also a great leader in civic affairs. His ability and profound scholarship have been

recognized frequently by the heads of our state and nation, who called upon him in times of crisis when his gentle kindness made him beloved by all.…His career long will be remembered as that of a great American and a great Catholic bishop.[28]

The motivation behind Hanna's retirement as archbishop and his withdrawal from many other significant positions, including administrative chairman of the NCWC and president of the California Commission of Immigration and Housing, is shrouded in mystery; his own explanation—that he was motivated by "his advancing years and desire to be relieved of the burdens of his office"[29]—is problematic. The *Monitor,* for example, suggested an earlier date for the announcement when reporting on March 9, "His Excellency, the Most Reverend Edward J. Hanna, D.D. *some time ago* [emphasis mine] offered his resignation to the Holy See."[30] Moreover, the archbishop's resignation took his family totally by surprise. One of Hanna's nieces wrote to archdiocesan officials shortly following the announcement, "Is Uncle so completely incapacitated that he must resign? The news comes as a great surprise and quite an upset. Would you like to wire us his condition?"[31]

Hanna's resignation caught the archdiocese off guard as well. None of the Archepiscopal Council Meeting Minutes mention Hanna's departure. He had presided at the January 23, 1935, meeting; the March 4 minutes read, "In the absence of Archbishop Hanna the coadjutor archbishop called a meeting of the members of the Council." The March 26 minutes read simply, "The Most Rev. John Joseph Mitty, Archbishop (presiding)."[32] The March 5 resignation date leaves some unanswered questions.

Hanna's move to Rome, which became permanent, is also mysterious. The chancellor of the archdiocese and Mitty's secretary, Thomas Connolly, corresponded with numerous people with the understanding that Hanna would be in San Francisco; there is no indication that he knew of the archbishop's impending departure for Rome. For instance, in March 1935 Hanna was granted honorary membership in the Sodality of Notre Dame des Malades, and Connolly wrote the Sodality, saying that he would inform Hanna of his membership, "immediately upon his return." In February Connolly responded to an invitation from a local charitable endeavor, stating Hanna "will be pleased to serve as Honorary Chairman of the General Committee of Arrangements for the Catholic Council of Social Work, planned for May 7 and 8 in San Francisco."[33] As late as September 1935, Hanna's secretary Thomas Millett wrote, "Archbishop Hanna is at presently residing in Europe and I can not [sic] definitely state when he will return."[34]

Among the many uncertainties, some facts are clear. For instance, it is clear that the apostolic delegate, Archbishop Amleto Cicognani, had contacted both Mitty and John Cantwell in Los Angeles concerning Hanna. In February 1934 Cicognani wrote to Cantwell, stating that he was backing off from an earlier plan to forcibly remove Hanna:

> I note that your Excellency agrees substantially with my opinion regarding the danger of enforcing a removal or withdrawal. After considering your Excellency's letter, I have decided not to go through with my plan of having the Sacred Congregation write directly to the person concerned [Hanna]. I am writing to Archbishop Mitty today to inquire if the Archbishop [Hanna] intends to visit Rome this year, and if he does what his definite plans are. If he does not intend to visit Rome, I shall request the Sacred Congregation to authorize me to summon him to the Delegation.[35]

One year later, in late February, Cicognani again wrote to Cantwell, stating that he had received Hanna's resignation but would not make it public while Hanna was hospitalized, although now that the resignation was in hand, Cantwell could "speak freely to Archbishop Mitty about the matter." Cicognani thanked Cantwell for his assistance:

> I wish to thank your Excellency most cordially for your good offices in this matter. Your Excellency's gracious and valued cooperation will be appreciated no less by the Holy See than by myself. I am sorry that I had to call upon your Excellency for such a distasteful task. Now that it is over, I trust your Excellency will forget the unpleasant part and think only of the good which you have accomplished. I am glad to know that

the task was lightened considerably by the attitude of the Archbishop.[36]

The exact nature of the "distasteful task" that Cantwell was asked to perform is uncertain, but it seems likely that Cantwell, and probably Mitty, were told to arrange for Hanna's departure from the archdiocese. There is some indication that Hanna knew of the delegate's actions. Cicognani's reference to "the attitude of the Archbishop" suggests that Hanna cooperated with the plan. Moreover, in a letter to Hanna acknowledging his resignation from the National Longshoremen's Board of 1934, President Roosevelt describes the resignation as "submitted due to the fact that you are leaving the country for some time."[37] Since Hanna had obviously told Roosevelt and/or Secretary of Labor Frances Perkins that he was leaving the country, Hanna had apparently known of his impending move to Rome when he resigned from the board.

When Hanna arrived in Rome in April 1935, he took up residence at the Villa San Francesco, operated by Franciscan Tertiary brothers on the Via Dei Monti Parioli.[38] Arrangements for his life there were made through the Sacred Consistorial Congregation. In a letter to Cicognani, the congregation referred to Hanna's situation as a "delicate issue" and to its "understanding [of] the necessity of his [Hanna's] continued residence in Italy," and concluded, "If we succeed to persuade him that he should never leave, so much the better."[39] Working through the congregation, Mitty arranged for Hanna to receive a monthly stipend of $250 through the administration of the Apostolic Delegate; Hanna's mail was also routed to the congregation. Mitty corresponded with Father Joseph Breslin at the North American College as the Roman point man: "All things considered, I think it best for him [Hanna] to remain where he is and I am counting upon you to use your influence to keep him there." In a veiled reference to possible interference, he concluded, "There is just the possibility that some visitor may arrange to take him back here, or something of that kind."[40]

Extant data from the period of Hanna's retirement in Rome provide more clues as to why he retired so abruptly and without warning. Significant evidence points to senility or an undiagnosed case of what today is called Alzheimer's Disease. John Lardner,

Sulpician superior of St. Patrick's, the archdiocesan seminary, said that when Hanna visited the seminary, his demeanor had been "inconsistent, even childish." His visit, he noted, "reminds me of the days when my mother used to make me mind the baby. He cannot be still for five minutes."[41] One observer described Hanna in November 1935:

> I lived with the old man [Hanna] for about a month and he is as simple as a child; he spent most of his time in the chapel and saying his office and prayers. He has to be shown his room, having lost his sense of direction; he asks the same questions five times in a half hour; he forgets everything. But he does exactly what you tell him; he never moves except on order; he is completely dependent but is as easy to manage or to have around as anybody I have ever met. What he needs is a good devoted Catholic man to keep him company—he hates to be alone—and to think and do for him. If he has that he is safe and presentable in any company.[42]

Observations in the early 1940s point to Hanna's failing mental faculties. In March 1943 Howard Carroll, assistant to the NCWC general secretary Michael Ready, wrote Mitty, relaying the firsthand observations of Carroll's brother Walter, a priest who lived in Rome:

> You might tell Archbishop Mitty that he [Hanna] is quite well physically,...[but] his physical habits are those of a baby and this means that a brother must be constantly with him....He has not said Mass for over a year because of lack of memory. He has no idea what he just did, where he was or what he is to do next....He doesn't know there is a war on and is living entirely in the past. He told me for instance that he frequently goes to the North American College and they are always very wonderful to him there.[43]

Carroll's account was consistent with that of Edward Kennedy, an Associated Press war correspondent who visited Villa San Francesco and wrote that Hanna "has lived in Rome throughout the war and almost wholly oblivious of it, for he is passing the closing years of his life in a peace which his mind has fashioned."[44]

Despite these accounts, extant letters indicated that he was clear-headed during his latter days in San Francisco and his first years in Rome. In addition, his work with the State Relief Commission, State Planning Board, his leadership of the fact-finding commission that settled the 1933 cotton strike, and especially his chairmanship of the National Longshoremen's Board demonstrate his ability to function mentally. In letters to family members and to Mitty written between 1936 and 1944, the content is clear and Hanna's handwriting is consistent with that of his mature years. In February 1944, less than six months before his death, Hanna wrote to Mitty, "I am glad to hear you are getting along well. As for myself I can relate the same. My state of health is what is what [sic] one may expect at my age. For the rest, I am well taken care of, and nothing [is] wanting to me."[45]

Historians have generally concluded that Hanna's retirement was due to his mental condition. Frederick Zwierlein states that Hanna was retired for giving "evidence of senility in the pulpit." Francis Weber is less harsh but comes to the same conclusion: "His [Hanna's] brilliant mind played mean tricks on him. Not that he had lost it. Just that it often failed to focus clearly on reality. Somewhat like failing eyes that see, but only through a mist."[46]

There is some evidence that Hanna was retired to Rome because of inappropriate behavior with a woman. A few months after Hanna arrived in Rome, a woman named Marie came to the Eternal City searching for the archbishop. Correspondence between Joseph Hurley and Archbishop Edward Mooney of Detroit, Hanna's successor as chairman of the NCWC Administrative Committee, reported, "Hanna is now hiding at the Villa [San Francesco] and M[arie] is looking high and low for him. The danger is that at any moment, the old man may go back to Rome in search for her." Joseph Breslin, the man Mitty had assigned to watch over Hanna, was told to watch for the woman in order to "whisk Eddie out of town." Breslin moved Hanna from Villa San Francesco to a Cistercian monastery at Casamare, used as a facility for "problem priests," an act that drew the ire of some observers: "It is a tragedy that he [Hanna] should be in such a place. He [Breslin] could easily have gone up to the place run by the Irish Sisters at Fiesole, or could have taken or sent [Hanna] on a trip to Ireland, or to the Riviera; any place but to put him in an institution which may be considered primitive or correctional."[47] Hurley, while supporting Hanna, alluded to possible wrongdoing: "I refuse to believe that Hanna has been guilty of anything except indiscretions. He will still put his arms around anybody within sight. And if there are some proofs [sic] about the past, the old fellow is all right now."[48]

The theory about indiscreet behavior is supported by two kinds of data. First, rumors of this kind were common at the time and still exist today. In 1963 the Rochester priest Charles Shay said that Hanna was removed from his position because he "was showing too much affection for a woman in the chancery office."[49] Similarly, Frederick Zwierlein wrote of Hanna's "indiscreet acts of charity."[50] Second, hard facts show that Hanna was increasingly kept under wraps in Rome, to the extent that Mitty was forced to use an intermediary in 1942 to find out Hanna's condition. The ongoing war and Hanna's probably deteriorating mental condition might explain his inaccessibility, but one would think that even in these circumstances his successor would be able to deal directly with him. Additionally, Hanna's family was kept from contacting him. His sister, Mother Anne Hanna, wrote to Mitty in January 1943,

> I knew that Brother [Hanna] had received no word from home since October 1941. The Christmas letter sent at the end of November was returned to me, July 1942, marked "service suspended"; and I made no further attempt to reach him, except through prayers. While I accept God's holy will with all my heart, the total loss of all means of intercourse has been a heart pang.[51]

Until appropriate archival resources are made available, certainty about the reasons for Hanna's retirement and his permanent residence in Rome remain out of reach.

Regardless of the reasons for his retirement, Hanna was able to function and to celebrate some important events during his residence in Rome. On May 30, 1935, Hanna marked his golden jubilee in the priesthood by celebrating a Mass in the chapel of the

North American College. On this occasion, Rochester friend and fellow Fortnightly Club member Edward Miner sent greetings from the club and the city: "Yours has been a life, rich in love and friendship of your fellows, and no man could ask for greater affection or reverence then what has come to you through the years of your service."[52] Later that year Hanna celebrated a Thanksgiving Day Mass at the American Church of Santa Susanna in Rome.[53] He also associated with the North American College, where a retreat he led in 1936 inspired one student to remark: "Just being near him, listening to him, asking him questions, gives me a greater spiritual 'hypo' than an hour's strenuous meditation. There's not a fellow here who would not gladly give his life for *our own* [writer's emphasis] Archbishop Hanna."[54]

Death and Return to San Francisco

Edward Hanna's long life road, which took him from Rochester to San Francisco to Rome, ended with his death on July 10, 1944. Mitty's announcement, which was published in the San Francisco newspapers, described Hanna as " a recognized leader" in service to all:

He was an outstanding citizen and a distinguished churchman. His long life was one of devotion to his country and to his church. His learning, kindness, generosity and good will to men and women of every race and creed won all who knew him to his singularly attractive personality.[55]

Hanna's funeral was held in Rome at the North American College Chapel on July 13, with Bishop Paolo Giobbe as celebrant. Cardinals Pietro Fumasoni-Biondi, Camillo Caccia-Dominioni, and Alessandro Verde and three U.S. Army chaplains were in attendance. A few days later a requiem Mass was celebrated at the Church of Santa Susanna.[56] On July 18 another requiem Mass was celebrated at St. Mary's Cathedral in San Francisco. Mitty was the celebrant, Bishops Robert Armstrong (Sacramento), Thomas Connolly (auxiliary of San Francisco), and Thomas Gorman

(Reno) attended, and Bishop Duane Hunt (Salt Lake) preached the funeral oration. Hunt enumerated Hanna's many accomplishments, describing him as "the gifted scholar, the magnetic orator, the charming and gracious gentleman, the stately ambassador of Christ," who as a young man heard the voice of God directing him "to turn away from the world, to forsake the joys and pleasures proper to other men and to leave all things and to follow the Master." He spoke of Hanna's "versatile genius" that led him to serve in many public capacities, bringing to each effort "his sense of fair play" and "God's justice in the affairs of men," and applauded Hanna's ecumenical efforts, especially his condemnation of anti-Semitism:

> All we know is that a well-worn path led to his door and that up that path come [sic] people of all ranks and classes, of all creeds and colors. Came Catholics and Protestants alike, Jews and Gentiles, priests and laymen, bankers and beggars, saints and sinners, the successes of life and the failures. No one was too lofty or too poor to approach the archbishop. And to each he gave the same captivating smile of welcome. Each left with gratitude in his heart and blessing in his soul.[57]

News of Hanna's death generated praise from many quarters. The Irish freedom fighter and future president Eamon de Valera expressed his gratitude for Hanna's continual promotion of the Irish cause in the United States. Californians who had worked with Hanna, such as Robert Sproul, president of the University of California at Berkeley and Herbert Fleishhacker, a fellow member on the California Commission of Immigration and Housing, spoke of his ability to carry his spiritual leadership into the civic realm.[58] The San Francisco *Call-Bulletin*'s obituary read in part: "This kindly and earnest man of religion had a genius and instinct for human understanding,...an amazing capacity for commanding attention of the community, and an inspiring capacity for winning the respect of the community."[59]

The wide range of religious leaders mourning Hanna's death testified to his ecumenism. The Reverend Edgar A. Lowthern, pastor of Temple Methodist Church, stated:

Nothing was alien to Archbishop Hanna's interest. He made San Francisco a better place in which to live, by his spiritual and civic leadership. He was truly a great man. He had a genius for friendship and comfort among all kinds of people, rich and poor, educated and uneducated.[60]

Edward Lambe Parsons, retired Episcopal bishop of California, called Hanna "a distinguished leader, not only of his own faith, but of all faiths. He was universally beloved in San Francisco for his many good works." Rabbi Irving Reichart stated: "Archbishop Hanna was the people's Archbishop....He was a true shepherd of his flock, a priest who knew and loved the people of San Francisco, who cooperated personally in every worthwhile civic, cultural and religious movement."[61]

Because of the war in Europe, Hanna was initially interred in a vault at the North American College; when the war ended, Mitty arranged to have Hanna's body returned to San Francisco, accompanied by Monsignor Egisto Tozzi, pastor of All Souls Church in South San Francisco, who was sent to Rome for that purpose. The *SS President Monroe*, carrying Hanna's body, sailed from Rome on July 1, 1947, and arrived in San Francisco on August 18. Special services were held at the cathedral on August 20, then Edward Hanna was laid to rest in the mausoleum at Holy Cross Cemetery in Colma, south of San Francisco. Edward Hanna, archbishop for the people, had reached his final home.[62]

Conclusion

The fact that Archbishop Hanna's retirement and death are shrouded in some mystery does not detract from the brilliance of a career lived in unselfish service of church and state. An astute academic and seminary professor, Hanna was a leading theologian in the United States before fears of modernism shifted his efforts in other directions. His early work in Rochester with Italian immigrants and with labor-management issues continued and flourished when he moved to San Francisco. Mayors, governors, and presidents selected him to resolve labor disputes, to arbitrate workers' wages, and to provide leadership on numerous significant commissions and panels. His compassion led him to become actively involved in various charitable organizations. He was also active in the Church, on both local and national levels. A major proponent of Catholic education, he made schools a high priority in the archdiocese. Because he shunned the personal spotlight to benefit the collective good, he was much beloved by the people of the archdiocese and by his fellow priests. On the national level, Hanna served with distinction as administrative chairman of the National Catholic Welfare Conference, guiding this nascent episcopal body in lobbying for Catholic rights and issues. In all phases of life and ministry, Edward Hanna truly was an archbishop for the people.

NOTES

Introduction

1. Vincent P. Lannie, *Public Money and Parochial Education* (Cleveland: Press of Case Western Reserve University, 1968).

2. John Tracy Ellis, *The Life of James Cardinal Gibbons* (Westminster, MD: Christian Classics, 1987), 2:500.

3. Sara-Alice Quinlan, *In Harvest Fields by Sunset Shores* (San Francisco: Gilmartin Company, 1926), 5.

4. The history of the Catholic hierarchy in the United States has been analyzed most prominently in its relationship to the Vatican. Gerald Fogarty, SJ, has explored this relationship in two significant works. *The Vatican and the American Hierarchy from 1870 to 1965* (Wilmington, DE: Michael Glazier, 1985) provides detailed accounts of numerous issues that have arisen since Vatican I between the American hierarchy and the Vatican, including the Third Plenary Council of Baltimore (1884), numerous issues associated with Americanism, the establishment of the apostolic delegation, promotion of *romanità*, the attempted suppression of the NCWC, the relationship of the American government to the Vatican, and the question of religious liberty as illustrated in the case of John Courtney Murray, SJ. In Fogarty's *Patterns of Episcopal Leadership* (New York: Macmillan, 1989), part of the six-volume bicentennial history of the American Church, contributors focus on the specific contributions of American prelates from John Carroll to Paul Hallinan as a way of understanding the relationship between the hierarchy and the state in America. Fogarty suggests that "freedom from government interference led to episcopal absolutism both in the manner in which bishops were chosen and in the way dioceses were governed." He concludes saying that the story of the American Catholic hierarchy is "a history which reveals the periods of the ebb and flow of papal centralization." A second historian, Bernard Cooke, in his edited volume, *The Papacy and the Church in the United*

States, concentrates more significantly on the historical development of the role of the papacy in its relationship to the American Church.

In addition to an analysis of the relationship between the American Church and the Vatican, the historical record is replete with biographies of historically significant twentieth-century prelates who were contemporaries of Hanna. James O'Toole describes *romanitá* in its fullest expression and the "militant and triumphant" episcopal attitude through his biography of Cardinal William Henry O'Connell of Boston. Edward Kantowicz highlights episcopal centralization in his history of the life and career of Cardinal George Mundelein of Chicago. An example of episcopal advocacy for the poor and the persecuted church is presented in James Gaffey's aforementioned life of Bishop Francis Clement Kelley of Oklahoma. The lives of many other prominent prelates, including Archbishop Patrick Riordan, Hanna's predecessor in San Francisco, have been chronicled by historians.

5. Arthur S. Link and Richard L. McCormick, *Progressivism* (Arlington Heights, IL: Harlan Davidson, 1983), 2.

6. William Halsey, *The Survival of American Innocence: Catholicism in an Era of Disillusionment, 1920–1940* (Notre Dame, IN: University of Notre Dame Press, 1980), 1–7.

7. Robert F. McNamara, "Archbishop Hanna, Rochesterian," *Rochester History* (April 1963): 1–24; idem, *The Diocese of Rochester in America 1868–1993*, 2nd ed. (Rochester, NY: Roman Catholic Diocese of Rochester, 1998).

8. Richard Gribble, CSC, "Edward Hanna," *The New Revised Catholic Encyclopedia* (Detroit: Gale Corporation associated with the Catholic University of America Press, 2002), 6:634; idem, "Advocate for Immigrants: The Church and State Career of Archbishop Edward J. Hanna," *Southern California Quarterly* 83, no. 3 (fall 2001): 285–316; idem, "Social Catholicism Engages the American State: The Contribution of Edward J. Hanna," *Journal of Church and State* 42 (autumn 2000): 737–58; "Church, State, and the American Immigrant: The Multiple Contributions of Archbishop Edward J. Hanna," *U.S. Catholic Historian* 16, no. 4 (fall 1998): 1–18; idem, "Countering Federalization of Education in the United States," *Records of the American Catholic Historical Society of Philadelphia* 108, nos. 3–4 (fall–winter 1997–98): 23–52; idem, "The Rough Road to San Francisco: The Story of Edward Hanna, 1907–1915," *Southern California Quarterly* 78, no. 3 (fall 1996): 225–42.

9. R. Scott Appleby, *"Church and Age Unite!" The Modernist Impulse in American Catholicism* (Notre Dame, IN: University of Notre Dame Press, 1992), 146–47; Thomas J. Shelley, *Dunwoodie: The History of St.*

Joseph's Seminary, Yonkers, New York (Westminster, MD: Christian Classics, 1993), 148–71; Michael J. DeVito, *The New York Review* (New York: United States Catholic Historical Society, 1977), 260–91; Gerald Fogarty, SJ, *American Catholic Biblical Scholarship* (San Francisco: Harper & Row, 1989), 132–35, 138–39; James Gaffey, *Citizen of No Mean City: Archbishop Patrick Riordan of San Francisco (1841–1914)* (Wilmington, NC: Consortium Books, 1976), 281–302.

10. Douglas Slawson, "The Attitudes and Activities of American Catholics Regarding the Proposals to Establish a Federal Department of Education between World War I and the Great Depression" (PhD diss., Catholic University of America, 1981); idem, *The Foundation and First Decade of the National Catholic Welfare Council* (Washington, DC: Catholic University of America Press, 1992), 85–88, 100–111, 192–202, 241–55; idem, "The National Catholic Welfare Conference and Church-State Conflict in Mexico, 1925–1929," *The Americas* 47, no. 1 (July 1990): 55–93; idem, "The National Catholic Welfare Conference and the Mexican Church-State Conflict of the Mid-1930s: A Case of Déjà Vu," *Catholic Historical Review* 80, no. 1 (1994): 58–96; Thomas J. Shelley, "The Oregon School Case and the National Catholic Welfare Conference," *Catholic Historical Review* 75, no. 3 (July 1989): 439–57; John B. Sheerin, *Never Look Back: The Career and Concerns of John J. Burke* (New York: Paulist Press, 1975), 108–54; M. Paul Holsinger, "The Oregon School Bill Controversy, 1922–1925," *Pacific Historical Review* 37 (1968): 327–41; David B. Tyack, "The Perils of Pluralism: The Background of the Pierce Case," *American Historical Review* 74 (1968): 74–98.

11. Richard Gribble, CSC, "Edward Hanna and Labor Arbitration in San Francisco, 1916–1923," *The Californians* 9, no. 3 (November–December 1991): 35–40; Michael Kazin, *Barons of Labor* (Urbana: University of Illinois Press, 1987), especially pp. 253–58; William Issel and Robert W. Cherny, *San Francisco 1865–1932: Politics, Power and Urban Development* (Berkeley: University of California Press, 1986), 53–79.

12. Christina A. Ziegler-McPherson, "Americanization: The California Plan: The Commission of Immigration and Housing of California and Public Policy, 1913–1923" (PhD diss., Stanford University, 1999); Anne Marie Woo-Sam, "Domesticating the Immigrant: California's Commission of Immigration and Housing and the Domestic Immigration Policy Movement, 1910–1945" (PhD diss., University of California, Berkeley, 1999).

13. David F. Selvin, *A Terrible Anger: The 1934 Waterfront and General Strikes in San Francisco* (Detroit: Wayne State University Press, 1996).

14. John J. Mitty to "The Clergy, Religious and Laity of the Archdiocese of San Francisco," n.d. [1935], General Correspondence, Hanna File, Archives, Archdiocese of San Francisco (hereafter AASF), Menlo Park, California.

Chapter 1: The Rochester Priest

1. Lawrence J. McCaffrey, "Irish Textures in American Catholicism," *Catholic Historical Review* 78, no. 1 (January 1992): 2.

2. There are many monographs, collected works, and essays that outline in detail the anti-Catholic animus of nineteenth-century America. Among the best sources are: Ray Allen Billington, *The Protestant Crusade, 1800–1860: A Study of the Origins of American Nativism* (New York: Rinehart & Company, 1952); Gustavus Myers, *History of Bigotry in the United States* (New York: Random House, 1943); James J. Kenneally, "The Burning of the Ursuline Convent: A Different View," *Records of the American Catholic Historical Society of Philadelphia* (hereafter *Records*) 90 (1979): 15–22; Michael Feldberg, *The Philadelphia Riots of 1844: A Study of Ethnic Conflict* (Westport, CT: Greenwood Press, 1975); James F. Connelly, *The Visit of Archbishop Gaetano Bedini to the United States of America (June 1853–February 1854)* (Rome: Gregorian University Press, 1960); and Mark J. Hurley, *The Unholy Ghost: Anti-Catholicism in the American Experience* (Huntington, IN: Our Sunday Visitor, 1992).

3. The best complete history of the northern Know-Nothing Party is Tyler Anbinder, *Nativism and Slavery: The Northern Know Nothings and the Politics of the 1850s* (New York: Oxford University Press, 1992).

4. Two notable late nineteenth-century incidents illustrate the ways in which many German Catholics in America resisted assimilation to American Catholic ways. In 1886 Peter Abbelen, a priest from Milwaukee, wrote his "Memorial," which asked for greater clarification of the status of German national parishes in the United States. Later in 1891 the St. Raphael's Verein, headed by General Secretary Peter Paul Cahensly, generated its "Lucerne Memorial," which made very specific requests of the Vatican to stop "leakage" of German Catholics in America to Protestantism. Both memorials were rejected almost unanimously by the American hierarchy. These documents raised resentment within the Church among the various nationalities that now called the United States home. See Colman J. Barry, OSB, *The Catholic Church and German Americans* (Milwaukee: Bruce Publishing Company, 1953), 44–85; and Philip Gleason, *The Conservative Reformers: German-American Catholics*

and the Social Order (Notre Dame, IN: University of Notre Dame Press, 1968), 131–82.

5. The best source for a detailed history of the American Protective Association (APA) is Donald L. Kinzer, *An Episode in Anti-Catholicism: The American Protective Association* (Seattle: University of Washington Press, 1964). Its period of influence was short, 1887–1896, but quite virulent.

6. Patrick W. Carey, "American Catholic Romanticism, 1830–1888," *Catholic Historical Review* 74 (October 1988): 594; Joseph P. Chinnici, OFM, *Living Stones: The History and Structure of Catholic Spiritual Life in the United States* (New York: Macmillan, 1989), 91–133. Chinnici argues that Hecker, John Keane, and Walter Elliott promoted a theological view that corresponded to their political ideas. A positive anthropology, which emphasized God's immanence in the person and the nation, was the result.

7. While Hanna always acknowledged and gloried in his Irish heritage, he claimed no knowledge of his roots from Ulster Orangemen.

8. *Union and Advertiser* (Rochester), December 4, 1912; Church Records, Immaculate Conception Church, Rochester, New York, copy in Hanna Files, Archives, Diocese of Rochester (hereafter ADR), Rochester, New York; Alan E. Currie to Robert McNamara, May 24, 1962, Robert McNamara Private Papers (hereafter MPP); *Rochester Evening Times*, October 21, 1912; Academy of the Sacred Heart Personnel Records, Rochester, New York, copy in Hanna Files, ADR.

9. Edward Hanna Clergy Record, Diocese of Rochester, Hanna Files, ADR; Austin Hanna, interview with Robert McNamara, April 12, 1962; *Rochester Herald*, May 31, 1915; James Cantwell to John J. Burke, CSP, November 8, 1922, Cantwell to Mother Augustine, October 10, 1918, Cantwell to Pierre de Chaignon La Rose, December 11, 1916, Chancery Correspondence, AASF.

10. *Monitor* (San Francisco), n.d. [1912], clipping in Hanna Files, ADR.

11. *Rochester Herald*, October 22, 1912; *Rochester Evening Times*, October 21, 1912.

12. It should be noted that McQuaid's promotion of Catholic education was consistent with the general attitude of the American hierarchy in this area. The plenary councils of 1852, 1866, and 1884 all promoted Catholic education, especially the establishment of Catholic schools. In 1852 the Pastoral Letter (#10) read: "Encourage the establishment and support of Catholic schools; make every sacrifice which may be necessary for this object." In 1866 the Bishop's Pastoral (#27) read: "We recur to the

subject of the education of youth, to which in the former plenary council we already directed your attention, for the purpose of reiterating the admonition we then gave, in regard to the establishment and support of parochial schools." In 1884 the bishops (#34) stated: "We have in view, to multiply our schools, and to perfect them. We must multiply them till every Catholic child in the land should have within his reach the means of education....No parish is complete till it has schools adequate to the needs of its children, and the pastor and the people of such a parish should feel that they have not accomplished their entire duty until the want is supplied." See Hugh J. Nolan, *Pastoral Letters of US Catholic Bishops*, vol. 1, *1792–1940* (Washington, DC: National Conference of Catholic Bishops, 1983), 180, 199, 225.

13. *Rochester Herald*, May 31, 1915, clipping, Hanna Files, ADR.

14. *Union Advertiser* (Rochester), June 27, 1879.

15. Quoted in Ronald C. White Jr. and C. Howard Hopkins, *The Social Gospel: Religion and Reform in Changing America* (Philadelphia: Temple University Press, 1976), 262.

16. Paul M. Minus, *Walter Rauschenbusch American Reformer* (New York: Macmillan, 1988), 29; *The Sheaf* (newsletter from St. Bernard's Institute) 35, no. 3 (n.d.): 2.

17. *Monitor*, n.d. [1912], clipping, Edward Hanna File, Archives Archdiocese of Los Angeles (hereafter AALA), San Fernando, California.

18. *Boston Republic*, December 7, 1912, clipping, Hanna Files, ADR.

19. McNamara, "Archbishop Hanna, Rochesterian," 5–8.

20. *Rochester Democrat and Chronicle*, October 5, 1879.

21. Edward Hanna to Bernard McQuaid, August 20, 1880, McQuaid Papers, ADR.

22. *Monitor*, June 5, 1915.

23. DeVito, *New York Review*, 262; Edward Hanna to Bernard McQuaid, August 24, 1882, McQuaid Papers, ADR.

24. Quoted in *The Sheaf* 35, no. 3 (n.d.): 2. The letters are Walter Rauschenbusch to Munson Ford, August 20, 1882, and December 12, 1884, respectively. The only remaining extant correspondence concerning Rauschenbusch that Hanna wrote came at the time of the former's death in 1918. In a letter to Charles Dewey in Rochester, Hanna seems critical of Rauschenbusch's social method: "How he could sympathize with the awfulness of cruelty of course I do not understand. He saw there was something wrong with our 'Industrial System' and instead of taking the greater way of reform, he narrowed himself to a system, and you and I know that the whole world cannot be squeezed into any one theory." In a letter to Rauschenbusch's widow he stated, "Rauschenbusch was true, just,

simple in faith and really courageous." It seems that Hanna did not understand nor fully appreciate Rauschenbusch's contribution to the Social Gospel. See Edward Hanna to Charles Dewey, August 6, 1918, A. D515 Box 2, Charles Dewey Papers, University of Rochester Archival Library (hereafter URL), Rochester, New York.

25. Quoted in George Hurley to Bernard McQuaid, January 6, 1884, McQuaid Papers, ADR.

26. Edward Hanna to Bernard McQuaid, August 9, 1884, McQuaid Papers, ADR.

27. Edward Hanna to Bernard McQuaid, June 12, 1885, McQuaid Papers, ADR.

28. The career of Edward Pace at the Catholic University of America is chronicled in C. Joseph Nuesse, *The Catholic University of America: A Centennial History* (Washington, DC: Catholic University of America Press, 1990).

29. *Rochester Evening Times*, October 21, 1912. See also Edward Christoph, "Archbishop Edward Hanna's Scholastic Disputation of 1886," unpublished essay, 1949, Hanna Papers, ADR.

30. Edward Hanna to Bernard McQuaid, December 15, 1886, and July 8, 1887, McQuaid Papers, ADR.

31. John Tracy Ellis, *The Formulative Years of the Catholic University of America* (Washington, DC: American Catholic Historical Association, 1946), 219, 334–35; *Monitor*, June 5, 1915; *The Republic* (Boston), December 7, 1912, clipping in Hanna Papers, ADR. Although there is no extant data to verify it, it is highly probable that the influence of Francesco Satolli and Edward Pace was applied in Hanna's invitation to Catholic University. Satolli was closely allied with Pope Leo XIII who had granted approval of the university in 1887. Pace, a classmate of Hanna's and co-awardee of the doctorate at the hands of the pope had been sent to Rome to be educated for the university's faculty, spending the whole of his academic career there. See Nuesse, *Catholic University*, 54. It should be noted that Hanna's association with Catholic University continued at a distance. During the rectorship of Bishop Denis O'Connell, who had been Hanna's rector at the North American College the latter part of his tenure there (1885 to 1895), Hanna tried to convince McQuaid to take up a collection for the university, but Hanna reported to O'Connell that "he [McQuaid] wouldn't take up a collection even for your sake." See Edward Hanna to Denis O'Connell, November 19, 1905, O'Connell Papers, Archives, the Catholic University of America (hereafter ACUA), Washington, DC. In November 1915 Hanna was elected to the Board of Trustees at Catholic

University. See J. F. Regis Canevin to Edward Hanna, November 16, 1915, Hanna Files, AASF.

32. *Union and Advertiser* (Rochester), December 4, 1912.

33. Edward Hanna, Sermon, February 3, 1889, Hanna Papers, ADR.

34. Edward Hanna, Sermon, "The Doctrine of Christ," January 9, 1898, Hanna Papers, ADR.

35. *Rochester Evening Times*, October 21, 1912, clipping in Hanna Files, ADR; Robert McNamara, interview with William Stauder, February 11, 1947, MPP.

36. Edward Hanna, Sermon, October 15, 1899, Hanna Papers, ADR.

37. Edward Hanna, Sermons, February 3, 1889, and "First Sunday of Lent," 1888, Hanna Papers, ADR.

38. Edward Hanna, Sermon, Septuagesima Sunday, 1889, Hanna Papers, ADR.

39. *Monitor*, April 5, 1915.

40. Souvenir Program of the Consecration of Edward Hanna, December 4, 1912, Hanna Papers, ADR.

41. *San Francisco Examiner*, December 17, 1912.

42. Joseph White, *The Diocesan Seminary in the United States* (Notre Dame, IN: University of Notre Dame Press, 1989), 177.

43. Robert McNamara, "St. Bernard's Seminary 1893–1968," *The Sheaf* (Publication of St. Bernard's Seminary) 15: 3–12. When McQuaid purchased the land Hanna congratulated his ordinary: "May our dear Lord bless and help you on your every endeavor in prosecuting this work so dear to your heart, so calculated to advance the Kingdom among our people." See Edward Hanna to Bernard McQuaid, May 5, 1887, McQuaid Papers, ADR.

44. McNamara, "St. Bernard's Seminary 1893–1968," 12–13.

45. Frederick J. Zwierlein, "American College in Rome, 1859–1955: Criticism and Supplement," *Social Justice Review* 50 (September–October 1957): 168; Robert McNamara, interview of J. F. Goggin, November 6, 1949, MPP. Goggin's comment is verified by William F. Stauder, another former student of Hanna's. Speaking of Hanna he stated, "A good man and a good teacher, even though he could deal out 'baloney.'" See Robert McNamara, interview of William F. Stauder, February 11, 1947, MPP.

46. St. Bernard's Seminary Catalog, 1908–1911, MPP.

47. Robert McNamara, interview with Dr. Joseph J. Baierl, February 4, 1947, MPP.

48. Ibid.

49. Michael Ryan (1863–1935) was a Canadian native who met Hanna in Rome while the former was a student at the Irish College. He taught philosophy at St. Bernard's from 1899 to 1913.

50. Robert McNamara, interview with Edward Byrne, July 15, 1946, MPP.

51. Robert McNamara, interviews with Dr. Joseph J. Baierl, February 4, 1947, and with Frederick Zwierlein, February 17, 1948, MPP. Under the guidance of its general editors, Charles G. Herbermann, Edward A. Pace, Conde B. Pallen, Thomas J. Shahan, and John J. Wynne, SJ, the first *Catholic Encyclopedia* volume was published in 1907. Eventually there were fifteen volumes, two supplements, and an index to this massive project.

52. Robert McNamara, interview with Frederick Zwierlein, February 17, 1948, MPP.

53. *Monitor,* July 15, 1944.

54. *Rochester Democrat and Chronicle,* October 22, 1912.

55. Frederick J. Zwierlein, *The Life and Letters of Bishop McQuaid* (Rochester, NY: Art Print Shop, 1927), 3:451–52.

56. Robert McNamara, interview with Edward Byrne, July 15, 1946, MPP; Edward Hanna to Denis O'Connell, November 19, 1905, O'Connell Papers, ACUA.

57. Edward Hanna to Denis O'Connell, November 19, 1905, O'Connell Papers, ACUA.

58. *Rochester Herald,* October 22, 1912; Gerd Korman, *Industrialization, Immigrants and Americanizers: The View from Milwaukee, 1866–1921* (Madison: State Historical Society of Wisconsin, 1967), 148–49; Anne Marie Woo-Sam, "Domesticating the Immigrant: California's Commission of Immigration and Housing and the Domestic Immigration Policy Movement, 1910–1945" (PhD diss., University of California, Berkeley, 1999), 67.

59. *Rochester Evening Times,* October 21, 1912, and December 20, 1912.

60. Blake McKelvey, *The Quest for Quality (1890–1925)* (Cambridge, MA: Harvard University Press, 1956), 142 and 154; *Union and Advertiser* (Rochester), December 4, 1912.

61. Philip P. McGuire, "Striking Events in the Life of the Most Reverend Edward Joseph Hanna, D.D., Archbishop of San Francisco," 1926, Hanna Papers, AALA. Hanna also had contact with the pope concerning Italians as the two spoke about the "Italian question" when the

priest was in Rome in 1906 during his sabbatical year. See Edward Hanna to Bernard McQuaid, n.d. [1906], Hanna Papers, ADR.

62. Edward Hanna, "The Doctrine of Christ," January 9, 1898, Hanna Papers, ADR.

63. *Rochester Evening News,* October 21, 1912; *Rochester Herald,* August 8, 1910; McKelvey, *Quest for Quality,* 287.

64. "An Investigation of the Conditions Existing in the Clothing Factories of Rochester, New York," 1913, Rochester Chamber of Commerce, Rochester Public Library, p. 2. The other committee members, all leading citizens of Rochester, were: Granger A. Hollister, Reverend Henry H. Stebbins, Herbert W. Bramley, Henry W. Morgan, Roland B. Woodward, and Dr. Lucius L. Button (who was added after the committee was first formed).

65. Ibid., pp. 9, 18–22. Some of the specifics of the report were: (1) Ventilation—86% good or excellent, 7% fair, 7% poor; (2) Heating—92.7% good or excellent, 6.3% poor; (3) Light, natural—95% good or excellent, (4) Light, artificial—87% excellent, 5% good, 8% poor; (5) Cleanliness—19.7% good, 60.9% fair, 17.9% poor; (6) Toilets—99.8% of men have adequate toilets (cleanliness 33.8% excellent, 37.8% good, 17% fair, 11.4% poor) 99.1% of women have adequate toilets (cleanliness 36.3% excellent, 40% good, 19.6% fair, 6.8% poor).

66. Henry W. Morgan to Edward J. Hanna, January 7, 1913, Hanna File, AASF.

67. *Union and Advertiser,* May 28, 1910.

68. *San Francisco Examiner,* December 17, 1912; *Rochester Herald,* n.d. [1912], clipping, Hanna Papers, ADR.

69. *Monitor,* n.d. [1913], clipping, Hanna Papers, ADR.

70. *San Francisco Examiner,* December 17, 1912; *Rochester Herald,* n.d. [1912], clipping, Hanna Papers, ADR.

71. *San Francisco Examiner,* December 17, 1912; Mason Gray to Edward Hanna, July 28, 1915, Chancery Correspondence, AASF; *The Sheaf* 35, no. 2 (winter 1992): 2.

72. Tom O'Connor to Robert McNamara (telegram), April 2, 1966, MPP. Bishop McQuaid was the official chaplain, but from the outset Hanna took on the duties of chaplain and was very active with the Knights.

73. Stephen Thomas, "Aspects of the History of a Club: Thirty Years of Fortnightly, 1948–1978," unpublished essay; Blake McKelvey, "Rochester's Literary and Book Clubs," *Rochester History* 48, nos. 1–2 (January and April 1986): 7. Besides Fitch, the other six original members of the Fortnightly Club were a who's who of Rochester society: Martin Cook (attorney), Myron Thomas (pastor of Plymouth Congregational

Church), Dr. Max Landsberg (rabbi of Congregation B'rith Kodesh), Newton Mann (Unitarian minister), Charles E. Rider (businessman), and William Peck (journalist and historian).

74. The papers Hanna gave were: January 10, 1899, "Savonarola"; February 20, 1890, "Cardinal Wiseman"; December 10, 1901, "Translation"; March 31, 1903, "Education of the Masses—Italians"; November 29, 1904, "Machiavelli"; February 6, 1906, "The New Apologetic in the Roman Catholic Church"; March 5, 1907, "The French Church Imbroglio"; March 3, 1908, "Coleridge—His Life and Philosophy"; November 23, 1909, "Columbus"; February 7, 1911, "The Spirit of the Middle Ages"; February 20, 1912, "Dante."

75. Edward Hanna to Charles Dewey, May 5, 1913, A. D515 Box 2, Charles Dewey Papers, URL.

76. Joseph Brennan, "Let Us Sing Praises of Famous Men: Edward Hanna, Algernon Crapsey, Max Landsberg," paper delivered at the Fortnightly Club, Rochester, New York, March 5, 2002, pp. 11–12; McKelvey, "Rochester's Literary and Book Clubs," 7.

77. Brennan, "Let Us Sing Praises of Famous Men," appendix; Meeting Minutes, Fortnightly Club, Book #2, Rochester, New York.

78. Edward Hanna to Charles Dewey, November 7, 1916, A. D515, Box 2, Charles Dewey Papers, URL. In another touching note to Dewey, on the occasion of the death of a member of the club, Hanna wrote, "Aside from your dear self there was no one to whom I could speak so simply and frankly. I could talk with him [the deceased] about prayer, asceticism, about Church policy, about the problems of mind and heart, about politics and the thousand questions of everyday. He could listen sympathetically and he could always understand even though we were miles apart in our conclusions. How often in your old library we talked, we three, and I always left feeling better because your lives touched mine." See Edward Hanna to Charles Dewey, September 12, 1918, A. D515, Box 2, Charles Dewey Papers, URL.

79. Meeting Minutes Fortnightly Club, Book #2, Rochester, New York. Records show that Hanna attended meetings on September 25, 1914, November 23, 1915, April 16, 1918, April 17, 1923, and April 27, 1926.

Chapter 2: The Rough Road to San Francisco

1. *Testem benevolentiae*, in *Documents of American Catholic History*, vol. 2, ed. John Tracy Ellis (Wilmington, DE: Michael Glazier, 1987),

538. The Vatican worried that the contentions condemned would water down the faith and lead the faithful astray from traditional orthodoxy.

2. There are many outstanding monographs and articles that tell the complete story of the Americanist crisis. See Thomas McAvoy, CSC, *The Great Crisis in American Catholic History, 1895–1900* (Chicago: Henry Regnery Company, 1957); Gerald P. Fogarty, SJ, *The Vatican and the Americanist Crisis: Denis J. O'Connell, American Agent in Rome, 1885–1903* (Rome: Gregorian University Press, 1974); Robert Emmett Curran, SJ, *Michael Augustine Corrigan and the Shaping of Conservative Catholicism in America, 1878–1902* (New York: Arno Press, 1978); Margaret M. Reher, "Pope Leo XIII and 'Americanism,'" *Theological Studies* 34 (1973): 679–89; Philip Gleason, "The New Americanism in Catholic Historiography," *U.S. Catholic Historian* 11, no. 3 (summer 1993): 1–18; Gerald P. Fogarty, SJ, "The Catholic Hierarchy in the United States between the Third Plenary Council and the Condemnation of Americanism," *U.S. Catholic Historian* 11, no. 3 (summer 1993): 19–35; Thomas Wangler, "Americanist Beliefs and Papal Orthodoxy, 1884–1899," *U.S. Catholic Historian* 11, no. 3 (summer 1993): 37–51; Margaret M. Reher, "Phantom Heresy: A Twice-Told Tale," *U.S. Catholic Historian* 11, no. 3 (summer 1993): 93–105.

3. The spiritual foundation of Americanism was given by Isaac Hecker, founder of the Paulists. For Hecker, American Catholicism had been chosen to lead the world into the new age. In *Testem*, Leo did not condemn political Americanism, the concept of the separation of church and state and consequent patriotic American ideas of society. The document did condemn ecclesiastical Americanism, where it was felt that the faith was being compromised to accommodate people. The authority and wisdom of the Church were to be maintained and honored. Leo rejected Hecker's notion of the merit of passive virtues while extolling the active evangelical counsels of poverty, celibacy, and obedience.

4. Michael V. Gannon, "Before and After Modernism: The Intellectual Isolation of the American Priest," in *The Catholic Priest in the United States: Historical Investigations*, ed. John Tracy Ellis (Collegeville, MN: Saint John's University Press, 1971), 293–383. Gannon gives possible reasons for this intellectual renaissance (see pp. 326–29).

5. Quoted in John Ratte, *Three Modernists* (New York: Sheed & Ward, 1967), 20.

6. Many monographs exist that describe modernism with specific reference to Tyrrell, Loisy, and von Hügel. See Bernard M. G. Reardon, *Roman Catholic Modernism* (London: A & C Black, 1970); David G. Schultenover, *George Tyrrell: In Search of Catholicism* (Shepherdstown, WV: Patmos Press, 1981); Lawrence Barmann, *Baron Friedrich von Hügel and the*

Modernist Crisis in England (Cambridge: Cambridge University Press, 1972); John Ratte, *Three Modernists* (New York: Sheed & Ward, 1967); Alfred Loisy, *My Duel with the Vatican: The Autobiography of a Catholic Modernist* (New York: Greenwood Press, 1968); Marvin O'Connell, *Critics on Trial: An Introduction to the Catholic Modernist Crisis* (Washington, DC: Catholic University of America Press, 1994).

7. For information pertinent to Sullivan, see Michael B. McGarry, CSP, "Modernism in the United States: William Laurence Sullivan, 1872–1935," *Records of the American Catholic Historical Society of Philadelphia*, 90 (1979): 33–52; R. Scott Appleby, "Modernism as the Final Phase of Americanism: William L. Sullivan, American Catholic Apologist," *Harvard Theological Review* 81, no. 2 (1988): 171–92; and Margaret M. Reher, "Americanism and Modernism—Continuity or Discontinuity," *U.S. Catholic Historian* 1 (1980–81): 87–103. For information pertinent to Slattery, see Stephen J. Ochs, *Desegregating the Altar* (Baton Rouge: Louisiana State University Press, 1990), 119–34; and William L. Portier, "Modernism in the United States: The Case of John R. Slattery (1851–1936)" (paper presented at the American Academy of Religion, 1990).

8. See Reher, "Americanism and Modernism," 90–92; Gannon, "Before and After Modernism," 338–39; and Coleman Barry, OSB, *The Catholic University of America 1903–1909* (Washington, DC: Catholic University of America Press, 1950), 176–83.

9. See R. Scott Appleby, *"Church and Age Unite!" The Modernist Impulse in American Catholicism* (Notre Dame, IN: University of Notre Dame Press, 1992). Thomas McAvoy, CSC, wrote, "Because of the sparseness of Theological and Scriptural writings among the Catholics in the United States it would be difficult to say that the condemned Modernism formally existed in this country." See Thomas McAvoy, "The Catholic Minority after the Americanist Controversy," *Review of Politics* 21, no. 1 (January 1959): 72–73.

10. Jay P. Dolan, *The American Catholic Experience* (Garden City, NY: Doubleday, 1985), 317. James Connelly, CSC, "History of the Congregation of Holy Cross in the United States" (booklet, Notre Dame, Indiana, 1992). John Zahm, CSC, *Evolution and Dogma* (Chicago: D. H. McBride & Co., 1896). The Holy Cross community wanted to minimize problems. Father Gilbert Francais, superior general, and Father Louis L'Etorneau, provincial of the American Province, ordered Zahm to remove the book. In a rather ironic turn of events, Zahm was then appointed as American provincial of the congregation.

11. During his tenure as rector of the North American College, O'Connell hosted regular discussions at his Roman apartment, dubbed

"Liberty Hall." These discussions centered on the concepts of Americanism. Besides Zahm, other regular members of the group were John Slattery, Franz Kraus, and Alfred Loisy.

12. Modernism in the United States has its roots in the Americanist movement. Contemporary scholarship has challenged the earlier "phantom heresy" theory promoted by Thomas McAvoy and Felix Klein. The historian Christopher Kauffman sees a connection between the movements through the new apologetic voiced by Alphonse Magnien, SS, and articulated by John Hogan, SS. William Portier demonstrates a link through Slattery and his affiliation with the Americanists, especially Denis O'Connell. Margaret Reher has stated, "The fresh wave of intellectualism that surged through the 'elite' of the American clergy in the early 1900s was, at least partially, due to the encouragement given progressive thought by the Americanists in the previous decade." See McAvoy, *The Great Crisis;* Felix Klein, *Americanism: A Phantom Heresy* (Atchison, KS: Aquin Book Shop, 1951); Christopher Kauffman, *Tradition and Transformation in Catholic Culture* (New York: Macmillan, 1988), 153–224; Portier, "Modernism in the United States," 92; and Reher, "Americanism and Modernism," 99.

13. It is ironic that Corrigan, the leader of the conservative element in the Americanist crisis, would have invited the Sulpicians, a progressive community based in the Gallican tradition, to head the faculty at St. Joseph's. Corrigan felt the Sulpicians could provide better educational opportunities for his seminarians than the secular clergy.

14. Michael DeVito, "Principles of Ecclesial Reform according to the New York Review (1905–1908)" (PhD diss., Fordham University, 1974), 30–31. See also DeVito's book version of his dissertation, *New York Review* (New York: United States Catholic Historical Society, 1977), 1–61, which discusses the *Review's* inception and early days.

15. James Gaffey, *Citizen of No Mean City: Archbishop Patrick Riordan of San Francisco (1841–1914)* (Wilmington, NC: Consortium Books, 1976), 277–87. The other two men listed on the *terna* were Bishop Thomas Conaty, rector of the Catholic University of America, as *dignior* and Father James Cleary of Minneapolis as *dignus.*

16. Patrick Riordan to Bernard McQuaid, April 4, 1907, McQuaid Papers, ADR.

17. Patrick Riordan to Bernard McQuaide *[sic]*, April 18, 1907, McQuaid Papers, ADR.

18. Patrick Riordan to Denis O'Connell, May 18, 1907, O'Connell Papers, ACUA.

19. Patrick Riordan to Bernard McQuaide *[sic]*, May 18, 1907, McQuaid Papers, ADR.

20. Diomede Falconio to James (John) Farley, January 15, 1908, Farley Papers, Archives Archdiocese of New York (hereafter AANY), Yonkers, New York.

21. Thomas Coakley, "Position Paper," pp. 1–2, Miscellaneous Hanna File, ADR.

22. Andrew Meehan to J. F. Goggin, December 12, 1907, Meehan Papers, ADR. Meehan told Goggin of a recent conversation he had with Gotti where the cardinal had told him of a letter he had recently sent to Riordan in support of Hanna.

23. Bernard McQuaid to Patrick Riordan, September 18, 1907, Riordan Papers, AASF.

24. Patrick Riordan to Bernard McQuaid, December 27, 1907, McQuaid Papers, ADR.

25. Gerald P. Fogarty, SJ, *American Catholic Biblical Scholarship* (San Francisco: Harper & Row, 1989), 133.

26. James P. Gaffey, *Citizen of No Mean City*, 525. When Lepicier was given a copy of the first volume of the *Review* he was immediately on guard as references were made to works on the Index of Forbidden Books and several articles spoke of the progress and development of doctrine. See Thomas Coakley to Robert McNamara, June 22, 1946, MPP.

27. Edward Hanna to Bernard McQuaid, August 20, 1907, McQuaid Papers, ADR. Hanna, on vacation in Lake Placid, New York, wrote, "It was here I received the news about San Francisco. Of course something has happened and I surmise that the affair in Rome is not as yet settled....Someone in Rome has been giving information and this information has been forwarded to the Hearst newspapers. But to be candid, the news though not unexpected, finds me not prepared." This letter indicates that Hanna knew that his writings might be suspect. The Roman source may have been Lepicier but there is no extant documentation to verify this hypothesis.

28. Francis Duffy to Edward Hanna, January 8, 1905, O'Connell Papers, ACUA.

29. Alexis Lepicier (1863–1936) studied at *Propaganda Fide*, receiving doctorates in theology and philosophy. In 1892 he was appointed by Leo XIII to the chair of dogmatic theology at the Urban College, which was vacated by Francesco Satolli, who has been appointed as the first apostolic delegate to the United States. Lepicier's writings influenced the neoscholastic revival. His famous tract *De Beata Virgine Maria Matre Dei* was one of the earliest scholastic treatments of Marian theology.

30. Pope Pius X, *"Pascendi Dominici Gregis,"* in *The Papal Encyclicals 1903–1939*, ed. Claudia Carlen, IHM (Wilmington, NC: McGrath Publishing Company, 1981), #28, 71–98.

31. Andrew Meehan to Bernard McQuaid, November 8, 1907, McQuaid Papers, ADR.

32. Patrick Riordan to Bernard McQuaide [*sic*], November 8, 1907, McQuaid Papers, ADR.

33. *Rochester Democrat and Chronicle*, December 2, 1907.

34. Andrew Meehan to J. F. Goggin, December 2, 1907, Meehan Papers, ADR.

35. Andrew Meehan to Bernard McQuaid, December 17, 1907; Salvatore Brandi to Bernard McQuaid, December 28, 1907, McQuaid Papers, ADR.

36. Bernard McQuaid to Rafael Merry del Val, November 12, 1907, McQuaid Papers, ADR.

37. Andrew Meehan to Bernard McQuaid, January 4, 1908, McQuaid Papers, ADR. There is no extant letter that proves Meehan's claim. However, Andrew Breen, the one who would later admit to the accusations, was quoted in the *Rochester Herald*, January 14, 1908, as having informed Riordan of the charges he had levied against Hanna.

38. *Rochester Democrat and Chronicle*, January 13, 1908, Hanna Papers, ADR. Breen was ordained in 1893 in Rome. He returned immediately to Rochester and was a member of the founding faculty at St. Bernard's Seminary. Like Hanna, Breen had been groomed by McQuaid for his seminary position.

39. Bernard McQuaid to Andrew Breen, January 30, 1908, Breen Papers, ADR.

40. *Rochester Democrat and Chronicle*, February 4, 1908; *Post Express* (Rochester), February 26, 1909.

41. This was the claim of William F. Stauder who was a St. Bernard's student during the events narrated. See William F. Stauder, interview by Robert McNamara, February 11, 1947, MPP.

42. Bernard McQuaid to Daniel Hudson, CSC, February 18, 1908, Hudson Papers, Archives University of Notre Dame (hereafter AUND), Notre Dame, Indiana.

43. Bernard McQuaid to James (John) Farley, February 2, 1908, Farley Correspondence, AANY.

44. Bernard McQuaid to Daniel Hudson, CSC, February 18, 1908, Hudson Papers, AUND.

45. *Rochester Democrat and Chronicle*, January 14, 1908.

46. *Rochester Herald*, January 14, 1908.

47. Andrew Meehan to Bernard McQuaid, January 12, 1908, McQuaid Papers, ADR.

48. *Rochester Herald*, January 14, 1908, clipping, Breen Papers, ADR.

49. Robert McNamara, interviews with Edward Byrne, July 15, 1946; with J. F. Goggin, November 6, 1949; John J. Wynne to Robert McNamara, May 11, 1944, MPP.

50. *New York Review* 1, no.1 (June–July 1905): 1.

51. Michael J. DeVito, "*The New York Review* (1905–1908)," *The Priest* 34 (February 1978): 33.

52. Francis Duffy to Edward Hanna, January 8, 1905, O'Connell Papers, ACUA. Duffy refers to attacks of "the Philistines" that the *Review* can expect in the future.

53. Edward Hanna, "The Human Knowledge of Christ I," *New York Review* 1, no. 3 (October–November 1905): 303.

54. Ibid., 316.

55. *Pascendi Dominici Gregis*, #42. The document says that upon these three precepts modernists "wage unrelenting war."

56. Edward Hanna, "The Human Knowledge of Christ II," *New York Review* 2, no. 4 (December 1905–January 1906): 430.

57. Ibid., 429.

58. Ibid., 428–29; Pascendi, #13.

59. Edward Hanna, "The Human Knowledge of Christ III," *New York Review* 1, no. 5 (February–March 1906): 597–615.

60. *Pascendi*, #4.

61. Appleby, "*Church and Age Unite!*" 165.

62. Edward Hanna, "Absolution," in *Catholic Encyclopedia*, vol. 1 (New York: Robert Appleton Company, 1907), 61.

63. Robert F. McNamara interview with William F. Stauder, February 11, 1947, MPP. Stauder, as a student at St. Bernard's, recalls that Hanna stated that the power to forgive sins was not necessarily in the consciousness of the Church from the outset. He was challenged in this view by only one student who said that if the Church was not conscious of absolution from the beginning who or what could prevent any doctrine from being foisted upon her later?

64. Edward Hanna, "Penance," in *Catholic Encyclopedia*, 11:620.

65. Gannon, "Before and After Modernism," 349.

66. *Pascendi*, ## 13, 26, and 28.

67. *San Francisco Examiner*, January 13, 1908, and *Rochester Post Express*, January 13, 1908, clippings Hanna Papers, ADR.

68. Andrew Meehan to Bernard McQuaid, January 12, 1908, McQuaid Papers, ADR.

69. Patrick Riordan to Bernard McQuaid, January 13, 1908, McQuaid Papers, ADR.

70. *Rochester Herald*, January 18, 1908; *Rochester Post Express*, February 24, 1908, clippings, Hanna Papers, ADR.

71. Andrew Meehan to Bernard McQuaid, January 22, 1908, McQuaid Papers, ADR; McQuaid to Daniel Hudson, CSC, February 18, 1908, Hudson Papers, AUND.

72. *Pascendi*, #50.

73. Bernard McQuaid to "Most Eminent Cardinal," n.d. [1907–8], McQuaid Papers, ADR.

74. Robert F. McNamara interview with Francis Burns, n.d., MPP.

75. Bernard McQuaid to Cardinal Rafael Merry del Val (copy), November 12, 1907, McQuaid Papers, ADR. McQuaid wanted to assure the cardinal secretary of state that St. Bernard's was theologically sound and orthodox.

76. Ibid.

77. Bernard McQuaid to Andrew Breen, January 30, 1908, Breen Papers, ADR.

78. *Rochester Herald*, January 14, 1908, clipping, Hanna Papers, ADR.

79. Faculty Statement, December 8, 1907, Hanna Papers, ADR.

80. Statement of St. Bernard's Seminary Students, January 14, 1908, Hanna Papers, ADR.

81. Patrick Riordan to James (John) Farley, June 25, 1908, Farley Papers, AANY; Gaffey, *Citizen of No Mean City*, 543–44.

82. Robert F. McNamara interview with T. F. Coakley, June 22, 1946, MPP.

83. Salvatore Brandi to Bernard McQuaid, December 7, 1907; Andrew Meehan to McQuaid, December 17, 1907, McQuaid Papers, ADR.

84. Edward Hanna to Cardinal Girolamo Gotti, December 16, 1907, Hanna Papers, ADR.

85. Francesco Satolli to Edward Hanna, April 5, 1908, Riordan Papers, AASF; Patrick Riordan to Bernard McQuaid, January 13, 1908, McQuaid Papers, ADR. Riordan advised McQuaid that *Propaganda* wanted another article from Hanna. He wrote, "If this is done there will be no further delay." See also Gaffey, *Citizen of No Mean City*, 530.

86. Andrew Meehan to Bernard McQuaid, January 19, 1908, McQuaid Papers, ADR.

87. Edward Hanna, "The Human Knowledge of Christ IV," *New York Review* 3, nos. 4–5 (January–April 1908): 399.

88. Ibid., 391.

89. Edward Hanna, "The Power of the Keys," *New York Review* 3, nos. 4–5 (January–April 1908): 562. Several years later, in 1912, Hanna wrote an errata to his original article on "Absolution." The new wording clearly demonstrates an effort to move away from his previous position on development of doctrine: "Though it is clear that this power of absolution was granted to the Church, and therefore, known to the Apostles and their successors, the teaching body of the Church, from the very beginning, still it requires careful study to trace the tradition of this grant and its realization in the practice of the faithful back in the first centuries, or to invert this process, to follow the evidences of this practice from the first allusions to it in ecclesiastical writings down to the last word of the vast body of theological doctrine on this subject." See *Catholic Encyclopedia Errata*, 1912, p. 776.

90. Thomas Shelley, *Dunwoodie: The History of St. Joseph's Seminary, Yonkers, New York* (Westminster, MD: Christian Classics, 1993), 155. See pp. 148–71 for a more detailed account of the history of the *New York Review* and St. Joseph Seminary.

91. Andrew Meehan to J. F. Goggin, February 19, 1908, Meehan Papers, ADR. Satolli had told Meehan that some Vatican officials were disappointed in Hanna's second efforts.

92. Giovanni Genocchi to Patrick Riordan, August 5, 1908, Riordan Papers, AASF.

93. Ibid.

94. Edward Hanna, "Some Recent Books on Catholic Theology," *The American Journal of Theology* 10 (January 1906): 175. This is only one of several statements that speak of the process of development in Roman Catholic doctrine.

95. Ibid., 184

96. Patrick Riordan to John Ireland, October 21, 1908, Riordan Papers, AASF.

97. Quoted in *Rochester Herald*, September 14, 1908.

98. McNamara, "Archbishop Hanna, Rochesterian," 17; Colman Barry, *The Catholic University of America, 1903–1909:* Rectorship of Denis J. O'Connell (Washington, DC: Catholic University Press, 1950), 253–54.

99. Patrick Riordan to Daniel Hudson, CSC, July 28, 1911, Hudson Papers, AUND; Gaffey, *Citizen of No Mean City*, 313–14.

100. *Rochester Herald*, October 22, 1912.

101. Patrick Riordan to Edward Hanna, October 25, 1912, LBR (4a), AASF.

102. Patrick Riordan to Daniel Hudson, CSC, November 9, 1912, Hudson Papers, AUND.

103. *Union and Advertiser,* November 29, 1912; *Rochester Herald,* December 5, 1912.

104. Quoted in *Rochester Herald,* December 5, 1912.

105. Cathedral Calendar Souvenir, Consecration of Edward Hanna, December 4, 1912, Hanna Papers, ADR.

Chapter 3: The Archbishop of San Francisco

1. Tom Cole, *A Short History of San Francisco* (San Francisco: Lexikos, 1981), 36.

2. Ibid., 70, 94, 87.

3. Ibid., 108; Oscar Lewis, *San Francisco: Mission to Metropolis* (San Diego: Howell-North Books, 1980), 191; John Bernard McGloin, SJ, *San Francisco: The Story of a City* (San Rafael, CA: Presidio Books, 1978), 135.

4. Quoted in McGloin, *San Francisco,* 143.

5. McGloin, *San Francisco,* 208–12; Cole, *Short History of San Francisco,* 115–16; Lewis, *San Francisco,* 230; William Issel and Robert W. Cherny, *San Francisco, 1865–1932: Politics, Power, and Urban Development* (Berkeley: University of California Press, 1986), 174–76.

6. McGloin, *San Francisco,* 156.

7. Ibid., 299.

8. Issel and Cherny, *San Francisco, 1865–1932,* 174, 166–67.

9. Ibid., 197.

10. *San Francisco Examiner,* December 22, 1912.

11. *Monitor,* n.d. [1913], clipping, Hanna Papers, ADR; *Union and Advertiser* (Rochester), March 26, 1913.

12. Quoted in *Tidings* (Los Angeles), September 2, 1983, clipping, Hanna File, AALA.

13. *Monitor,* n.d. [1913], clipping, Hanna Papers, ADR.

14. *Rochester Herald,* May 31, 1915.

15. Edward Hanna to Charles Dewey, May 5, 1913, A. D515, Box 2, Dewey Papers, URL.

16. Memoranda Book H-29, AASF; Philip P. McGuire, "Striking Events in the Life of the Most Reverend Edward Joseph Hanna, D.D., Archbishop of San Francisco," 1926, pp. 15–16, Hanna Papers, AALA.

17. Patrick Riordan to Edward Hanna (Telegram), July 13, 1914, Hanna Papers, AASF; *Monitor,* September 15, 1944.

18. Report of the Commission of Immigration and Housing of California to Governor Hiram Johnson, July 10, 1914, Simon Lubin Papers, Bancroft Library, University of California, Berkeley (hereafter BL-UCB), Berkeley, California.

19. *Monitor*, January 10, 1914, July 15, 1944; McGuire, "Events in the Life of Edward Hanna," p. 16. The other members of the executive committee were Jesse W. Lilienthal, James D. Phelan, Albert Ehtgott, Raphael Weill, Walter MacArthur, Harry Bogart, Tim Reardon, F. K. Stevenot, Blanche I. Sanborn.

20. Memoranda Book, H-29, Archepiscopal Council Meeting Minutes, January 1, 1915, H-31, Manuscripts, AASF.

21. Thomas Shahan to Edward Hanna, May 12, 1915, Chancery Correspondence, AASF.

22. John Cantwell to Garrett Cotter, February 6, 1915, LB 51; John Cantwell to William Cantwell, May 20, 1915, LB 52, AASF.

23. Memoranda Book, H-29; Edward Hanna to John Bonzano, June 1, 1915, B-6, Manuscripts, AASF.

24. Pope Benedict XV to "The Suffragan Bishops," June 1, 1915, L-155, AASF.

25. *Monitor*, June 5, 1915; *San Francisco Examiner*, September 8, 1915, clipping, California History Room—San Francisco Public Library (hereafter CHR—SFPL), San Francisco, California.

26. Memoranda Book, H-29, AASF.

27. Quoted in *Monitor*, July 31, 1915.

28. *San Francisco Examiner*, September 8, 1915.

29. McGuire, "Events in the Life of Edward Hanna," p. 29.

30. *Monitor*, September 11, 1915.

31. Luetts Mayer to Edward Hanna, August 14, 1915, Chancery Correspondence, AASF.

32. Edward Hanna to Charles Dewey, October 6, 1915, A. D515, Box 2, Dewey Papers, URL; O. K. Cushing to Hanna, July 10, 1915, Chancery Correspondence, AASF.

33. Edward O'Day, "Bishop Edward J. Hanna," in *Varied Types*, ed. Edward O'Day, 128–32 (San Francisco: Town Talk Press, 1915), 128; *San Francisco Examiner*, March 9, 1935.

34. *Monitor*, n.d. [1912–1913], clipping, Hanna Papers, ADR.

35. *Boston Republic*, December 7, 1912, clipping, Hanna Papers, ADR.

36. *Monitor*, December 4, 1915.

37. McGuire, "Events in the Life of Edward Hanna," p. 10.

38. John J. Mitty, Sermon, August 1947, Hanna Papers, AASF.

39. The sermon series topics were: "The Spirit of the World Against the Spirit of Christ," "The Church and the Family," "Christ, the Child and the School," "The Church and the State," and "The Church and Labor."

40. Edward Hanna, Sermon, twenty-eighth International Eucharistic Congress, June 20–24, 1926, International Eucharistic Congress Files, Archives, Archdiocese of Chicago (hereafter AAC), Chicago, Illinois.

41. McGuire, "Events in the Life of Edward Hanna," pp. 53 and 68.

42. Edward Hanna, Sermon, "The Spirit of the World Against the Spirit of Christ," n.d. [Lent 1920], Hanna Papers, ADR.

43. Edward Hanna, Sermons, "No Title," January 22, 1928, and "Our Intellectual Heritage," *Monitor,* n.d., Clipping, Hanna Papers, AASF.

44. Edward Hanna, Sermon, "Our Intellectual Heritage," *Monitor,* n.d., clipping, Hanna Papers, AASF.

45. Edward Hanna, Sermon, n.d., Hanna Papers, AASF.

46. Edward Hanna to Angelo Rossi, January 10, 1931, L-165, AASF; Hanna, "Christmas Message," *NCWC Bulletin* 5, no. 7 (December 1923): 11.

47. Edward Hanna, Address, February 8, 1918, Simon Lubin Papers, BL-UCB.

48. *San Francisco Examiner,* May 10, 1926, and November 20, 1925, Clippings, CHR-SFPL; Edward Hanna, Sermon, "The Church and the Family," n.d., Lent 1920, Hanna Papers, ADR.

49. Edward Hanna, Sermon, "Christ, the Home, and the Child," December 1920, Hanna Papers, AASF.

50. Quoted in *San Francisco Examiner,* March 8, 1920.

51. *San Francisco Examiner,* October 17, 1921.

52. Edward Hanna, Sermon, "Christ, the Church, and the Home," December 1920, Hanna Papers, AASF. In this same sermon Hanna further stated, "If philosophy and statesmanship teach the permanence of the marriage bond, how much more clearly is it brought home to the christian *[sic]* conscience in the teaching of Christ Himself, and in the traditions of His Church? Christ not only blessed marriage as the great institution of nature,...He raised the marriage bond to the dignity of a sacrament."

53. Ibid.; *San Francisco Chronicle,* November 18, 1924.

54. Quoted in Edward O'Day, "Bishop Edward J. Hanna," 131.

55. NCWC Administrative Committee Meeting Minutes, September 27, 1923, NCWC Administrative Committee Papers, ACUA.

56. Quoted in *San Francisco Chronicle,* November 18, 1924.

57. Newspaper Clipping, n.d., Hanna File, AALA; Galley of Article on Edward Hanna, n.d. [1944], MPP; "A Layman's Friend," n.d., Hanna Papers, ADR; Edward Hanna, Essay for *NCWC Bulletin*, n.d. [January 1929], NCWC General Administration Papers, ACUA.

58. Gerald P. Fogarty, SJ, ed., *Patterns of Episcopal Leadership* (New York: Macmillan, 1989), 167–70.

59. James P. Gaffey, "Bishops on the Fringe: Patrick Riordan of San Francisco and Francis Clement Kelley of Oklahoma City," in ibid., 185.

60. Archepiscopal Council Meeting Minutes, August 14, 1915, April 18, 1916, November 28, 1917, H-31 Manuscripts; John Cantwell to Cardinal Giovanni Genocchi, December 10, 1917, James Cantwell to F. S. Maginnis, August 20, 1926, Chancery Correspondence, AASF.

61. *Monitor*, March 6, 1926, and March 20, 1926.

62. Archepiscopal Council Meeting Minutes, July 9, 1923, H-31, Manuscripts, AASF.

63. Parish Statistics, A-30, AASF; *Catholic Directories*, 1915–1935; Francis Weber, *Encyclopedia of California's Catholic Heritage, 1769–1999* (Mission Hills, CA: Saint Francis Historical Society, 2001), 272. Various sources differ on the number of parishes in the Archdiocese of San Francisco. Parish statistics in the archdiocese list 180 parishes and missions in 1915, but the *Catholic Directory* of 1915 lists 182. Parish statistics list 237 parishes and missions in 1936; the *Catholic Directory* for 1935 lists 222.

64. Archepiscopal Council Meeting Minutes, December 11, 1924, July 2, 1928, H-31, Manuscripts, AASF.

65. Ibid., February 12, 1916; John Cantwell to John Wynne, SJ, November 16, 1916, LB 59, AASF. Hanna's policy on confirmation was: For parishes where the sacrament was administered each year or every two years, a child "must have begun their fourteenth year." In all other parishes, "they must have entered their thirteenth year."

66. Memoranda Book, December 20, 1920, H-29 Manuscripts; James Cantwell to P. J. Kenedy and sons, December 4, 1922, Chancery Correspondence; Pietro Fumasoni Biondi to Edward Hanna, June 5, 1931, Apostolic Delegate Papers, AASF.

67. Memoranda Book, H-29, Manuscripts, W. W. Campbell to Edward Hanna, March 16, 1926, Chancery Correspondence, AASF.

68. *Monitor*, April 29, 1916, October 12, 1918, May 22, 1920, May 24, 1924; Memoranda Book, H-29, Manuscripts, AASF. Galley proof of article on Hanna, n.d., MPP; Itinerary of the California Holy Year Pilgrimage to Rome [1925], Chancery Correspondence, AASF.

69. Memoranda Book, H-29, Manuscripts; Archbishop Michael Kelly to Edward Hanna, June 17, 1928, Hanna Papers, AASF; *Monitor,* June 25, 1932; Weber, *Encyclopedia of California's Catholic Heritage,* 271.

70. *Call* (San Francisco), March 7, 1927, Clipping, CHR-SFPL.

71. *Monitor,* October 4, 1924, and May 31, 1924.

72. *Republic* (Boston), Clipping, December 7, 1912, Hanna Papers, ADR.

73. *Monitor,* May 31, 1924.

74. *San Francisco Examiner,* September 21, 1918.

75. Ibid., September 25, 1921.

76. Weber, *Encyclopedia of California's Catholic Heritage,* 208. The letter's reference to hanging a hat from the roof of the cathedral meant that a new cardinal would not be named until one of the four in the United States had died and his hat had been hung from the rafters of the cathedral as is the custom.

77. Rumors that Hanna would be made a cardinal surfaced in 1916, 1918, 1919, 1921, 1923, 1924, 1925, 1929, and 1930.

78. *San Francisco Examiner,* October 1, 1931.

79. Edward Hanna, Address, n.d., Hanna Papers, AALA.

80. *Monitor,* April 20, 1920.

81. Ibid., February 17, 1934.

82. McGuire, "Events in the Life of Edward Hanna," p. 109.

83. Ibid., pp. 168, 109, 158, and 133. Weber, *Encyclopedia of California's Catholic Heritage,* 270.

84. Quoted in Weber, *Encyclopedia of California's Catholic Heritage,* 271.

85. *Monitor,* May 15, 1926.

86. Edward Hanna to Angelo Rossi, September 26, 1932, L-165, AASF.

87. In 1904 at a national convention in St. Louis, three separate organizations, the Educational Seminary Faculties (1897), the Association of Catholic Colleges (1898), and the Parish School Conference (1902), merged to form the National Catholic Education Association. For more details, see Harold A. Buetow, *Of Singular Benefit: The Story of U.S. Catholic Education* (London: Macmillan, 1970), 181.

88. Francis Howard to Edward Hanna, February 23, 1918; P. K. Gordon to James Cantwell, June 3, 1918, Chancery Correspondence, AASF. Extant data does not indicate if Hanna ever was actively involved with the preparation of a catechism. Concurrently, Peter Yorke, an Irish-born priest who had become very popular in San Francisco through his advocacy for organized labor between 1900 and 1910, wrote a series of

religion textbooks that were popular and widely distributed in the archdiocese. See Jeffrey Burns, "¿Que es Esto? The Transformation of St. Peter's Parish, San Francisco: 1913–1970," in *American Congregations*, vol. 1, ed. James P. Wind and James W. Lewis, 396–462 (Chicago: University of Chicago Press, 1994), 405.

89. McGuire, "Events in the Life of Edward Hanna," p. 133.

90. John J. Mitty, Sermon, August 8, 1947, Hanna Papers, AASF.

91. "Mandate of Most Reverend Archbishop Concerning the Course of Study in Catholic Elementary and Grammar Schools," May 23, 1922, A-82, Manuscripts, AASF.

92. *Monitor*, September 22, 1922.

93. John Cantwell to Sister M. Veronica, February 17, 1916, LB 56; Cantwell to D. O. Crowley, August 2, 1916, LB 57; B. Ellen Burke to Edward Hanna, June 17, 1916, Chancery Correspondence, AASF.

94. James McHugh to Edward Hanna, January 14, 1929, A-19, Manuscripts, AASF.

95. Hanna carefully scrutinized reports from schools. When something was not to his satisfaction the principal and/or pastor received a letter, generally from John Cantwell, expressing the archbishop's dismay about some specific items and asking that significant efforts be made to rectify the situation as soon as possible.

96. As one example, in 1929 Hanna realized that a need was present for another Catholic college for women in San Francisco. Dominican sisters had petitioned the archbishop for permission to open a junior college in the city, but Hanna had already made arrangements with the Religious of the Sacred Heart to move their College of the Sacred Heart to San Francisco. Thus, Hanna asked the Dominicans to defer any openings until evidence for the need for another college was present. See James Cantwell to Sister M. Raymond, OP, March 11, 1929, Hanna Papers, AASF.

97. Annual Diocesan School Reports, 1915 to 1935, A-82, Manuscripts, AASF.

98. Joseph White, *The Diocesan Seminary in the United States* (Notre Dame, IN: University of Notre Dame Press, 1989), 171; James Gaffey, *Men of Menlo: Transformation of an American Seminary* (Lanham, MD: University Press of America, 1992), 2–9. Gaffey claims that the Sulpicians were superior spiritual formators but lacked in their ability to form San Francisco's seminarians intellectually.

99. Edward Hanna, Address, "A Message to the Schools," July 14, 1918, Hanna Papers, ADR; McGuire, "Events in the Life of Edward Hanna," p. 147, Hanna Papers, AALA; Edward Hanna, "The Message of

the Seminary," *The Catholic Educational Association Bulletin* 15 (November 1918): 614.

100. James Cantwell to John E. Knight, October 10, 1916, LB 58, AASF; Gaffey, *Men of Menlo*, 19.

101. Hanna, "Message of the Seminary," 615–18.

102. Hanna received many requests for incardination to the archdiocese and many additional requests for service to particular ethnic groups. Often he, through his representatives, would answer requests for service to particular groups by making reference to orders and congregations already present in the archdiocese who were engaged in the work, implying that additional personnel were not necessary. When individual requests for incardination were received, but quotas were filled, a general response was: "While the diocese of San Francisco cannot be considered in need of priests, especially as we have had a number ordained recently, and have others coming to us in the fall, still there is here, as elsewhere, need of first class priests." See John Cantwell to William Mullway, July 3, 1916, LB 57, AASF.

103. John Cantwell to Canon Garrett Cotter, July 3, 1916, LB 57, AASF.

104. John Cantwell to John Foley, DD, December 6, 1916, LB 59, AASF.

105. James Cantwell to William Harper, May 26, 1922, Chancery Correspondence; Archepiscopal Council Meeting Minutes, February 23, 1917, H-31, Manuscripts, AASF. See also Gaffey, *Men of Menlo*, 10. Hanna expected a reimbursement of $1,500 at a rate of $110 annually, beginning in the second year of ordination.

106. Gaffey, *Men of Menlo*, 18.

107. Thomas Millett to Nicholas Cooke, July 22, 1927, Chancery Correspondence, AASF.

108. Patrick Ryan to Nicholas Cooke, August 23, 1927, Hanna Papers, AASF.

109. Gaffey, *Men of Menlo*, 6–7, 16, 32.

110. Ibid., 16–17.

111. John Mahoney to Garret McEnerney, June 12, 1920, L-23; Archepiscopal Council Meeting Minutes, March 20, 1920, H-31, Manuscripts, AASF.

112. Memoranda Book, H-29, Manuscripts, AASF; *Monitor*, March 11, 1922.

113. Archepiscopal Council Meeting Minutes, October 14, 1921, H-31, Manuscripts, AASF; McGuire, "Events in the Life of Edward Hanna," p. 135, AALA.

114. The fund drive began well after some initial pledges were paid, but many others remained in arrears. In August 1925 Hanna initiated two separate letter writing campaigns asking for assistance from his pastors in collecting pledges. A typical letter read, "We are making a personal appeal to each pastor to aid us in collecting the balance of the Educational Fund. I know you will do all you can to help us in this undertaking when you realize that we have a million dollar debt on our new seminary, and are trying to avoid what has been done in other dioceses, namely apportioning the seminary debt to the various parishes." See James Cantwell to John Tobin, August 5, 1925, Chancery Correspondence, AASF.

115. Gaffey, *Men of Menlo*, 17.

116. The Catholic Educational Fund never found the appeal Hanna had hoped to generate, despite several writing campaigns to all pastors of the archdiocese urging them to press parishioners to fulfill pledges made when the campaign was initiated. The fund's failure to generate the desired monies did not stop construction of St. Joseph's, but other proposed projects were curtailed. In March 1928 Hanna officially canceled the drive and all pledges not paid to date. See James Cantwell to John Tobin, August 4, 1925; Cantwell to Mrs. G. V. Menchan Jr., March 13, 1928, Chancery Correspondence, AASF.

117. John Mahoney to Clarence Morris, March 25, 1921, and March 3, 1921, Chancery Correspondence, AASF. Until the 1921 and 1924 immigration restriction laws began to take hold, Catholics continued to flock to America's shores, arriving most prominently from Italy, Russia, Poland, and other eastern and southern European countries between 1880 and 1924.

118. Quoted in James Cantwell to Robert Drady, April 4, 1923; See also James Cantwell to Edward Hanna, April 4, 1923, Chancery Correspondence, AASF.

119. James Cantwell to John J. Burke, CSP, October 28, 1925, Chancery Correspondence, AASF.

120. *Monitor*, February 17, 1934.

121. California was the only state in the Union in 1925 that did not grant tax-exempt status to private nonprofit schools.

122. James Cantwell to John Dollard, March 14, 1924 [*sic*—1925]; Cantwell to John Coen, April 2, 1925, Chancery Correspondence, AASF.

123. James Cantwell to Charles W. Fay, October 9, 1926; Cantwell to Paul Scharrenberg, October 13, 1926; Cantwell to Charles Kenwick, October 21, 1926; Cantwell to R. G. Sproul, October 22, 1926; Cantwell to W. N. Burkhardt, October 13, 1926, Chancery Correspondence, AASF.

124. James Cantwell to Joseph Scott, June 4, 1928, Chancery Correspondence, AASF.

125. James Cantwell to Joseph Scott, June 4, 1928, Hanna Papers, AASF.

126. John Cantwell to Edward Hanna, March 27, 1933, Cantwell Correspondence, AASF. Cantwell's comments to Hanna are very interesting in light of the Los Angeles ordinary's words to Hanna only a few months earlier on the same subject. He wrote, "The more I think about our campaign for the exemption of our schools from taxation, the less enthusiastic I am about it." See John Cantwell to Edward Hanna, October 29, 1932, Cantwell Correspondence, AALA.

127. Edward Hanna to William Randolph Hearst, May 11 and May 16, 1933; Hanna to Dr. C. P. Deems, May 20, 1933, Chancery Correspondence, AASF.

128. "Plan of Campaign"; Charles N. Dempster's Argument in Favor of Amendment No. 47, A-29 Manuscripts, AASF.

129. *San Francisco Examiner,* June 20, 1933.

130. Edward Hanna, KGO Radio Talk, June 24, 1933, A-29 Manuscripts, AASF.

131. Edward Hanna to "Reverend Dear Father," June 28, 1933, A-29, Manuscripts, AASF.

132. Section 214 of the California Revenue and Taxation Code, which exempted private nonprofit schools from taxation, was enacted in 1945.

133. For additional information, see Gordon M. Seely, "Church-State Conflict and Catholic Schools in California," in *Catholic San Francisco: Sesquicentennial Essays,* ed. Jeffrey M. Burns, 237–44 (Menlo Park, CA: Archives of the Archdiocese of San Francisco, 2005).

134. *Monitor,* July 17, 1944.

135. Ibid., February 27, 1926; John Cantwell to Ernst Power, June 6, 1915, LB 52, AASF.

136. John J. Mitty, Sermon, August 12, 1944, Hanna Papers, AASF; Edward Hanna, "Message of the Seminary," 610; McGuire, "Events in the Life of Edward Hanna," p. 38, Hanna Papers, AALA.

137. Edward Hanna, "A Message to the Schools," July 14, 1918, Hanna Papers, ADR.

138. Edward Hanna, "Message of the Seminary," 614, 618.

139. Extant data is replete with examples of letters sent by Hanna's assistants in the chancery to priests demanding compliance with personal and parochial financial indebtedness. One typical letter read, "The Most Reverend Archbishop wishes to see you on Saturday morning. His Grace

feels much humiliated to have to write to you so often in reference to your bills." See James Cantwell to Samuel Tarrant, February 5, 1925, Chancery Correspondence, AASF.

140. Edward McGlynn was a faithful supporter of the socialist politician Henry George and his Single Tax Theory. In a protracted and often nasty dispute, Corrigan and McGlynn locked horns over the basic issue of a priest's loyalty and obedience to his local ordinary. When McGlynn persisted in his support for George and rejected Corrigan's order to desist, the archbishop excommunicated the priest. McGlynn was eventually reinstated by Pope Leo XIII but without the knowledge of Corrigan. The details of this conflict are presented in Robert Emmett Curran, SJ, *Michael Augustine Corrigan and the Shaping of Conservative Catholicism in America, 1876–1902* (New York: Arno Press, 1978), see especially pp. 168–255. See also Curran, "The McGlynn Affair and the Shaping of the New Conservatism in American Catholicism," *Catholic Historical Review* 66, no. 2 (April 1980): 184–204.

141. The San Francisco Archdiocesan Archives has many letters written by Hanna's vicars general and other close assistants who warned clergy against speaking on prohibition or any other controversial political topics. One typical letter read, "The Most Reverend Archbishop has instructed me to write to you that he does not wish you to take part in any public discussion in reference to prohibition, no matter what your private views may be." See James Cantwell to Edward McCarthy, February 8, 1924, Chancery Correspondence, AASF.

142. Archepiscopal Council Meeting Minutes, July 5, 1917, H-31, Manuscripts; Thomas Millett to Richard Meade, March 2, 1924, Hanna Papers, AASF. Millett wrote to Meade, who had recently failed a section of the periodic junior clergy exam: "The Most Reverend Archbishop wishes me to impress upon you the seriousness of this matter, and he trusts that you will make the proper preparations for the coming examination."

143. James Cantwell to John T. Egan, July 25, 1922, Chancery Correspondence, AASF.

144. James Cantwell to Joseph Crowley, SJ, January 18, 1928, Hanna Correspondence, AASF.

145. James Cantwell to J. Bernard Praught, October 26, 1932, Hanna Correspondence, AASF.

146. Edward Hanna to John Rogers, May 23, 1933, Chancery Correspondence, Hanna to Rogers, August 31, 1933, L166 Legal File, Hanna to Rogers, November 8, 1933, A6.1, AASF. Almost $81,000 was diverted, but Hanna allowed the parish to keep some funds for the land on

which the shelter stood and additional cash for maintenance. Extant records differ on the amount of money involved. In August Hanna asked for Rogers to return $47,812.63, but in November the balance stated was $58,000. Hanna stated to Rogers, "I am very sorry that this matter has dragged out so much and I am anxious to have it definitely finished as soon as possible."

147. John Cantwell to John Smyth, June 16, 1916, LB 57; James Cantwell to J. Viladomat, February 6, 1925, Chancery Correspondence; Charles R. Baschab to Edward Hanna, December 10, 1915, Diocesan Correspondence; Edward Hanna to Thomas Doran, June 30, 1931, Chancery Correspondence, AASF.

148. John Commiskey, SS, to Edward Hanna, March 9, 1935, Hanna Papers, AASF; Newspaper Clipping, "From the Pastor's Desk," November 9, 1975, Hanna Papers, AALA; Joseph Munier, interview by Robert McNamara, February 28, 1961, MPP.

149. Edward Hanna, Address, July 28, 1915, Hanna Papers, AASF.

150. Anonymous to Jeffrey Burns, February 27, 2001, Letter in Possession of the Author; Edward Hanna, "Reception of the Coadjutor," January 29, 1932, Hanna Papers, AALA.

151. James Gaffey claims that James Cantwell's influence on Hanna was great. He writes, "James Cantwell succeeded to his brother John's post and became the leading advisor to Hanna, wielding such influence that he virtually ruled the archdiocese." See Gaffey, *Men of Menlo*, 18.

152. John Cantwell to "Sister Superior," June 9, 1915, LB 52; John Cantwell to "The Catholic Clergy and Laity of the [Arch]diocese of San Francisco, January 29, 1916," Diocesan Correspondence; James Cantwell to Joseph [Illegible], OFM, Cap. March 21, 1923, Chancery Correspondence, AASF. Hanna, through Cantwell, informed religious when their efforts were inadequate. He was not afraid to inform provincials of his concerns.

153. Edward Hanna, Speech, "Religion and Democracy," July 23, 1918, Hanna Papers, AASF.

154. *San Francisco Examiner*, November 2, 1920.

155. *Monitor*, March 2, 1918.

156. *Monitor*, May 15, 1926; Edward Hanna, Baccalaureate Address, June 19, 1921, Hanna Papers, ADR.

157. *Monitor*, May 15, 1926.

158. Edward Hanna, Sermons, "The Church and the State," n.d. [1920], "Authority and Disorder," Hanna Papers, AASF.

159. *Monitor*, October 8, 1921.

160. *San Francisco Examiner*, November 20, 1925, Clipping, n.d. [1915], CHR-SFPL. In an interesting contrast to this whole discussion,

Hanna, while still in Rochester, registered his complaints with the American system in a sermon preached in 1899. "It is my personal opinion, that if we as a nation have a characteristic vice it is dishonesty. It is may hap *[sic]* more public than private, but dishonesty it certainly is. It shows itself in private life, etc.; it shows itself in our political life in the use of means to attain political ends that conform not with the morality expected of Christians in the loose motions we hold anent honesty in high places, yea and in low. But your good Catholic answers, if we do not do it we cannot succeed, if we do *not* [emphasis Hanna] get this corrupt money others will, as though another man's success through wrong doing affords a reason for my practice of dishonesty. Here is one of our dangers and a potent one in a democratic community where practical life has such fascination." See Edward Hanna, Sermon, October 15, 1899, Hanna Papers, ADR.

161. Edward Hanna, Sermons, October 10, 1915, Hanna Papers, AASF; *San Francisco Examiner*, October 1, 1915.

162. The best account of the Knights' efforts during World War I is presented in Christopher J. Kauffman, *Faith and Fraternalism: The History of the Knights of Columbus, 1882–1982* (New York: Harper & Row, 1982), 190–227.

163. *Monitor*, August 11, 1917; *San Francisco Chronicle*, April 8, 1917. One example of Hanna's overt patriotic stance is presented in a speech to the National Catholic Education Association, which met in San Francisco in 1918: "With banners unfurled, you call us to battle. To battle for God, to battle for Christ, to battle for truth, to battle for justice. To battle that our fellows may be truly free. To battle for the highest national ideals that have even been set before a people. To battle for the inheritance of light and of power which has been transmitted to us adown the centuries. To battle that our children may live in peace and grow unto the fullness of the age which is in Christ." See *San Francisco Examiner*, n.d. [1918], Clipping, CHR-SFPL.

164. John Cantwell to "Reverend and Dear Father," June 9, 1917, LB 60, AASF.

165. John Ryan to Edward Hanna, December 16, 1918, Chancery Correspondence; Mrs. George Kessler to Edward Hanna, June 21, 1916, Chancery Correspondence, AASF.

166. John Cantwell to General J. Franklin Bell, April 12, 1917, LB 60; John Cantwell to J. P. Tracy, September 8, 1915; Edward Hanna to Lindley M. Garrison, July 31, 1915, LB 53, AASF.

167. Edward Hanna to James Phelan (Telegram), June 15, 1917; Hanna to Newton Baker (Telegram), June 15, 1917, LB 60, AASF. Statistics showed that 39 percent of military personnel were Catholic, but Baker

provided a chaplain quota to Catholics of only 23 percent. Hanna wrote to Baker, "Of highest importance for happiness of Catholic troops [is] that their priests be with them in the hour of danger to minister the sacraments of their Church. To be deprived of such ministrations is considered a serious loss. The strain of administering sacraments is very serious on chaplains even though granted thirty[-]nine percent."

168. As one example, Chicago's *New World* moved from silence in January 1919 to a lack of confidence that the League would function as designed by mid-April. One editorial read, "A League of Nations has come out of the sessions. And the treaty is that enforced by consequences. These will not accomplish the world reconciliation which is essential to any sort of peace." See *New World* (Chicago), April 18, 1919.

169. *Monitor*, February 1, 1919, February 15, 1919, February 22, 1919, July 12, 1919, November 27, 1919.

170. McGuire, "Events in the Life of Edward Hanna," p. 83, Hanna Papers, AALA.

171. *Monitor*, May 22, 1920; *San Francisco Examiner*, September 2, 1920.

172. Frederick Koster to Edward Hanna, January 29, 1921; Herbert Hoover to Edward Hanna, January 8, 1921, Chancery Correspondence, AASF. Extant data do not reveal if the collection was actually conducted.

173. Wallace M. Alexander to Edward Hanna, January 8, 1919, Chancery Correspondence, AASF.

174. As one example of Hanna's use of prioritizing, his secretary, James Cantwell, wrote to an official of the Near East Relief Campaign, stating that while the archbishop supported the organization's efforts, "His Grace feels that nothing can be done at the present time for the Near East Relief, as there is a drive on for the relief of the women and children of Ireland." See James Cantwell to Frederick Buckalew, March 16, 1921, Chancery Correspondence, AASF.

175. During and especially after World War I, the *Monitor* ran numerous editorials that supported the Irish cause and attacked the British. On March 8, 1919, the paper stated, "The Irish cause is irrefutable." On December 27, 1919, an editorial read, "The trickery and treachery of the British Government has made the English word as wind in Ireland." On January 1, 1921, the paper reported, "Like Nero, Lloyd George fiddles as Ireland burns, and the champion of small nations keeps the home fires burning while his army of Black and Tans, drunken criminals for the most part, run amok through the length and breadth of Erin."

176. McGuire, "Events in the Life of Edward Hanna," p. 84.

177. *Monitor,* July 26, 1919. De Valera's first visit was directly associated with the fight for Irish freedom. The latter two were invitations to participate in annual memorial celebrations in honor of Father Peter Yorke.

178. *San Francisco Examiner,* June 18, 1916, Clipping, CHR-SFPL.

179. Andrew Gallagher to Edward Hanna, March 2, 1919; Morgan O'Brien to Edward Hanna, January 12, [1921]; A. J. Gallagher to "Dear Father," November 13, 1919, Chancery Correspondence; Memoranda Book, H-29, Manuscripts, AASF.

180. Lynn Dumenil, "The Tribal Twenties: 'Assimilated' Catholics' Response to Anti-Catholicism in the 1920s," *Journal of American Ethnic History* 11 (fall 1991): 21, 22, 34.

181. *Monitor,* October 4, 1924; Dumenil, "Tribal Twenties," 35 and 36. Dumenil quotes one San Francisco clergyman, Reverend Emmet O'Connor, about the Holy Name Society as "a most potent agency for the repression of Ku Kluxism."

182. *San Francisco Catholic,* July 25, 2003, p. 12.

183. *San Francisco Chronicle,* October 6, 1924.

184. *San Francisco Call,* October 6, 1924.

185. *San Francisco Chronicle,* October 6, 1924.

Chapter 4: An Archbishop for the People

1. Before it was popular, Hanna held the understanding of the Church as the "People of God," as expressed eloquently in Vatican II's "Dogmatic Constitution on the Church," *Lumen gentium,* chapter 2.

2. Tom Cole, *A Short History of San Francisco* (San Francisco: Lexikos, 1981), 120.

3. William Issel and Robert W. Cherny, *San Francisco, 1865–1932: Politics, Power, and Urban Development* (Berkeley: University of California Press, 1986), 182–86, 192–93.

4. Unsigned to Edward Hanna, October 1, 1919, Chancery Correspondence, AASF.

5. *Monitor,* n.d. [1913], Clippings, Hanna Papers, ADR.

6. Philip P. McGuire, "Striking Events in the Life of the Most Reverend Edward Joseph Hanna, D.D., Archbishop of San Francisco," 1926, p. 10, Hanna Papers, AALA.

7. *Monitor,* July 15, 1944.

8. Marie Lynch to Edward Hanna, January 10, 1919, Chancery Correspondence, AASF; *Monitor*, August 31, 1935.

9. *Monitor*, July 14, 1944.

10. Thomas Boyle to Edward Hanna, February 16, 1921; H. S. Braucher to Chester Rosekans, December 27, 1921, Chancery Correspondence, AASF; *Monitor*, August 31, 1935.

11. The Legal Aid Society's purpose was "to provide legal aid and assistance gratuitously to those who for any good reason may be unable to procure such assistance in other ways." See Miss E. F. McCarthy to John J. Cantwell, April 25, 1916, Legal Aid Society of San Francisco, B8.2, AASF.

12. Legal Aid Society of San Francisco Annual Report, n.d. [1926], Legal Aid Society of San Francisco, B8.2, AASF. Not only did McCarthy serve as secretary but she also provided Hanna with inside information of what was happening, reporting to the ordinary when "things do not seem to point in the direction The Most Reverend Archbishop wished them to" (see E. F. McCarthy to John J. Cantwell, April 25, 1916, Legal Aid Society of San Francisco, B8.2, AASF).

13. Marshall Hale to Edward Hanna, May 1, 1916, Chancery Correspondence, AASF.

14. James Cantwell to Marshall Hale, November 14, 1917; E. L. M. Tate-Thompson to Edward Hanna, May 26, 1920; Montaville Flowers to Edward Hanna, October 16, 1922, Chancery Correspondence, AASF.

15. W. F. Benedict to Edward Hanna, March 17, 1920; James Rolph to Edward Hanna, October 28, 1922; Helen Sanborn to Edward Hanna, March 24, 1916, Chancery Correspondence, AASF.

16. *San Francisco Examiner*, June 1, 1930, Clipping, CHR-SFPL.

17. Ibid., April 19, 1922, Clipping, CHR-SFPL.

18. Henry Mayer to Edward Hanna, August 12, 1920; W. F. Benedict to Hanna, March 17, 1920; James Rolph to Hanna, October 28, 1922, Chancery Correspondence, AASF.

19. James Cantwell to "Sister Superior," March 31, 1917, LB 60, AASF; *San Francisco Examiner*, September 15, 1932. This was an umbrella organization of twenty-nine national agencies of welfare and relief mobilization organized in 1929 by President Herbert Hoover. Newton D. Baker was appointed the body's chairman.

20. The National Conference of Catholic Charities was founded in 1910.

21. Illegible to Patrick Ryan, August 31, 1920; W. E. Corr to Edward Hanna, July 25, 1927, August 8, 1927, and August 26, 1927, Chancery Correspondence; Memoranda Book, H-29, AASF. Hanna was

often asked to speak to the National Conference of Catholic Charities on the question of immigration, an issue he knew very well from his active participation as vice president, and, after 1923, president of the California Commission of Immigration and Housing and his work as administrative chairman of the National Catholic Welfare Council. In January 1925 Hanna asked all pastors in the archdiocese to conduct a triduum, January 22–24, for the success of the Society for the Propagation of the Faith. The best account on the formation and promotion of Catholic Charities is provided in Mary J. Oates, *The Catholic Philanthropic Tradition in America* (Bloomington: Indiana University Press, 1995).

22. *Monitor*, October 6, 1917; R. George Green to Patrick Ryan, VG, June 1, 1920, Chancery Correspondence, AASF.

23. James Cantwell to A. M. Santandreau, February 13, 1917, LB 49, AASF.

24. James S. Fennell to Edward Hanna, January 6, 1921, Chancery Correspondence, AASF.

25. Richard E. Queen to Patrick Riordan, February 26, 1912, A-6, Manuscripts; Margaret Taylor to Edward Hanna, March 4, 1920, Chancery Correspondence, AASF.

26. John Hunt to John Mahoney, December 4, 1919; John Cantwell to John Hunt, November 22, 1916, Chancery Correspondence, AASF.

27. The Young Men's Institute (YMI) was established on March 4, 1883, at St. Joseph's Church in San Francisco. Six men founded the group for "the betterment of its members morally, intellectually, and socially." The YMI and the Young Ladies' Institute (YLI) raised money for seminarian education, scholarships for teaching brothers, assisting parochial schools and orphanages, and aiding in parish relief to the sick and downtrodden of society. See St. Joseph's Parish, "Golden Jubilee of Brothers' School" (1886–1936), AASF.

28. James Cantwell to Michael Walsh, December 12, 1919, Chancery Correspondence, AASF.

29. James Cantwell to Josephine T. Malloy, September 14, 1920, Chancery Correspondence, AASF.

30. Ibid.

31. Siena Club Meeting Minutes, April 4, 1913, Siena Club Alumnae, A8.99; Memoranda Book, H-29, AASF. The club's members often presented Hanna with spiritual bouquets as a way to say thanks for his interest and support of the group.

32. *Monitor*, February 17, 1934.

33. Ibid., November 14, 1914; *San Francisco Examiner*, November 2, 1920.

34. The sermons were entitled: "Christ, the Home and the Child," "Christ the School and the Child," and "Christ, the World and the Child."

35. James Cantwell to A. L. McMahon, OP, February 20, 1917; Francis A. Sprague to Edward Hanna, March 26, 1921, Chancery Correspondence, AASF.

36. Joseph J. Rosbrough, organizer of the International Rotary Club Week for Boys, complimented Hanna, "I note by the papers that you are deeply interested in boys' work." See Joseph J. Rosbrough to Edward Hanna, April 20, 1922, Chancery Correspondence, AASF.

37. Augustin Keane to Edward Hanna, July 30, 1915, September 15, 1915, and May 5, 1916, Chancery Correspondence, AASF.

38. Edward Hanna to John D. Mahoney, February 6, 1919, Chancery Correspondence, AASF.

39. Illegible Peixotto to Edward Hanna, September 15, 1920; George Patterson to John D. Mahoney, February 8, 1918; Oliver Olson to Hanna, February 9, 1925; John J. Hunt to John Mahoney, December 4, 1919, Chancery Correspondence, AASF.

40. *San Francisco Chronicle*, n.d., Clipping, CHR-SFPL.

41. Illegible to Edward Hanna, January 17, 1921, Chancery Correspondence, AASF.

42. Raymond O. Hansen to Edward Hanna, January 12, 1920; James Cantwell to William Culligan, SJ, April 15, 1918, Chancery Correspondence, AASF. Concerning the Church and the scouts Hanna stated, "Need I tell you that I am always deeply interested in the Catholic Scouting Movement, and I am glad that something finally is being done to make the movement in Catholic circles, not only national, but verily successful." See Edward Hanna to Bishop Francis Kelley, January 27, 1933, Chancery Correspondence, AASF.

43. General Letter, n.d. [1920], B 8.3, Manuscripts; Selah Chamberlain to Edward Hanna, May 9, 1935, Chancery Correspondence; Memoranda Book, H-29, AASF; *Monitor*, January 18, 1930.

44. Leroy R. Goodrich to Edward Hanna, April 13, 1931; Helen Dolman to Hanna, November 1, 1934; George Filmer to Hanna, February 18, 1927, Hanna Papers, AASF.

45. Edward Hanna, Statement, February 17, 1927, Hanna Papers, AASF.

46. Missionary Sisters of the Sacred Heart to Edward Hanna, n.d. [April 1921]; John Cantwell to Sister M. Helena, March 2, 1917, Chancery Correspondence, AASF.

47. John Cantwell to Sister Helena, August 28, 1917, LB 61, AASF.

48. John Cantwell to J. C. Astredo, November 5, 1916, Chancery Correspondence, AASF.

49. George Toule to Edward Hanna, August 9, 1919; James Cantwell to William McGough, October 22, 1924, Chancery Correspondence, AASF. It should be noted that James Cantwell succeeded his brother John as chancellor of the archdiocese when the latter was appointed bishop of Los Angeles in 1917.

50. James Cantwell to Sister Superior, December 23, 1918; Cantwell to James Rolph Jr., September 20, 1920, Chancery Correspondence; John Cantwell to B. C. Redahan, January 4, 1917, LB 59, AASF.

51. Harry Smith to Edward Hanna, August 29, 1918; Patrick L. Ryan to Hanna, December 7, 1915, Chancery Correspondence, AASF.

52. See *Rochester Herald*, May 31, 1915, clipping in Hanna Papers, ADR. Hanna was also well known for boarding San Francisco street cars and trolleys and traveling alone to events and speaking to fellow travelers along the way.

53. Hanna was not adverse to support people who, in his perception, had been wronged by major companies. In 1916, as one example, Hanna took the cause of a widow whose husband was killed in an accident while working for the Southern Pacific Railroad. The company made no effort to assist the woman, who was left penniless with a one-year-old son. Hanna also assured the superintendent of Holy Cross Cemetery in Colma that the archdiocese would provide a casket and pay all fees associated with the burial of those in the San Francisco Relief Home, a social service agency for the homeless. See James D. Mahoney to John Duffy, November 6, 1916; James Cantwell to "Superintendent Holy Cross Cemetery," March 22, 1919, Chancery Correspondence, AASF.

54. Minnie Martin to Edward Hanna, October 6, 1919; Simon Lubin to Hanna, July 12, 1918; James Mahoney to Thomas Powers, March 16, 1918, Chancery Correspondence, AASF.

55. James Cantwell to Mark Noon, November 23, 1919; Cantwell to Michael Williams, June 30, 1919; Arthur O'Connell to Mark Noon, July 24, 1919, Chancery Correspondence, AASF. Hanna became the advocate of many others in prison. In 1930 he took up the case of Henry Messier, who was serving a life sentence at San Quentin. Two years later he became the advocate for Rodney Selby, also at San Quentin. In both cases Hanna believed the evidence could not support the verdicts and asked that the prisoners' cases be reviewed and the men released.

56. A. C. Monahan to Edward Hanna, November 17, 1924; S. L. Marsh to Hanna, July 26, 1921, Chancery Correspondence; Thomas Millett to Bruno Hagspiel, SVD, April 24, 1930, Hanna Papers, AASF.

57. Clay O'Dell, "On Stony Ground: The Catholic Interracial Council in the Archdiocese of San Francisco" (PhD diss., University of Virginia, 2004), 26–27. It should be noted that during Hanna's tenure as archbishop the African American population in San Francisco was less than one percent of the total population. Additionally, while Hanna supported the sisters' efforts spiritually, he could not help the mission when it ran into hard financial times, claiming higher priorities for other projects.

58. James Flynn, "The History of Catholic Charities in the Archdiocese of San Francisco," pp. 1–2; Affiliated Catholic Charities List of 1932, A331, AASF.

59. William A. Proctor, "Location, Regulation, and Removal of Cemeteries in the City and County of San Francisco" (1950), pp. 1–4, CHR-SFPL.

60. Margaret Mahoney to Edward Hanna, February 22, 1915; Garret McEnerney to Hanna, May 8, 1915; Hanna to James J. Ryan, May 8, 1915, Diocesan Correspondence, AASF.

61. Report of the Law and Legislative Committee, October 9, 1924, Chancery Correspondence, AASF.

62. Ellen S. M. Grosejen to Cardinal Gasparri, October 9, 1925; James Cantwell to Loretta French, February 7, 1924, Chancery Correspondence, AASF.

63. John Mahoney to Edward Hanna, May 5, 1924; Joseph Sheehey to Board of Supervisors, May 26, 1924, Chancery Correspondence, AASF.

64. *San Francisco Chronicle*, September 13, 1924.

65. Report of the Law and Legislative Committee, October 9, 1924, Chancery Correspondence, AASF.

66. Ibid.; Proctor, "Location, Regulation, and Removal of Cemeteries," p. 5, CHR-SFPL.

67. McGuire, "Events in the Life of Edward Hanna," p. 163, AALA.

68. *San Francisco Examiner*, October 11, 1924. Hanna's comment was a reference to efforts made since 1880 to remove the cemeteries from the city.

69. Edward Hanna to "Dear Rev. Father," n.d. [November 1924], Chancery Correspondence, AASF.

70. McGuire, "Events in the Life of Edward Hanna," p. 165, AALA. The issue of cemetery removal would not die and was, in fact,

raised the very next year. Details concerning cemetery removal in San Francisco can be found in: Proctor, "Location, Regulation, and Removal of Cemeteries," CHR-SFPL.

71. Proctor, "Location, Regulation, and Removal of Cemeteries," pp. 6–7, CHR-SFPL.

72. A third group, the International Missionary Council, had its confluence with the WCC at New Delhi in 1961.

73. Quoted in *New Catholic Encyclopedia*, 2nd ed., vols. 10 and 14, ed. Berard Marthaler, OFM (Detroit: Gale Thompson, 2002), 165, 840–41.

74. Robert McNamara, interview with Edward Byrne, July 15, 1946, MPP.

75. Edward Hanna, Address, n.d., Hanna Papers, AALA.

76. Edward Hanna to Rabbi Samuel Koch, April 15, 1932, Chancery Correspondence; O. D. Foster to Hanna, February 1933, Hanna Papers, AASF.

77. C. R. Fisher to Edward Hanna, March 26, 1923; Everett R. Clinchy to Hanna, January 11, 1932. Chancery Correspondence; Paul Watson, SA, to Hanna, December 14, 1927, Hanna Papers, AASF. In *Zorach v. Clausen* in 1952 the U.S. Supreme Court ruled that public schools could grant release time to students to attend religious classes at churches and private schools.

78. Quoted in the *Los Angeles Times*, March 3, 1925, Clipping, Hanna Papers, AASF.

79. *Monitor*, November 28, 1931; Christina A. Ziegler-McPherson, "Americanization: The California Plan: The Commission of Immigration and Housing of California and Public Policy, 1913–1923" (PhD diss., Stanford University, 1999), 57.

80. *San Francisco Examiner*, January 2, 1920; John Cantwell to Martin Meyer, January 18, 1916, LB 55; Patrick Ryan to Leo J. Rabinowitz, August 8, 1925, Chancery Correspondence, AASF.

81. *San Francisco Examiner*, April 4, 1933.

82. Harold Zellerbach to Edward Hanna, May 26, 1930, Hanna Papers, AASF; *San Francisco Examiner* April 4, 1933; *Monitor*, November 7, 1931. Concerning anti-Semitism Hanna stated, "It is abhorrent to every caste, creed and religion to contemplate the children of a common Father being discriminated against because of race."

83. Martin Conboy to Edward Hanna, October 6, 1931, Hanna Correspondence, AASF. Some members of the elite selection committee were: Jane Addams, Bernard Baruch, Harry Emerson Fosdick, Bishop William Manning, New York Governor Franklin Roosevelt, and Mayor James Walker of New York City.

84. *Monitor,* November 7, 1931.

85. Ibid.

86. Newspaper Clipping, n.d. [November 1931]; James Rolph to Chairman of Archbishop Hanna Testimonial Dinner [Telegram], November 18, 1931, Hanna Papers, AASF. Extant records are filled with letters and telegrams congratulating Hanna on his reception of the Hebrew Medal.

87. *Herald Tribune* (New York), November 20, 1931, Clipping, NCWC Administrative Chairman Papers—Hanna, ACUA; *Monitor,* November 28, 1931.

88. Ibid.

89. *San Francisco Chronicle,* May 14, 1931. The whole citation read: "Edward Joseph Hanna—great spiritual leader, teacher, and scholar. One who[se] arbitrament is accepted by clashing factions in the warfare of industrial strife, and whose public-spirited leadership extends beyond any one city or any one faith; eager to promote the well-being of all who suffer and are afflicted, you are in truth a friend to mankind."

90. Rush Rhees to Edward Hanna, February 14, 1933; Hanna to Joseph T. Alling, March 7, 1933. Rush Rhees Papers, URL; *San Francisco Chronicle,* December 10, 1934.

91. Jeffrey Burns, *San Francisco: A History of the Archdiocese of San Francisco,* vol. 2, *1885–1945* (Strasbourg: Editions du Signe, 2001), 17.

92. Duane Hunt, Sermon, July 18, 1945, Hanna Papers, AASF; Lewis Francis Byington, *The History of San Francisco* (San Francisco: S. J. Clarke, 1931), 2:25.

93. Unsigned to Cardinal Eugenio Pacelli, n.d., Hanna Papers, AASF.

94. *San Francisco Chronicle,* March 9, 1935, Clipping, Hanna Papers, ADR.

95. NCWC News Service, August 11, 1947. Bishop Duane Hunt of Salt Lake, in his funeral oration for Hanna, stated, "To be strong and yet gentle; to be powerful and yet humble; to be happy, yet compassionate; to be devout, yet social minded; to be able to walk with the great and the near great, and yet to be intimate with the lowliest of God's creatures— there would be seen the qualities of a Christian gentleman. And such is His Grace, the Most Rev. Edward J. Hanna, the third Archbishop of the Archdiocese of San Francisco, the mother parish of California Catholicism." See Newspaper Clipping, July 24, 1944, Hanna Papers, AASF.

Chapter 5: Edward Hanna and Labor in San Francisco, 1915–1930

1. Pastoral Letter of 1884, #59 in Hugh Nolan, ed., *Pastoral Letters of the United States Catholic Bishops* (Washington, DC: United States Catholic Congress, 1984), 1:236.

2. The Knights of Labor, founded in 1869 in Philadelphia by Uriah S. Stephens, came to Canada in 1881. Taschereau wrote to *Congregation de Propaganda Fide* requesting its opinion on this "suspect" organization. In September 1884 *Propaganda* answered Taschereau saying the Knights should be considered as one of the societies proscribed by the Holy See. The complete story of the Knights is given in Henry J. Browne, *The Catholic Church and the Knights of Labor* (Washington, DC: Catholic University of America, 1949).

3. One significant person of this period who illustrates how Catholics supported workers' rights is Father John A. Ryan. His doctoral dissertation, *A Living Wage: Its Ethical and Economic Aspects* was published in 1906. It argued, in line with *Rerum novarum*, that justice demanded adequate wages for working people.

4. Michael Kazin, *Barons of Labor* (Urbana: University of Illinois Press, 1987) 21–22; Judd Kahn, *Imperial San Francisco—Politics and Planning in an American City, 1897–1906* (Lincoln: University of Nebraska Press, 1979), 14, 13.

5. Kahn, *Imperial San Francisco*, 154–76. The career of Abraham Ruef is given in Walton Bean, *Boss Ruef's San Francisco: The Story of the Union Labor Party, Big Business and the Graft Prosecutions* (Berkeley: University of California Press, 1952). Other important works that describe the San Francisco labor scene in this era are William A. Bullough, *The Blind Boss and His City* (Berkeley: University of California Press, 1979); Robert Edward Lee Knight, *Industrial Relations in the San Francisco Bay Area, 1900–1918* (Berkeley: University of California Press, 1960); William Issel and Robert W. Cherny, *San Francisco 1895–1932: Politics, Power and Urban Development* (Berkeley: University of California Press, 1986).

6. An entire discussion of the work of the Union Labor Party and that of Father Yorke is beyond the scope of this work. During the period 1900–1910 Yorke was very active on labor's behalf in San Francisco. He was influential in securing the rights of labor and unions through his efforts in the 1901 Teamsters and Waterfront workers' strike, the 1907 Carmen's strike, and his support of labor in the long process of graft prosecutions in

San Francisco, 1906–1909. Using *Rerum novarum* as his qualifying document, Yorke never wavered from his support of labor's cause. Some historians such as Mary Lyons ("Peter C. Yorke: Advocate of the Irish from the Pulpit to the Podium," in *Religion and Society in the American West*, ed. Carl Guarneri and David Alvarez [Lanham, MD: University Press of America, 1987], 401–22) and Timothy Sarbaugh ("Father Yorke and the San Francisco Waterfront," *Pacific History* 25 [1981]: 28–35) have argued that Yorke acted as an Irish nationalist rather than one who followed the edicts of Leo XIII. Nationalism was certainly present here as is evident by Yorke's personal polemic *The Leader* and the texts of his many speeches, yet Yorke quoted *Rerum novarum* numerous times in his championing of unionism, just wages, and the right to strike. The Union Labor Party under Mayors Eugene Schmitz and P. H. McCarthy held control of San Francisco's political scene from 1901 to 1911, save the Edward Taylor administration of 1907–1909. Only the aforementioned graft prosecutions interrupted the continuity of the party. The best and most complete monographs on Yorke and labor, including information on the Union Labor Party, are Joseph Brusher, SJ, *Consecrated Thunderbolt* (Hawthorne, NJ: Joseph F. Wagner, 1973); Bernard Cronin, *Father Yorke and the Labor Movement in San Francisco, 1900–1910* (Washington, DC: Catholic University of America Press, 1943); and Richard Gribble, CSC, *Catholicism and the San Francisco Labor Movement, 1896–1921* (San Francisco: Mellen University Press, 1993).

7. William Issel, "Business Power and Political Culture in San Francisco, 1900–1940," *Journal of Urban History* 16, no. 1 (November 1989): 67.

8. Steven M. Avella, "California Catholics and the Gubernatorial Election of 1934," in *FDR, the Vatican, and the Roman Catholic Church in America, 1933–1945*, ed. David B. Woolner and Richard G. Kurial (New York: Palgrave Macmillan, 2003), 71.

9. Issel, "Business Power," 56, 57. Catholic leaders often claimed to represent more than half the city's residents. Statistics show, however, the claim was a bit exaggerated. The 1906 census showed 34 percent of San Franciscans were Catholic (but 81 percent of all church members). In 1916 Catholics were 42 percent and in 1936 they numbered 28 percent.

10. James Rolph served as mayor of San Francisco (1911–1930) and governor (1930–1934) in a long career of public service in the state of California.

11. Issel, "Business Power," 67.

12. Edward Hanna, Sermon, "The Church and the State," n.d. [Lent 1920], Hanna Papers, ADR.

13. *San Francisco Examiner,* June 29, 1934.

14. Newspaper Clipping, n.d. Hanna File, AASF.

15. John Bernard McGloin, *San Francisco: The Story of a City* (San Rafael, CA: Presidio Press, 1978), 304–8; Tom Cole, A *Short History of San Francisco* (San Francisco: Lexikos, 1981), 118; William Issel and Robert W. Cherny, *San Francisco 1865–1932: Politics, Power and Urban Development* (Berkeley: University of California Press, 1986), 178. From the outset the guilt of Mooney and Billings was suspect. Mooney was slated for execution; Billings was given a life sentence. Both men were released from prison in 1939. It was clear at the time that no substantial evidence existed to warrant their convictions.

16. Robert C. Francis. "A History of Labor on the San Francisco Waterfront" (PhD diss., University of California, Berkeley, 1934), 149.

17. A 1915 agreement between the ILA and the WEU stated that a minimum sixty-day "cooling off period" was necessary before any announced strike could be initiated. Only twenty-two days elapsed between the announcement of the strike on May 9 and the actual walkout on June 1.

18. Frederick Koster to "Merchants of San Francisco," July 3, 1916, James Rolph Papers, California Historical Society Library (hereafter CHSL), San Francisco, California.

19. Quoted in Kazin, *Barons of Labor,* 239.

20. The other members of the group were C. R. Johnson of Union Lumberyard, George M. Rolph (no relation to the mayor) of California and Hawaiian Sugar Refining, C. F. Michaels of Langly and Michaels Wholesale Drugs, and Wallace M. Alexander, attorney-at-law. Hugh M. Webster was named confidential secretary of the committee.

21. "The San Francisco Open-shop Movement," *San Francisco Argonaut,* August 12, 1916, p. 33.

22. William Sproule to James Rolph, August 17, 1916, Rolph Papers, CHSL.

23. Steven C. Levi, "San Francisco's Law and Order Committee, 1916," *Journal of the West* 12 (1973): 55.

24. "Waterfront Situation," *Labor Clarion* (San Francisco), July 14, 1916, p. 1.

25. "The Condition of Labor," *Leader* (San Francisco), August 12, 1916, p. 4.

26. Ibid., September 2, 1916, p. 4.

27. For a more complete analysis of the Law and Order Committee, especially with respect to its impact on the eight-hour day in San Francisco, see Steven Levi, "The Battle for the Eight Hour Day in

San Francisco," *California History* 57 (1978–79): 342–53; and idem, "San Francisco's Law and Order Committee, 1916," 53–70.

28. Kazin, *Barons of Labor,* 239.

29. *Monitor,* August 19, 1916, p. 4.

30. Ibid.

31. James Rolph to Chamber of Commerce, SFLC, BTC, and Waterfront Workers' Federation, August 10, 1916, Rolph Papers, CHSL.

32. Issel and Cherny, *San Francisco 1865–1932,* 40. The others named by Cherny and Issel were: William Crocker, Wallace M. Alexander, Milton Esberg, and Charles H. Kendrick.

33. *Monitor,* January 14, 1914.

34. Ibid.

35. *San Francisco Examiner,* n.d. [1916], Clipping, A. M66, Edward Miner Papers, URL.

36. Harry Davis to James Rolph, August 11, 1916, Rolph Papers, CHSL.

37. P. H. McCarthy to James Rolph, August 11, 1916, Rolph Papers, CHSL.

38. *Leader,* August 12, 1916.

39. *San Francisco Chronicle,* August 22, 1916.

40. *Leader,* August 26, 1916.

41. *Monitor,* July 29, 1916.

42. *Bulletin* (San Francisco), September 5, 1916.

43. Ibid.

44. Ibid.

45. James Rolph to Frederick Koster, July 10, 1916, Rolph Papers, CHSL.

46. James Rolph, Speech, September 4, 1916, Rolph Papers, CHSL.

47. Ibid.

48. Francis, "History of Labor," 51.

49. Olaf Tveitmoe to James Rolph, December 8, 1916, Rolph Papers, CHSL.

50. Steven C. Levi, "Miner Chipman and the Law and Order Committee of the San Francisco Chamber of Commerce, 1917," *Pacific Historian* 18 (1974): 55.

51. *Monitor,* August 9, 1919.

52. Ibid., February 8, 1919.

53. Ibid., April 20, 1921.

54. *Rerum novarum,* issued in 1891 by Pope Leo XIII, is considered by Catholic social historians as the foundational document of contemporary Roman Catholic social thought. While supportive of organized labor

and collective bargaining, the encyclical also promoted private property in its condemnation of socialism.

55. *Monitor,* March 27, 1920, pp. 1, 6.

56. Edward Hanna to John Burke, December 1920, Chancery Correspondence, AASF.

57. "The Open-shop," *New World* (Chicago), January 14, 1921, p. 4.

58. "Getting Something out of Labor Day," *Tablet* (Brooklyn), September 2, 1922, p. 6.

59. Church groups and other organizations denounced the actions of the Klan during the 1920s. Internal corruption precipitated the Klan's demise, but even before this its polemics against Catholics were condemned by many. The *Monitor* comments on the denunciations of the Klan by various groups in several issues. See May 13, 1922, July 22, 1922, August 19, 1922, and March 10, 1923, for examples.

60. Edward Hanna, Max Sloss, and George Bell, "Supplementary Wage Award and Decision on Petition for Rehearing of the Building Trades Arbitration Board," January 18, 1921, Hanna Papers, AASF.

61. Builders Exchange of San Francisco to Edward Hanna, Max Sloss, and George Bell, April 29, 1921, Hanna Papers, AASF.

62. "Arguments for Increase in Wages for Fifteen Crafts," Building Trades Council of San Francisco, 1921, #29, #3, Hanna Papers, AASF.

63. John S. Partridge, "In the Matter of the Arbitration between the Builders Exchange and the Building Trades Council," San Francisco, 1921, #4, Hanna Papers, AASF.

64. Ibid., #3.

65. "Report of Reinforcing Iron Workers to the Impartial Arbitration Board," January 10, 1921, Hanna Papers, AASF.

66. *San Francisco Examiner,* April 1, 1921.

67. Quoted in Kazin, *Barons of Labor,* 258.

68. Hanna, Sloss, and Bell, "Supplementary Wage Award," n.d., Hanna Papers, AASF.

69. P. H. McCarthy to Charles Gompertz, June 16, 1921, Hanna Papers, AASF.

70. *Monitor,* June 25, 1921.

71. Varnishers and Polishers Local Union No. 134 to Industrial Board of Commissioners, October 27, 1921, Hanna Papers, AASF.

72. Edward McGee to Bell, Hanna, and Sloss, April 16, 1921, Hanna Papers, AASF.

73. Hanna, Bell, and Sloss, "Supplementary Wage Award," n.d., Hanna Papers, AASF.

74. *San Francisco Chronicle,* October 1, 1921; *San Francisco Examiner,* December 23, 1921.

75. *San Francisco Examiner,* December 23, 1921.

76. *San Francisco Chronicle,* December 23, 1921.

77. General Contractors of San Francisco to Impartial Wage Board, October 28, 1922, Hanna Papers, AASF.

78. "General Report on the Cost of Living in San Francisco," Report of the Industrial Association of San Francisco, October 1, 1922, Hanna Papers, AASF.

79. Building Trades Council of San Francisco to Edward Hanna, Henry Brandenstein, and C. F. Michaels, October 28, 1922, Hanna Papers, AASF.

80. Edward Hanna, "Testimony before Impartial Wage Board," November 17, 1922, Hanna Papers, AASF.

81. In another Labor Day address, September 1, 1923, Hanna continued his moderate tone. While insisting on fair wages and healthful working conditions, he emphasized the responsibility of workers to achieve "that high degree of honest performance which the laborers' remuneration *[sic]* demands." Philip P. McGuire, "Striking Events in the Life of the Most Reverend Edward Joseph Hanna, D.D., Archbishop of San Francisco," 1926, p. 154, Hanna Papers, AALA.

82. M. W. F. McAllister, "Testimony before Impartial Wage Board," November 22, 1922, Hanna Papers, AASF.

83. Edward Hanna, "Testimony," November 17, 1922, Hanna Papers, AASF.

84. The molders' union dispute led to violence when in December 1922 workers went on strike against the open shop. The strike was not called off officially until 1934. Some molders worked on an open-shop basis, others used the closed shop. For more information, see Ira Cross, *History of the Labor Movement in California* (Berkeley: University of California Press, 1935), 253.

85. Bulletin No. 2236 of General Contractors of San Francisco, December 5, 1922, Hanna Papers, AASF.

86. "General Report of Cost of Living in San Francisco," December 1, 1922, Hanna Papers, AASF.

87. "Summary of General Economic Conditions," Unpublished Report, 1923, Hanna Papers, AASF.

88. Builders Exchange to Impartial Wage Board, November 28, 1922, Hanna Papers, AASF.

89. Edward Dwyer to Hanna, December 1, 1922, Hanna Papers, AASF.

90. Cement Finishers' Union Local No. 580 to Impartial Wage Board, November 22, 1922, Hanna Papers, AASF.

91. "Building Trades Wage Scale," January 1, 1923, Hanna Papers, AASF.

92. *San Francisco Examiner*, December 23, 1922.

93. *San Francisco Chronicle*, October 27, 1926.

94. Union Leaders to Edward Hanna, Max Sloss, and Selah Chamberlain, November 18, 1926, Collection 11, Box 16 #2, ACUA.

95. *San Francisco Chronicle*, November 18, 1926.

96. *Labor Clarion*, November 26, 1926.

97. *San Francisco Chronicle*, November 18, 1926.

98. *San Francisco Chronicle*, December 10, 1926.

99. *Labor Clarion*, January 21, 1927.

100. *San Francisco Chronicle*, November 12, 1928.

101. Thomas Doyle, E. E. Fitzgerald, and Charles Gurvey to Edward Hanna, November 24, 1928, Collection 11, Box 16 #22, ACUA.

102. BTC Representatives to Edward Hanna, December 10, 1928, Collection 11, Box 16 #22, ACUA.

103. *San Francisco Chronicle*, December 31, 1928.

104. Ibid., April 1, 1929.

105. *San Francisco Examiner*, June 6, 1931.

106. In the fall of 1931 the Industrial Association asked Hanna to again chair the board, but due to his active involvement with the California Unemployment Commission he declined the invitation. A fifth board was formed in October with Dean Willard E. Hotchkiss of Stanford University as chair.

107. *San Francisco Examiner*, April 21, 1933.

108. Edward Hanna to "Reverend and Dear Father," April 17, 1933, Chancery Correspondence, AASF. Hanna's reference to the pope was with respect to the 1931 publication of *Quadragesimo anno*.

109. *San Francisco Chronicle*, May 10, 1933; *San Francisco News*, May 9, 1933, Clipping A-10, Manuscripts, AASF.

Chapter 6: An Advocate for Immigrants

1. J. Donald Fisher, "A Historical Study of the Migrant in California" (master's thesis, University of Southern California, 1945), 5; George T. Brown and David E. Shi, *America*, brief ed. (New York: W. W. Norton, 1997), 2:605.

2. Quoted in Alexander Saxton, *The Indispensable Enemy: Labor and the Anti-Chinese Movement in California* (San Francisco: California Historical Society, 1973), 274–75.

3. Maldwyn A. Jones, *American Immigration* (Chicago: University of Chicago Press, 1992), 217.

4. Ibid., 275.

5. Moses Rischin, "Immigration, Migration and Minorities in California," in *Essays and Assays: California History Reappraised*, ed. George H. Knoles (San Francisco: California Historical Society, 1973), 70–71.

6. Fisher, "Historical Study of the Migrant in California," 11, 13–14. See also Rischin, "Immigrants, Migration and Minorities," 68. In 1890, 41 percent of Californians in total lived in cities of ten thousand people or more. Only Massachusetts, Rhode Island, New York, New Jersey, Maryland, and Connecticut ranked ahead in urban population.

7. Quoted in Rischin, "Immigrants, Migration and Minorities," 65.

8. *San Francisco Examiner*, November 2, 1920, March 14, 1917.

9. Leslie W. Koepplin, *A Relationship of Reform: Immigrants and Progressives in the West* (New York: Garland, 1990), 125.

10. Quoted in Frank B. Lenz, "The International Immigration Congress," *Immigrants in America Review* 1, no. 3 (1915): 55; *San Francisco Examiner*, November 2, 1920.

11. Lenz, "International Immigration Congress," 55; Anne Marie Woo-Sam, "Domesticating the Immigrant: California's Commission of Immigration and Housing and the Domestic Immigration Policy Movement, 1910–1945" (PhD diss., University of California, Berkeley, 1999), 67.

12. C. C. Browning to "Archbishop Hanna," January 31, 1916, Diocesan Correspondence; W. E. Corr to Edward Hanna, August 8, 1927, Hanna Papers, AASF.

13. John Cantwell to William Colligan, SJ, November 12, 1915, LB 54; Edward Hanna to "To Whom It May Concern," November 28, 1919, Chancery Correspondence, AASF; *Monitor*, May 3, 1919.

14. James Cantwell to Francis Bruno, July 7, 1917, LB 61; John Cantwell to Mother Reginald, August 17, 1916, LB 58; John Cantwell to Joseph Galli, August 31, 1915, LB 53, Manuscripts, AASF.

15. James Cantwell to Albert Ascoli, February 21, 1918, Chancery Correspondence; John Cantwell to R. M. Piperoni, February 19, 1917, LB 59, Manuscripts, AASF. Hanna's chancery staff wrote numerous letters to Italian clergy asking their assistance in discouraging their parishioners from seeking the sacraments, especially marriage, at Sts. Peter and Paul.

16. Memoranda Book, H-29; Rag A. Pedrini to Edward Hanna, September 28, 1927, Chancery Correspondence, AASF.

17. Alessandro Baccari Jr., Vincenza Scarpaci, and Gabriel Zavatlano, SDB, *Saints Peter and Paul: The Chronicles of "The Italian Cathedral of the West," 1884–1984* (San Francisco: Sts. Peter and Paul Church, 1985), 98–99. The church was bombed on January 30, 1926, May 9, 1926, October 29, 1926, and January 9, 1927. On March 6, 1927, another attempt failed, killing the bomber and mortally wounding an accomplice. No clear-cut motive was ever discovered for the bombings, although the International Workers of the World (IWW) or "Wobblies" were suspected, due to their creed, "No God, No Master."

18. *San Francisco Examiner*, October 6, 1922.

19. McGuire, "Events in the Life of Edward Hanna," p. 139, Hanna Papers, AALA.

20. California Secretary of State to Eugenio Pascelli [*sic*—Pacelli], n.d. [1929], Hanna Papers, AASF.

21. *San Francisco Chronicle*, October 18, 1924.

22. John McGreevy, *Catholicism and American Freedom: A History* (New York: W. W. Norton, 2003), 172. McGreevy states, "Many American intellectuals also fell under Mussolini's spell during the 1920s and 1930s, but American Catholic bishops, often former Roman seminarians with personal experience of hostility between the Vatican and the Italian State, were especially prone to marvel at Mussolini's ability to defuse Church-State tension."

23. William Barry Smith, "The Attitude of American Catholics Towards Italian Fascism between the Two World Wars" (PhD diss., Catholic University of America, 1969), 5–7. See also John P. Diggins, *Mussolini and Fascism: The View From America* (New York: Prometheus Books, 1972), especially pp. 5–73 for a more detailed account.

24. *San Francisco Chronicle*, November 20, 1925.

25. *Monitor*, August 31, 1929; *San Francisco Examiner*, June 6, 1931. There were some significant American Catholics who opposed Mussolini as well. John Ryan rejected fascism as contrary to the moral order because of its rejection of freedom of speech, press, and assembly. Francis Duffy, the famous World War I chaplain, was quoted in 1928: "Less Benito Mussolini and more Thomas Jefferson would be a right good dose for Italy at the present time." The Paulist monthly, *The Catholic World*, under its editor James Gillis, was the only major American Catholic publication that opposed Mussolini from the outset, as early as 1923. See Smith, "Attitude of American Catholics Towards Italian Fascism," 59, 62, 77–85, 184.

26. The Japanese mission in San Francisco was an outgrowth of the work of Father Albert Breton, a priest of the Foreign Mission Society of Paris. He worked with Japanese Sisters of the Presentation to assist Japanese immigrants in San Francisco. See *Monitor*, September 6, 1913.

27. John Cantwell to E. B. Ledvina, October 5, 1917; James Cantwell to James Walsh, MM, June 6, 1918, Chancery Correspondence, AASF.

28. Father John, OFM, to Edward Hanna, September 17, 1915, Diocesan Correspondence; Paul Marella to Hanna, March 31, 1933, Apostolic Delegate Correspondence, AASF.

29. John Cantwell to P. J. O'Connor, September 4, 1915, LB 53; Cantwell to J. C. Cebria, February 6, 1917, LB 59; Cantwell to J. Volcarie Alonso, January 15, 1915, LB 51, Manuscripts, AASF.

30. *San Francisco Chronicle*, n.d. [1926], Clipping in Edward Miner Papers, URL. See also Woo-Sam, "Domesticating the Immigrant," 66–67. She says, "[Hanna] played an important role in the Commission's move for Mexican restriction in 1926."

31. *San Francisco Chronicle*, March 10, 1926. See also Don Mitchell, *Lie of the Land: Migrant Workers and the California Landscape* (Minneapolis: University of Minnesota Press, 1996), 104.

32. *San Francisco Chronicle*, March 10, 1926.

33. Quoted in Mark Reisler, *By the Sweat of Their Brow: Mexican Immigrant Labor in the United States* (Westport, CT: Greenwood Press, 1976), 158.

34. V. S. McClatchy to Edward Hanna, February 23, 1929, Hanna Papers, AASF.

35. Mitchell, *Lie of the Land*, 104.

36. Julie G. Arce to Edward Hanna, n.d. [1929], Our Lady of Guadalupe File, AASF.

37. Moises Sandoval, *On the Move: A History of the Hispanic Church in the United States* (Maryknoll, NY: Orbis Books, 1990), 44; Manuel Gamio, *Mexican Immigration to the United States: A Study of Human Migration and Adjustment* (New York: Dover Publications, 1971), 118.

38. John J. Mitty to Amleto Cicognani, October 8, 1932; Sister Josefina to Edward Hanna, n.d. [January 1930], Carmelite Sisters of Cristo Rey, Box 2; Charles Murphy to John Mitty, July 26, 1933, Perpetual Adoration Sisters, Box 7, AASF.

39. Woo-Sam, "Domesticating the Immigrant," 34; California Commission of Immigration and Housing, Annual Report, 1915, p. 5, BL-UCB.

40. Christina A. Ziegler-McPherson, "Americanization: The California Plan: The Commission of Immigration and Housing of California and Public Policy, 1913–1923" (PhD diss., Stanford University, 1999), 48, 50–51.

41. Samuel E. Wood, "The California State Commission of Immigration and Housing: A Study of Administrative Organization and the Growth of Function" (PhD diss., University of California, Berkeley, 1942), 104. Wood provides a detailed description of how Simon Lubin worked with Johnson and the legislature in the formation of the commission.

42. Report of the Commission of Immigration and Housing of California to Governor Hiram Johnson, July 10, 1914; Simon Lubin et al. to Hiram Johnson, July 10, 1914; Meeting Minutes, Commission of Immigration and Housing of California, October 3, 1913, and December 5, 1913, Simon Lubin Papers, BL-UCB.

43. Quoted in Wood, "California State Commission," 104.

44. Ibid., 129.

45. Ziegler-McPherson, "Commission of Immigration and Housing of California," 57.

46. Edward Hanna to Simon Lubin, January 16, 1914, Simon Lubin Papers, BL-UCB.

47. Quoted in Douglas Sackman, "Domestic Arrangements: The Commission of Immigration and Housing and the Alienation of Mexican Labor in California's Citrus Industry, 1914–1936" (paper delivered at the West Coast meeting of the American Historical Association, Portland, Oregon, August 9, 1997).

48. A tabulation of official meetings of the commission between October 3, 1913, and April 5, 1926, the last recorded meeting, indicates the agency convened one hundred times. In those thirteen years Hanna missed twenty-four meetings. See Wood, "California State Commission," 114.

49. Simon Lubin et al. to Hiram Johnson, July 10, 1914; Commission of Immigration and Housing of California, First Annual Report [July 1915], Simon Lubin Papers, BL-UCB.

50. Wood, "California State Commission," 169–70.

51. California Immigration and Housing Bulletin 1, no. 6 (September 1920), California Immigration and Housing Papers, BL-UCB.

52. Ziegler-McPherson, "Commission of Immigration and Housing of California," 67.

53. Edward Hanna to Simon Lubin, December 18, 1913, Simon Lubin Papers, BL-UCB.

54. Hanna's influence on the commission members was considerable. Meeting minutes of the commission reveal the pastoral and sensitive nature of Hanna's hand in the commission's deliberations. Additionally, it appears that Hanna became convinced during the commission's initial whirlwind of meetings throughout the state, when the initial six surveys were completed, that assimilation could best be obtained by meeting the special needs of people. His work and experience in Rochester with Italian immigrants were highly influential in making his ultimate conclusion. See Meeting Minutes, Commission of Immigration and Housing of California, January to June 1914, Commission of Immigration and Housing of California Papers, BL-UCB.

55. Pamphlet, "Americanization of Foreign-Born Women," p. 24, 1917, Commission of Immigration and Housing of California; First Annual Report [1914], Simon Lubin Papers, BL-UCB. In 1916 the Bureau of Immigrant Education was established with a three-fold program: home education for women, labor camp education, and general citizenship education.

56. Simon Lubin et al. to Hiram Johnson, July 10, 1914; Pamphlet, "A Report on Housing Shortages" [1923], sponsored by the Commission of Immigration and Housing of California, Simon Lubin Papers, BL-UCB.

57. In August 1913 a labor camp dispute at the Wheatland hop ranch owned by Ralph Durst left four men dead. Before the commission was formally organized it was charged with the task of discovering what precipitated the disturbance. Cletus Daniel claims that this event was the catalyst that transformed the commission into a group seeking reform of inadequate housing and unsanitary conditions, the two things determined to be the cause of the conflict. See Wood, "California State Commission," 184; and Cletus E. Daniel, *Bitter Harvest: A History of California Farmworkers 1870–1941* (Ithaca, NY: Cornell University Press, 1981), 91.

58. Simon Lubin et al. to Hiram Johnson, July 10, 1914; Clipping *Fresno Republican*, February 3, 1923, Simon Lubin Papers, BL-UCB.

59. Daniel, *Bitter Harvest*, 96.

60. Commission of Immigration and Housing of California, First Annual Report [1915] and Ninth Annual Report [1923], Simon Lubin Papers, BL-UCB. In its first nine years of operation the department adjusted over thirty-eight thousand complaints. See Wood, "California State Commission," 146.

61. Woo-Sam, "Domesticating the Immigrant," 80; *San Francisco Examiner*, April 14, 1919.

62. Commission of Immigration and Housing of California, Ninth Annual Report [1923], Simon Lubin Papers, BL-UCB.

63. Richardson's proposed budget cut financing to several state agencies, including the Bureau of Labor Commissioners, Industrial Accident Commission, and the Industrial Welfare Commission. The total planned savings was $583,324. The $182,576 budget of the Immigration and Housing Commission was to be totally eliminated. See Budget Schedule, State of California, 1923, Hanna File, AASF.

	Current Budget	*Proposed*	*Decrease*
Bureau of Labor Commissioners	$347, 807	$288,000	$59,807
Immigration and Housing	$182,576	$0	$182,576
Industrial Accident Commission	$800,461	$543,820	$256,641
Industrial Welfare	$115,360	$31,060	$84,300
	$1,446,204	$862,880	$583,324

64. Hanna served as administrative chairman of the National Catholic Welfare Council (NCWC) from its inception in 1919 until 1935. In 1922 a campaign led by Cardinal William O'Connell (Boston) and Archbishop Dennis Dougherty (Philadelphia) was initiated to eliminate the NCWC. Hanna directed the fight that eventually led the Vatican to rescind its order to scuttle the council. His recent fight made him the logical choice to head the commission's battle against Governor Richardson.

65. Edward Hanna et al. to Friend Richardson, n.d. [February 7, 1923], Hanna Papers, AASF.

66. Industrial Relations, Commission of Immigration and Housing, F 3743:20, California State Archives (hereafter CSA), Sacramento, California. The commission members in 1923 were: Edward Hanna, president; John S. Chambers, vice president; George Hollis, secretary; J. H. McBride and G. B. Ocheltree.

67. Clippings, *Fresno Republican*, February 3, 1923; *Sacramento Bee*, February 8, 1923, Simon Lubin Papers, BL-UCB.

68. *San Francisco Call*, March 1, 1921.

69. W. J. Barron to J. D. Dermody, May 5, 1921, NCWC General Secretary Files—Burke, ACUA. When Hanna left San Francisco for retirement in Rome, Mrs. Hattie W. Richards Butler was elected president of the California Commission of Immigration and Housing.

70. Restriction legislation had been in process for several decades. The Chinese Exclusion Acts of 1882, 1892, and 1902 were the first. A series of literacy acts were passed in Congress in 1896, 1913, and 1915 but

each was vetoed by the sitting president. Woodrow Wilson's veto of the 1917 Literacy Act was overridden by Congress and became law.

71. The creation of the California State Department of Industrial Relations in 1927 eliminated the autonomy of several state commissions and agencies, including the Commission of Immigration and Housing, which continued as a policy-making body only. Samuel Wood has commented about these events, "Theoretically, the Commission still existed as a policy-determining body. Actually, however, its power in this regard was nil, since it had no control [in] the execution of such a policy." See Wood, "California State Commission," 114.

72. A. E. Monteith to Edward Hanna, December 10, 1937, Hanna File, AASF. It should be noted that Anne Marie Woo-Sam, while noting Hanna's contributions to the commission, states that he spent less time formulating policy than Lubin and attended fewer meetings of the commission than its other members. See Woo-Sam, "Domesticating the Immigrant," 67.

Chapter 7: Head of the National Church— The NCWC and Domestic Issues

1. As described in chapter 2 the condemnations of Americanism (1899) and modernism (1907) created a death pall on American scholarship and ended for a significant period collective meetings of the hierarchy, which had been somewhat regular during the nineteenth century.

2. Joseph McShane, SJ, *"Sufficiently Radical": Catholicism, Progressivism, and the Bishops' Program of 1919* (Washington, DC: Catholic University of America Press, 1986), 72; Christopher J. Kauffman, *Faith and Fraternalism: The History of the Knights of Columbus 1882–1982* (New York: Harper & Row, 1982), 190–227. The banner of Catholicism's response to the war before the 1917 meeting was carried principally by the Knights of Columbus. Kauffman describes the efforts of the Knights to establish recreation centers in Europe and the United States for use by service personnel.

3. McShane, *"Sufficiently Radical,"* 72. The complete history of the War Council's efforts is given in Michael Williams, *American Catholics in the War: National Catholic War Council 1917–1921* (New York: Macmillan, 1921). The endeavors of all churches to aid the war cause is presented in John F. Piper Jr., *The American Churches in World War I* (Athens: Ohio University Press, 1985).

4. Douglas Slawson, *The Foundation and First Decade of the National Catholic Welfare Council* (Washington, DC: Catholic University of America Press, 1992), 45–69.

5. Ibid., 70–95. Slawson's book is the most recent and comprehensive history of the early years of the conference. The NCWC was initially organized with four departments: education, Catholic press, social action, and lay organizations (home missions was a fifth department added in 1920). NCWC Administrative Committee Meeting Minutes, September 25, 1919, Administrative Committee Papers, ACUA. The episcopal chairmen were: education—Archbishop Austin Dowling of St. Paul; legislation—Archbishop Dennis Dougherty of Philadelphia; social action—Bishop Peter Muldoon of Rockford, Illinois; lay organizations—Bishop Joseph Schrembs, then bishop of Toledo, Ohio; and press and publicity—Bishop William Russell of Charleston, South Carolina.

6. Report of the Chairman of the NCWC Administrative Committee, September 22–23, 1920, NCWC Administrative Committee Paper, ACUA.

7. The NCWC Administrative Committee met December 9–10, 1919, April 14, 1920, July 28–29, 1920, and September 22–23, 1920.

8. NCWC Administrative Committee Meeting Minutes, January 26, 1922, NCWC Administrative Committee Papers, ACUA.

9. Robert Grady to Edward Hanna, November 22, 1920, Hanna Papers, AASF.

10. John Burke to Edward Hanna, February 23, 1921, Hanna Papers, AASF.

11. Edward Hanna to John Burke, November 6, 1920, NCWC Administrative Committee Papers, ACUA.

12. Edward Hanna to John Burke, n.d. [December 1920], NCWC Administrative Committee Papers, ACUA.

13. John Burke to Edward Hanna, November 17, 1920, NCWC Administrative Committee Papers, ACUA.

14. *NCWC Bulletin* 2, no. 6 (February 1921): 2.

15. Report of the NCWC Administrative Committee Chairman, NCWC Annual Report, September 1923, NCWC Administrative Committee Papers, ACUA.

16. Edward Hanna to Reverend and Right Reverend Members of the Council, May 4, 1920, NCWC Administrative Committee Meeting Minutes, ACUA. Hanna continued to promote the need for the NCWC throughout his tenure as Administrative Committee Chairman. In December 1927 he wrote, "Never in the history of the development of Christ's cause in the United States has anything been done of so great

importance as the work of the National Catholic Welfare Conference. It has not only united bishops, priests and people from east and west, and from north and south, but it has given unto the cause of education and unto the cause of social service a new impetus and a new life. It has made our faithful people throughout the land realize more and more the glory of their task, and also the great value of united action in the realization of our ideals." See Edward Hanna to John Burke, December 15, 1927, NCWC Administrative Committee Papers, ACUA. In November 1932 he wrote, "Without the Conference, the Church would have no recognized voice in the national affairs as such of our country—and particularly such national matters as affect the state of religion and the immediate well-being of the Church." See Report of the NCWC Administrative Committee Chairman, n.d. [November 1932], NCWC Annual Report, NCWC Papers, ACUA.

17. Edward Hanna to John Burke, February 17, 1921, NCWC Administrative Committee Papers, ACUA.

18. John Burke to Edward Hanna, February 12, 1921, NCWC Administrative Committee Papers, ACUA; *Monitor*, March 27, 1920.

19. Editorial, "Well Deserved Tribute," *Indiana Catholic and Record*, n.d., Clipping found in NCWC Administrative Committee Papers, ACUA.

20. John Burke to Edward Hanna, September 8, 1931, NCWC Administrative Committee Papers; Pope Pius XI to William O'Connell et al. [all cardinals], August 10, 1927, NCWC International Affairs Papers, ACUA.

21. Report of NCWC Administrative Committee Chairman, September 22–23, 1920; List of Allotments and Payments, NCWC, 1920–1923, n.d. [1923], NCWC Annual Reports, ACUA.

22. Report of NCWC Administrative Committee Chairman, September 22–23, 1920, NCWC Annual Reports; Edward Hanna to U.S. Catholic Bishops, n.d., enclosed in John Burke to Edward Hanna, November 27, 1920, NCWC Administrative Committee Papers, ACUA.

23. John Burke to Edward Hanna, December 13, 1920, NCWC Administrative Committee Papers, ACUA.

24. NCWC Administrative Committee Meeting Minutes, January 26, 1922, NCWC Administrative Committee Papers; Report of the Administrative Committee Chairman, n.d. [September 1923], NCWC Annual Reports, ACUA.

25. Reports of the NCWC Administrative Committee Chairman, November 1933 and November 1934, NCWC Annual Reports, ACUA. As one example: in November 1934 Hanna was mandated to operate the

NCWC on a budget of $125,000, which was $65,000 less than the budget for 1930.

26. Letter of the Hierarchy to Woodrow Wilson, April 1917, in Raphael Huber, *Our Bishops Speak* (Milwaukee: Bruce Publishing Company, 1952), 173–74. In part the letter from the War Council read: "Standing firmly upon our solid Catholic tradition and history from the very foundation of the nation, we affirm in this hour of stress loyalty and patriotism toward our country, our government and our flag....Now that war has been declared, we bow in obedience to the summons to bear our part in it, with fidelity, with courage, and with the spirit of sacrifice, which as loyal citizens we are bound to manifest for the defense of the most sacred rights and the welfare of the whole nation....We are all true Americans, ready as our age, our ability, and our condition permit to do whatever is in us to do, for the preservation, the progress and triumph of our beloved country."

27. Linley V. Gordon to John Burke, April 16, 1921; Burke to Gordon, April 20, 1921; Edward Hanna to John Burke [Telegram], April 26, 1921, NCWC General Secretary Papers, ACUA.

28. *Monitor*, June 18, 1921, December 3, 1921, December 17, 1921, January 7, 1922.

29. NCWC Administrative Committee Statement, n.d. [April 25, 1921], NCWC General Secretary Papers, ACUA.

30. Report of the NCWC Administrative Committee Chairman, September 21–22, 1921, NCWC Annual Reports, ACUA.

31. Statement of the NCWC Administrative Committee, November 1921, in Huber, *Our Bishops Speak*, 262.

32. *San Francisco Chronicle*, November 9, 1921.

33. Statement of the NCWC Administrative Committee, February 11, 1922, General Secretary Executive Department Papers, ACUA.

34. *NCWC Bulletin*, Christmas 1923, Clipping found in NCWC Administrative Committee Papers, ACUA; *NCWC Bulletin* 6, no. 1 (June 1924): 3.

35. *Monitor*, June 25, 1932. See also Charles A. McMahon, "Resignation of Archbishop Hanna," *Catholic Action* 17, no. 4 (April 1935): 10.

36. The suppression order was actually issued on February 25, less than three full weeks after Pius XI took office.

37. Slawson, *National Catholic Welfare Council*, 137–38.

38. *New York World*, June 14 and 19, 1922, Clippings found in NCWC Meeting Minutes, 1919–1922, ACUA. The paper reported four probable reasons for the Consistorial Congregation's actions: (1) the

action of Cardinal William O'Connell and Archbishop Dennis Dougherty who saw no reason for the NCWC; (2) the expense of supporting the organization; (3) opposition from wealthy Catholics who disliked John Ryan's open-shop proposal; (4) opposition of the Knights of Columbus.

39. Slawson, *First Decade of the National Catholic Welfare Council*, 138. Several bishops, including O'Connell, Dougherty, and John Keane (Dubuque), were known to be hostile to the NCWC. See John B. Sheerin, CSP, *Never Look Back: The Career and Concerns of John J. Burke* (New York: Paulist Press, 1975), 71 and 83. Sheerin comments, "Several of the bishops...suspected Cardinal O'Connell of having a hand in the suppression."

40. Austin Dowling to John Burke, April 1, 1922, NCWC Meetings of Bishops, ACUA.

41. NCWC Administrative Committee Meeting Minutes, April 6, 1922, NCWC Administrative Committee Papers, ACUA. *Acta* was the official Vatican organ that published papal documents and decrees of the Roman curia and various congregations.

42. Ibid.; Slawson, *First Decade of the National Catholic Welfare Council*, 144; Cardinal Peter Gasparri to Joseph Schrembs [Telegram], April 8, 1922, NCWC Administrative Committee Meeting Minutes, ACUA.

43. Petition of the NCWC Administrative Committee to Pope Pius XI, April 25, 1922, Hanna Papers, AASF.

44. Ibid.

45. NCWC Administrative Committee to "Your Grace," April 29, 1922, NCWC Administrative Committee Meeting Minutes; *New York World*, June 14, 1922, Clipping found in NCWC Meetings of Bishops, ACUA.

46. NCWC Administrative Committee Meeting Minutes, April 26, 1922, ACUA. See also James O'Toole, *Militant and Triumphant: William Henry O'Connell and the Catholic Church in Boston, 1859–1944* (Notre Dame, IN: University of Notre Dame Press, 1992), 199–200. O'Toole states, "O'Connell opposed...the NCWC [thinking it] an infringement on the authority of individual bishops and finding it dangerously radical in promoting social welfare programs."

47. Slawson, *First Decade of the National Catholic Welfare Council*, 137.

48. Joseph Schrembs to Peter Muldoon, May 9, 1922, Hanna Papers, AASF; William O'Connell to Muldoon, May 3, 1922, NCWC Administrative Committee Meeting Minutes, ACUA.

49. Louis Walsh to Edward Hanna, February 19, 1923, Hanna Papers, AASF. It should be noted that Walsh held significant personal pique toward O'Connell, who was Walsh's predecessor in Portland and

left the diocese with major economic irregularities that Walsh only discovered later. For a full picture of the conflict between these two men, see O'Toole, *Militant and Triumphant*, 194–202.

50. Quoted in Sheerin, *Never Look Back*, 83.

51. *New York World*, June 21, 1922; Slawson, *First Decade of the National Catholic Welfare Council*, 145–78.

52. Decree of the Sacred Consistorial Congregation, June 22, 1922, NCWC Meetings of Bishops, 1919–1922, ACUA. Some of the nine points were: (1) possibly hold meetings at longer intervals, (2) all meetings are voluntary, (3) meetings do not have the force of law, (4) minutes of meeting will be communicated to Rome, (5) possibly change the name of the organization away from Council, possibly to Committee. A summary of all nine points is found in Slawson, *First Decade of the National Catholic Welfare Council*, 175–76.

53. John Burke to Edward Hanna [Telegram], June 26, 1922; Hanna to Burke [Telegram], June 26, 1922, NCWC Meetings of Bishops, 1919–1922, ACUA.

54. Edward Hanna to Joseph Schrembs, August 12, 1922; Hanna to John Burke, August 12, 1922, NCWC Dissolution, NCWC Meetings of Bishops, 1919–1922, ACUA.

55. Edward Hanna to Consistorial Congregation, January 24, 1923, NCWC Administrative Committee Papers, ACUA.

56. Slawson, *First Decade of the National Catholic Welfare Council*, 176, 186–91, 206–7; NCWC Administrative Committee Meeting Minutes, September 22, 1923, ACUA.

57. Memorandum on the Question of Birth Control, July 1, 1933, NCWC General Secretary Papers, Executive Department, ACUA.

58. Ellen Chesler, *Woman of Valor: Margaret Sanger and the Birth Control Movement in America* (New York: Simon & Schuster, 1992), 200.

59. Leslie Woodcock Tentler, "A Bitter Pill: American Catholics and Contraception," *Commonweal* 81, no. 8 (April 23, 2004): 12.

60. Report of the NCWC Administrative Committee Chairman, September 21–22, 1920, NCWC Annual Reports, ACUA.

61. Statement of the NCWC Administrative Committee, January 26, 1922, NCWC General Secretary Papers, Executive Department, ACUA.

62. John Burke to Edward Hanna, December 13, 1920, NCWC Administrative Committee Papers, ACUA.

63. Pamphlet, "A Friendly Word with Catholics concerning Birth Control," n.d. [1922], NCWC Family Life Bureau Papers, NCWC General Secretary, Executive Department, ACUA.

64. Report of the NCWC Administrative Committee Chairman, September 27–28, 1922, NCWC Annual Reports, ACUA.

65. John Burke to Edward Hanna, February 9, 1924, Hanna Papers, AASF.

66. Some of the titles of these information sheets were: "A Natural Menace," "Birth Control and the Labor Movement," "Authoritative Medical Report on Birth Control Methods," and "The Protestant Episcopal Church Records Its Condemnation of Contraception."

67. Chesler, *Woman of Valor*, 212.

68. John Burke to Edward Hanna, December 5, 1925; NCWC Administrative Committee Meeting Minutes, April 13, 1926, NCWC Administrative Committee Papers, ACUA.

69. Report of the NCWC Administrative Committee Chairman, n.d. [November 1928], NCWC Annual Reports, ACUA.

70. John Burke to M. R. Ward, January 24, 1929, NCWC General Secretary Papers, ACUA.

71. Chesler, *Woman of Valor*, 213, 415.

72. Report of the NCWC Administrative Committee Chairman, n.d. [November 1930], NCWC Annual Reports, ACUA.

73. NCWC Administrative Committee Meeting Minutes, April 14, 1931; Report of the NCWC Administrative Committee Chairman, n.d. [November 1931], NCWC Annual Reports; John Burke to Edward Hanna, February 13, 1931, NCWC Administrative Committee Papers, ACUA. Some Protestant and Jewish groups began to promote relaxation of federal penal laws against mailing of birth control materials.

74. John Burke to Edward Hanna, May 23, 1932, NCWC Administrative Committee Papers, ACUA.

75. John Burke to Edward Hanna, February 27, 1935, Hanna Papers, AASF. Ellen Chesler describes how the Birth Control Lobby worked with John Ryan on the Gillette bill. The lobby believed that Ryan carried sufficient weight with the bishops that his opinion might sway the group. She claims that Ryan was somewhat open to the Gillette initiative if its drafting was modified. She quotes John Noonan stating that Ryan did not want to be more rigorous on the issue than constraints by the hierarchy required him to be. Sanger's often irreverent comments toward the Church, however, forced Ryan and, therefore, the NCWC to stiffen its opposition. See Chesler, *Woman of Valor*, 332–35. The idea that Ryan would be open on birth control is not verified by his earlier record on the subject. In 1907 in an essay in the *Catholic Encyclopedia* he identified neo-Malthusianism as "intrinsically immoral" in its "perversion of natural faculties and functions."

He also wrote against the practice in a 1916 essay in the *Ecclesiastical Review* and in 1920 in *Catholic Charities Review*.

76. David O'Brien, *American Catholics and Social Reform: The New Deal Years* (New York: Oxford University Press, 1968), 139–40. O'Brien provides a detailed account of the SAD's role during the New Deal years in pages 120–49.

77. Peter Dietz to Edward Hanna, December 14, 1920, Chancery Correspondence, AASF.

78. *NCWC Review* 13, no. 1 (January 1931): 5.

79. Edward Hanna to John Burke, November 28, 1930, NCWC Administrative Committee Papers, ACUA.

80. Report of the NCWC Administrative Committee Chairman, n.d. [November 1932], NCWC Annual Reports, ACUA.

81. Statement of the Hierarchy of the United States, November 12, 1931, in Huber, *Our Bishops Speak*, 195.

82. Statement of NCWC Administrative Committee on the Present Crisis, April 25, 1933, in Huber, *Our Bishops Speak*, 275.

83. Jeffrey M. Burns, *American Catholics and the Family Crisis, 1930–1962* (New York: Garland Publishing, 1988), 19–25.

84. The national bureaucratic approach was centered about the Family Life Bureau, an agency of the Social Action Department of the National Catholic Welfare Conference. This bureau was founded in 1931 with Father Edgar Schmiedeler, OSB, as director. The bureau operated from a supradiocesan perspective. It recommended what should be done but did not perform the action itself. The personalist sacramental approach takes radical personalism as its philosophical foundation. *Integrity* magazine, between 1946 and 1956, under the direction of its editors Ed Willock and Carol Jackson, taught that family renewal lay at the heart of social reconstruction. *Integrity*'s concept of personalism was rooted in the ideas of Emmanuel Mounier, Peter Maurin, Dorothy Day, and Paul Hanly Furfey. All stressed the personal pursuit of perfection. Personalists sought reform through personal change not legislative, organizational, or institutional reconstruction. Burns's third category, the internal educational approach, was manifested most profoundly in the Cana Conference and marriage counseling centers. Alphonse Clemens is the sociologist most associated with the marriage counseling centers. Cana itself started in 1943 as a retreat for married couples. The specialized environmental approach was manifest in the Christian Family Movement (CFM), started by Pat and Patty Crowley in the early 1940s. CFM used the Cardinal Josef Cardijn method for Catholic Action, "observe, judge, act," and applied it to the environment in which the family was present. While Cana tried to remedy problems

from inside the family, CFM tried to change the environment. See Burns *American Catholics and the Family Crisis*, 122–310. Also, for a detailed history of CFM, see Jeffrey M. Burns, *Disturbing the Peace: A History of the Christian Family Movement, 1949–1974* (Notre Dame, IN: University of Notre Dame Press, 1999).

85. Ibid., 128–30, 170–77, 213–20, 279–310. Father (later Cardinal) Josef Cardijn of Belgium was the architect of the "observe, judge, act" concept of Catholic Action, applying it in the work of his Young Christian Workers group. A complete history of the Christian Family Movement is given in Burns, *Disturbing the Peace.*

86. The influence of the Industrial Revolution on the family was stated by the Catholic sociologist Paul Mundie in this way: The pre–Industrial Revolution Era was characterized by "great stability and solidarity," a time when all contributed to the whole. Thus, families contributed an undivided wage. In the post–Industrial Revolution Era, with the onset of factory life, family members contributed to a divided wage. Individualism overtook the communal family effort. Children in many ways became an economic liability. See Paul J. Mundie, "Family in Transition," *American Catholic Sociological Review* 2 (March 1941): 41.

87. Edgar Schmiedeler, OSB, "Conserving the Family," *Catholic Action* 14 (January 1932): 12.

88. "The Christian Family: A Statement of the American Hierarchy," November 21, 1949, in *Catholic Mind* 48 (1950): 124.

89. Statement of Hierarchy of the United States on the Economic Crisis, April 26, 1933, in Huber, *Our Bishops Speak*, 281.

90. Report of the NCWC Administrative Committee Chairman, September 27–28, 1922, NCWC Annual Reports, ACUA.

91. Through the efforts of Bishop John Cantwell of Los Angeles, the Legion of Decency was formed in November 1933 to monitor films and to pressure motion picture makers into producing films of better quality and greater moral integrity. An episcopal committee, chaired by John T. McNicholas of Cincinnati, supervised the Legion's operations, which were so highly successful that in June 1934 Hollywood producers, who felt the loss of revenues from the absence of Catholics at films, petitioned the bishops and asked for direction. Within two years all U.S. dioceses had a chapter of the Legion, which evaluated movies and published results for the faithful. The complete story of the Legion is told in James M. Skinner, *The Cross and the Cinema: The Legion of Decency and the National Catholic Office of Motion Pictures, 1933–1970* (Westport, CT: Praeger Publications, 1993). See also John T. McNicholas, "The Episcopal Committee and the Problem of Evil Motion Pictures," *The*

Ecclesiastical Review 91, no. 2 (August 1934): 113–19; and Hugh C. Boyle, "The Legion of Decency: A Permanent Campaign," *The Ecclesiastical Review* 91, no. 4 (October 1934): 367–70.

92. Many fine monographs chronicle the plight of African American Catholics. The best summary history is found in Cyprian Davis, OSB, *The History of Black Catholics in the United States* (New York: Crossroad, 1990). An excellent analysis of the struggle for African Americans to become priests is found in Stephen Ochs, *Desegregating the Altar: The Josephites and the Struggle for Black Priests, 1871–1960* (Baton Rouge: Louisiana State University Press, 1990). Other volumes on this general subject are Lawrence E. Lucas, *Black Priest/White Church: Catholics and Racism* (Trenton, NJ: African World Press, 1990); and Diana L. Hayes and Cyprian Davis, OSB, eds., *Taking Down Our Harps: Black Catholics in the United States* (Maryknoll, NY: Orbis Press, 1998).

93. *Monitor*, June 11, 1921, and August 2, 1919.

94. Report of the NCWC Administrative Committee Chairman, n.d. [November 1929], NCWC Annual Reports, ACUA.

95. See Michael Ready to Franklin Roosevelt, March 6, 1933, General Secretary Files, NCWC Papers, ACUA.

96. John Burke to Edward Hanna, January 7, 1933, NCWC Administrative Committee Papers, ACUA.

97. Peter Gasparri to Edward Hanna, February 20, 1924, Hanna Papers, AASF; Cardinal Carlo Perosi to Hanna, June 19, 1929, found in Report of NCWC Administrative Committee Chairman, n.d. [November 1929], NCWC Annual Reports, ACUA.

98. Quoted in Report of the NCWC Administrative Committee Chairman, n.d. [November 1931], NCWC Annual Reports, ACUA.

99. *NCWC News Service*, August 11, 1947.

Chapter 8: The NCWC and Immigration

1. *New Republic* quoted in John Higham, *Strangers in the Land: Patterns of American Nativism 1860–1925* (New Brunswick, NJ: Rutgers University Press, 1992), 302. Madison Grant, *The Passing of the Great Race* (New York: Scribner, 1916).

2. Robert S. Divine, *American Immigration Policy, 1924–1952* (New Haven, CT: Yale University Press, 1957), 9–11. In 1924 the historian Roy L. Garis wrote, "It is evident beyond doubt that the immigrant from Northern and Western Europe is far superior to the one from Southern

and Eastern Europe." See Roy L. Garis, "America's Immigration Policy," *The North American Review* 220 (September 1924): 75.

3. Quoted in Roy L. Garis, *Immigration Restriction: A Study of the Opposition to Aid Regulation of Immigrants into the United States* (New York: Macmillan, 1928), 169–70. Higham, *Strangers in the Land*, 307–8, 313–14, 318.

4. Gerald Fogarty, SJ, ed., *Patterns of Episcopal Leadership* (New York: Macmillan, 1989), 86.

5. Marvin O'Connell, "John Ireland," in Fogarty, *Episcopal Leadership*, 142–43; Richard M. Linkh, *American Catholicism and European Immigrants (1900–1924)* (New York: Center for Migration Studies, 1975), 68–72.

6. Linkh, *Catholicism and Immigrants*, 49–58. The first settlement house was opened in Cincinnati by Bishop William Elder in 1897. By 1912 Cincinnati's Santa Maria Institute was performing a variety of functions. Guardian Angel Mission was opened near Chicago's famous Hull House in 1910 and St. Rose's Settlement in New York City was established in 1912.

7. Ibid., 72.

8. Ibid., 170–71. James Gillis, CSP, "Editorial," *The Catholic World* 118 (December 1923): 401–6. It is important to note that the call for a more lenient attitude toward immigrants was not held by Catholics alone. The essayist Herbert Horwill wrote, "If any country in the world is under a moral obligation to adopt a tolerant and even generous attitude to immigration, it is surely the United States." Fred Rindge of the International YMCA commented, "It is for us, very largely, to decide whether our future citizens shall be assets or liabilities. And there is much cause for encouragement." See Herbert Horwill, "America's New Immigration Policy," *The Contemporary Review* (London) 121 (April 1922): 468; and Fred H. Rindge Jr., "The Immigrant: Asset or Liability?" *Missionary Review of the World* 46 (August 1923): 606.

9. Edward Roddy, "The Catholic Newspaper Press and the Quest for Social Justice" (PhD diss., Georgetown University, 1961), 194.

10. Catholic Yearbook 1928, special section "Immigration," p. 570.

11. Reports of the NCWC Administrative Committee Chairman, September 1920 and September 1923, NCWC Annual Reports, ACUA. It should be noted that during World War I the National Catholic War Council established several community houses, called Everyman's Clubs, in various parts of the country to allow people of different ethnic backgrounds to come together on an informal basis. These agencies taught English and operated as employment agencies.

12. The bureau was to conduct all business with the U.S. government, including departments and bureaus, and the diplomatic and consular offices of foreign governments. It was a clearinghouse for persons and agencies throughout the United States, both Catholic and non-Catholic, in matters relating to immigration, emigration, naturalization, and allied subjects in the general field of Catholic Action. The bureau's full injunction for operation is given in its annual report of 1923, NCWC Papers, ACUA.

13. Hanna wrote that recognition would "promote closer international relations between Catholics, bring a kindlier treatment of them in foreign ports and lead the foreign-born here to realize more deeply their indebtedness to the Catholic Church." See Report of the Administrative Committee Chairman, September 21–22, 1921, NCWC Annual Reports, ACUA.

14. These satellite offices, save Philadelphia, were opened in 1921. A small office in Juarez, Mexico, across the border from El Paso opened in January 1923. The Philadelphia office opened in 1922 and closed in 1927 but only after Hanna personally visited and apparently convinced Archbishop Dennis Dougherty of the necessity of the closure. For information on the appointment of Mohler, see Douglas Slawson, *The Foundation and First Decade of the National Catholic Welfare Council* (Washington, DC: Catholic University of America Press, 1992), 74–75.

15. Bureau of Immigration, NCWC Annual Report, November 1928, ACUA.

16. Ibid., November 1923. On May 4, 1923, a representative of the Protestant evangelical societies sent a letter to the NCWC representative on Ellis Island describing "the splendid follow-up work for newly arrived immigrants of Roman Catholic affiliations, which your Welfare Council [*sic*—Conference] is doing."

17. Slawson, *First Decade of the National Catholic Welfare Council*, 75. The decline of the St. Raphael's Society prompted the bureau to make overtures to several European nations, including Poland, Germany, Belgium, Holland, England, Ireland, Scotland, Austria, Hungary, and Yugoslavia to set up their own emigrant aid societies.

18. Bureau of Immigration, NCWC Annual Report, November 1923, ACUA; Linkh, *Catholicism and Immigrants*, 161. The Bureau of Immigration was not the only agency that followed the progress of immigrants. The Home Mission Council, a group of forty-three affiliated Protestant immigrant groups, comprising twenty-seven denominations, organized to follow up on Protestant immigrants to America. See

Raymond E. Cole, "A Church Program for the Immigrant," *Missionary Review of the World* 46 (January 1923): 29–32.

19. The genesis of the 1921 bill is interesting. Albert Johnson's House Committee on Immigration pushed through an initiative that banned immigration for two years (with a few exceptions) but the Senate version of 3 percent based on the 1910 census was passed. Woodrow Wilson pocket vetoed the measure, but in May 1921 Warren Harding signed the bill. Essayist George Creel called the law a "bungling, ineffective stop-gap." See George Creel, "Close the Gates," *Colliers* 69 (May 6, 1922): 9.

20. John Higham, *Send These to Me: Immigrants in Urban America*, rev. ed. (Baltimore: Johns Hopkins University Press, 1984), 55.

21. Higham, *Strangers in the Land*, 311.

22. One letter to John Burke from a private citizen did suggest that the NCWC should fight the 1921 bill "through a massive publicity campaign." See Joseph Doherty to John Burke, March 2, 1921, NCWC General Secretary Files, ACUA.

23. Quoted in Divine, *American Immigration Policy*, 14. For more complete details on the 1924 National Origins Law, see Higham, *Strangers in the Land*, 324, and idem, *Send These to Me*, 55–56.

24. Quoted in Martin Marty, *Modern American Religion*, vol. 2, *The Noise of Conflict, 1919–1941* (Chicago: University of Chicago Press, 1991), 88. Restrictionists hailed the 1924 law. The opinion of Roy L. Garis is illustrative: "Indeed, the time is opportune for Americans to insist on an American policy, regardless of what our employers of cheap labor and our foreign born want. We have catered to them too long already and in consequence have been throwing away our birthright. The vital thing is to preserve the American race, as far as it can be preserved, and build it up with Nordic stock; intelligent, literate, easily assimilated, appreciatory and able to carry on our American institutions. The percentage law based on the census of 1890 will in time automatically bring about such a result." See Garis, "America's Immigration Policy," 76.

25. Quoted in Linkh, *Catholicism and Immigrants*, 179–80.

26. Slawson, *First Decade of the National Catholic Welfare Council*, 237.

27. John Burke to Edward Hanna, January 8, 1924, A-6 Manuscripts Collection, AASF.

28. John Burke to Edward Hanna, January 12, 1924, NCWC General Secretary Files—Burke, ACUA.

29. The initiative was introduced just before Christmas 1923 and the hearings on the bill began immediately after Christmas. Thus, Mohler had to submit his brief quickly, before the hearings ended, and with little

input from the Administrative Committee, something Hanna hoped to be able to provide.

30. Bruce Mohler to Chairman of the Committee on Immigration and Naturalization, House of Representatives, January 7, 1924, A-6 Manuscripts Collection, AASF.

31. Ibid.

32. Nonquota status was given to immigrants in special circumstances for education and specialized work for government and industry.

33. John J. Burke to Edward Hanna, June 2, 1924, A-6 Manuscripts Collection, AASF; Meeting Minutes for the NCWC Administrative Committee, May 1, 1924; NCWC Annual Report 1924, ACUA.

34. The 1890 census quota was 164,666 and the national origins quota was 153,714. See Divine, *American Immigration*, 26–27.

35. Divine, *American Immigration*, 26–51. Divine presents a detailed description and analysis of the national origins debate.

36. Report of the NCWC Administrative Committee Chairman, September 1925, NCWC Annual Reports, ACUA.

37. In 1926 the bureau was actively reviewing 105 initiatives, geared toward softening the restriction policy, which were introduced into Congress. The bureau also distributed a pamphlet that explained to others its work and purpose.

38. NCWC Administrative Committee Meeting Minutes, April 27, 1927, NCWC Papers; Bruce M. Mohler to Rev. T. W. Drumm, December 12, 1929, NCWC International Affairs Papers, ACUA.

39. No extant data reveals precisely what Hanna meant by this comment.

40. Bruce Mohler to Edward Hanna, April 28, 1925, A-6 Manuscripts Collection, AASF.

41. Bruce Mohler to Edward Hanna, February 9, 1928, A-6 Manuscripts Collection, AASF.

42. NCWC Annual Report 1924, Bureau of Immigration, NCWC Papers, ACUA.

43. John Burke to Bishop Edwin Byrne, April 22, 1927, NCWC General Secretary Files—Burke; Burke to Edward Hanna, March 2, 1928, NCWC Numerical Files—Hanna, ACUA.

44. NCWC Annual Report, Bureau of Immigration, November 1928, NCWC Papers, ACUA.

45. NCWC Annual Report, Bureau of Immigration, July 1, 1932, to June 30, 1933, NCWC Papers; Bruce Mohler to John Burke, February 16, 1931, NCWC General Secretary Files—Burke, ACUA.

46. NCWC Annual Report, Bureau of Immigration, September 1926, NCWC Papers, ACUA.

47. Divine, *American Immigration*, 87–88.

48. Several different ideas were proposed to further restrict immigration in the wake of Hoover's new policy of interpreting who would be a public charge. Albert Johnson in 1931 suggested that immigration be suspended save relatives of American citizens and resident aliens. Senator David Reed's proposal went further, suspending all immigration save relatives of citizens alone. Secretary of State Henry Stimson recommended a flat 90 percent reduction of all immigration. The Stimson proposal was actually debated in Congress, but the measure was stymied by a few staunch opponents.

49. Divine, *American Immigration*, 77, 88–90. Franklin Roosevelt maintained the public charge policy during his first two terms but in a less stringent form. This policy changed the composition of immigration to the United States. The national origins law established a ratio of 5 to 1 in favor of countries of northwestern Europe, but between 1931 and 1940 the actual distribution of European immigrants was 57 percent from northwestern countries and 43 percent from southeastern nations. Between 1931 and 1940 528,431 immigrants were admitted, but taking into account emigration of aliens, the net increase in the decade was only 68,693.

50. Quoted in ibid., 86.

51. John A. Ryan, "Ethical Aspects of Some International Problems," *America* 49 (May 20, 1933): 155.

52. NCWC Annual Report, Bureau of Immigration, July 1, 1932, to June 30, 1933, NCWC Papers, ACUA. Some of the specific measures introduced under Roosevelt were: (1) State Department will issue student visas where previously visas were granted for permanent residents only. (2) State Department withdrew its strict policy of demanding more than reasonable proof of support as a prerequisite for granting a visa to husbands and fathers of dependents residing in the United States. (3) Secretary of labor was granted authorization to issue nonquota visas to Western Hemisphere–born husbands and wives of American citizens. (4) Department of Labor amended its drastic regulations that forbade immigrant students from engaging in any kind of gainful occupation.

53. Ibid.

Chapter 9: The NCWC and the Drive to Federalize Education

1. Marvin Lazerson, "Understanding American Catholic Educational History," *History of Education Quarterly* 17, no. 3 (fall 1977): 297–317. Lazerson gives a review of issues, personalities, and proclamations concerning education in American Catholic history. Quoting Vincent P. Lannie he views Catholic educational historiography as dominated by a vision of "Church and School Triumphant."

2. Quoted in Harold Buetow, *Of Singular Benefit: The Story of U.S. Catholic Education* (London: Macmillan, 1970), 146.

3. "Pastoral Letter to the Laity," October 17, 1829, in *Pastoral Letters of the United States Catholic Bishops*, ed. Hugh J. Nolan (Washington, DC: United States Catholic Conference, 1984), 1:39. The complete history of the provincial and plenary councils of Baltimore is given in Peter Guilday, *A History of the Councils of Baltimore, 1791–1884* (New York: Macmillan, 1932).

4. At this time two major encounters between Catholic leaders and American society were centered on the issue of education. Between 1840 and 1842 Bishop John Hughes in New York waged a battle to procure public money for Catholic schools, an effort that was at least partially successful. More serious, however, was the Philadelphia riots of 1844, which were generated in large part by a conflict between Bishop Francis Kenrick and the public schools over the use of the King James Version of the Bible in class. The riots resulted in the destruction of two churches and a seminary, plus several deaths. See Vincent P. Lannie, *Public Money and Parochial Education* (Cleveland: Press of Case Western Reserve University, 1968); Michael Feldberg, *The Philadelphia Riots of 1844* (Westport, CT: Greenwood Press, 1975); Vincent P. Lannie and Bernard C. Diethorn, "For the Honor and Glory of God: The Philadelphia Bible Riots of 1840 [*sic*—1844]," *History of Education Quarterly* 8 (spring 1968): 44–106; Elizabeth B. Geffen, "Violence in Philadelphia in the 1840s and 1850s," *Pennsylvania History* 36 (October 1969): 381–410.

5. Buetow, *Of Singular Benefit*, 146–52. "Pastoral Letter," fifth Sunday after Easter, 1843, in Nolan, *Pastoral Letters*, 141. With nativism and anti-Catholic animus common in the period, the bishops wisely demonstrated their conformity with mainstream American belief.

6. "Pastoral Letter," Feast of the Ascension, 1852, in Nolan, *Pastoral Letters*, 180; Buetow, *Of Singular Benefit*, 149.

7. McMaster, a zealous convert to Catholicism, created a furor with his indictment of the American public school system and his perception that the hierarchy was doing little to stem its influence on Catholic youth. He was a staunch opponent of the "Poughkeepsie Plan" whereby the local parochial school was used as a public school during normal school hours with religious education for Catholic youth provided after the school day. This same basic plan would be used in 1891 by Archbishop John Ireland (St. Paul) in two parishes, Stillwater and Faribault, as a method to keep funds-strapped Catholic schools alive. See Daniel F. Reilly, *The School Controversy (1891–1893)* (Washington, DC: Catholic University of America Press, 1943), for a complete chronology and analysis of these events. In response to McMaster's comments, submitted by his agent, Ella B. Edes, *Propaganda* sent a questionnaire to the American hierarchy asking why Catholics attended public schools and what to do about parents who refused to send their children to parochial schools. The results of the survey were given to the Congregation of the Inquisition, which spoke with Pope Pius IX, who issued the "Instruction of 1875."

8. "The Instruction of 1875," in *Catholic Education in America: A Documentary History*, ed. Neil G. McCluskey, SJ (New York: Teachers' College, Columbia University, 1964), 121–26. Thomas T. McAvoy, "Public Schools vs. Catholic Schools and James McMaster," *Review of Politics* 28 (January 1966): 19–46.

9. "Pastoral Letter," December 7, 1884, in Nolan, *Pastoral Letters*, 221–25.

10. Alan Dawley, *Struggles for Justice: Social Responsibility and the Liberal State* (Cambridge, MA: Harvard University Press, 1991).

11. *Rerum novarum* is considered the formative document for contemporary Roman Catholic social teaching. Its precepts, the right of workers to organize, just wages, adequate rest from labor, including reasonable daily work hours, and state responsibilities to workers, became the base on which reformers such as John A. Ryan based their writings and call for action.

12. Lynn Dumenil, "'The Insatiable Maw of Bureaucracy': Anti-statism and Education Reform in the 1920s," *The Journal of American History* 77, no. 2 (September 1990): 505. Teacher salaries averaged $871 per year, with Mississippi at the low end ($291) and New Jersey at the top ($1282). The average worker salary was $1144. For more explanation on the state of public education in America in the postwar period, see David B. Tyack and Elisabeth Hansot, *Managers of Virtue: Public School Leadership in America, 1820–1920* (New York: Basic Books, 1982); and David B.

Tyack, *The One Best System: A History of American Urban Education* (Cambridge, MA: Harvard University Press, 1974.

13. William Halsey, *The Survival of American Innocence: Catholicism in an Era of Disillusionment, 1920–1940* (Notre Dame, IN: University of Notre Dame Press, 1980), 2. Halsey defines innocence as "the belief in a rational and predictable cosmos, the belief in a moral structure inherent in the universe, the belief in progress and a didactic or 'genteel' rendering of cultural, especially literary art forms." When this period of American innocence was present is not precisely defined by Halsey, but the later nineteenth century is suggested. American Catholics struggled to maintain their earlier understanding of a rational and structured world amid the multiple and significant changes that overtook society in the postwar period.

14. Quoted in Martin Marty, *Modern American Religion*, vol. 2, *The Noise of Conflict, 1919–1941* (Chicago: University of Chicago Press, 1986), 94–95.

15. Dumenil, "The Tribal Twenties: 'Assimilated' Catholics' Response to Anti-Catholicism in the 1920s," *Journal of American Ethnic History* 11 (fall 1991): 21–49. Dumenil describes and analyzes the impact of anti-Catholic animus in the 1920s.

16. The origins of the various education initiatives proposed in Congress during the 1920s are described in Erwin Stevenson Selle, *The Organization and Activities of the National Education Association: A Case Study in Educational Sociology* (New York: Teachers' College, Columbia University, 1932); and Albertina Adelheit Abrams, "The Policy of the National Education Association toward Federal Aid to Education (1857–1953)" (PhD diss., University of Michigan, 1954).

17. Dumenil, "'The Insatiable Maw of Bureaucracy': Anti-Statism and Education Reform in the 1920s," *The Journal of American History* 77, no. 2 (September 1990): 501.

18. U.S. Congress, Senate S.4987, 65th Congress, 2nd session, 1918. Additional provisions of the Smith proposal were: (1) the Department of Education would have at least three assistant secretaries and a solicitor in the Justice Department, (2) the new department would comprise the Bureau of Education and any other educational commissions or boards that the president might transfer to it, (3) the department was directed to undertake studies in illiteracy, immigrant education, public school education, public health education, and preparation of adequately trained teachers.

19. Buetow, *Of Singular Benefit*, 180–81. The Catholic school system of 1920, with its 5,800 schools and 1.7 million students in a total Catholic population of 17.7 million, represented a greater than 50 percent rise in schools and almost a doubling of students since 1900. As stated in

chapter 3, support and assistance for this burgeoning system was provided by the formation of the NCEA in 1904. The NCEA was deliberative and informative, not legislative. It eventually comprised seven departments: (1) major seminary, (2) minor seminary, (3) college and university, (4) superintendents, (5) secondary schools, (6) primary schools, (7) special education. Its goals, articulated in 1917, were fivefold: (1) education is the cooperation by human agencies with the Creator for the attainment of his purpose in regard to the individual who is to be educated and in regard to the social order of which the student is a member; (2) the development of the student's physical, intellectual, and moral capacities is primary; (3) performance of religious duties ensures fulfillment of other obligations; (4) religious training should permeate all so that "its influence will be felt in every circumstance of life"; and (5) an education that unites intellectual, moral, and religious elements is the best training for citizenship.

20. NCEA Executive Board Meeting Minutes, National Catholic Education Association *Bulletin* 15 (November 1918): 16–17.

21. William Henry O'Connell, "The Reasonable Limits of State Activity," National Catholic Education Association *Bulletin* 16 (November 1919): 62–66.

22. The latter change, removal of the word *parochial*, did nothing for Catholic schools since they were private as well as parochial and, thus, still would not qualify for the federal appropriation. It should be noted that parochial schools often taught immigrants in their vernacular languages as a means to maintain culture and the faith. A full discussion of this policy is provided in Fayette Veverka, *For God and Country: Catholic Schooling in the 1920s* (New York: Garland Press, 1988), especially pp. 73–82.

23. Dumenil, "'The Insatiable Maw of Bureaucracy,'" 512. She writes, "While the department of education bill did not threaten private schools in the same manner [as the 1922 Oregon School Law] Catholic leaders tended to view it as an entering wedge, a first step in control and even elimination of the parochial schools."

24. NCWC Administrative Committee Meeting Minutes, September 25, 1919, ACUA.

25. Dumenil, "'The Insatiable Maw of Bureaucracy,'" 499–524. Dumenil argues that antistatism was the principle most used to defeat all the various forms of the original Smith bill.

26. John J. Burke to Edward Hanna, February 23, 1921, Burke Private Files, NCWC General Secretary Papers, ACUA.

27. Paul Blakely, SJ, "Silver Threads and Smith Bill Gold," *America* 24 (October 23, 1920): 21; idem, "The Unmendable Smith Bill," *America* 24 (January 22, 1921): 341. Blakely's statement appears to refer to all

schools, public and private. No public discussion of the idea of Catholic schools receiving federal funds, something more accessible with a Federal Department of Education, was initiated.

28. *Monitor,* June 5, 1920.

29. NCWC *Catholic News Sheet,* May 31, 1920.

30. Ibid., January 17, 1921.

31. Douglas Slawson, "The Attitudes and Activities of American Catholics regarding the Proposals to Establish a Federal Department of Education between World War I and the Great Depression" (PhD diss., Catholic University of America, 1981), 231.

32. Newsletter, Grand Lodge of Masons of New York State, January 17, 1922, NCWC General Secretary Files, ACUA.

33. John Burke to Edward Hanna, February 13, 1922, NCWC General Secretary Files, ACUA.

34. John Burke to James Munro, May 10, 1921, NCWC General Secretary Files, Sterling-Towner, ACUA.

35. The NCWC was severely hampered in its fight against Sterling-Towner at this time due to its own struggle for survival as described in chapter 7.

36. John Burke to Edward Hanna, February 13, 1922, NCWC General Secretary Files, ACUA.

37. John Burke to Edward Hanna, March 1, 1922, NCWC General Secretary Files, ACUA. In an interesting and somewhat contradictory tactic, Hanna in a May 27, 1922, pastoral letter on education to the Archdiocese of San Francisco wrote, "Without Christian schools for the little ones of the flock, the faith of the next generation will be imperiled." Hanna's comment, consistent with traditional Catholic fears, demonstrates that the possible loss of Catholic schools remained an underlying tenet to Catholic opposition to federalization of education. See Philip P. McGuire, "Striking Events in the Life of the Most Reverend Edward Joseph Hanna, D.D., Archbishop of San Francisco," 1926, p. 133, Hanna Papers, AALA.

38. Editorial, "The N.E.A., the Masons, and Federal Schools," *America* 29 (June 30, 1923): 254; Paul Blakely, SJ, "The Crusade for the Towner-Sterling Bill," *America* 29 (July 21, 1923): 334.

39. Slawson, "Attitudes and Activities," 241. There is at least one indication that Harding was on Burke's side in the fight against a Federal Department of Education. The general secretary reported the president's words in conversation, "Father Burke, you will have to fight. I don't know whether you will succeed ornot *[sic]*, but you will have to fight." John Burke to Edward Hanna, February 13, 1922, NCWC General Secretary Files, ACUA.

40. NCWC Education Department, Sterling-Towner File, ACUA. The file gives a list of individuals and groups in opposition to Sterling-Towner. It is probable that the rivalry among educators who were competing for the education secretary position may have been the catalyst that caused others such as Butler, Lowell, and Angell to oppose the federalization drive.

41. William Guthrie, "The Oregon Compulsory Public School Law," April 21, 1924, P115, Manuscripts, AASF. Several fine articles have fully described the Oregon school case in detail. See David B. Tyack, "The Perils of Pluralism: The Background of the Pierce Case," *American Historical Review* 74 (1968): 74–98; M. Paul Holsinger, "The Oregon School Bill Controversy, 1922–1925," *Pacific Historical Review* 37 (1968): 327–41; Edmond G. Drouin, "The U.S. Supreme Court and Religious Freedom in American Education in Its Decisions Affecting Church-Related Elementary and Secondary Schools During the First Three Quarters of the Twentieth Century" (PhD diss., Catholic University of America, 1980), 144–58; Thomas J. Shelley, "The Oregon School Case and the National Catholic Welfare Conference," *Catholic Historical Review* 75, no. 3 (July 1989): 439–57; Lloyd P. Jorgenson, "The Oregon School Law of 1922: Passage and Sequel," *Catholic Historical Review* 54 (October 1968): 455–66.

42. Guthrie, "Oregon Compulsory Public School Law." The initiative passed 115,506 to 102,685.

43. Quoted in Holsinger, "Oregon School Bill Controversy," 335; *Monitor*, January 27, 1923.

44. Guthrie, "Oregon Compulsory Public School Law."

45. Alexander Christie to Edward Hanna, n.d. [December 1922], Hanna Papers, AASF.

46. Quoted in Shelley, "Oregon School Case," 443.

47. The NCWC, although sympathetic, could not in the fall of 1922 economically support Archbishop Christie in his fight. Recall the problems the nascent body had in collecting assessments from bishops. Christie had asked for funds since "the campaign has exhausted our resources." See Shelley, "Oregon School Case," 443. In August 1922 Hanna directed Burke "to give every aid possible through the staff of the National Catholic Welfare Council...by furnishing them [Oregon] with suitable literature for defensive distribution." NCWC Administrative Committee Meeting Minutes, August 11, 1922, ACUA.

48. It seems that Gibbons took a less active role than Dowling. As treasurer of the NCWC Dowling was responsible for raising the money from the nation's bishops to finance the campaign. See Shelley, "Oregon

School Case," 444. Also see NCWC Administrative Committee Meeting Minutes, January 11, 1923, ACUA.

49. NCWC Administrative Committee Meeting Minutes, January 11, 1923, ACUA.

50. Charles N. Lischka, "The Appeal of the Oregon School Law," *NCWC News Bulletin* 6, no. 11 (April 1925): 11–13.

51. Edward Hanna to Cardinal Peter Gasparri, January 24, 1923; Hanna to Consistorial Congregation, January 24, 1923, NCWC General Secretary Papers—Burke Private File, ACUA.

52. John Burke to Edward Hanna, February 26, 1923, NCWC General Secretary Papers; NCWC Administrative Committee Meeting Minutes, April 12, 1923. See also Shelley, "Oregon School Case," 445–47.

53. NCWC Administrative Committee Meeting Minutes, April 12, 1923, ACUA. In the end Hanna was angered that Kavanaugh's bill totaled over $25,000. See Shelley, "Oregon School Case," 447.

54. Peter Muldoon to Edward Hanna, February 5, 1923, Hanna Papers, AASF. Another comment about the Knights is even more revealing. John Carroll, bishop of Helena, Montana, wrote Austin Dowling, who was in charge of raising funds for the court battle, "The Knights are able and anxious to give their money as I have the best of reasons to know. We should not delude ourselves about that. They believe it would be the greatest feather in their cap 'to save the schools of Oregon and the nation' while their God-appointed defenders were quarreling about lawyers and haggling about the price." See John P. Carroll to Austin Dowling, July 21, 1923, Hanna Papers, AASF.

55. Quoted in Shelley, "Oregon School Case," 447.

56. Christopher J. Kauffman, *Faith and Fraternalism: The History of the Knights of Columbus, 1882–1982* (New York: Harper & Row, 1982), 283–84. Christie had met with the Knights on January 7, 1923, in Chicago, four days prior to the NCWC Administrative Committee meeting. This is when the $10,000 was promised to fight the battle in Oregon. However, when the NCWC offered to finance the litigation the Knights initially balked until the matter was clarified. Christie actually received the Knights' money in February.

57. J. P. Kavanaugh to Edward Hanna, April 1, 1924, Hanna Papers, AASF.

58. NCWC Administrative Committee Meeting Minutes, May 1, 1924, ACUA.

59. Shelley, "Oregon School Case," 454.

60. John Burke to Edward Hanna, June 2, 1925, NCWC Administrative Committee Papers, ACUA.

61. *NCWC News Service*, August 11, 1947.

62. National Education Association of the United States, "Addresses and Proceedings of the Sixty-Sixth Annual Meeting" (Washington, DC, 1924), 188.

63. James H. Ryan to Senator William E. Borah, January 23, 1924, Education Department Files—Sterling-Reed, ACUA; James H. Ryan, "The Sterling-Reed Bill: A Criticism," *Catholic Educational Review* 22 (June 1924): 358.

64. James H. Ryan to Senator William E. Borah, January 23, 1924, NCWC Education Department Files—Sterling-Reed, ACUA; James H. Ryan, "The Proposed Monopoly in Education," *Atlantic Monthly* 133 (February 1924): 172–79.

65. U.S. Congress, H.R. 6562, 68th Congress, First Session, NCWC Education Department Files—Sterling-Reed, ACUA.

66. John Burke to Edward Hanna, January 12, 1924, NCWC Administrative Committee, Hanna Papers; NCWC Administrative Committee Meeting Minutes, May 1, 1924, ACUA.

67. "The Supreme Court Affirms the Right of Private Religious Schools," June 1, 1925 in John Tracy Ellis, ed., *Documents of American Catholic History*, Vol. II (Wilmington, DE: Michael Glazier, 1987), 615–16.

68. John Burke to Edward Hanna, January 16, 1926; Burke to Hanna, January 27, 1926; Hanna to Burke, January 28, 1926; Burke to Hanna, February 13, 1926, NCWC Administrative Committee, Hanna Papers, ACUA.

69. "Memorandum Before Congress on Behalf of the Cathedral Academy of Albany, New York," March 10, 1926; John Burke to Members of the Hierarchy, February 27, 1926, NCWC Education Department Files—Curtis-Reed; John Burke to Edward Hanna, March 2, 1926, NCWC Administrative Committee, Hanna Papers, ACUA.

70. NCWC Administrative Committee Meeting Minutes, April 13, 1926, September 13, 1926, ACUA; Editorial, "The Federal Education Bill!" *America* 36 (December 18, 1926): 228.

71. James H. Ryan, "Dangers of Federalism," *NCWC News Bulletin* (November 1927): 10; NCWC Education Department Files—Curtis-Reed, ACUA.

72. Statement to House Committee on Education, Summary, April 25–28 and May 2, 1928, NCWC Education Department Files—Curtis-Reed, ACUA.

73. Slawson, "Attitudes and Activities," 480–81. The inauguration of Herbert Hoover as president on March 4, 1929, gave proponents of

federalization of education hope that a new administration might be sympathetic to their cause. These hopes were quickly dashed, however, when Dr. Ray Lyman Wilbur, secretary of the interior, announced, "A Department of Education similar to the other departments of Government is not required." The National Advisory Committee on Education, formed in June 1929, became the group to promote the concept of a Federal Department of Education after ten years of legislative attempts had failed.

74. Dumenil, "'The Insatiable Maw of Bureaucracy,'" 500.

Chapter 10: The NCWC and the International Community

1. *Monitor,* February 15, 1919.

2. Ibid., November 15, 1919.

3. Richard Gid Powers, *Not Without Honor: The History of American Anticommunism* (New York: Free Press, 1995), 29. For more information on the Red Scare phenomenon after World War I, also see 25–33, and 40–42; M. J. Heale, *American Anticommunism: Combating the Enemy Within, 1830–1970* (Baltimore: Johns Hopkins University Press, 1990), 60–78; Robert K. Murray, *Red Scare: A Study in National Hysteria 1919–1920* (Minneapolis: University of Minnesota Press, 1955); Seymour J. Mandelbaum, *The Social Setting of Intolerance: The Know-Nothings, the Red Scare, and McCarthyism* (Chicago: Scott, Foresman and Company, 1964).

4. *Monitor,* January 25, 1920.

5. In May 1923 Archbishop John Zepliak of Petrograd, Monsignor Constantine Butchkavitch, and several other Catholic priests were tried and convicted as enemies of the state in a Moscow courtroom. The priests were accused of holding views contrary to the new Soviet government through their refusal to cooperate with several state proclamations. The indictment said that the clergy "had tried cleverly to distort the laws and to find a juridical basis for refusing compliance." See *New York Times,* May 27, 1923, Section VIII, page 3, for a summary of the trial.

6. "Conditions in Russia," Statement of Hierarchy of the United States, September 25, 1924 in Raphael Huber, *Our Bishops Speak* (Milwaukee: Bruce Publishing Company, 1952), 186.

7. Leo V. Kanawada, Jr., *Franklin D. Roosevelt's Diplomacy and American Catholics, Italians and Jews* (Ann Arbor, MI: UMI Research Press, 1982), 4. See also Powers, *Not Without Honor,* 118–19.

8. John Burke to Edward Hanna, January 30, 1933, NCWC Administrative Committee Files, ACUA.

9. Edward Hanna to John Burke, February 11, 1933, NCWC Administrative Committee Files, ACUA.

10. John Burke to Edward Hanna, February 27, 1933, NCWC Administrative Committee Files, ACUA.

11. Paul Marella to J. M. Gannon, March 10, 1933, NCWC Office of the General Secretary Papers, ACUA. The bishops contacted were in Boston; Baltimore; Chicago; Cincinnati; Milwaukee; New York; Philadelphia; St. Louis; St. Paul, Minnesota; San Francisco; Cleveland; Erie, Pennsylvania; Fall River, Massachusetts; Fort Wayne, Indiana; Kansas City; Omaha; Pittsburgh; and Toledo.

12. Cardinal Dougherty's Response to Russian Recognition Questionnaire, n.d. [March 1933], NCWC Office of the General Secretary Papers, ACUA.

13. John T. McNicholas to John Burke, February 7, 1933, NCWC Office of the General Secretary Papers, ACUA.

14. NCWC Administrative Committee Meeting Minutes, April 25, 1933, NCWC Administrative Committee Papers, ACUA.

15. Summary of American Commentary on the Recognition of Soviet Russia by the United States Government, NCWC General Secretary Files, n.d. [November 1933], ACUA.

16. Kanawada, *Roosevelt's Diplomacy and American Catholics*, 8–9; George Q. Flynn, *American Catholics and the Roosevelt Presidency, 1932–1936* (Lexington: University of Kentucky Press, 1968), 123–49; Thomas Blantz, *George N. Shuster: On the Side of Truth* (Notre Dame, IN: University of Notre Dame Press, 1993), 84; Wilfrid Parsons, SJ, "An Open Letter to M. Litvinov," *America* 50 (November 4, 1933): 107–8.

17. Recognition was given with the proviso that the Soviets would soften their stand against public worship. This condition was placed in the agreement as a result of Catholic pressure on Roosevelt. See Kanawada, *Roosevelt's Diplomacy and American Catholics*, 3.

18. There are no extant sources where Gillis expressed any reaction to America's recognition of the Soviet Union. His public silence is unusual since he was an active commentator on domestic and international affairs in his capacity as editor of *The Catholic World*, but this certainly does not mean that he approved of the move.

19. John Burke to Edward Hanna, October 5, 1933, NCWC Administrative Committee Papers; John Burke to William Phillips, September 30, 1933, NCWC General Secretary Files, ACUA.

20. C. W. Curier to Edward Hanna, September 25, 1915, Hanna Papers, AASF; Memorandum of Rene Capistran Garza to NCWC Administrative Committee, September 14, 1926, NCWC Administrative Committee Papers, ACUA.

21. John Sheerin, CSP, *Never Look Back: The Career and Concerns of John J. Burke* (New York: Paulist Press, 1975), 108.

22. In early January 1916 sixteen Americans were pulled from a train in Chihuahua and gunned down by forces loyal to General Villa. The act led to a call in Congress for military action against Mexico. However, calmer voices prevailed. See *New York Times*, January 13, 1916.

23. *San Francisco Examiner*, January 14, 1916.

24. Some of the specifics of the Queretaro Constitution relevant to the church were: Article 3, which forbade parochial education; Article 27, which nationalized all land, including ecclesiastical property, thereby placing religious temporalities in the hand of government; and Article 130, which declared the priesthood to be a profession that required civil registration of practitioners, allowed states the right to regulate the number of functioning clergymen, and confined the ministry to native-born Mexicans. See Douglas Slawson, "The National Catholic Welfare Conference and the Church-State Conflict in Mexico, 1925–1929," *The Americas* 47, no. 1 (July 1990): 56–57. Additionally, see Christopher J. Kauffman, *Faith and Fraternalism: The History of the Knights of Columbus, 1882–1982* (New York: Harper & Row, 1982), 289.

25. Slawson, "NCWC in Mexico, 1925–1929," 57. Slawson's comment speaks of the Patronato Real used by the monarchs of Spain to control church and state in the New World. The best complete text on this system is Eugene W. Shiels, *King and Church: The Rise and Fall of the Patronato Real* (Chicago: Loyola University Press, 1961).

26. *Monitor*, May 1, 1920.

27. Slawson, "NCWC in Mexico, 1925–1929," 57–58.

28. Ibid., 59; Annual Report of the NCWC Administrative Committee Chairman, n.d. [September 1925], NCWC Administrative Committee Papers, ACUA.

29. John Burke to Edward Hanna, February 13, 1926, and March 2, 1926, Hanna Papers, AASF.

30. Slawson, "NCWC in Mexico 1925–1929," 61.

31. Statement of the NCWC Administrative Committee on Mexican Injustice to the Church, April 15, 1926, in Huber, *Our Bishops Speak*, 269–70.

32. Ibid. The bishops encouraged Catholics to even meet with non-Catholics to present a more united front in their protest to the U.S. government.

33. Edward Hanna to Calvin Coolidge, April 15, 1926, Hanna Papers, AASF.

34. NCWC Administrative Committee Meeting Minutes, April 15, 1926, NCWC Administrative Committee Papers, ACUA.

35. Slawson, "NCWC in Mexico, 1925–1929," 62–63.

36. Edward Hanna et al. to Calvin Coolidge, April 23, 1926, Hanna Papers, AASF.

37. Slawson, "NCWC in Mexico, 1925–1929," 66.

38. NCWC News Sheet, April 19, 1926; Pamphlet, "Organization and By-Laws," n.d. [1926], NCWC Administrative Committee Papers, ACUA.

39. John Burke to Edward Hanna, April 21, 1926, and April 30, 1926, NCWC Administrative Committee Papers, ACUA; Slawson, "NCWC in Mexico, 1925–1929," 63–64.

40. Slawson, "NCWC in Mexico, 1925–1929," 65.

41. John Burke to Edward Hanna, May 16, 1926 [Telegram], Hanna Correspondence, AASF. Burke provided specifics on the two premises of the expulsion, namely, that Caruana entered Mexico illegally and that he had violated the constitution. "Archbishop Caruana's entrance into Mexico was in every way legal. A month ago it was made the subject of an investigation by [the] Mexican government and even its officials, eager and determined to find it illegal had to abandon their efforts. Archbishop Caruana gave no disturbant interviews to the press since he went into Mexico. That the Archbishov [sic] has violated article one hundred thirty of [the] present constitution which forbids a priest or minister to officiate at a religious service function without [the] permission of the civil authorities is not true [,] for the archbishop has taken care never to officiate in public and has been scrupulously careful not to violate even the most unjust provisions of [the] Mexican constitution."

42. Edward Hanna to U.S. Secretary of State [Frank Kellogg], May 19, 1926, Hanna Correspondence, AASF.

43. *San Francisco Chronicle*, July 2, 1926.

44. Edward Hanna to Frank Kellogg, July 7, 1926, Hanna Correspondence, AASF.

45. John Burke to Edward Hanna, July 7, 1926, NCWC Administrative Committee Papers, ACUA.

46. Pietro Fumasoni-Biondi to Edward Hanna, July 8, 1926; Hanna Statement, n.d. [1926], Chancery Correspondence, AASF.

47. Sheerin, *Never Look Back*, 112–16. Soon after the Liga began its overt opposition to the government the Knights of Columbus in the United States began to lobby the American government for action in Mexico. The order generated a "Mexican Fund." Christopher Kauffman, historian of the Knights, says that the order was clearly associated with the Cristero Rebellion, but there is no evidence of a direct financial link. See Kauffman, *Faith and Fraternalism*, 295.

48. Annual Report of the NCWC Administrative Committee Chairman, n.d. [September 1926], NCWC Annual Reports; Memorandum of Rene Capistran Garza to NCWC Administrative Committee, September 14, 1926, NCWC Administrative Committee Papers, ACUA.

49. Garza, an idealistic Mexican Catholic layman and attorney, was one of the original leaders of the "Liga Nacional de Defensa de la Libertad Religiosa," the foundational group associated with the Cristero Rebellion of 1926.

50. Meeting Minutes of the NCWC Administrative Committee, September 13, 1926, NCWC Administrative Committee Papers, ACUA.

51. In part the letter read, "We, the bishops of the United States of America,…send our greetings of sympathy and affection to you…bishops of the United States of Mexico, and to your heroic people. We, our clergy and laity, are watching with eagerness and entire sympathy your magnificent fight against a tyrannical government. We applaud your wisdom, moderation, and firmness; and are filled with admiration of the calmness, courage, and endurance of the Mexican people. You are showing to the whole world the true spirit of martyrs, ready to endure and suffer all for the sake of Christ. You are also showing yourselves the real champions in Mexico of religious and civil liberty. You are fearlessly resisting armed force in defense of the inalienable rights of man." See "Letter of Sympathy from the Hierarchy of the United States to the Archbishops, Bishops, Priests, and Laity of Mexico," in Huber, *Our Bishops Speak*, 188.

52. M. Elizabeth Ann Rice, OP, *The Diplomatic Relations Between the United States and Mexico, as Affected by the Struggle for Religious Liberty in Mexico, 1925–1929* (Washington, DC: Catholic University of America Press, 1959), 105; John Burke to Joseph Schrembs, December 12, 1926, NCWC International Affairs Papers, ACUA.

53. Bishop Francis Clement Kelley of Oklahoma City was the primary author, with a supporting committee of Cardinal Patrick Hayes of New York, Archbishop Austin Dowling of St. Paul, Cardinal John Glennon of St. Louis, and Bishop Joseph Schrembs, then bishop of Cleveland.

54. "Pastoral Letter on Mexico," in Huber, *Our Bishops Speak*, 66.

55. Ibid., 76.

56. Cardinal Donato Sbarretti to Edward Hanna, February 7, 1927, found in Meeting Minutes of NCWC Administrative Committee, April 27, 1927, NCWC Administrative Committee Papers, ACUA.

57. Pope Pius XI to William O'Connell et al. [All Cardinals], August 10, 1927, NCWC International Affairs, ACUA.

58. Edward Hanna to John Burke, March 12, 1927, NCWC Administrative Committee Papers, ACUA.

59. In 1926 a general religious strike suspended all public religious services. In what became known as the Cristero Rebellion, Catholic insurgents burned schools, attacked troop trains, and even murdered some school teachers. The states of Jalisco, Michoacan, and Colima echoed with the cry, "Viva Cristo Rey." The tension was lessened largely through the mediation of Dwight W. Morrow, who became the U.S. ambassador to Mexico in 1927. The Mexican government eventually compromised on some of its most anti-clerical measures. Some ninety thousand Mexicans died during the ensuring three-year conflict. For more information on the Cristero Rebellion, see Jean A. Meyer, *The Cristero Rebellion: The Mexican People between Church and State* (Cambridge: Cambridge University Press, 1976).

60. Slawson, "NCWC in Mexico, 1925–1929," 71.

61. NCWC News Sheet, September 12, 1927, NCWC Administrative Committee Papers, ACUA.

62. Quoted in John Burke, Memorandum, November 26, 1927, Hanna Papers, AASF. See also Sheerin, *Never Look Back*, 118.

63. Slawson, "NCWC in Mexico, 1925–1929," 56.

64. John Burke, Summary of Interview, December 20, 1927, and December 29, 1927, Hanna Papers, AASF.

65. Slawson, "NCWC in Mexico, 1925–1929," 76–80; John Burke to Edward Hanna, January 7, 1928, NCWC Administrative Committee Papers, ACUA.

66. John Burke, interview with Archbishop Martin Tritschler, January 18, 1928, NCWC Administrative Committee Papers, ACUA.

67. Edward Hanna to John Burke, March 15, 1928, NCWC General Secretary Papers—Burke, ACUA.

68. Slawson, "NCWC in Mexico, 1925–1929," 80–82.

69. Ibid., 84–85; Summary of Interview, John Burke, Archbishop Ruiz y Flores and President Plutarco Calles, May 22, 1928, Hanna Correspondence, AASF.

70. John Burke to Edward Hanna, June 26, 1928, Hanna Correspondence, AASF.

71. Edward Hanna to John Burke, July 2, 1928, NCWC Administrative Committee Papers, ACUA.

72. Edward Hanna, Statement of NCWC Administrative Committee Chairman, July 19, 1928, NCWC Administrative Committee Papers, ACUA; Rice, *Diplomatic Relations between the United States and Mexico, 1925–1929*, 141–42.

73. Slawson, "NCWC in Mexico, 1925–1929," 86.

74. Ibid., 89–91.

75. Statement of Archbishop Leopoldo Ruiz y Flores, June 21, 1929, Hanna Correspondence, AASF. On the same occasion President Portes Gil commented, "I am glad to take advantage of this opportunity to declare publicly and very clearly that it is not the purpose of the constitution, nor of the laws, nor of the Government of the Republic to destroy the identity of the Catholic Church or any other, or to interfere in any way with its spiritual functions." See Statement of President Emilio Portes Gil, June 21, 1929, Hanna Correspondence, AASF.

76. Statement of John Burke, June 22, 1929, Hanna Papers, AASF.

77. Statement of Archbishop Pietro Fumasoni-Biondi, June 22, 1929, Hanna Papers, AASF.

78. Annual Report of NCWC Administrative Chairman, n.d. [November 1929], NCWC Annual Reports, ACUA.

79. Meeting Minutes, NCWC Administrative Committee, April 15, 1931, and November 9, 1931, NCWC Administrative Committee Papers, ACUA.

80. Kelley wrote two long books on the church's struggles in Mexico. See *The Mexican Question: Some Plain Facts* (New York: Paulist Press, 1926) and *Blood-Drenched Altars: Mexican Study and Comment* (Milwaukee: Bruce Publishing Company, 1935).

81. Meeting Minutes, NCWC Administrative Committee, April 5, 1932, and November 17, 1932, NCWC Administrative Committee Papers, ACUA.

82. "Protest of the Hierarchy of the United States against the Continued Persecution of the Church in Mexico," January 12, 1933, in Huber, *Our Bishops Speak*, 201.

83. Meeting Minutes, NCWC Administrative Committee, November 13, 1933, NCWC Administrative Committee Papers, ACUA.

84. On March 4, 1933, Roosevelt declared, "In the field of world policy, I would dedicate this nation to the policy of the good neighbor—the neighbor who resolutely respects himself and, because he does so, respects the rights of others—the neighbor who respects his obligations and respects the sanctity of his agreements in and with a world of neighbors." See

Franklin Roosevelt, *The Public Papers and Addresses of Franklin D. Roosevelt* (New York: Russell and Russell, 1969), 2:14.

85. Flynn, *American Catholics and Roosevelt*, 150.

86. Kanawada, *Roosevelt's Diplomacy*, 23; Flynn, *American Catholics and Roosevelt*, 32–36, 170–72. The NCWC issued two separate statements on the crisis. "Anti-Christian Tyranny in Mexico" (November 1934) called for an end to United States indifference. "Government's Silence on Mexico" (May 1935) called on the president to be consistent in his defense of the principles of freedom of conscience, religious worship, and education. America could not be blind to the removal of these freedoms in Mexico. See Huber, *Our Bishops Speak*, 205–9, 307–9.

87. E. David Cronon, "American Catholics and Mexican Anti-Clericalism," *Mississippi Valley Historical Review* 45 (1958–59): 206. See also Douglas Slawson, "The National Catholic Welfare Conference and the Mexican Church-State Conflict of the Mid-1930s: A Case of Déjà Vu," *Catholic Historical Review* 80, no. 1 (January 1994): 58–96.

88. Slawson, "NCWC and Mexican Conflict in the 1930s," 63–64.

89. "Statement of the Hierarchy of the United States on Anti-Christian Tyranny in Mexico," November 15, 1934, in Huber, *Our Bishops Speak*, 207–8.

90. *Monitor*, December 8, 1934.

91. Quoted in Slawson, "NCWC and Mexican Conflict in the 1930s," 66. Also see Kauffman, *Faith and Fraternalism*, 300–301, for a more detailed description of the Knights' actions at this time.

92. Kanawada, *Roosevelt's Diplomacy*, 30–35; Kauffman, *Faith and Fraternalism*, 306. The full story of the Knights' campaign in Mexico is given by Kauffman, *Faith and Fraternalism*, pp. 287–314.

93. John Burke to Edward Hanna, January 30, 1935, NCWC General Secretary Files—Burke, ACUA.

94. "Resolution on Religious Persecution in Mexico," January 31, 1935, found in NCWC Administrative Committee Papers, ACUA.

95. John Burke to Edward Hanna, February 2, 1935, Hanna Correspondence; John Mitty to John Burke, February 1, 1935, Mitty Correspondence, AASF.

96. *New York Times*, February 2, 1935, clipping found in Hanna Correspondence, AASF.

97. Slawson, "NCWC and Mexican Conflict in the 1930s," 75–83.

98. Edward Hanna to Michael Curley, March 6, 1935, Hanna Correspondence, AASF. Hanna wrote, "I wish to say that every member of the Administrative Committee has presented his opinion, and that

everyone of them voted that the Administrative Committee should not publicly support the Borah Resolution."

    99. Slawson, "NCWC and Mexican Conflict in the 1930s," 69–71, 72, 83–87.

    100. Ibid., 92–95.

Chapter 11: Servant of the State in the 1930s

    1. Many fine books look at religious fundamentalism in the United States. Two excellent examples are George M. Marsden, *Fundamentalism and American Culture: The Shaping of Twentieth-Century Evangelicalism, 1870–1925* (Oxford: Oxford University Press, 1980). See pages 184–88 about the Scopes trial. Also see Marsden, *Fundamentalism and Evangelicalism* (Grand Rapids, MI: William B. Eerdmans, 1991).

    2. The full story of the affair between Stephenson and Madge Oberholtzer is related in Wyn Craig Wade, *The Fiery Cross: The Ku Klux Klan in America* (New York: Simon & Schuster, 1987), 239–48. See also Kenneth T. Jackson, *The Ku Klux Klan in the City, 1915–1930* (New York: Oxford University Press, 1967), 157–59.

    3. Arthur S. Link, William A. Link, and William B. Catton, *American Epoch: A History of the United States since 1900*, vol. 1, *1900–1945* (New York: Alfred A. Knopf, 1987), 228.

    4. James Gillis, "Editorial Comment," *Catholic World* 134 (December 1931): 363.

    5. David A. Shannon, *Between the Wars: America 1919–1941* (Boston: Houghton Mifflin, 1965), 149.

    6. The Agricultural Adjustment Act (AAA) of May 13, 1933, the first branch of the three-pronged attack, aimed to establish a better balance between the prices of agricultural products (which had dropped significantly and in the process bankrupted many farmers) and industrial products so as to bring them into the same ratio as existed in the period from 1909 to 1914. The legislation did raise farm prices, but the renewed prosperity of farmers eventually forced sharecroppers off the land with a consequent loss of livelihood. Unemployment was attacked by the establishment of the Federal Emergency Relief Administration and the Public Works Administration (PWA) both of which produced numerous government jobs. Initially, however, in order to free capital for use in the economy the Emergency Banking Act was passed by Congress on March 9, which was followed by the more "reform"-minded legislation of the Glass-Steagall

Banking Act in June 1933, which established the Federal Deposit Insurance Corporation (FDIC) to insure funds and restore consumer confidence.

7. General Hugh S. Johnson, administrator of the NRA, worked with committees representing each industry. Fair codes of practice within the industry, desired by capital, were worked out and labor standards were set, which in many cases eliminated sweat shops and child labor. Before the codes were negotiated Johnson asked the nation to accept an interim blanket code, which set work standards of 35–40 hours per week, a minimum pay of 30–40 cents per hour, and the elimination of child labor.

8. Roosevelt appointed James Farley (New York) as postmaster general and Thomas Walsh (Montana) as attorney general.

9. Roosevelt had effectively quoted from the two foundational social encyclicals, *Rerum novarum* (1891) and *Quadragesimo anno* (1931), in his campaign speeches, which misled many into thinking that the New Deal was based on the Church's social teaching. Roosevelt was a shrewd politician and courted the Catholic vote throughout his administration. David O'Brien has correctly stated, "The New Deal was essentially a political procedure seeking simultaneously to satisfy the frantic demands of savagely conflicting interests and to reestablish a workable economic order." See David O'Brien, *American Catholics and Social Reform: The New Deal Years* (New York: Oxford University Press, 1968), 234.

10. Several authors have fully discussed the support given by the Church to the initial efforts of Roosevelt. See O'Brien, *American Catholics and Social Reform*, 47–69; George Q. Flynn, *American Catholics and the Roosevelt Presidency 1932–1936* (Lexington: University of Kentucky Press, 1986), 36–60, 78–102; Aaron Abell, *American Catholicism and Social Action: A Search for Social Justice, 1865–1950* (Garden City, NY: Hanover House, 1960), 230–40. It should be noted that not all Catholics supported the New Deal, even in this early stage. Al Smith and Frederick Kenkel, editor of the Central Verein's *Central Blatt and Social Justice*, for example, saw Roosevelt's policy as socialism.

11. Francis L. Broderick, *Right Reverend New Dealer: John A. Ryan* (New York: Macmillan, 1963), 211–43.

12. Thomas Blantz, CSC, *A Priest in Public Service: Francis J. Haas* (Notre Dame, IN: University of Notre Dame Press, 1982), 66–88.

13. "Report and Recommendations of the California State Unemployment Commission," November 9, 1932, p. 23, BL-UCB.

14. Ibid., p. 24.

15. Ibid.

16. Quoted in William Issel and James Collins, "The Catholic Church and Organized Labor in San Francisco 1932–1938," *Records of the American Catholic Historical Society of Philadelphia* 190, nos. 1 and 2 (1998): 83.

17. Edward Hanna to James Rolph, August 28, 1931, Chancery Correspondence, AASF.

18. "Report and Recommendations of the California State Unemployment Commission," November 9, 1932, pp. 25–26, BL-UCB.

19. Ibid., p. 39. Comparison of California against national averages shows similar trends. While the percentage employed in California dropped 41 percent, it dropped only 36 percent nationally. While the average weekly salary dropped 21 percent in California, it plummeted 30 percent nationally.

20. Ibid., p. 32.

21. State Unemployment Commission Meeting Minutes, September 3, 1931, and September 15, 1931, Industrial Relations #3275–14, CSA. Extant records show that between September 1931 and November 1932 the commission met seventeen times, not counting a series of hearings throughout the state.

22. "Report and Recommendations of the California State Unemployment Commission," November 9, 1932, pp. 29–30, BL-UCB.

23. Edward Hanna to James Rolph, December 19, 1931, Hanna Correspondence, AASF.

24. Abstract of Hearings on Unemployment before the California State Unemployment Commission (April–May 1932), pp. 5–14, BL-UCB.

25. "Report and Recommendations of the California State Unemployment Commission," November 9, 1932, p. 26, BL-UCB.

26. Ibid., p. 28.

27. Ibid., p. 54.

28. Edward J. Hanna to James Rolph, Jr., December 19, 1931, Hanna Files, AASF.

29. "Report and Recommendations of the California State Unemployment Commission," November 9, 1932, p. 54, BL-UCB.

30. Sanford A. Mosk, "Unemployment Relief in California under the State Emergency Relief Administration," in *Essays in Social Economics in Honor of Jessica Blanche Peixotto*, ed. Sanford A. Mosk (Berkeley: University of California Press, 1935), 253–54.

31. *San Francisco Chronicle*, September 9, 1934.

32. Mosk, "Unemployment Relief in California," 258.

33. *San Francisco Chronicle*, September 9, 1934.

34. Administrative Appointments Book, Governor James Rolph, F3638:11, CSA.

35. Edward Hanna to James Rolph, April 1, 1933, Chancery Correspondence, AASF.

36. Quoted in Edward Hanna to Harry Hopkins, July 20, 1933, Chancery Correspondence, AASF.

37. *San Francisco Chronicle*, November 23, 1933.

38. Mosk, "Unemployment Relief in California," 272.

39. Edward Hanna to Frank Merriam, August 1, 1934, Chancery Correspondence, AASF.

40. Edward Hanna to Edward Maher, January 5, 1934; L. L. Pendleton to Edward Hanna, May 9, 1934, Chancery Correspondence, AASF.

41. Areas where the board was to look at development were: transportation facilities, water supplies, beach protection, forest conservation, small farm development, land reclamation, acquisition of lands for public buildings, and development of military defense.

42. The original members of the commission were: Archbishop Hanna, John C. Austin, Joseph Mesmer, William Fox, Earl Lee Kelly, Harry A. Hopkins, Vincent S. Brown, Dr. Julius B. Harris, Mrs. Edmund Brown. See Chronological History, State Planning Board in California, n.d., F 3444–1, CSA.

43. Edward Hanna to Frank Merriam, March 21, 1935; John C. Austin to Edward Hanna, March 13, 1935, Chancery Correspondence, AASF.

44. More complete coverage and analysis of the 1933 California cotton strike is related in Cletus Daniel, *Bitter Harvest: A History of California Farmworkers, 1870–1941* (Ithaca, NY: Cornell University Press, 1981), 167–221; and Don Mitchell, *Lie of the Land: Migrant Workers and the California Landscape* (Minneapolis: University of Minnesota Press, 1996), 130–55. A short but excellent summary of the principal events in the strike is provided in Kevin Starr, *Endangered Dreams: The Great Depression in California* (New York: Oxford University Press, 1996), 74–75.

45. Daniel, *Bitter Harvest*, 179; Mitchell, *Lie of the Land*, 130–31, 134, 142.

46. Mitchell, *Lie of the Land*, 134.

47. Daniel, *Bitter Harvest*, 181.

48. Mitchell, *Lie of the Land*, 141.

49. Daniel, *Bitter Harvest*, 177; Mitchell, *Lie of the Land*, 148.

50. Daniel, *Bitter Harvest*, 183; Mitchell, *Lie of the Land*, 143; *San Francisco Chronicle*, October 9, 1933.

51. Daniel, *Bitter Harvest*, 194.

52. Mitchell, *Lie of the Land*, 143, 147.

53. *San Francisco Chronicle*, October 10, 1933.

54. Daniel, *Bitter Harvest*, 194; *San Francisco Examiner*, October 10, 1933.

55. *Sacramento Bee*, October 11, 1933.

56. Daniel, *Bitter Harvest*, 202; *San Francisco Examiner*, October 11, 1933.

57. *San Francisco Chronicle*, October 12, 1933; *San Francisco Examiner*, October 12, 1933, and October 13, 1933.

58. *San Francisco Examiner*, October 14, 1933. Originally, Rolph appointed the dean of Berkeley's law school, O. K. McMurray, but he was unable to serve. It is not clear from extant data why he could not fulfill the appointment.

59. Daniel, *Bitter Harvest*, 212.

60. *San Francisco Examiner*, October 21, 1933.

61. Daniel, *Bitter Harvest*, 214–15.

62. *San Francisco Chronicle*, October 23, 1933; Mitchell, *Lie of the Land*, 152–53.

63. Mitchell, *Lie of the Land*, 153.

64. Starr, *Endangered Dreams*, 84–85.

65. Robert W. Cherny, "Constructing a Radical Identity: History, Memory, and the Seafaring Stories of Harry Bridges," *Pacific Historical Review* 70, no. 4 (2001): 571.

66. Franklin Roosevelt to Edward Hanna [Telegram], June 26, 1934, Chancery Correspondence, AASF.

67. Edward Hanna to Franklin Roosevelt [Telegram], June 27, 1934, Chancery Correspondence, AASF.

68. *San Francisco Examiner*, June 29, 1934.

69. Eustace L. Williams, "Padre of the Strike," *Today* (August 4, 1934): 5.

70. *San Francisco News*, June 28, 1934. The article stated additionally, "Probably no Catholic prelate has a more brilliant record than he in untangling snares between groups of citizens, bringing warring factions together for the advancement of the communities' interests, creating understanding and good feeling, and establishing public relief upon a firm foundation."

71. Issel and Collins, "Catholic Church in San Francisco," 82.

72. Quoted in ibid., 85–86.

73. Ibid.

74. Starr, *Endangered Dreams*, 91–100.

75. Ibid., 102–3.

76. Mike Quinn, *The Big Strike* (Olema, CA: Olema Publishing Company, 1944), 187.

77. Jaime Garcia de Alba, "Apostle of the Dock: Archbishop Edward J. Hannah's *[sic]* Role as Chairman of the National Longshoremen's Board during the 1934 San Francisco Waterfront Strike," *Ex Post Facto*, publication of San Francisco State University 10 (spring 2001): 45; Quinn, *Big Strike*, 132.

78. Garcia de Alba, "Apostle of the Dock," 45.

79. *San Francisco Examiner*, July 14, 1934, clipping, CHR-SFPL.

80. Quinn, *Big Strike*, 146; Garcia de Alba, "Apostle of the Dock," 46; "Awards and Recommendations, National Longshoremen's Board," October 1934, Hanna Papers, AASF.

81. *San Francisco Chronicle*, July 31, 1934.

82. Ibid.

83. Williams, "Padre of the Strike," 5.

84. "Award and Recommendations of the National Longshoremen's Board," October 1934, Hanna Papers, AASF.

85. *San Francisco News*, June 29, 1934.

86. Ibid.; *San Francisco Examiner*, June 29, 1934.

87. Edward Hanna, Statement, n.d. [1934], National Longshoremen's Board, A 27.3, AASF.

88. David F. Selvin, *A Terrible Anger: The 1934 Waterfront and General Strikes in San Francisco* (Detroit: Wayne State University Press, 1996), 138.

89. Garcia de Alba, "Apostle·of the Dock," 48–49.

90. Edward Hanna, Statement, n.d. [1934], National Longshoremen's Board, A 27.3, AASF.

91. Ibid.

92. "Award and Recommendations of the National Longshoremen's Strike," October 1934, Hanna Papers, AASF.

93. Ibid.; Garcia de Alba, "Apostle of the Dock," 50–51.

94. "Award and Recommendations of the National Longshoremen's Strike," October 1934, Hanna Papers, AASF.

95. Quoted in Garcia de Alba, "Apostle of the Dock," 50.

96. Harrison B. Robinson to Edward Hanna, October 17, 1934, Hanna Correspondence, AASF.

97. Garcia de Alba, "Apostle of the Dock," 50.

98. Frances Perkins to Edward Hanna, November 27, 1934; Franklin Roosevelt to Hanna, December 7, 1934, Hanna Correspondence, AASF; *San Francisco Chronicle*, March 9, 1935. Perkins wrote in

part, "The public service you have rendered helped thousands of people and was most effective. I want you to know of my sincere appreciation for your patriotic service."

Chapter 12: The Final Years: Retirement and Death

1. Tom Cole, *A Short History of San Francisco* (San Francisco: Lexikos, 1981), 123.

2. Ibid., 123–26.

3. Ibid. ; John Bernard McGloin, SJ, *San Francisco: The Story of a City* (San Rafael, CA: Presidio Press, 1978), 197.

4. *Monitor*, February 13, 1932.

5. Ibid., February 6, 1932; Cardinal Andrew Fruhwirth, Statement, January 29, 1932, Mitty Papers, AASF.

6. Jeffrey M. Burns, "John Joseph Mitty (1884–1963)," in *The Encyclopedia of American Catholic History*, ed. Michael Glazier and Thomas Shelley (Collegeville, MN: Liturgical Press, 1997), 967–68; Edward Hanna, Address, October 7, 1926, Hanna Sermons, AASF.

7. John J. Mitty to Edward Hanna, August 25, 1931, Hanna Correspondence, AASF.

8. John J. Mitty to Edward Hanna, November 30, 1931, and December 4, 1931, Hanna Correspondence, AASF.

9. Edward Hanna to John J. Mitty [Telegram], February 6, 1932; Newspaper Clipping, n.d. [April 1932], Mitty Papers, AASF.

10. John Burke to Edward Hanna [Telegram], February 4, 1932, Hanna Correspondence; Ambrose P. Dunnigan to Edward Hanna, February 12, 1932, Mitty Papers, AASF.

11. John J. Mitty to Edward Hanna [Telegram], February 4, 1932, Mitty Papers, AASF.

12. Edward Hanna, Sermon, n.d. [April 1935], Mitty Papers; Newspaper Clipping, n.d. [April 1935], Hanna Correspondence, AASF.

13. John Cantwell to Edward Hanna, October 27, 1932, A-29 Manuscripts, AASF.

14. John Mitty to John Burke, November 2, 1932, and November 29, 1932, NCWC General Secretary Files—Burke, ACUA; Thomas Millett to John Mitty, November 8, 1932, Hanna Correspondence, AASF.

15. John Mitty to John Burke, December 5, 1932, NCWC General Secretary Files—Burke, ACUA.

16. John Mitty to John Burke, December 22, 1932, NCWC General Secretary Files—Burke, ACUA; Mitty to Burke, January 23, 1933, Chancery Correspondence, AASF.

17. John Mitty to John Burke, February 1, 1935, Mitty Correspondence; Mitty to James Hanna, March 11, 1935, Hanna Correspondence, AASF.

18. Thomas Connelly to "Father Cornelius," March 14, 1935, Chancery Correspondence; Amleto Cicognani to John Mitty, March 30, 1935, Hanna Correspondence, AASF.

19. *Monitor,* March 9, 1935.

20. Ibid.; *San Francisco Examiner,* March 9, 1935.

21. Angelo Rossi, Press Release, March 8, 1935; Frank F. Merriam to Edward Hanna, March 13, 1935, Hanna Letters of Appreciation File, AASF.

22. Albert Boynton to Edward Hanna, March 12, 1935; Christine Regan and Margaret B. Code to Edward Hanna, March 17, 1935, Hanna Letters of Appreciation File, AASF.

23. Irving F. Reichart to Edward Hanna, March 11, 1935, Hanna Letters of Appreciation File, AASF.

24. Quoted in *NCWC News Service,* August 11, 1947, found in Chancery Correspondence, AASF.

25. Edward Hanna to John Burke, March 5, 1935, NCWC Administrative Committee Papers, ACUA.

26. Michael Ready to Edward Hanna, December 7, 1935, NCWC Administrative Committee Files, ACUA.

27. Ralph Hayes to Edward Hanna, March 9, 1935, Hanna Letters of Appreciation File, AASF.

28. Quoted in *Los Angeles Times,* March 9, 1935, Edward Hanna File, AALA.

29. Quoted in *Monitor,* July 15, 1944.

30. Ibid., March 9, 1935.

31. Margaret Finnigan to James Cantwell [Telegram], March 9, 1935, Hanna Correspondence, AASF.

32. Archepiscopal Meeting Minutes, January through March 1935, A-29 Manuscripts, AASF.

33. Thomas Connelly to Rev. Z. Frechette, March 25, 1935; Connelly to Edward Wien, February 18, 1935, Chancery Correspondence, AASF.

34. Quoted in Thomas Connelly to Elizabeth Longan, September 17, 1935, Chancery Correspondence, AASF.

35. Amleto Cicognani to John Cantwell, February 3, 1934, Cantwell Correspondence, AALA.

36. Amleto Cicognani to John Cantwell, February 27, 1935, Cantwell Correspondence, AALA.

37. Franklin Roosevelt to Edward Hanna, December 7, 1934, General Hanna Correspondence, AASF.

38. Robert McNamara, "Recollections," April 4, 1935, MPP; Francis Weber, *Magnificat: The Life and Times of Timothy Cardinal Manning* (Mission Hills, CA: Saint Francis Historical Society, 1999), 47.

39. Sacred Consistorial Congregation to Amleto Cicognani, May 5, 1935, Apostolic Delegate Correspondence, AASF.

40. John Mitty to Joseph Breslin, June 17, 1935, General Hanna Correspondence, AASF.

41. Quoted in James Gaffey, *Men of Menlo: Transformation of an American Seminary* (Lanham, MD: University Press of America, 1992), 19.

42. Joseph Hurley to "Doc" [Edward Mooney], November 14, 1935, Mooney Papers, Archives Archdiocese of Detroit (hereafter AAD), Detroit, Michigan.

43. Quoted in Howard Carroll to John J. Mitty, March 15, 1943, General Hanna Correspondence, AASF.

44. Newspaper Clipping, n.d. [1944], Hanna File, AALA.

45. Edward Hanna to John Mitty, February 1, 1944, General Hanna Correspondence, AASF. Earlier in 1942 Hanna wrote to Mitty, "I can tell you about myself that I was never better than I am now. The brothers are taking the best care of me....I do not want for anything." In April 1939 Hanna wrote Mitty relating his attendance at events concerning the death of Pope Pius XI and the election of Pius XII. See Edward Hanna to John Mitty, February 1, 1944, December 4, [1942], n.d. [April 1939], General Hanna Correspondence, AASF.

46. Zwierlein, "The American College in Rome, 1859–1955," part II, 206; "From the Pastor's Desk," November 9, 1975, clipping found in Hanna File, AALA. Weber is more blunt in another source stating: "Because of what would now be diagnosed as Alzheimer's Disease, the Archbishop [Hanna] had agreed to retire in 1935 and take up residence in Rome." See Weber, *Magnificat*, 47.

47. Joseph Hurley to "Doc" [Edward Mooney], October 18, 1935, and November 14, 1935, Mooney Papers, AAD.

48. Joseph Hurley to "Doc" [Edward Mooney], November 14, 1935, Mooney Papers, AAD.

49. Charles Shay, interview with Robert McNamara, May 28, 1963, MPP. Shay served in various Rochester parishes from 1937 to 1965.

50. Zwierlein, "American College in Rome, 1859–1955," part II, 206.

51. Mother Anne Hanna to John Mitty, January 24, 1943, General Hanna Correspondence, AASF.

52. Edward Miner to Edward Hanna, May 29, 1935, Edward Miner Papers, A.M. 66, URL.

53. Newspaper Clipping, November 25, 1935, found in General Hanna Correspondence, AASF.

54. Michael O. Driscoll, Diary, October 26, 1936, MPP.

55. *San Francisco Examiner,* July 11, 1944.

56. *Rochester Register,* July 23, 1944; Henry Grady to John Mitty, August 5, 1944, Return of Body File, Hanna Papers, AASF.

57. *San Francisco Examiner,* July 19, 1944.

58. Cathedral Calendar, Rochester, July 20, 1944, Hanna Papers, ADR; *San Francisco Examiner,* July 11, 1944, Clipping, SFPL.

59. Quoted in *Monitor,* July 15, 1944.

60. *San Francisco Examiner,* July 11, 1944, Clipping, SFPL.

61. Ibid.

62. *San Francisco Examiner,* April 28, 1947, and August 21, 1947.

SELECTED BIBLIOGRAPHY

Archival Repositories

Archives of the Archdiocese of Chicago (AAC), Chicago, Illinois

Archives of the Archdiocese of Detroit (AAD), Detroit, Michigan

Archives of the Archdiocese of Los Angeles (AALA), San Fernando, California

Archives of the Archdiocese of New York (AANY), Yonkers, New York

Archives of the Archdiocese of San Francisco (AASF), Menlo Park, California

Archives of the Catholic University of America (ACUA), Washington, DC

Archives of the Diocese of Rochester (ADR), Rochester, New York

Archives of the University of Notre Dame (AUND), Notre Dame, Indiana

Bancroft Library, University of California, Berkeley (BL-UCB), Berkeley, California

California Historical Room, San Francisco Public Library (CHR-SFPL), San Francisco, California

California Historical Society Library (CHSL), San Francisco, California

California State Archives (CSA), Sacramento, California

Robert McNamara Personal Papers (MPP), Rochester, New York

University of Rochester Archival Library (URL), Rochester, New York

Primary Sources

Ellis, John Tracy, ed. *Documents of American Catholic History*. 3 vols. Wilmington, DE: Michael Glazier, 1987.

Hanna, Edward. "Absolution." In *The Catholic Encyclopedia*, vol. 1. New York: Robert Appleton, 1907, 61–66.

———. "Contrition." In *The Catholic Encyclopedia*, vol. 4. New York: Robert Appleton, 1907, 337–40.

———. "The Human Knowledge of Christ I." *The New York Review* 1, no. 3 (October–November 1905): 303–16.

———. "The Human Knowledge of Christ II." *The New York Review* 1, no. 4 (December 1905–January 1906): 425–36.

———. "The Human Knowledge of Christ III." *The New York Review* 1, no. 5 (February–March 1906): 597–615.

———. "The Human Knowledge of Christ IV." *The New York Review* 3, nos. 4–5 (January–April 1908): 391–400.

———. "Penance." In *The Catholic Encyclopedia*, vol. 11. New York: Robert Appleton, 1907, 618–35.

———. "The Power of the Keys." *The New York Review* 3, nos. 4–5 (January–April 1908): 561–68.

———. "Purgatory." In *The Catholic Encyclopedia*, vol. 12. New York: Robert Appleton, 1907, 575–80.

———. "The Message of the Seminary." *The Catholic Educational Association Bulletin* 15 (November 1918): 610–22.

———. "Some Recent Books on Catholic Theology." *American Journal of Theology* 10, no. 1 (January 1906): 175–84.

Huber, Raphael, OFM Conv. *Our Bishops Speak: National Pastorals and Annual Statements of the Hierarchy of the United States, Resolutions of Episcopal Committees and Communications of the Administrative Board of the National Catholic Welfare Conference, 1919–1951*. Milwaukee: Bruce Publishing Company, 1952.

McCluskey, Neil G., SJ, ed. *Catholic Education in America: A Documentary History*. New York: Teachers' College, Columbia University, 1964.

Nolan, Hugh, ed. *Pastoral Letters of the United States Catholic Bishops*. Washington, DC: United States Catholic Conference, 1984.

Secondary Sources

"An Alarm and Warning." *America* 34, no. 12 (January 2, 1926): 271–73.

Appleby, R. Scott. *"Church and Age Unite!" The Modernist Impulse in American Catholicism.* Notre Dame, IN: University of Notre Dame Press, 1992.

———. "Modernism as the Final Phase of Americanism: William L. Sullivan, American Catholic Apologist." *Harvard Theological Review* 81, no. 2 (1988): 171–92.

Athearn, Leigh. *"The California State Relief Administration"* (pamphlet). Los Angeles, 1939.

Avella, Steven M. "California Catholics and the Gubernatorial Election of 1934." In *FDR, the Vatican, and the Roman Catholic Church, 1933–1945,* ed. David B. Woolner and Richard G. Kurial, 67–92. New York: Palgrave Macmillan, 2003.

Baccari, Alessandro, Jr., Vincenza Scarpaci, and Gabriel Zavatlano, SDB. *Saints Peter and Paul Church: The Chronicles of 'The Italian Cathedral' of the West, 1884–1984.* San Francisco: Sts. Peter and Paul Church, 1985.

Ball, James B. "Theologies of Social Transformation: A Study of Walter Rauschenbusch and Gustavo Gutierrez." PhD diss., University of Notre Dame, 2003.

Barry, Colman J., OSB. *The Catholic University of America, 1903–1909: Rectorship of Denis J. O'Connell.* Washington, DC: Catholic University of America Press, 1950.

Beckley, Harlan. *Passion for Justice: Retrieving the Legacies of Walter Rauschenbusch, John Ryan and Reinhold Niebuhr.* Louisville, KY: John Knox Press, 1992.

Bischoff, Henry, SJ. "National Conference of Bishops: A Look at the Past." *The American Ecclesiastical Review* 154 (January–June 1966): 384–96.

Blakely, Paul, SJ. "The Crusade for the Towner-Sterling Bill." *America* 29 (July 21, 1923): 333–34.

———. "Silver Threads and Smith Bill Gold." *America* 24 (October 23, 1920): 21–22.

———. "The Unmendable Smith Bill." *America* 24 (January 22, 1921): 341–42.

Blantz, Thomas, CSC. *George N. Shuster: On the Side of Truth.* Notre Dame, IN: University of Notre Dame Press, 1993.

———. *A Priest in Public Service: Francis J. Haas.* Notre Dame, IN: University of Notre Dame Press, 1982.

Blied, Benjamin J. "Rev. Andrew E. Breen, D.D., Priest, Professor, Author." *Salesianum* 48 (October 1953): 172–79.

Brechin, Gray. *Imperial San Francisco: Urban Power, Earthly Ruin.* Berkeley: University of California Press, 1999.

Brennan, Joseph. "Let Us Sing the Praises of Famous Men: Edward Hanna, Algernon Crapsey, Max Landsberg." Paper delivered at the Fortnightly Club, Rochester, New York, March 5, 2002.

Broderick, Francis L. *Right Reverend New Dealer: John A. Ryan.* New York: Macmillan, 1963.

Brusher, Joseph, SJ. *Consecrated Thunderbolt: Father Yorke of San Francisco.* Hawthorne, NJ: Joseph F. Wagner, 1973.

Buetow, Harold A. *Of Singular Benefit: The Story of U.S. Catholic Education.* London: Macmillan, 1970.

Burns, Jeffrey M. *American Catholics and the Family Crisis, 1930–1962.* New York: Garland Publishing, 1988.

———, ed. *Catholic San Francisco: Sesquicentennial Essays.* Menlo Park, CA: Archives of the Archdiocese of San Francisco, 2005.

———. "¿Que es Esto? The Transformation of St. Peter's Parish, San Francisco, 1913–1970." In *American Congregations*, vol. 1, ed. James P. Wind and James W. Lewis, 396–462. Chicago: University of Chicago Press, 1994.

———. *San Francisco: A History of the Archdiocese of San Francisco*, vol. 2, *1885–1945.* Strasbourg: Editions du Signe, 2001.

Byington, Lewis Francis. *The History of San Francisco.* San Francisco: S. J. Clarke, 1931.

Carey, Patrick W. "American Catholic Romanticism, 1830–1888." *Catholic Historical Review* 74 (October 1988): 590–606.

Cassidy, Francis P. "Catholic Education in the Third Plenary Council of Baltimore I." *Catholic Historical Review* 34 (October 1948): 257–305.

———. "Catholic Education in the Third Plenary Council of Baltimore II." *Catholic Historical Review* 34 (January 1948): 414–36.

Cecil, Lord Hugh Richard Heathcote. *Nationalism and Catholics.* London: Macmillan, 1919.

Cherny, Robert W. "Constructing a Radical Identity: History, Memory, and the Seafaring Stories of Harry Bridges." *Pacific Historical Review* 70, no. 4 (2001): 571–99.

Chesler, Ellen. *Woman of Valor: Margaret Sanger and the Birth Control Movement in America.* New York: Simon & Schuster, 1992.

Chinnici, Joseph P., OFM. *Living Stones: The History and Structure of Catholic Spiritual Life in the United States.* New York: Macmillan, 1989.

Cole, Raymond E. "A Church Program for the Immigrant." *Missionary Review of the World* 46 (January 1923): 29–32.

Cole, Tom. *A Short History of San Francisco.* San Francisco: Lexikos, 1981.

Cooper, John M. *Breaking the Heart of the World: Woodrow Wilson and the Fight for the League of Nations.* Cambridge: Cambridge University Press, 2001.

Creel, George. "Close the Gates." *Colliers* 69 (May 6, 1922): 9–10.

Cronon, E. David. "American Catholics and Mexican Anti-Clericalism." *Mississippi Valley Historical Review* 45 (1958–59): 201–30.

Cross, Ira. *History of the Labor Movement in California.* Berkeley: University of California Press, 1935.

Curran, Robert Emmett. *Michael Augustine Corrigan and the Shaping of Conservative Catholicism in America 1878–1902.* New York: Arno Press, 1978.

Daniel, Cletus. *Bitter Harvest: A History of California Farmworkers, 1870–1941.* Ithaca, NY: Cornell University Press, 1981.

Daniels, Josephus. *The Wilson Era: Years of War and After 1917–1923.* Westport, CT: Greenwood Press, 1974.

Dawley, Alan. *Struggles for Justice: Social Responsibility and the Liberal State.* Cambridge, MA: Harvard University Press, 1991.

DeSauliners, Lawrence. *The Response in American Catholic Periodicals to the Crisis of the Great Depression, 1930–1935.* Lanham, MD: University Press of America, 1984.

DeVito, Michael J. "The *New York Review*, 1905–1908: An Attempt at Aggiornamento." *Priest* 34 (February 1978): 30–37.

————. The *New York Review, 1905–1908.* New York: United States Catholic Historical Society, 1977.

————. "Principles of Ecclesial Reform according to the *New York Review* (1905–1908)." PhD diss., Fordham University, 1974.

Diggins, John P. *Mussolini and Fascism: The View from America.* Princeton, NJ: Princeton University Press, 1972.

Divine, Robert A. *American Immigration Policy, 1924–1952.* New Haven, CT: Yale University Press, 1957.

Dolan, Jay P. *The American Catholic Experience.* Garden City, NY: Doubleday, 1985.

Drouin, Edmond G. "The U.S. Supreme Court and Religious Freedom in American Education in Its Decisions Affecting Church-Related Elementary and Secondary Schools During the First Three Quarters of the Twentieth Century." PhD diss., Catholic University of America, 1980.

Dumenil, Lynn. "'The Insatiable Maw of Bureaucracy': Anti-Statism and Education Reform in the 1920s." *The Journal of American History* 77, no. 2 (September 1990): 499–524.

————. "The Tribal Twenties: 'Assimilated' Catholics' Response to Anti-Catholicism in the 1920s." *Journal of American Ethnic History* 11 (fall 1991): 21–49.

Eliel, Paul. *The Waterfront and General Strikes of 1934.* San Francisco: Hooper Printing Company, 1934.

Fisher, J. Donald. "A Historical Study of the Migrant in California." Master's thesis, University of Southern California, 1945.

Flynn, George Q. *American Catholics and the Roosevelt Presidency 1932–1936.* Lexington: University of Kentucky Press, 1968.

Fogarty, Gerald P., SJ. *American Catholic Biblical Scholarship.* San Francisco: Harper & Row, 1989.

————, ed. *Patterns of Episcopal Leadership.* New York: Macmillan, 1989.

————. *The Vatican and the American Hierarchy from 1870 to 1965.* Wilmington, DE: Michael Glazier, 1985.

Francis, Robert C. "A History of Labor on the San Francisco Waterfront." PhD diss., University of California, Berkeley, 1934.

Gaffey, James P. *Citizen of No Mean City: Archbishop Patrick Riordan of San Francisco (1841–1914).* Wilmington, NC: Consortium Books, 1976.

———. *Francis Clement Kelley and the American Catholic Dream.* 2 vols. Bensonville, IL: Heritage Foundation, 1980.

———. "The Life of Patrick William Riordan Second Archbishop of San Francisco, 1841–1914." PhD diss., Catholic University of America, 1965.

———. *Men of Menlo: Transformation of an American Seminary.* Lanham, MD: University Press of America, 1992.

Gamio, Manuel. *Mexican Immigration to the United States: A Study of Human Migration and Adjustment.* New York: Dover Publications, 1971.

Gannon, Michael V. "Before and After Modernism: The Intellectual Isolation of the American Priest." In *The Catholic Priest in the United States: Historical Investigations,* ed. John Tracy Ellis, 293–383. Collegeville, MN: St. John's University Press, 1971.

Garcia de Alba, Jaime. "Apostle of the Dock: Archbishop Edward J. Hannah's *[sic]* Role as Chairman of the National Longshoremen's Board during the 1934 San Francisco Waterfront Strike." *Ex Post Facto,* publication of San Francisco State University 10 (spring 2001): 38–55.

Garis, Roy L. *Immigration Restriction: A Study of the Opposition to Aid Regulation of Immigrants into the United States.* New York: Macmillan, 1928.

Gorrell, Donald K. *The Age of Social Responsibility: The Social Gospel in the Progressive Era, 1900–1920.* Macon, GA: Mercer University Press, 1988.

Guchteneere, R. de. *Judgment on Birth Control.* London: Sheed & Ward, 1946.

Halsey, William. *The Survival of American Innocence: Catholicism in an Era of Disillusionment, 1920–1940.* Notre Dame, IN: University of Notre Dame Press, 1980.

Handy, Robert T., ed. *The Social Gospel in America, 1870–1920.* New York: Oxford University Press, 1966.

Heale, M. J. *American Anticommunism: Combating the Enemy Within, 1830–1970.* Baltimore: Johns Hopkins University Press, 1990.

Higham, John. *Send These to Me: Immigrants in Urban America.* Rev. ed. Baltimore: Johns Hopkins University Press, 1984.

———. *Strangers in the Land: Patterns of American Nativism 1860–1925.* New Brunswick, NJ: Rutgers University Press, 1992.

Holsinger, M. Paul. "The Oregon School Bill Controversy, 1922–1925." *Pacific Historical Review* 37 (1968): 327–41.

Hunt, Rockwell D. *California and Californians*, vol. 4. San Francisco: Lewis Publishing Company, 1926.

Issel, William. "Business Power and Political Culture in San Francisco, 1900–1940." *Journal of Urban History* 16, no. 1 (November 1989): 52–77.

———. "Citizens outside the Government: Business and Urban Policy in San Francisco and Los Angeles, 1890–1932." *Pacific Historical Review* 57, no. 2 (May 1988): 117–45.

———. "Liberalism and Urban Policy in San Francisco from the 1930s to the 1960s." *Western Historical Quarterly* 22, no. 4 (November 1991): 431–51.

Issel, William, and Robert W. Cherny. *San Francisco, 1865–1932: Politics, Power, and Urban Development.* Berkeley: University of California Press, 1986.

Issel, William, and James Collins. "The Catholic Church and Organized Labor in San Francisco 1932–1958." *Records of the American Catholic Historical Society of Philadelphia* 109, nos. 1 and 2 (1998): 81–112.

Jaffe, Julian F. *Crusade against Radicalism: New York during the Red Scare, 1914–1924.* Port Washington, NY: Kennikat Press, 1972.

Jones, Maldwyn A. *American Immigration.* Chicago: University of Chicago Press, 1992.

Jorgenson, Lloyd P. "The Oregon School Law of 1922: Passage and Sequel." *Catholic Historical Review* 54 (October 1988): 455–66.

Joyce, James A. *Broken Star: The Story of the League of Nations (1919–1939).* Swansea, MA: C. Davies, 1978.

Kanawada, Leo V., Jr. *Franklin D. Roosevelt's Diplomacy and American Catholics, Italians and Jews.* Ann Arbor, MI: UMI Research Press, 1982.

Kauffman, Christopher J. *Faith and Fraternalism: The History of the Knights of Columbus, 1882–1982.* New York: Harper & Row, 1982.

————. *Tradition and Transformation in Catholic Culture: The Priests of Saint Sulpice in the United States from 1791 to the Present.* New York: Macmillan, 1988.

Kazin, Michael. *Barons of Labor.* Urbana: University of Illinois Press, 1987.

Kelley, Francis Clement. *Blood-Drenched Altars: Mexican Study and Comment.* Milwaukee: Bruce Publishing Company, 1935.

————. *The Mexican Question: Some Plain Facts.* New York: Paulist Press, 1926.

Knight, Robert Edward Lee. *Industrial Relations in the San Francisco Bay Area 1900–1918.* Berkeley: University of California Press, 1960.

Knock, Thomas J. *To End All Wars: Woodrow Wilson and the Quest for a New World Order.* New York: Oxford University Press, 1992.

Knoles, George H. *Essays and Assays: California History Reappraised.* San Francisco: California Historical Society, 1973.

Koepplin, Leslie W. *A Relationship of Reform: Immigrants and Progressives in the West.* New York: Garland, 1990.

Korman, Gerd. *Industrialization, Immigrants and Americanizers: The View from Milwaukee, 1866–1921.* Madison: State Historical Society of Wisconsin, 1967.

Lenz, Frank B. "The International Immigration Congress." *Immigrants in America Review* 1, no. 3 (1915): 55.

Levi, Stephen. "The Battle for the Eight Hour Day in San Francisco." *California History* 57 (1978–79): 342–53.

————. "Miner Chipman and the Law and Order Committee of the San Francisco Chamber of Commerce, 1917." *Pacific Historian* 18 (1974): 47–60.

————. "San Francisco's Law and Order Committee, 1916." *Journal of the West* 12 (1973): 53–70.

Lewis, Oscar. *San Francisco: Mission to Metropolis.* San Diego: Howell-North Books, 1980.

Link, Arthur S., William A. Link, and William B. Catton. *American Epoch: A History of the United States since 1900*, vol. 1, *1900–1945.* New York: Alfred A. Knopf, 1987.

Link, Arthur S., and Richard L. McCormick. *Progressivism.* Arlington Heights, IL: Harlan Davidson, 1983.

Linkh, Richard M. *American Catholicism and European Immigrants (1900–1924)*. New York: Center for Migration Studies, 1975.

Lischka, Charles N. "The Appeal of the Oregon School Law." *NCWC News Bulletin* 6, no. 11 (April 1925): 11–13.

———. "The Case Against a Federal Department of Education." *NCWC Review* 12, no. 2 (February 1930): 9–10.

Mandelbaum, Seymour J. *The Social Setting of Intolerance: The Know-Nothings, the Red Scare and McCarthyism*. Chicago: Scott, Foresman and Company, 1964.

Marty, Martin. *Modern American Religion*, vol. 2, *The Noise of Conflict*, 1919–1941. Chicago: University of Chicago Press, 1991.

McCaffrey, Lawrence J. "Irish Textures in American Catholicism." *Catholic Historical Review* 78, no. 1 (January 1992): 1–18.

McGarry, Michael B., CSP. "Modernism in the United States: William Lawrence Sullivan, 1872–1935." *Records of the American Catholic Historical Society of Philadelphia* 90 (1979): 33–52.

McGloin, John Bernard, SJ. *San Francisco: The Story of a City*. San Rafael, CA: Presidio Press, 1978.

McGreevey, John. *Catholicism and American Freedom: A History*. New York: W. W. Norton, 2003.

McKelvey, Blake. *The Quest for Quality (1890–1925)*. Cambridge, MA: Harvard University Press, 1956.

———. "Rochester's Literary and Book Clubs." *Rochester History* 48, nos. 1–2 (January and April 1986): 3–19.

McKeown, Elizabeth. "The National Bishops Conference: An Analysis of Its Origins." *Catholic Historical Review* 66 (1980): 565–83.

McMahon, Charles A. "Resignation of Archbishop Hanna." *Catholic Action* 17, no. 4 (April 1935): 9–11, 14.

McNamara, Robert F. "Archbishop Hanna, Rochesterian." *Rochester History* (April 1963): 1–24.

———. *The Diocese of Rochester in America 1868–1993*, 2nd ed. Rochester, NY: Roman Catholic Diocese of Rochester New York, 1998.

———. "St. Bernard's Seminary 1893–1968." *The Sheaf* (Publication of St. Bernard's Seminary, Rochester, New York) 15 (1968).

McShane, Joseph, SJ. *"Sufficiently Radical": Catholicism, Progressivism, and the Bishops' Program of 1919*. Washington, DC: Catholic University of America Press, 1986.

McWilliams, Carey. *California and the Challenge of Growth II*. Berkeley: University of California Press, 1964.

Men of California. San Francisco: Western Press Reporter, 1925.

Meger, Jean. *The Cristero Rebellion: The Mexican People between Church and State, 1926–1929*. Cambridge: Cambridge University Press, 1976.

Millard, Bailey. *History of the San Francisco Bay Region*. 3 vols. San Francisco: American Historical Society, 1924.

Minus, Paul M. *Walter Rauschenbusch American Reformer*. New York: Macmillan, 1988.

Mitchell, Don. *Lie of the Land: Migrant Workers and the California Landscape*. Minneapolis: University of Minnesota Press, 1996.

"Modernism in the Church in America." *American Ecclesiastical Review* 38 (January 1908): 1–10.

Montavan, William F. "Shall the National Origins Law Be Enforced?" *NCWC News Bulletin* 10, no. 12 (May 1929): 4–5, 26.

Mosk, Sanford A. "Unemployment Relief in California under the State Emergency Administration." In *Essays in Social Economics in Honor of Jessica Blanche Peixotto*, ed. Sanford A. Mosk. Berkeley: University of California Press, 1935.

Murray, Robert K. *Red Scare: A Study in National Hysteria, 1919–1920*. Minneapolis: University of Minnesota Press, 1955.

"The N.E.A., the Masons, and Federal School." *America* 29 (June 30, 1923): 254–55.

Nickel, George. "Matter of Communication in Administration in the California State." *Survey* 75 (January 1939): 11–12.

Noonan, John T., Jr. *Contraception: A History of its Treatment by the Catholic Theologians and Canonists*. Cambridge, MA: Belknap Press of Harvard University, 1966.

Nuese, C. Joseph. "The National Catholic Welfare Conference." In *The Catholic Church USA*, ed. Louis Putz, CSC, 138–52. Chicago: Fides Publishers, 1956.

O'Brien, David. *American Catholics and Social Reform: The New Deal Years.* New York: Oxford University Press, 1968.

O'Connell, Marvin. *Critics on Trial: An Introduction to the Catholic Modernist Crisis.* Washington, DC: Catholic University of America Press, 1994.

O'Connell, William Henry. "The Reasonable Limits of State Activity." *National Catholic Education Association Bulletin* 16 (November 1919): 62–66.

O'Day, Edward. "Bishop Edward J. Hanna." In *Varied Types*, ed. Edward O'Day, 128–32. San Francisco: Town Talk Press, 1915.

O'Dell, Clay. "On Stony Ground: The Catholic Interracial Council in the Archdiocese of San Francisco." PhD diss., University of Virginia, 2004.

O'Toole, James. *Militant and Triumphant: William Henry O'Connell and the Catholic Church in Boston, 1859–1944.* Notre Dame, IN: University of Notre Dame Press, 1992.

Parsons, Wilfrid, SJ. "An Open Letter to M. Litvinov." *America* 50 (November 4, 1933): 107–8.

———. *Mexican Martyrdom.* New York: Macmillan, 1936.

Piper, John F. *The American Churches in World War I.* Athens: Ohio University Press, 1985.

Powers, Richard Gid. *Not Without Honor: The History of American Anticommunism.* New York: Free Press, 1995.

Purnell, Jennie. *Popular Movements and State Formation in Revolutionary Mexico: The Agranistas and Cristeros of Michoacan.* Durham, NC: Duke University Press, 1998.

Olin, Spencer C. "European Immigrant and Oriental Alien: Acceptance and Rejection by the California Legislature of 1913." *Pacific Historical Review* 33 (August 1966): 303–15.

Peitz, Darlene A. *Solidarity or Hermeneutic: A Revisionist Reading of the Theology of Walter Rauschenbusch.* New York: P. Laney, 1992.

Quinn, Mike. *The Big Strike.* Olema, CA: Olema Publishing Company, 1944.

Ranchietti, Michele. *The Catholic Modernists.* London: Oxford University Press, 1969.

Ratte, John. *Three Modernists.* New York: Sheed & Ward, 1967.

Reher, Margaret M. "Americanism and Modernism—Continuity or Discontinuity." *U.S. Catholic Historian* 1 (1980–81): 87–103.

Reisler, Mark. *By the Sweat of Their Brow: Mexican Immigrant Labor in the United States.* Westport, CT: Greenwood Press, 1976.

Rice, M. Elizabeth Ann, OP. *The Diplomatic Relations between the United States and Mexico, as Affected by the Struggle for Religious Liberty in Mexico, 1925–1929.* Washington, DC: Catholic University of America Press, 1959.

Roddy, Edward G. "The Catholic Newspaper Press and the Quest for Social Justice." PhD diss., Georgetown University, 1961.

Ryan, James H. "Dangers of Federalism." *NCWC News Bulletin* (November 1927): 10.

———. "The Sterling-Reed Bill: A Criticism." *Catholic Educational Review* 22 (June 1924): 346–58.

Ryan, John. "The Attitude of the Church Toward Birth Control." *Catholic Charities Review* 4, no. 10 (December 1920): 299–301.

———. "Ethical Aspects of Some International Problems." *America* 49 (May 20, 1933): 155–56.

———. "Family Limitation." *American Ecclesiastical Review* 54 (1916): 684–96.

Sackman, Douglas. "Domestic Arrangements: The Commission of Immigration and Housing and the Alienation of Mexican Labor in California's Citrus Industry, 1914–1936." Paper delivered at the West Coast Meeting of the American Historical Association, Portland, Oregon, August 5, 1997.

Sandoval, Moises. *On the Move: A History of the Hispanic Church in the United States.* Maryknoll, NY: Orbis Books, 1990.

Sanger, Margaret. *Margaret Sanger: An Autobiography.* New York: W. W. Norton, 1938.

———. *Woman and the New Race.* New York: Blue Ribbons Books, 1920.

Saxton, Alexander. *The Indispensable Enemy: Labor and the Anti-Chinese Movement in California.* San Francisco: California Historical Society, 1973.

Schmiedeler, Edgar, OSB. *"Conserving the Family." Catholic Action* 14 (January 1932): 12–13.

Seely, Gordon M. "Church-State Conflict and Catholic Schools in California." In *Catholic San Francisco: Sesquicentennial Essays*, ed. Jeffrey M. Burns, 237–44. Menlo Park, CA: Archives of the Archdiocese of San Francisco, 2005.

Selvin, David F. *A Terrible Anger: The 1934 Waterfront and General Strikes in San Francisco.* Detroit: Wayne State University Press, 1996.

Shanaberger, Manuel Scott. "The Reverend Dr. Edward McGlynn: An Early Advocate of the Social Gospel in the American Catholic Church: An Intellectual History." PhD diss., University of Virginia, 1993.

Shannon, David A. *Between the Wars: America 1919–1941.* Boston: Houghton Mifflin, 1965.

Sharpe, Dores Robinson. *Walter Rauschenbusch.* New York: Macmillan, 1942.

Shelley, Thomas J. *Dunwoodie: The History of St. Joseph's Seminary, Yonkers, New York.* Westminster, MD: Christian Classics, 1993.

———. "John Cardinal Farley and Modernism in New York." *Church History* 61, no. 3 (September 1992): 350–61.

———. "The Oregon School Case and the National Catholic Welfare Conference." *Catholic Historical Review* 75, no. 3 (July 1989): 439–57.

Sheerin, John B., CSP. *Never Look Back: The Career and Concerns of John J. Burke.* New York: Paulist Press, 1975.

Slawson, Douglas. "The Attitudes and Activities of American Catholics regarding the Proposals to Establish a Federal Department of Education between World War I and the Great Depression." PhD diss., Catholic University of America, 1981.

———. *The Foundation and First Decade of the National Catholic Welfare Council.* Washington, DC: Catholic University of America Press, 1992.

———. "The National Catholic Welfare Conference and the Church-State Conflict in Mexico, 1925–1929." *The Americas* 47, no. 1 (July 1990): 55–93.

———. "The National Catholic Welfare Conference and the Mexican Church-State Conflict of the Mid-1930s: A Case of Déjà Vu." *Catholic Historical Review* 80, no. 1 (1994): 58–96.

Smith, William Barry. "The Attitude of American Catholics towards Italian Fascism Between the Two World Wars." PhD diss., Catholic University of America, 1969.

Starr, Kevin. *Endangered Dreams: The Great Depression in California.* New York: Oxford University Press, 1996.

Tangeman, Michael. *Mexico at the Crossroads: Politics, the Church, and the Poor.* Maryknoll, NY: Orbis Books, 1995.

Tentler, Leslie Woodcock. "A Bitter Pill: American Catholics and Contraception." *Commonweal* 81, no. 8 (April 23, 2004): 11–17.

Tyack, David B. "The Perils of Pluralism: The Background of the Pierce Case." *American Historical Review* 74 (1968): 74–98.

Veverka, Fayette. *For God and Country: Catholic Schooling in the 1920s.* New York: Garland Press, 1988.

Wade, Wyn Craig. *The Fiery Cross: The Ku Klux Klan in America.* New York: Simon & Schuster, 1987.

Walsh, James P., ed. *The San Francisco Irish 1850–1976.* San Francisco: Irish Literary and Historical Society, 1978.

Weber, Francis. *Encyclopedia of California's Catholic Heritage, 1769–1999.* Mission Hills, CA: Saint Francis Historical Society, 2001.

———. *Magnificat: The Life and Times of Timothy Cardinal Manning.* Mission Hills, CA: Saint Francis Historical Society, 1999.

White, Joseph. *The Diocesan Seminary in the United States.* Notre Dame, IN: University of Notre Dame Press, 1989.

White, Ronald C., Jr., and C. Howard Hopkins. *The Social Gospel: Religion and Reform in Changing America.* Philadelphia: Temple University Press, 1976.

Wood, Samuel E. "The California Commission of Immigration and Housing: A Study of Administrative Organization and the Growth of Function." PhD diss., University of California, Berkeley, 1942.

Woo-Sam, Anne Marie. "Domesticating the Immigrant: California's Commission of Immigration and Housing and the

Domestic Immigration Policy Movement, 1910–1945." PhD diss., University of California Berkeley, 1999.

Ziegler-McPherson, Christina A. "Americanization: The California Plan: The Commission of Immigration and Housing of California and Public Policy, 1913–1923." PhD diss., Stanford University, 1999.

Zwierlein, Frederick J. *The Life and Letters of Bishop McQuaid*, vol. 3. Rochester, NY: Art Print Shop, 1927.

———. "American College in Rome 1859–1955: Criticism and Supplement." *Social Justice Review* 50 (September–October 1957): 164–69, 200–206.

———. "One Hundred Years of Catholics in Rochester." In *Centennial History of Rochester, New York*, vol. 4, ed. Edward R. Foreman, 189–276. Rochester, NY, 1934.

INDEX